D0850362

The Company That Changed Itself

The Company That Changed Itself

R&D and the Transformations of DSM

Arjan van Rooij

AMSTERDAM UNIVERSITY PRESS

This book is published in cooperation with the Foundation for the History of Technology (SHT). The mission of the foundation is to develop and communicate knowledge that increases our understanding of the critical role of technology in the history of the western world. Since 1988 SHT supports scholarly research in the history of technology. Among others this resulted in large scale national and international research programs and numerous individual projects. The organization also coordinates the international research network Tensions of Europe. For more information see www.histech.nl.

This book has been made possible by the generous financial support of DSM.

Cover design: Chaim Mesika, Hilversum, The Netherlands
Layout: PROgrafici, Goes, The Netherlands
Photos: DSM Central Archives, Heerlen, The Netherlands; p. 4:
Foundation for the History of Technology, Eindhoven, The Netherlands:
collection A.A. Weijts.

ISBN 9789053569559
NUR 680

Amsterdam University Press, Amsterdam, 2007

Table of contents

Foreword

The pace of technological change has always been fast in the chemical industry. But a look back in history reveals more than just the speed of change; it also reveals the long-term continuities that shape a company. DSM is not the company it was a hundred years ago and it is not the company it was ten years ago. And yet there is one characteristic that has been a constant in the company's history: the build-up of technological capabilities and organisational structures for the longer term. It is a feature that has shaped DSM's transformations and will continue to do so in the future. This book documents an important part of the company's history and helps us to understand the interaction between change and continuity.

This book is not about R&D as such; it is about the results of R&D and the relationships between R&D and business. Companies have been facing these critical issues ever since they established R&D laboratories in the late nineteenth century, and they will continue to face them in the twenty-first century. This historical study shows how complex these issues are and how DSM's response to them has evolved over the years. Crucially, this book underlines that we cannot afford to become complacent but need to continue to work hard to build mutual commitment between R&D and business.

This book also shows that no company can innovate on its own. In the case of DSM, this is as true today as it was when the company was founded and when it took its first steps into the chemical industry. DSM has always nurtured an openness and receptiveness towards its environment, and these have served the company well. The changes in the last decade have been particularly striking, with an increasing geographical spread of R&D activities, decentralised R&D governance and a systematic sourcing of external research and new business development opportunities within the framework of an open innovation model.

After more than a century, DSM is as vibrant as ever and very well placed to contribute to the sustainable development of society and industry through its constant innovations.

Jan Zuidam
Deputy Chairman of the DSM Managing Board

Preface

In 1998, Jacques Joosten (Director of Corporate Technology at DSM) initiated a project to write a history of DSM's research activities, with the aim of gaining a better understanding of the role of industrial research in the company's development. He commissioned the Foundation for the History of Technology (Eindhoven, The Netherlands) to write this history. Ton van Helvoort, Eric van Royen, Judith Schueler and Frank Veraart carried out the research and wrote reports on aspects of the history of research at DSM. Harry Lintsen compiled and edited a book on the basis of their work, which was published in 2000.[1]

This collective volume, written in Dutch, was aimed at a broad audience. I have reworked and extended it, and the result is this book. My reworking of the material has resulted in a stronger emphasis on R&D projects. I have also placed more emphasis on R&D in relation to established businesses. Additional research has deepened the cases mentioned in the Dutch book, and I have added two cases (caprolactam and fine chemicals). The scope of the lysine case has also been extended to include research on other amino acids, and attention is paid to the links between lysine and fine chemicals.

The reworking and extensions provide a fresh perspective on the development of DSM and the role of industrial research in this development. The case of DSM may also appeal to an international audience. The company's long and colourful history provides new insights into the history of R&D and the analysis of innovation processes.

I have been fortunate in being able to use the material that had already been collected and the reports that formed the basis of the collective volume.[2] I also used material collected by Piet Vincken. His unpublished manuscript on the history of DSM enabled me to resolve several loose ends.[3] Ernst Homburg supplied me with his research on the establishment of caprolactam production and on industrial research at DSM in the 1990s. Our joint work on the history of DSM's fertiliser business also provided input for this book.[4] The urea case draws on my own previous work in this field and was part of my dissertation.[5] Finally, I am grateful to Wim Hoogstraten (former director of DSM's patents department) for compiling some patent statistics.

I researched and wrote this book between September 2003 and September 2005. An able committee, consisting of Ernst Homburg (Maastricht University), Jacques Joosten (DSM), Siep Schaafsma (formerly DSM Research) and Keetie Sluyterman (Utrecht University) guarded both the process and the content of the work. I have profited from their comments, suggestions and critical questions. Siep's careful reading of drafts helped me to avoid many chemical errors and provided me with useful pointers for further research. He also provided me with quantitative data on the development of DSM's research. At Eindhoven, Mila Davids and Jan Korsten acted as a sounding board for early testing of my ideas and took many organisational aspects of the project off my hands. Mila's many remarks forced me to be more critical and precise. In the final stages of the work Vikas Sonak (DSM) took a fresh view of the project and the draft chapters, which clarified and improved the text. Henk Rhebergen did an excellent job editing the text.

Last but not least, I want to thank all the people who were willing to talk to me about the development of DSM and its research (see the sources at the end of this book for a complete list of interviews). Their enthusiasm and humour have been a continuous source of inspiration. Several of them also read parts of the manuscript and provided invaluable comments and corrections. Herman de Rooij, Ruud Selman, Dick Venderbos and Jan Zuidam took time to read the complete manuscript and provided useful comments and critiques. It has been a privilege to have been able to work in this way.

Notes

1   H. Lintsen, Ed. (2000). *Research tussen vetkool en zoetstof: zestig jaar DSM Research 1940-2000*. Eindhoven/Zutphen: Stichting Historie der Techniek/Walburg Pers.

2   See the sources for a list of these reports. In those cases where my text draws on these reports, I refer to the reports themselves, and not to the underlying sources.

3   P.F.G. Vincken (2000). *Van Staatsmijnen in Limburg tot DSM Chemie*. Unpublished manuscript.

4   E. Homburg, with contributions by A. van Rooij (2004). *Groeien door kunstmest. DSM Agro 1929-2004*. Hilversum: Verloren.

5   A. van Rooij (2004). *Building Plants: Markets for Technology and Internal Capabilities in DSM's Fertiliser Business, 1925-1970*. Amsterdam: Aksant. Dissertation Eindhoven University of Technology.

I

Introduction: Research and Business in the Chemical Industry

"Industrial research is wonderful – if it pays off."[1]

Industrial research, or research and development (R&D), is a striking feature of innovation processes. In the twentieth century, large and well-equipped laboratories, staffed by large numbers of researchers, replaced the lone inventor of the nineteenth century. Companies spent large amounts of money on these laboratories, aiming to improve existing technologies and to drive diversification.

But does it pay to do industrial research? Many products that are now ubiquitous, such as nylon, plastics and the transistor, would never have existed without the work of company-owned R&D laboratories. The companies that pioneered these innovations have profited enormously from their investments in these facilities. On the other hand, many projects have failed or produced unexpected results. Because of this, the effectiveness of R&D and its role in the development of a company are often questioned. The role of management, not just the management of the R&D organisation but above all the company's top management and the management of its manufacturing organisation, is an important factor in this debate. Are R&D and business aligned? The relationship between R&D and other company functions, in particular marketing and production, has often been strained.

This book confronts two essential questions in relation to R&D. First: what roles does industrial research play in a company's development? And second: how does management direct the development of the company's research activities? These two questions are essential but also complex to research and answer. This book uses a historical method and follows the chronological development of a number of R&D projects, which leads to an understanding of the complexity and persistency of these issues.

This book analyses the Dutch chemical company DSM in depth. The company is over a hundred years old and has transformed itself several times. Having started life as a coal-mining company, it branched out into fertilisers, subsequently diversified into bulk chemicals and then became a company active in fine chemicals and high performance materials.[2] (Figure 1.1.) These three transformations reflect a striking and distinguishing characteristic of the company. Although DSM did not pioneer R&D as a method of invention and innovation, either in the chemical industry or in the Netherlands, it has built one of the largest industrial research facilities in the country and has spent large amounts of money on R&D. The case of DSM offers an excellent opportunity to study the role of industrial research and the way in which it is managed.

This introduction sets the stage for the next chapters. First the literature is reviewed to identify what roles R&D played in the development of companies and how the management of these companies affected the R&D organisation. The focus will be on the chemical industry, drawing examples from the electrical and other industries to call attention to systematic aspects of industrial research. Building on the review of the literature, the second part of this introduction will position DSM as a case study and outline the design of this book.

Figure 1.1. An overview of the development of DSM's main activities.

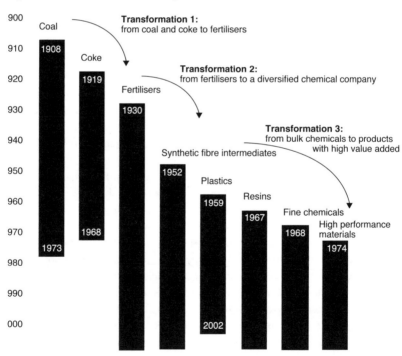

Note: start years refer to years when production started. End years refer to closure in the cases of coal and coke, and sale in the case of plastics.

The History of Industrial Research: Patterns and Themes

The German dyestuffs industry was one of the first industries in which companies started to do industrial research. For some time, German companies had simply copied the innovations of their French and British competitors who were leading the industry. In 1877, a patent law was enacted in Germany that made it impossible to copy innovations as they now could be protected by patents. German firms developed industrial research as an answer, recruiting scientists and building laboratories to develop new products and processes and improve existing ones. The enactment of the patent law, a threat to the established route to innovation, was decisive in pushing companies towards R&D.[3]

In the United States, threats played a similarly important role in the creation of the first R&D laboratories. American Telephone & Telegraph (AT&T) responded to the threat that radio posed to telephone services with the establishment of an industrial research laboratory in 1911.[4] Du Pont, an American chemical company and one of the first in the country to establish research facilities in 1902 and 1903, responded with R&D to the intention of some of its most important customers, the American army and navy, to enter its main business: explosives and particularly gunpowder. Du Pont continued to diversify by taking over innovative companies but increasingly vigorous anti-trust policies made this a difficult route to take in the 1920s, pushing Du Pont further towards R&D.[5]

In general, large companies in chemicals and electronics pioneered industrial research and Germany and the United States were the leading countries. Threats, often commercial and/or technological, prompted firms to establish research laboratories. Historians have mainly studied pioneering companies, consequently focusing on the period between roughly 1870 and 1920 and on organisational themes. In this period, companies had to find ways to organise and integrate industrial research laboratories in their organisations as a new form of technology development and innovation.[6]

In the Netherlands, the electronics company Philips and the Bataafsche Petroleum Maatschappij (BPM), the operational company of Royal Dutch/Shell in the Netherlands, established the first industrial research laboratories in the 1910s. At BPM, industrial research emerged gradually and as a reaction to competitive pressures to improve Borneo oil, one of its most important products at that time. At Philips, management intervened actively and reacted to a technological threat in its main business, the production of light bulbs, by establishing a research laboratory.

The First World War catalysed the development of industrial research in the Netherlands as Dutch companies were cut off from their raw materials, their markets, or both. Several of them diversified into new businesses and established research laboratories to help diversification. Some of these laboratories did not survive the end of the war, but in the 1920s the number of R&D laboratories started to grow and it continued to grow in the 1930s, while older laboratories grew in size.[7]

As the example of the Netherlands shows, by 1920 R&D was on the map in industry in general and an increasing number of companies started to do industrial research. The reasons for starting an industrial research laboratory shifted from specific threats to somewhat diffuse ideas about keeping up with the competition and industry standards. Increasingly, companies established research laboratories because their competitors had done so, and because they feared they would lag behind or that their standing would be harmed. This process continued above all in the 1930s, when R&D became an accepted and integral part of business.[8]

In the 1920s, pioneering companies turned to fundamental research, work that was not directly aimed at industrial applications but at gaining a thorough understanding of the problem under study. Du Pont, for instance, started such a programme. It led to the development of neoprene, a synthetic rubber, and nylon. In the United States, the Second World War catalysed the turn to fundamental research. Large-scale projects funded by the federal government underlined the importance of R&D in general, and of fundamental research in particular. The successes, coupled to a belief that fundamental research would inevitably yield new products and processes, convinced many companies to invest in this type of research after the war. Federal spending also continued. R&D became an industry.[9]

In the Netherlands, the same pattern of growth can be seen. Philips started fundamental research before the war and invested heavily in this type of research after the war. Other companies also increased their R&D expenditure, and some of them started fundamental research programmes and invested in generic research such as analysis using the latest and most advanced technologies. Government R&D spending also increased, although it never came to occupy the central place it did in the United States.[10]

Industrial research grew in size and scope after the Second World War, but the tide turned towards the end of the 1960s. The effectiveness of research, and above all fundamental research, in generating new products and processes came under scrutiny. At Du Pont, for instance, the involvement of the research organisation in large scale, government-run projects of the Second World War had increased the management's confidence in research. Fundamental research seemed to be the key to new products and processes. The 1950s and 1960s produced no new breakthrough products and technologies, however, and towards the 1970s the research organisation was refocused on commercial objectives, although Du Pont continued to invest heavily in R&D.[11]

David Hounshell argues that the Du Pont pattern is typical of many American companies: they all went through a period of fundamental research after the Second World War but refocused their priorities in the late 1960s and in the 1970s.[12] A similar conclusion was drawn from an analysis of managerial perspectives on research in the British chemical industry, and Ernst Homburg describes a similar pattern for the Netherlands. After about 1965, the spectacular growth of the size and scope of industrial research in the Netherlands stagnated and some companies started to cut back on research. Emphasis was now put on the market, as wages had increased, competition had intensified and saturation had become imminent on some markets. After 1965, companies cut back on fundamental research in particular, a process that continued in the 1980s and 1990s.[13]

Another issue that emerged at several companies in the late 1960s was the isolated position of research. Kees Boersma and Marc de Vries have shown that research at Philips drifted away from manufacturing and marketing after the Second World War. Homburg also cites the example of Philips and argues that such isolation was partly caused by the increased scale of industrial research after the Second World War.[14] Highlighting the examples of the Radio Corporation of America (RCA) and Alcoa, large American corporations in electronics and aluminium, respectively, Margaret Graham argues that centralised research facilities became generally isolated in the 1950s and 1960s. Many companies centralised their previously decentralised technical activities and research. The research environment became highly competitive as increased federal spending prompted many institutions and companies to set up research facilities or to broaden the scope of existing facilities. Research laboratories, moreover, were increasingly staffed with highly educated people, who were also more theoretically oriented than the previous generation of researchers and more loyal to their discipline than to the companies that employed them. Graham argues that corporate research, the research undertaken at centralised laboratories under the direct supervision of top management, became a 'counterculture', an island populated by fundamental researchers.[15]

Both Philips and RCA were large companies that operated with several divisions and a central (corporate) research laboratory, but Alcoa remained functionally organised. In their book about research at Alcoa, Graham and Bettye Pruitt note that the establishment of divisions had a negative effect on a company's ability to carry out long-term research, particularly in the case of small, long-term projects that top management did not sponsor directly. This suggests that increased involvement of divisional business managers pushed research to the short term.[16]

Several recent studies of American industrial research practices in the 1980s and 1990s show that companies focused research more on the short term than the long term, and formulated clear commercial and technological objectives for projects. They conducted less fundamental research, but increasingly cooperated in R&D with universities, research institutes and competitors. These studies emphasise the contrast with earlier periods, and argue that in the 1950s and 1960s industrial research was typically centralised, technology-driven and knowledge-driven, and closed off from other company activities, particularly manufacturing and marketing. In the 1980s, however, the cost and technological complexity of projects increased, while management became increasingly concerned about the commercial pay-off from industrial research. Many companies began to focus their R&D efforts on business activities and decentralised research. Laboratories were set up at business unit level and divisional management became responsible for much of the funding of research. The overall aim was to link R&D with the company's businesses. Research should not be undertaken to generate knowledge but to create new businesses or to improve existing products and processes.[17]

Decentralisation, increased cooperation and an increased focus on the short term are central themes that emerge from the literature on R&D in the 1980s. In management-oriented literature, increasing linkages between research and business are becoming the norm, and views on the practices of the 1950s and 1960s have become quite harsh. Roli Varma characterises the development of R&D management as a development from an 'autonomous model' to a 'linkage model'. According to Varma, industrial research in the 1950s and 1960s was free from influence from business management, production and marketing, but progressed to a model with more linkages between all company functions. Philip Roussel, Kamal Saad and Tamara Erickson, consultants with Arthur D. Little, a firm with many clients in the chemical industry, describe basically the same development but characterise it as a succession of three 'generations' of R&D management. Both Varma and Roussel et al. see the involvement of business management, marketing and production as a good thing.[18]

The way in which the interface between research and the rest of the company was organised and how it developed over time are important themes, and the influence of business management is a crucial factor in this relationship. The short review of the history of R&D presented here also shows a pattern in the development of industrial research. In some countries and industries, industrial research developed sooner than in others, but by the end of the First World War research was on the map everywhere. The build-up phase was followed by an expansion phase, typically after the Second World War, with increasing emphasis on fundamental research and an increasing isolation of the research organisation. In the late 1960s, the emphasis shifted to markets, where it has stayed although research expenditures have gone through some ups and downs. Moreover, companies increasingly started to cooperate in research and started to decentralise their laboratories in the 1980s.

These patterns in the history of R&D seem to have been caused by economics, as is clear in the shift of the late 1960s. Ernst Homburg, however, argues that firms also often copied each other's strategic decisions on industrial research. According to Homburg, firms hold each other in a blindfolded embrace, not sure where to go, just 'groping along the track'. The diffusion of contemporary management thinking through, for instance, research management associations, personal contacts and consultants, led firms to move in the same directions. Homburg argues, more or less implicitly, that the difference between leaders and followers became increasingly blurred over the course of the twentieth century.[19]

The Roles of Industrial Research in the Firm

Meeting Threats and Enabling Diversification

From the historical literature on R&D, two main roles of industrial research emerge. First, R&D enabled companies to diversify and take up new lines of business; companies conduct research to enter a new business. Several Dutch companies started doing research during the First World War to help them establish new businesses. David Hounshell and John Smith's well-known study of Du Pont similarly shows how research helped the process of diversification.[20] Second, R&D enabled companies to meet threats; companies conduct research to support existing lines of business. Industrial research developed as a response to specific threats of a commercial, technological or other nature.

Diversification is one of the best-researched themes in the history of R&D and has received more attention than responsive, threat-induced research, although the latter has remained an important role of industrial research laboratories. In the dyestuffs industry, for instance, much of the work for new laboratories consisted of screening the work of competitors using the information published in patents or obtained through analysing products.[21] Competitors often pose the main threat to a company. Responding to the innovations or other actions of competitors and defending the firm's commercial and technological position is therefore an important role of an industrial research laboratory. This response typically entails cost reduction or product (quality) improvements.

Threat-induced research will often be performed in relation to existing businesses to maintain or improve market position. William Utterback has built on the well-known life cycle concept to argue that different types of innovation are needed in different segments of the life cycle of a technology or a product. In the uncoordinated stage, a high rate of product innovations combines with a low rate of process innovations. This stage is followed by a segmental stage, during which a high rate of process innovations combines with a low rate of product innovations, and finally by a systematic stage with a medium rate of process innovations and a low rate of product innovations. On the whole, products become increasingly standardised and competition on price becomes increasingly important.[22]

Utterback links market development to innovation processes. Particularly in the systematic phase, the options for improvement are limited, perhaps requiring a different organisation and conduct of research. Moreover, Utterback's model points to increasing technological maturity over time, or in other words, decreasing opportunities for innovation. Jeffrey Plotkin argues that chemical technology had reached the point of maturity by 1980. Efficient processes had been developed for most large-volume petrochemical products. The scale of plants had increased so much that the problems of scale-up and the risk involved in building a first-of-a-kind plant became prohibitive, while the economics of new processes were not attractive enough to shut down existing capacity (Plotkin speaks of 'shutdown economics'). In response, companies redirected their research away from process research but this redirection also reinforced maturity.[23]

In contrast to Plotkin, Joseph Bower argues in his book on the petrochemical industry around 1980 that new technology improved feedstock and energy efficiencies. In this way technology continued to have a large impact on the industry.[24] Both Plotkin and Bower, however, point to the need to analyse research on existing products and not just focus on diversification. An analysis of both areas is necessary to understand the role of industrial research in the development of a company.

The Roles of Industrial Research and Innovation Strategy
As threat-induced research is linked with existing businesses, it also has a strategic dimension. Research enabling diversification is similarly linked with the strategies pursued by companies. Graham distinguishes two broad strategic categories in relation to industrial research: long-term, opportunity-generating work; and short-term, generic cost reduction. The first category can be linked to (possible) diversification, while the second can be linked to the maintenance of existing businesses and technologies.[25]

Louis Galambos, on the other hand, recognises formative and adaptive innovations in his analysis of the Bell System. He argues that Bell pursued both types of innovation at the same time, with the adaptive work focused on improving and systemising existing technologies, while the formative work focused on creating new technologies and shaping the direction of the telephone industry.[26]

Chris Freeman has tried to capture the different strategic roles of research with a taxonomy of innovation strategies. He distinguishes between six strategies, but the crucial three are the offensive, defensive and imitative strategies. A firm that pursues an offensive innovation strategy aims at achieving a breakthrough and being the first to market a new product. This risky, highly research-intensive strategy is the exception rather than the rule. A firm that pursues a defensive innovation strategy is likely to invest almost as much in research as an offensive firm, but does not try to be first. A defensive company follows (at short distance) behind the leaders in the industry, tries to appropriate a breakthrough, and improves this breakthrough if possible. Finally, a firm that pursues an imitative innovation strategy conducts less research and does not try to catch up with the leaders in the industry but follows at some distance. Low costs, and the technological activities necessary to achieve low costs, are essential in this strategy.[27]

Freeman's taxonomy has the advantage that it separates strategic goals more clearly from the actual research work than the concepts of Galambos and Graham. As in taxonomy, however, innovation strategies are ideal types, occasionally with porous boundaries. Also, Freeman's imitative strategy should not be understood as a strategy where firms simply 'imitate' the innovations of others but as a strategy where low costs are emphasised.

In Freeman's taxonomy, enabling diversification can be linked to either an offensive or defensive innovation strategy, depending on whether a firm diversifies to establish a leading position or to catch up; or depending on whether the diversification embodies a breakthrough or an entry into a well-established field. A diversification might be called imitative when a firm enters a business in order not to miss the bandwagon and enjoys some specific advantage that enable it to compete. Meeting threats constitutes a defensive strategy: a firm responding to a change in its competitive or broader social and economic environment. The role of industrial research here is to maintain the firm's existing businesses and technologies, and if possible to improve them.

In R&D history, offensive diversification and offensive companies have received a lot of attention. Hounshell and Smith, for instance, analyse Du Pont, a company that invested heavily in R&D and grew into one of the largest and most innovative chemical companies in the world.[28] Defensive companies have been studied much less, and therefore are an appropriate subject to analyse alongside threat-induced research: that is, the maintenance of existing businesses and technologies.

Other Roles of Industrial Research
Meeting threats and enabling diversification are not the only roles of industrial research that have been identified. Michael Dennis argues that R&D heightened entry barriers because firms wanting to enter a research-intensive industry had to invest in research themselves. This relates to the argument of Homburg that pioneering companies put R&D on the map, thereby forcing others to follow. Wolfgang Wimmer has shown this process in his study of the pharmaceutical industry in Germany between

1880 and 1935, where the success of the research-intensive strategy of Bayer forced other, less research-focused companies to increase their investments in R&D.[29]

Industrial research also heightened entry barriers by making product development proprietary, mainly through patenting. This enabled firms to increase their profits or control the rate and direction of technical change. Based on a case study from the American radio industry in the 1910s and 1920s, Leonard Reich argues that companies tried to patent as much, and as close as possible to their competitor's main businesses and core technologies. The extensive research that lay at the basis of this patenting drive was, according to Reich, rather undirected and sometimes barely connected to current commercial interests. Nevertheless, such patenting provided a defence against competitors and could lead to new business opportunities. It also created leverage in cross-licensing deals that were necessary when no single company could manufacture a product without infringing on another company's patents.[30]

In strong contrast with the example of Reich, Peter Spitz argues in his history of the petrochemical industry that in the 1950s and 1960s firms abandoned their control of technology by extensive licensing, leading to substantially increased competition in the market. Spitz argues that licensing is one of the factors that caused the industry to become very competitive, which in turn strained the profitability of companies.[31]

Reich suggests that companies defended themselves with patents, but these companies operated offensively; they wanted to be the first and tried to monopolise markets and technologies. Again some large, innovative and offensive companies figure prominently in Reich's work. The extent of control is a function of an industry's structure. In the petrochemical industry, the leaders had a hard time maintaining their lead as many defensive companies followed quickly in their footsteps and threatened to overtake their positions. Engineering contractors (companies specialised in engineering and construction of plants and suppliers of technology) also played an important role in this process as they had no production interests.[32]

The desire of offensive companies to control the rate and direction of technological change suggests that these companies increasingly relied on in-house technological capabilities to innovate. There were also options to absorb outside sources of knowledge and technology, ranging from independent inventors and private laboratories to engineering contractors and the acquisition of innovative companies. Smith argues that absorbing outside inventions was a crucial skill in American industrial research in the 1920s. In economics, recent studies have emphasised the importance of tracking the development of technology outside the boundaries of the firm and of identifying possible options for acquisition. Research, and technological capabilities in general, play a crucial role in this process and essentially contribute to absorptive capacity. From an innovation strategic perspective, absorbing outside innovations will typically be defensive. It might even be imitative when a company pursues a low-cost strategy and has the opportunity to acquire a plant to catch up with the state of the art.[33]

Table 1.1 summarises the various roles of research discussed here and the relationship with innovation strategy. It suggests that industrial research in the role of 'enabler of diversification' can serve different innovation strategies, whereas in other roles it is tied more to one particular strategy. This in turn suggests that the importance of these roles varies from one company to another.

Outside the strategy perspective, in his history of R&D at Bayer, Georg Meyer-Thurow points to the training function of industrial research. In the early years of this company's research laboratory, management often recruited a chemist for its production activities from research, thereby generating a high labour turnover and giving the laboratory the task of training chemists that joined the company. Ulrich Marsch shows that the German chemical company Griesheim-Elektron made the inventing chemist also responsible for development work, and if this work was successful he or she was also made responsible for managing production.[34]

Table 1.1. Roles of research in the development of a company and innovation strategy.

Role of industrial research	Innovation strategy		
	Offensive	Defensive	Imitative
Enabling diversification	X (establish a lead)	X (catch up)	X (bandwagon)
Meeting threats		X	
Controlling technological change	X		
Increasing / developing absorptive capacity		X	X

Business Management and Industrial Research

Business managers often played an important role in the practice of R&D. Homburg mentions the example of Jurgens, one of the forerunners of Unilever, where local business management frustrated every effort to coordinate and manage research. In her analysis of RCA, by contrast, Graham points to the importance of RCA's long-time top manager. He believed that research was necessary in order to compete and innovate, and provided a setting in which research could flourish. Either positively or negatively, business management played an important role in industrial research.[35]

There is also a link between the pattern identified in the history of R&D and management ideas about the role and importance of research. Successful projects, as well as ideas about the importance and management of research, fuelled the expansion of fundamental research after the Second World War. This faith was shaken in the late 1960s and many companies redirected their efforts to market-oriented research. Many other factors played a role in this switch, but the role of management cannot be neglected. Galambos, writing about the pioneering phase of industrial research, even argues that the momentum a research organisation creates can take the place of short-term, market-related business economic considerations.[36]

Graham and Hounshell have tried to identify the key challenges that research and business managers face when dealing with R&D. Graham argues that corporate research has often been poorly understood by business managers, leading to tensions and unrealistic demands being placed on research. She argues that uncertainty is a defining feature of R&D projects, and is a feature that makes them hard to manage. When outcomes are uncertain, setting strict targets and just pouring in money and personnel has little effect. At some point, on the other hand, outcomes can become more certain and then an intensive and targeted effort might lead to results. However, it is difficult to determine when projects have arrived at that point. Research managers are fighting on two fronts: internally they have to decide which projects are viable, manage a broad array of possible outcomes and technologies in the uncertain phase of projects; at the same time they need to find support for projects from business management, who are by nature focused more on the short term than on the long term. According to Graham, the interface between research and business management is crucial but difficult because of the nature of R&D. Some tension between research and business is unavoidable, and this tension can even be a source of creativity in research. Corporate R&D should develop a 'technical vision': a view of technological opportunities matched to the company's capabilities that enables business managers to select the most promising lines of business. According to Graham, R&D can develop this vision in the area of tension between research and business.[37]

Hounshell argues that three persistent problems have haunted R&D management ever since companies started to build research laboratories. He argues that the question of the best organisation of research has remained open since the late nineteenth century. Hounshell sees the movements from centralised to decentralised research as cyclic and, in an analysis like that of Homburg, influenced by bandwagon behaviour. Closely related to the question of the organisation of research is the question of finding a balance between short-term and long-term research. Finding this balance is difficult because firms cannot invest in research strictly on a short-term basis, but the results of long-term research are highly uncertain and unpredictable. This unpredictability is the final structural problem Hounshell identifies, arguing that no models have yet been developed that can capture the complex issue of research results quantitatively.[38]

Hounshell illustrates his three persistent problems with the case of Du Pont, a company that pioneered return on investment calculations and that tried to use quantitative data in the decision-making process whenever possible. Du Pont tried to use a formal, quantitative research management system but with limited success. The system worked reasonably well for short-term projects, but management found that long-term projects could be better judged on the merits of the research itself, a system that remained in place until the 1960s. This system relied on management's ability to understand research, and when they lost that ability, a quantitative system was again implemented. Hounshell strongly argues that this was an act of 'desperation' because he sees no alternative to informed judgement in the management of research.[39]

Both Graham and Hounshell suggest that the management of R&D remains an open-ended process. This contrasts with the ideas of Varma and Roussel et al., as they suggest that companies have developed, or at least can develop, excellent R&D management structures. They imply a somewhat linear view of the development of industrial research, from a situation where business management and research diverged to a situation where they (increasingly) converged. The work of Graham shows that such convergence is difficult and also that divergence makes research useful for companies. This debate provides a route to analyse research management.[40]

The Development of Technological Capabilities in Firms

Industrial research contributes to a firm's technological and organisational competence: it enables a firm to develop technology and to organise this activity. Hounshell argues that organisational capabilities are vital in the diversification process and for the company's long-term success.[41] Apart from the training of personnel, the roles of industrial research are built on technology (patents, a new process, an improved product etc.). The technology that R&D generates, fuels the performance of its roles in the development of a company.

Through projects, R&D builds organisational and technological capabilities. Gary Pisano argues that research projects have a dual output: they generate technology a firm can use, but at the same time they generate generic knowledge, particularly about how to conduct R&D better and faster; in other words, research projects build organisational capabilities. Pisano argues that projects may also generate fundamental knowledge that may be used in later projects but that technological knowledge is for the most part project-specific and cannot easily be transferred. For Pisano, industrial research is path dependent and cumulative: technology that was developed in the past enables a firm to start new projects but, at the same time, limits the options that may come into view.[42]

Pisano's model also shows why research is unpredictable. The dual output of R&D projects leads to secondary effects which in turn often make it hard to predict the outcome of research projects beforehand, particularly in the case of long-term projects, and to measure the returns from research afterwards. When the primary objective of a project fails, there may still be a payoff later: through a spin-off, through generic knowledge accumulated, or through the ability to continue a line of research.[43]

Pisano's study is tied in with a resource-based view of the firm. Following the pioneering work of Edith Penrose, firms are conceptualised as bundles of resources and competences that determine the direction of diversification. As such, firms do not branch out in all directions but tend to specialise in a few broad market areas or technologies. Penrose calls these market and technology bases, respectively. Path dependencies again play an important role.[44]

In a study of the American chemical firm Hercules Powder Company, established in 1912 as a result of an anti-trust suit brought against Du Pont, Penrose has tried to analyse the development of capabilities. She argues that from the company's main line of business in 1912, explosives and specifically black powder and dynamite, it diversified into paints by building on experience in nitrocellulose, an important intermediate for its main line of business but a compound that could be used in paints as well. The research department of Hercules, established in 1919, also contributed to a shift in technology and market base. The research department investigated the chemical processing of wood to manufacture resins, turpentine and pine oil. Although it involved different technologies and markets, Penrose argues that there was a relationship with Hercules' existing lines of business through generic experience in chemistry.[45]

Penrose analyses the shifting technology bases of Hercules by identifying the elements of existing bases that enable new bases to grow. Specific bodies of knowledge were important in the case of this firm. Such bodies of knowledge can also be related to generic types of research work. Important in this respect are product and process research, development and engineering. Product research aims at new or improved products while process research aims at new or improved processes. Development can be undertaken to improve products but is also a form of continued process research, intended to make preliminary process designs. The process can need custom equipment for which designs are made during process research. The process is also scaled-up from laboratory equipment to industrial size. Pilot plants may provide an intermediate step, enabling research on a scale of several tons per day for instance, and enabling preliminary market scans with the output of the plant. Pilot plants can also be used to improve products. Engineering, finally, leads to a design for an industrial-size plant. Engineering involves establishing the configuration of the process and the way in which the equipment should be placed, and it also entails making the drawings and specifications that are necessary to construct a plant.[46]

Analysing shifts in technology and market bases is important for understanding the role of industrial research in the development of a company. Following Penrose's approach, the challenge in analysing the growth of technological capabilities is to specify which elements of existing technology and market bases enable building of new bases. Following Pisano's approach, an analysis of research projects and technology development can provide the input to shifting technology bases. Pisano's dual output model also points to the importance of spin-offs from specific projects and generic knowledge and capabilities for building technology bases.

Design of the Book

So far, this chapter has reviewed the literature on R&D to specify patterns in the roles and management of industrial research. Through this review of the literature, the outline of the book can be detailed further. This chapter started out with two questions: the roles of industrial research in the development of a company, and the management of industrial research. Now DSM as a case study has to be positioned and specified.

DSM's Three Transformations
DSM differs from the companies typically chosen for R&D case studies. Historians have often studied large American or German companies that pioneered R&D in the period between roughly 1870 and 1920; companies such as Du Pont, for instance. Much less has been written about the period after 1920, and particularly about the period after 1980.

DSM decided to establish a research laboratory in 1938, well after the pioneering phase of 1870-1920. Although the company grew into one of the largest companies in the Netherlands, it did not belong to the class of R&D pioneers in the chemical industry and in the Netherlands, nor did it belong to the largest and most innovative companies in the chemical industry for a long time in its history. Measured by sales, DSM ranked seventeenth in the top fifty of the world's largest chemical firms in 1974, at a time when the company's chemical businesses were going through a substantial expansion process. By this measure, the industry's leaders were about three times larger than DSM. On the other hand, DSM was more

The main building of DSM's Central Laboratory (Geleen, the Netherlands) in June 1954. Although the rural setting suggests otherwise, the Central Laboratory was built on DSM's main production site, close to the production plants. The building is still being used for research purposes today.

Table 1.2. Top 50 chemical producers in the world, 1974.

Ranking	Company	Country	Sales
			Million dollars
1	BASF	West Germany	8,542
2	Hoechst	West Germany	7,795
3	ICI	UK	7,331
4	Bayer	West Germany	7,180
5	Du Pont	US	6,910
17	DSM	The Netherlands	2,645
50	Beecham	UK	1,044

J. Wei, T. W. F. Russel & M. W. Swartzlander (1979). *The Structure of the Chemical Industry.* McGraw-Hill. Table 5.16, 172-173.

Note: sales for DSM exclude energy.

THE COMPANY THAT CHANGED ITSELF

than twice as large as the smallest company in this list. (Table 1.2.)

DSM is also an interesting case study in itself. The Dutch state established DSM in 1902 as a coal-mining company but the company diversified in the 1910s and 1920s by building two large coke oven plants for the production of coke, an industrial fuel. From the production of coal and coke, DSM entered the chemical industry in 1930 by starting the production of nitrogen fertilisers. The company bought the necessary technology from engineering contractors but started to build internal technological capabilities at the same time and in 1938 decided to establish the Central Laboratory, a central R&D organisation.

In the 1930s, DSM established a foothold in the chemical industry through fertiliser production and the establishment of its R&D organisation. After the Second World War, the company expanded and diversified further into the chemical industry. First, DSM started producing caprolactam, an intermediate for nylon; later the company moved into plastics and resins. Its R&D organisation expanded and diversified at the same pace. The company also established an engineering department (Chemiebouw) and a licensing subsidiary (Stamicarbon) shortly after the war. Chemiebouw and Stamicarbon played an important role in DSM's innovation processes. Chemiebouw supported innovation and R&D with engineering capabilities; Stamicarbon developed into an extra outlet for research alongside DSM's own production organisation.

As DSM's chemical businesses expanded, the company's coal-related businesses declined. The coke oven plants closed in the late 1960s, and the last pit stopped production in 1973. The company now depended on its chemical businesses and had a large research organisation. DSM had diversified, but mainly produced bulk chemicals: products that are manufactured in large volumes but with relatively low profit margins. In the 1980s, management took action and focused the company on markets in which DSM had a strong commercial and technological position, and started a search for products with a higher value-added than bulk chemicals. The company reinforced its activities in fine chemicals and high-performance materials and both gradually became central in DSM's portfolio. The importance of activities in fertilisers and synthetic fibre intermediates declined, and recently the company sold its activities in bulk plastics.[47]

Over the course of its long history, DSM went through three transformations: from coal and coke to fertilisers; from fertilisers to a wide variety of chemicals; and finally towards products with high value-added (Figure 1.1.). These three transformations distinguish DSM from other chemical companies. Quite a few European companies diversified from coke and coke oven gas to fertilisers in the 1920s and expanded in the chemical industry after the Second World War, but not many of them have gone through a second and a third transformation. DSM provides much material for an analysis of the role of in-house research in the development of a firm.

As part of the second transformation, the company took on the name of DSM in 1969. Before that year, this name had been used as an international trade name only. DSM was an abbreviation of Dutch State Mines, a name that reflected what had been the official Dutch name: Staatsmijnen in Limburg. The change of name reflected that the company had moved away from coal.[48]

DSM's Products

As DSM transformed itself from one business to another and to the next, it is important to analyse the shifts in its market and technology bases. Following Pisano and Penrose, the method of this book will focus on R&D projects. However, the choice of R&D projects should not be limited to diversification. Historical studies often focus on diversification, while much less has been written on the crucial role of R&D in the maintenance of existing businesses. In this book, R&D is analysed in relation to diversification and in relation to the maintenance of existing businesses over the years.

This book does not analyse all of DSM's R&D and all of the company's lines of business. Exemplary products have been chosen as case studies that reveal contrasting characteristics of the role and management of R&D, and of the company's three transformations. In short, products have been chosen that reveal the nature of innovation processes at DSM.

The choice of products to analyse for DSM's first transformation is straightforward. The establishment of fertiliser production is analysed, followed by the process through which the company started to build internal capabilities. The improvement of the acquired ammonium sulphate process, and the development of a mixed fertiliser process on the basis of acquired patents, are central. This work also provides an entry into the decision-making process that led to the establishment of the Central Laboratory, DSM's formal R&D organisation. Finally, the development of an alcohol process shows the first careful steps in fields outside fertilisers.

After the Second World War, expansion and diversification characterised the development of DSM's chemical businesses and of its R&D. The development of urea processes reflects this expansion. Urea developed into the main export fertiliser and DSM built a large production capacity for this product over the years. The company worked from its established capabilities in fertilisers to develop production technology for urea, but the Central Laboratory eventually propelled DSM into a position of technological leadership.

The case of caprolactam, an intermediate for the synthetic fibre nylon, shows the diversification in DSM's chemical businesses and in its research.

After starting the production of alcohol, DSM took a second, and much more important, step outside fertilisers with caprolactam. It involved a different branch of chemistry and required a broader scope in R&D than urea and other fertilisers. Caprolactam reflects the drive to broaden the Central Laboratory's scope, and shows how this broadened scope mattered for R&D and the company. Through caprolactam, DSM built a new technology base and took an important step towards its second transformation.

The caprolactam technology base was vital for the development of a process for the synthesis of lysine, an amino acid. This project failed in the market and this failure had important effects on the development of research policies in the 1970s. The lysine project, however, also had important technological spin-offs in the field of fine chemicals. In this way, caprolactam enables the analysis of a chain of R&D-based diversifications and links the second to the third transformation.

The second transformation, from a fertiliser producer to a diversified chemical company, rested on several other products besides caprolactam, in particular polyethylene (a type of plastic), melamine (an intermediate for resins) and EPDM (a type of synthetic rubber). Like caprolactam, these products show the diversification in business and the increased scope of research. DSM's fertiliser technology base provided a link with melamine (through urea) while polyethylene technology provided a link to EPDM synthetic rubbers and other diversifications in the field of plastics after 1970.

Caprolactam, polyethylene, melamine and EPDM overlap as cases of DSM's innovation processes. Caprolactam is preferred here because of the links with lysine and fine chemicals. In addition, it was DSM's first major step outside fertilisers after the Second World War, and the technology base built in relation to caprolactam also fed polyethylene. Major developments in polyethylene, EPDM and melamine are reviewed, however, to balance the picture of DSM and its R&D organisation. DSM recently divested its activities in bulk plastics such as polyethylene, but before that, these products were a significant part of the company's turnover and its R&D budget.

To analyse DSM's third transformation, this book will focus on fine chemicals in the period after 1970. In addition, the case of Dyneema®, a strong and stiff polyethylene fibre, shows the development of a product in the field of high performance materials. Today, Dyneema® is one of DSM's most remarkable products. It originated from fundamental polymer research in the late 1950s but was commercialised in the late 1980s. Dyneema's® long history provides an interesting insight into the changing role of R&D and changing managerial expectations.

Alongside fine chemicals and Dyneema®, research on urea and caprolactam is followed from 1970 until 1990. The contrast between these two products is interesting. Urea declined in importance for DSM as a fertiliser and today is manufactured only as an intermediate for melamine production. Caprolactam, in contrast, remained an important business for DSM. Urea and caprolactam are interesting cases to analyse the role of research in the maintenance, or decline, of existing businesses.

EPDM and melamine have also remained important products for DSM. The company also invested heavily in the expansion and diversification of its plastics business until the 1990s. Caprolactam is preferred here because of its role in DSM's second transformation. It is then followed further to analyse the role of R&D in the maintenance of existing businesses.

This book ends in 1990. The material presented here provides a sufficient basis for analysing the role of R&D in DSM's three transformations as well as its role in the maintenance of existing businesses. In the period between 1930 and 1990, moreover, management views of R&D went through a full cycle: from high faith to a more critical view in the 1970s, and again to more faith in the 1980s. This cycle can also be seen in DSM's research expenditure. (See graph A2 in the appendix.) A short epilogue reviews some trends in the role and management of industrial research at DSM in the 1990s. In this way the book tries to build a bridge from historical analysis to current practices, and tries to extend the cycle of R&D to the present.

The book is structured chronologically. The chapters follow a format and start with an analysis of business strategy and research organisation, followed by an analysis of research work. The first chapter considers DSM's entry into the chemical industry, the initial build-up of capabilities and the establishment of the Central Laboratory. The next chapter deals with the period 1945-1970 and analyses urea, caprolactam and lysine, as well as the changing organisational structure of research and the shifting strategies. The last two chapters deal with the 1970s and 1980s respectively, again analysing urea and caprolactam but also Dyneema and the build-up of DSM's business and research in fine chemicals. The book closes with answers to the central research questions and a short epilogue on the 1990s.

Notes

1   Let's Pin a Dollar Sign on Industrial Research. *Chemical Engineering* (15 December 1958), 88.

2   The terms 'bulk' and 'fine' chemicals are used following the classification of Charles Kline. In this taxonomy, high-volume products are distinguished from low-volume products, and specification products are distinguished from performance products. Specification products are sold on the basis of chemical composition, while performance chemicals are sold because

they perform a certain function. The difference between high- and low-volume products is important because size brings specific problems in plant design and operation. Scale and product characteristics lead to a four sector classification of the chemical industry:

	Specification products	Performance products
Large scale production	Bulk chemicals	Pseudo-commodities
Small scale production	Fine chemicals	Specialties

The boundaries between different sectors are porous but a classification is useful to define how terms are used. DSM also adopted Kline's four sector model. (C. H. Kline (1976). Maximising Profits in Chemicals. *Chemtech* 6 (February), 110-117. Figure 2, 113. J. A. Bigot (1980). Heden en toekomst van de Nederlandse fijnchemie. *Chemisch Magazine* (November 1980), m 729-m 732. Figure 1, m 729).

3   E. Homburg (1992). The Emergence of Research Laboratories in the Dyestuffs Industry. *British Journal for the History of Science* 25, 91-111.
4   L. S. Reich (1985). *The Making of American Industrial Research: Science and Business at GE and Bell, 1876-1926.* Cambridge: Cambridge University Press.
5   D. A. Hounshell & J. K. Smith (1988). *Science and Corporate Strategy: Du Pont R&D, 1902-1980.* Cambridge: Cambridge University Press. D. A. Hounshell (1996). The Evolution of Industrial Research in the United States. R. S. Rosenbloom & W. J. Spencer, Eds. *Engines of Innovation: U.S. Industrial Research at the End of an Era.* Boston: Harvard Business School Press, 13-85, in particular 21-26.
6   Reich 1985, op. cit. Hounshell & Smith 1988, op. cit. C. Reinhardt (1997). *Forschung in der chemischen Industrie: die Entwicklung synthetische Farbstoffe bei BASF und Hoechst, 1863 bis 1914.* Freiburg: Dissertation Technische Universität Freiburg. W. Wimmer (1994). *"Wir haben fast immer was Neues": Gesundheitswesen und Innovationen der Pharma-Industrie in Deutschland, 1880-1935.* Berlin: Duncker & Humblot. Dissertation Freie Universität Berlin. K. Boersma (2002). *Inventing Structures for Industrial Research. A History of the Philips Nat. Lab. 1914-1946.* Amsterdam: Aksant. Dissertation Eindhoven University of Technology.
7   E. Homburg (2003). *Speuren op de tast. Een historische kijk op industriële en universitaire research.* Maastricht: Universiteit Maastricht. Inaugural lecture 31 October 2003. 16-22. Also: J. J. Hutter (1984). Nederlandse Laboratoria 1860-1940, een kwantitatief overzicht. *Tijdschrift voor de geschiedenis der geneeskunde, natuurkunde, wiskunde en techniek* 9(4), 150-174, particularly graph 1, 153.
8   Homburg 2003, op. cit. particularly 22-23.
9   Hounshell 1996, op. cit. 36-47. See also D. C. Mowery & N. Rosenberg (1998). *Paths of Innovation: Technological Change in 20th-Century America.* Cambridge: Cambridge University Press, 20-30.
10 Homburg 2003, op. cit. 37-38. J. Faber (2003). Het Nederlandse Innovatie Systeem, 1870-1970. *NEHA Jaarboek* 66, 208-232, in particular 226-229.
11 Hounshell & Smith 1988, op. cit.
12 D. A. Hounshell (1992). Du Pont and the Management of Large-Scale Research and Development. P. Galison & B. Hevly, Eds. *Big Science: The Growth of Large-Scale Research.* Stanford: Stanford University Press, 236-261. Hounshell 1996, op. cit.
13 J. R. Anchor (1985). Managerial Perceptions of Research and Development in the UK Chemicals Industry, 1955-1981. *Chemistry and Industry* (1 July 1985), 426-430, (15 July 1985), 459-464, (5 August 1985), 498-504. Homburg 2003, op. cit. 31, 44-45. For general statistics

on the Netherlands see: R. P. van de Kasteele (1979). *R&O: research en ontwikkeling en de Nederlandse onderneming*. Deventer: Kluwer. Graph 3.5.1, 32 and graph 3.5.2, 34.

14 Homburg 2003, op. cit. 39. K. Boersma & M. de Vries (2003). De veranderende rol van het Natuurkundig Laboratorium van het Philipsconcern gedurende de periode 1914-1994. *NEHA Jaarboek* 66, 287-313, in particular 300-306, more in particular 304.

15 M. B. W. Graham (1985a). Industrial Research in the Age of Big Science. *Research on Technological Innovation, Management and Policy* 2, 47-79. M. B. W. Graham (1985b). Corporate Research and Development: The Latest Transformation. *Technology in Society* 7, 179-195. M. B. W. Graham (1988). *The Business of Research: RCA and the VideoDisc*. London: Cambridge University Press.

16 M. B. W. Graham & B. H. Pruitt (1990). *R&D for Industry: A Century of Technical Innovation at Alcoa*. New York: Cambridge University Press, 500.

17 E. Corcoran (1992). Redesigning Research: Trends in Industrial Research. *Scientific American* 266(6), 72-80. H. I. Fusfeld (1994). *Industry's Future: Changing Patterns of Industrial Research*. Washington: American Chemical Society. R. Varma (1995). Restructuring Corporate R&D: From Autonomous to Linkage Model. *Technology Analysis and Strategic Management* 7(2), 231-247. R. Varma (2000). Changing Research Cultures in U.S. Industry. *Science, Technology, & Human Values* 25(4), 395-416.

18 Varma 1995, op. cit. Varma 2000, op. cit. P. A. Roussel, K. N. Saad & T. J. Erickson (1991). *Third Generation R&D: Managing the Link to Corporate Strategy*. Boston: Harvard Business School Press.

19 Homburg 2003, op. cit. English phrase from: E. Homburg (2004). *Groping Along the Track: A Historical Perspective on Industrial and Academic Research*. CONTEC lecture, Eindhoven University of Technology, 1 April 2004.

20 Hounshell & Smith 1988, op. cit. Homburg 2003, op. cit. 18-19.

21 C. Reinhardt (1998). An Instrument of Corporate Strategy: The Central Research Laboratory at BASF, 1868-1914. E. Homburg, A. S. Travis & H. G. Schröter, Eds. *The Chemical Industry in Europe, 1850-1914: Industrial Growth, Pollution and Professionalization*. Dordrecht: Kluwer Academic Publishers, 239-259. Particularly 256.

22 J. M. Utterback (1994). *Mastering the Dynamics of Innovation: How Companies Can Seize Opportunities in the Face of Technological Change*. Boston: Harvard Business School Press, 83-101. Also: J. M. Utterback & W. J. A. Abernathy (1990). A Dynamic Model of Process and Product Innovation. C. Freeman, Ed. *The Economics of Innovation*. Cheltenham: Edward Elgar, 424-441. Originally published in Omega 1975, 3(6).

23 J. S. Plotkin (2003). Petrochemical Technology Development. P. H. Spitz, Ed. *The Chemical Industry at the Millennium: Maturity, Restructuring, and Globalization*. Philadelphia: Chemical Heritage Press, 51-84, particularly 51-53.

24 J. L. Bower (1986). *When Markets Quake: The Management Challenge of Restructuring Industry*. Boston, MA: Harvard Business School Press, 20.

25 Graham 1985b, op. cit. 181.

26 L. Galambos (1992). Theodore N. Vail and the Role of Innovation in the Modern Bell System. *Business History Review* 66(1), 95-126.

27 C. Freeman (1974). *The Economics of Industrial Innovation*. Harmondsworth: Penguin Books. First edition. 254-282. This taxonomy did not change profoundly in the second and third edition of the book.

28 Hounshell & Smith 1988, op. cit.

29 M. A. Dennis (1987). Accounting for Research: New Histories of Corporate Laboratories and the Social History of American Science. *Social Studies of Science* 17, 479-518, in particular 487. Homburg 1992, op. cit. 107, 109. Wimmer 1994, op. cit.

30 Reich 1985, op. cit. 4. Hounshell 1996, op. cit. 40. L. S. Reich (1977). Research and the Struggle to Control Radio: A Study of Big Business and the Uses of Industrial Research. *Business History Review* 51(2), 230-235. Also: D. F. Noble (1977). *America by Design.* New York: Knopf, 95. P. Erker (1990). Die Verwissenschaftlichung der Industrie: Zur Geschichte der Industrieforschungen in den europäischen und amerikanischen Elektrokonzernen. *Zeitschrift für Unternehmensgeschichte* 35(2), 73-94, in particular 92.

31 P. H. Spitz (1988). *Petrochemicals: The Rise of an Industry.* New York: Wiley. Particularly 540-541.

32 See A. van Rooij (2004). *Building Plants: Markets for Technology and Internal Capabilities in DSM's Fertiliser Business, 1925-1970.* Amsterdam: Aksant. Dissertation Eindhoven University of Technology.

33 W. M. Cohen & D. A. Levinthal (1990). Absorptive Capacity: A New Perspective on Learning and Innovation. *Administrative Science Quarterly* 35, 128-152. J. K. Smith (1990). The Scientific Tradition in American Industrial Research. *Technology & Culture* 31, 121-131, in particular 126-127. Also: N. R. Lamoreaux & K. L. Sokoloff (1999). Inventors, Firms and the Market for Technology in the Late Nineteenth and Early Twentieth Century. N. R. Lamoreaux, D. M. G. Raff & P. Temin, Eds. *Learning by Doing in Markets, Firms and Countries.* Chicago: Chicago University Press, 19-57. Van Rooij 2004, op. cit. 21-34.

34 G. Meyer-Thurow (1982). The Industrialization of Invention: A Case Study from the German Chemical Industry. *Isis* 73, 363-383, in particular 370. U. Marsch (2000). *Zwischen Wissenschaft und Wirtschaft: Industrieforschung in Deutschland und Großbritanniën 1880-1936.* Paderborn: Ferdinand Schöningh, 83.

35 Graham 1988, op. cit. 48 and further. Homburg 2003, op. cit. 19.

36 Galambos 1992, op. cit.

37 Graham 1988, op. cit. 4-5, 220-227. Graham & Pruitt 1990, op. cit. 10, 501-504

38 D. A. Hounshell (1998). Measuring the Return on Investment in R&D: Voices from the past, Visions of the Future. *Assessing the Value of Research in the Chemical Sciences: Report of a Workshop.* Washington: National Academy Press. Chemical Sciences Roundtable, National Research Council, 6-17.

39 Hounshell 1998, op. cit. 14.

40 Roussel et al. 1991, op. cit. Varma 1995, 2000, op. cit. Homburg 2003, op. cit.

41 Hounshell 1996, op. cit. 26.

42 G. P. Pisano (2000). In Search of Dynamic Capabilities: The Origins of R&D Competence in Biopharmaceuticals. G. Dosi, R. R. Nelson & S. G. Winter, Eds. *The Nature and Dynamics of Organizational Capabilities.* New York: Oxford University Press, 129-154.

43 Cf. Hounshell 1998, op. cit. 13.

44 E. T. Penrose (1959). *The Theory of the Growth of the Firm.* Oxford: Basil Blackwell.

45 E. Penrose (1971). The Growth of the Firm. A Case Study: The Hercules Powder Company. *Growth of Firms, Middle East Oil and Other Essays.* London: Frank Cass & Co. Ltd., 43-63. Originally published in: Business History Review 1960, 34, 1-23.

46 Van Rooij 2004, op. cit. 20-21.

47 E. Homburg (2000). Epiloog. DSM Research op weg naar de 21e eeuw. H. Lintsen, Ed. *Research tussen vetkool en zoetstof: zestig jaar DSM Research 1940-2000.* Eindhoven/Zutphen: Stichting Historie der Techniek/Walburg Pers, 118-135.

48 Naam is alléén DSM. *DSM Nieuws* 1969, 18(25), 1. F. A. M. Messing (1988). *Geschiedenis van de mijnsluiting in Limburg: Noodzaak en lotgevallen van een regionale herstructurering 1955-1975.* Leiden: Martinus Nijhof, 97.

2

From Works Laboratories to Centralised Research

Late in 1940, DSM's researchers moved to a new, large and spacious laboratory building. Their relocation constituted an important change: the new building housed a centralised research organisation. However, DSM's centralised research department grew out of its existing research organisation and out of its existing research effort. DSM was established as a coal-mining company in 1902 and branched out into coke in 1919 and into fertilisers in 1930. Works laboratories at one of the coke oven plants and at the fertiliser works conducted not only routine quality control but also some research. The initiative to establish a central research organisation came from these laboratories. The works laboratory of the fertiliser works in particular proved crucial for the establishment of DSM's central research department.

In 1940, a dedicated research organisation was nothing new. Pioneering companies in the chemical industry had set the example in the late nineteenth century, and in the Netherlands in the 1910s. These pioneering companies often responded to a specific commercial or technological threat. DSM responded to a diffuse threat. The company thought that centralised industrial research ensured competitiveness. Pioneering companies had put industrial research on the map and DSM adapted to a well-established practice.

The development of research from works laboratories to a centralised and dedicated research department is central to this chapter. The step towards centralised research is analysed from an organisational perspective, focusing on how and why it grew out of works laboratories, and from the perspective of the research work done in the 1930s, focusing on how continuity was built between the works laboratories and centralised research.[1]

Coal and Coke: The Establishment and Development of DSM in the 1910s and 1920s

At the end of the nineteenth century, private companies gave coal-mining in Limburg a boost. Coal had been mined in this region for a long time, but the entry of these companies, mostly with Belgian and German expertise and capital, marked the beginning of large-scale industrial coal-mining in the Netherlands. The involvement of Belgian and German groups sparked a debate about the question of whether or not the Dutch State should intervene and perhaps even take up coal-mining itself. The result of this debate was the establishment of DSM in 1902. The State fully owned DSM and gave the company the right to exploit the coalfields in Limburg that had not yet been granted to private companies.

Planning for the first mine started quickly after DSM had been established. The company mined its first coal in 1908 and soon opened additional pits. Exploratory drilling showed that DSM's second field contained bituminous coal, a type of coal that was suitable for the manufacture of coke but difficult to sell as an energy source for households. Coke was a fuel used for a variety of industrial purposes and in blast furnaces. It was produced by heating bituminous coal without letting in air or oxygen (so-called dry distillation). A gas similar to the well-known coal-based town gas was produced as a by-product. At the end of the nineteenth century, engineering contractors developed industrial plants which gave operators the opportunity to recover and exploit the gas. It was used to supply the heat necessary to distil coal, but could also be sold to surrounding villages and cities. Coke oven plants of this type had other by-products as well.[2]

When it became clear that DSM's second field would produce bituminous coal, management soon considered taking up coke manufacture. In 1910, they decided to build a coke oven plant, but construction of the pit and its adjacent installations took priority. In 1914, the well-known German engineering contractor Hinselmann was hired to build a coke oven plant. To supervise the work of Hinselmann, and to manage the future production of coke, DSM appointed Daan Ross van Lennep, an engineer who had worked in the town gas industry.

The outbreak of the First World War delayed the construction of the coke oven plant, but in 1919 DSM started production and a year later the installation operated at full capacity. The company expanded the coke oven plant as the production of bituminous coal increased. Another bituminous coal field also came into production in 1926. Evence Coppée, like Hinselmann a specialist engineering contractor, built a second, very large, coke oven plant on that site. The installation started production in 1929.

Through these two coke oven plants, DSM became a large manufacturer of coke and also produced substantial amounts of several by-products. Such diversification was explicit policy. DSM's operating results in coal were rather poor and new businesses based on internally-available raw materials were welcome. Frits van Iterson in particular held this view. He had been a professor of mechanical engineering at Delft Technical College (Netherlands, now Delft University of Technology) before he was appointed to DSM's top management in 1914. In this managing board, Van Iterson became responsible for above-ground installations, including the manufacture of coke and by-products, and soon became the driving force behind DSM's diversification. Van Iterson held the opinion that the company ought to maximise the value of its raw materials. Coke manufacture made the company less dependent on the cyclic fluctuations of the coal market. DSM also tried to sell coke oven gas to surrounding municipalities, but this proved to be difficult in the early 1920s. Towns and cities often operated their own facilities to produce town gas and were reluctant to buy coke oven gas from DSM. In the 1920s, however, another feedstock-driven diversification came into view: large scale nitrogen fertilisers.

Nitrogen Fertilisers: DSM's Entry into the Chemical Industry

Ammonia is the key intermediate for the production of nitrogen fertilisers. From the middle of the nineteenth century, the town gas industry, and later the coke industry, formed the main source of supply. Both these industries extracted ammonia from the gas they produced. Most of it went

DSM's first coke oven plant, called Emma, in June 1926. In the foreground are the batteries of ovens in which coal was distilled. The resulting coke was discharged from the ovens and transported to the tower in the back, where it was cooled down, creating a characteristic steam plume. Coke oven plants produced coke, an industrial fuel, and coke oven gas, an important energy source and starting point for chemical operations. Production of coke pulled DSM into the chemical industry.

into the production of ammonium sulphate, the result of a reaction of ammonia and sulphuric acid. The amounts were relatively small, as ammonia production was linked to town gas or coke production, but could be substantial in the case of large coke oven plants. DSM produced ammonium sulphate as a by-product of coke manufacture as well, and dwarfed other Dutch producers because of the scale of the coke oven plants.

In the early 1920s, the French engineering contractor Claude, followed by its German competitor Linde, and soon by several other companies as well, developed processes to extract hydrogen from coke oven gas. Hydrogen was an interesting product at that time. In 1913, the German chemical company BASF had put on stream the first ammonia synthesis plant in the world. BASF manufactured ammonia from its elements, hydrogen and nitrogen. Several engineering contractors followed BASF's breakthrough and developed ammonia synthesis processes. Nitrogen could be produced from atmospheric air by cooling it to low temperatures, but the supply of hydrogen was more difficult. The technologies from Claude and Linde brought a cheap and abundant supply of hydrogen into view: coke oven gas.

There were many coke oven plants around the world and particularly in Europe. With the availability of ammonia synthesis processes, and technologies to extract hydrogen from coke oven gas, a route to nitrogen fertilisers was open to manufacturers of coke. Moreover, the fertiliser mar-

Graph 2.1 Use of nitrogen fertilisers in the Netherlands, 1922/23-1939/40.

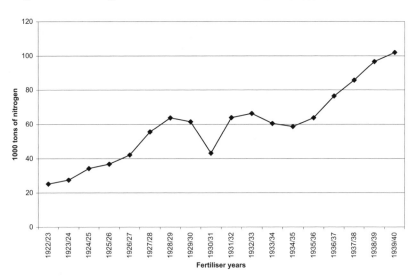

Source: RAL, 17.26/ 19B inv. no. 387: De Nederlandse markt voor stikstofmeststoffen sedert 1921/22, ca. 1955. Note: Fertiliser years ran from 1 July in one year to 1 July in the following year.

THE COMPANY THAT CHANGED ITSELF

ket grew in the 1920s and particularly in the Netherlands (see graph 2.1). Most coke manufacturers already knew the fertiliser market as they often produced ammonium sulphate as a by-product. The route via ammonia synthesis would boost production tremendously, however.

As a large manufacturer of coke, DSM was interested in the large-scale manufacture of fertilisers. For Van Iterson, the route to fertilisers via ammonia synthesis was interesting primarily because it would use internally-available feedstock and energy. Fertiliser production would consume large amounts of coke oven gas and also a large part of the electricity that the company generated in its own power station. Fertilisers opened up the possibility of making more money out of the coal and coke operations. Calculations of profits also showed promising results, but a thorough analysis of the market and DSM's possible position was not made. DSM simply assumed there was a market for its greatly expanded production.

At the end of 1925, the option of large-scale fertiliser manufacture took concrete shape for the first time, but it took several years before Van Iterson and Ross van Lennep detailed the final plans. Internal development of the necessary technology was not considered because DSM did not have the capability to do so, and because ammonia and fertiliser technologies were available from several engineering contractors.[3] DSM chose to hire one of these contractors: the Belgian company AMMONIAQUE SYNTHÉTIQUE ET DÉRIVÉS (ASED), a joint venture of Coppée and Montecatini. Coppée was an experienced engineering contractor that had worked for DSM before; Montecatini was the leading company of the Italian chemical industry and had developed its own ammonia synthesis technology. ASED built an ammonia plant for DSM, as well as a plant for the manufacture of ammonium sulphate. Construction of the new plants started in 1928.

DSM also took steps in the late 1920s to build a market for its fertilisers. The company developed close relationships with farmers' cooperatives in the Netherlands, who controlled the Dutch market, and built a network of sales agents abroad. In May 1930, DSM's fertiliser works, called the SBB (*Stikstofbindingsbedrijf*, Dutch for 'nitrogen fixation works'), shipped its first ammonium sulphate. Prices fell dramatically, however, because many other coke producers had decided to build an ammonia plant and boost their fertiliser production (Graph 2.2.). Most of them produced mainly ammonium sulphate and the market was oversupplied. IG Farbenindustrie, the conglomerate into which BASF had merged with some other major German chemical companies in 1925, took the lead in establishing a fertiliser cartel and this cartel stabilised prices after 1932. Moreover, the Dutch government restricted imports of nitrogen fertilisers in 1934, after many other countries had done the same in the early 1930s. Finally, the Dutch fertiliser industry established a central sales office in 1935 (called central sales office for nitrogen fertilisers: *Centraal Stikstofverkoopkantoor*,

CSV). This sales office united Dutch producers and also became the sole importer of nitrogen fertilisers.[4]

The cartel, import limitations and the CSV stabilised the fertiliser market. The SBB in the meantime cut its production costs, expanded production and diversified. In August 1931, DSM hired Uhde, a German contractor with extensive interests in fertiliser technologies, to engineer and construct a nitric acid plant and a plant for the manufacture of calcium ammonium nitrate. Nitric acid was an intermediate necessary for the manufacture of this fertiliser.

For the SBB, the first half of the 1930s was difficult but fertiliser production incurred no losses and profitability improved substantially after 1935.[5] The SBB performed well in comparison to DSM's other activities. Feedstock-driven diversification paid off in this way. Coal led to coke and, through coke oven gas, to ammonia and fertilisers. The availability of technology gave DSM the means to pursue this feedstock-driven course as engineering contractors built both the coke oven plants and the large-scale fertiliser production plants.

The course DSM took with its diversifications into coke and fertilisers shows that the Dutch government gave the company the freedom to develop its own policies. DSM was fully state-owned but in 1913 government instructed top management to run the company like a private business. Unlike other state-owned companies, DSM had no monopoly but

Graph 2.2. Prices of ammonium sulphate and calcium ammonium nitrate in the Netherlands.

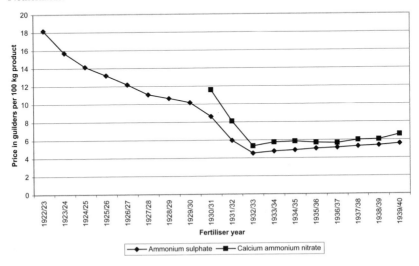

Source: RAL, 17.26/19B inv. no. 387: Het stikstoverbruik in Nederland. Bogers, 15 December 1950.

THE COMPANY THAT CHANGED ITSELF

competed with other businesses. To meet this competition, the company was given more freedom than the Dutch postal, telegraph and telephone services for instance, where the involvement of the Dutch government was much more direct. The instructions of 1913 were to remain the framework for the relations between DSM and the Dutch state until the late 1980s, when the government privatised part of the company.[6]

Keeping Up: The Establishment of the Central Laboratory

Works Laboratories at DSM

When the first coke oven plant started in 1919, DSM established a works laboratory near this plant for routine control of raw materials, intermediates and end products. This laboratory checked the quality of the coal used for coking, and also (among others) the by-product, ammonium sulphate. In the 1920s, the works laboratory of the coke oven plant also started to work for the mines. It tested air samples, which enabled control of ventilation and was important for the safety of the miners. Almost 7,000 samples were tested in 1928. The works laboratory also tested the strength of concrete and other materials. Shaft derricks, cooling towers and other buildings were often designed in-house and made of reinforced concrete. Tests of building materials were important when DSM undertook expansion and revamping projects.[7]

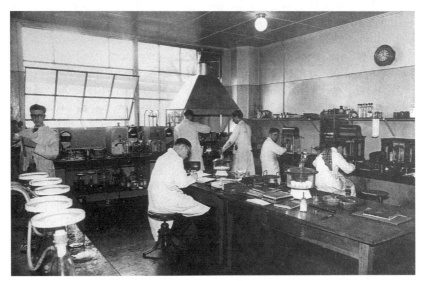

The works laboratory of the Emma coke oven plant in 1923. The production of coke, coke oven gas and by-products was checked and supported by analysis. This routine work took up most of the time in the laboratory, but some research was conducted as well, although on a limited scale.

The expansion of the tasks and workload of the works laboratory led top management to upgrade this facility to a 'Central Laboratory' around 1928. The name reflected the central position the works laboratory had developed in DSM's organisation. DSM hired Honoré Pieters in November 1928 to head the Central Laboratory. Pieters had studied at Delft Technical College and had worked at the analytical laboratory of this technical college before joining DSM.[8]

Under Pieters, DSM's Central Laboratory conducted some research in the late 1920s and in the 1930s, alongside the routine checks that constituted its main task. The laboratory helped DSM's production units solve problems and also worked on improvements of technologies in use. Research was conducted to improve the removal of sulphur compounds from coke oven gas, for instance, leading to the so-called wet-purification process. The laboratory also worked on the improvement of analysis techniques, which could improve the speed and efficiency of its service work. Research work was small-scale, however. Service research was the Central Laboratory's primary task.[9]

Besides the Central Laboratory, DSM established a Central Experimental Station (*Centraal Proefstation*) in 1929, focused on supporting DSM's mining operations. The Central Experimental Station conducted service work and some research, particularly in relation to mechanical engineering problems. The Experimental Station investigated the transportation of coal in the mines and coal classification, among others. It was also involved in research on electric welding. Besides mechanical engineering, physics was an important discipline at the Central Experimental Station.[10]

Besides the Central Laboratory and the Central Experimental Station, DSM had a sizeable technical organisation in relation to its coal operations for planning and executing projects. DSM was a large, technology-oriented company.[11] This organisation and its capabilities also played a role in the establishment of large-scale fertiliser manufacture. DSM constructed the buildings necessary to house the installations ASED supplied and designed the infrastructure around the plant. DSM also had a lot of experience in supervising the work of contractors. Still, the start of large-scale fertiliser manufacture presented a challenge to DSM. Van Iterson wanted to hire engineers and chemists who had the ability to comprehend the processes used in the SBB's plants. In 1930, Van Iterson hired three academically-trained chemical engineers to oversee the production of ammonia and solve operational problems to guarantee continuous production. These three engineers, Jan van Aken, Johan Goris and Herman Zelders, came from the Dutch company ENKA, a manufacturer of synthetic fibres.[12]

The ammonia plant had Van Iterson's special attention. He wanted to hire a physicist to work in the gas and air separation section of the ammonia plant. With cryogenic technology, using extremely low temperatures, hydrogen and nitrogen were manufactured there. Van Iterson could not find a physicist, but his contacts suggested Gé Berkhoff, an academically-trained chemist. Berkhoff was hired in 1929 but he first worked at the cryogenic laboratory of Leiden University. He was subsequently transferred to Willebroek in Belgium, where ASED operated plants comparable to those they were building for DSM. Berkhoff then came to the SBB, where he coached Van Aken, Goris and Zelders.

In the early 1930s, the SBB established its own works laboratory for routine quality control of fertiliser production. Soon after its start-up, the ammonia plant operated fairly smoothly and the SBB manufactured fertilisers without major problems. Berkhoff was appointed head of the SBB's works laboratory, and both Goris and Zelders came along with him. Van Aken was transferred to the staff department of the SBB. A final organisational addition to the SBB was the establishment of a patent department in 1932.

Bold Plans: Towards a Dedicated Research Organisation

In a short period of time, DSM built a large fertiliser works and learnt the day-to-day routine of fertiliser production. This was no small achievement. By the 1930s, however, chemical companies and firms in other industries

The works laboratory of the SBB nitrogen fixation works. The laboratory's main task was routine production control, but it was also responsible for two diversifications and an important improvement in ammonium sulphate manufacture. The SBB works laboratory was an important building block for the Central Laboratory.

had established large, independent research laboratories, intended to improve existing products and processes and to work on diversification. In a report on the activities of the Central Laboratory between 1920 and 1929, Pieters noted that research was a very important activity of his laboratory, but that it was sometimes hampered by inadequate facilities and a shortage of personnel, in particular qualified personnel.[13]

In December 1928, a few months after the construction of the SBB had started, top management considered research to be of the highest importance for the company. Drawing on the examples of IG Farben in Germany and Philips in the Netherlands, DSM's top management argued that 'An industry of a large size can only flourish through private research (...).' Nevertheless, the time had not come to establish a research laboratory because the fertiliser works was still under construction.[14]

Seven years later, Pieters and Berkhoff put the question of whether or not DSM should establish a dedicated research organisation back on the agenda. In 1935 they proposed merging the Central Laboratory with the SBB's works laboratory. The Central Laboratory would then become the works laboratory for DSM's first coke oven plant, complementing the works laboratory that had in the meantime been established at the company's second coke oven plant. The remaining parts of the Central Laboratory would be merged with the works laboratory of the SBB into a new organisation that should be located near fertiliser production. This organisation would become responsible for all material testing, routine production control of fertilisers, and research for both the coke and fertiliser operations. Pieters and Berkhoff proposed bringing together the chemists working in DSM's laboratories in a centralised organisation. Their focus on chemists reflects the establishment and early growth of the SBB. Pieters and Berkhoff argued that in this way better use could be made of the available personnel, instruments and library. Moreover, they argued that the close contact between chemists was an important advantage.[15]

Top management responded to Pieters and Berkhoff's proposal by establishing a committee, chaired by Berkhoff. Although Van Iterson was not part of this committee, he actively involved himself with the issue Pieters and Berkhoff had put on the agenda. Van Iterson visited several companies to familiarise himself with R&D practice. He emphasised that industrial research was necessary 'to keep up': DSM should establish a dedicated research organisation to prevent the company from becoming uncompetitive.[16] In contrast, R&D pioneers like Du Pont and BASF often started doing industrial research because of a specific commercial or technological threat. For instance, the enactment of the German patent law was one of the reasons why German dyestuff firms built laboratories in the late 1870s and 1880s. For DSM there was no compelling reason to set up a research department. Van Iterson believed that industrial research was a necessity to remain competitive. Berkhoff and others shared this view. The case of DSM shows that R&D had become an accepted part of business strategy in the chemical industry. The company adapted itself to established practices.

In 1938, Berkhoff's committee drafted a plan for DSM's new research organisation. The new plan no longer argued for a merger between the Central Laboratory and the SBB's works laboratory but proposed a reorganisation of all research work at DSM. Works laboratories at both coke oven plants and at the SBB would become responsible for routine production control. The Central Experimental Station would remain independent and concentrate on issues related to coal-mining. All other work would be centralised in a new laboratory, to be located at the SBB, and to be called the Central Laboratory, taking over this name from Pieters' laboratory.

The committee also proposed expanding research work substantially. In 1938 the number of people working in all of DSM's laboratories totalled 147. The committee planned that this number would more than double to 342 by 1941, with the new Central Laboratory accounting for 204 people. A large new building would have to be built. In addition, the committee proposed constructing a new building for the Central Experimental Station to improve its facilities. These were 'bold plans', Berkhoff recalled in 1990.[17]

Although the plans were bold for DSM, leading Dutch industrial firms and leading nitrogen fertiliser producers were conducting research on a larger scale than DSM. Among the SBB's direct competitors were companies like IG Farben, ICI from Great Britain and Montecatini from Italy. All had large research facilities. In 1938, IG Farben employed 124 academically-trained people alone at its ammonia laboratory in Oppau, where BASF had put on stream the first ammonia synthesis plant in the world. In the Netherlands, Philips employed 476 people in research in 1939. In the same year, the Bataafsche Petroleum Maatschappij (BPM), the Dutch operating arm of Royal Dutch/Shell, employed 1165 people at their research centre in Amsterdam.

DSM did not lag behind other coke companies that diversified into fertilisers in the 1920s and 1930s. There were two other producers of nitrogen fertilisers in the Netherlands: the Maatschappij tot Exploitatie van Kooks-ovengassen (Mekog) in IJmuiden, which started production in 1929; and the Compagnie Neérlandaise de l'Azote (CNA) in Sluiskil, which started production in 1930. CNA opened a small laboratory in 1930, soon after production started. This laboratory mainly worked on improving the ammonia plant. Mekog leaned heavily on BPM, one of its major shareholders, and lacked independent innovative capacity before the Second World War.

Berkhoff's committee also drafted ambitious plans for the content of the Central Laboratory's research. Besides research on existing products and processes, work was planned that aimed at utilising the available raw materials to establish new lines of business. The use of nitric acid for the production of dyes and explosives was one of the topics considered. Research on new products and processes was also planned, as well as fundamental research and some product research. Fundamental research would be focused on catalysis and crystallisation, for instance. Catalytic processes were the basis of the production of ammonia and nitric acid, two crucial intermediates for the production of fertilisers. Crystallisation was an important process in the production of ammonium sulphate.[18] Fundamental research aimed at gaining a deep understanding of topics that were of high industrial relevance. The choice of topics for fundamental research was not based on scientific interest or just plain curiosity on the part of researchers. Moreover, catalysis and crystallisation were difficult to research for universities because their organisations were oriented towards scientific disciplines.[19]

In 1938, top management approved the plans to organise a central research department. They also approved the plans to build new facilities for the Central Laboratory and the Central Experimental Station. In November 1940, the first wing of the Central Laboratory's building was put into use (at Geleen). In 1942, the new facilities of the Central Experimental Station were put into use (at Treebeek).[20]

With the new Central Laboratory, DSM had a dedicated research department and had adapted itself to the established practice of R&D in the chemical industry. Organisationally, the Central Laboratory grew out of decentralised works laboratories. A decentral initiative, moreover, set DSM on the track of a centralised and dedicated research organisation. The proposal of Pieters and Berkhoff from 1935 put the issue of research back on the agenda and formulated an outline of a dedicated organisation.

Development of the Central Laboratory's Organisation
After the Central Laboratory's building had been put into use, three departments were set up in 1941: Organic Products, Physical Chemistry and General Chemistry. The organisation was disciplinary and based on main branches of chemistry. Unlike the Organic Products and Physical Chemistry departments, the General Chemistry department was generic and was involved in, for example, chemical analysis. It also conducted research on corrosion, a common problem in chemical plants. In 1938, a permanent fertiliser pilot plant had been established at the SBB to investigate production problems on scale. This installation remained the responsibility of the SBB to enable a close cooperation between research and production, and

Figure 2.1. Organisational structure of DSM's chemical sector after 1942.

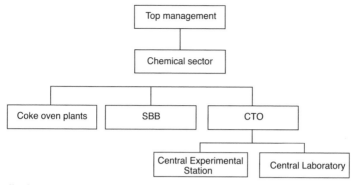

Note: all other units outside the chemical sector have been excluded from this diagram.

to enable training of production personnel.[21]

The organisation of the Central Laboratory changed through the splitting up of the General Chemistry and Physical Chemistry departments. Around 1944, Corrosion Research and Coal Research, mainly aimed at coke and related subjects, split off from General Chemistry. Inorganic Chemistry, mainly aimed at fertilisers, and Chemical Technology, mainly aimed at generic process research and equipment, split off from the Physical Chemistry Department. The name of the Organic Products department changed to Organic Chemistry, marking the completion of the reorganisation.[22]

In 1940, Berkhoff was appointed research director of the Central Laboratory and Pieters was appointed as his deputy. Berkhoff had been hired for production support in the ammonia plant but his role in the establishment of the Central Laboratory shows that he developed a strategic role in the 1930s. His appointment as research director completed this development.

The Central Laboratory, the SBB and the coke oven plants organisationally belonged to a chemical sector (*Chemische Bedrijven*), headed by Ross van Lennep, who in turn reported to Van Iterson in top management. In 1942, DSM merged the Central Laboratory, the Central Experimental Station and the SBB's patent department into the Central Technological Research Organisation (*Centrale Technische Onderzoekingsdienst*, CTO). Berkhoff was appointed head of CTO on 1 January 1943 and continued to report to Ross van Lennep. Pieters became responsible for finance, personnel and other support functions of the Central Laboratory.[23] (See also figure 2.1.)

The outbreak of the Second World War seriously hindered the buildup of the Central Laboratory. Staff was kept to a minimum to prevent the laboratory's involvement in the German war effort. Diversification seemed to be impossible, so researchers focused on the processes in the SBB's plants. The ammonia and nitric acid processes were studied and catalysis research was taken up. The Central Laboratory also worked on products that could substitute scarce materials. Goris worked on a process for synthetic rubber in cooperation with staff engineers from the SBB. The success of these products was limited. For instance, rubber processors tried to make bicycle tyres from DSM's synthetic rubber but the quality of the tyres was poor and the processing of the rubber difficult.[24]

Although the war hindered the development of the Central Laboratory, the laboratory could work without major interference from the Germans and could steadily grow in size to a workforce of about 200 at the end of the war. By contrast, the laboratories of BPM were cut off from the rest of Royal Dutch/Shell and from its feedstocks. Researchers were posted to government agencies and to other companies, while researchers at Amsterdam provided their services to other Dutch firms. At Philips, the research organisation started to function as a safe haven for researchers and scientists who were faced with the prospect of unemployment or forced labour in Germany.[25]

From Passive to Active: Research at the SBB's Works Laboratory and the Establishment of the Central Laboratory

In its plan of 1938, Berkhoff's committee argued that the establishment of a new Central Laboratory followed from the development of DSM and from the work of the laboratories the company was already operating. The day-to-day operations of DSM asked for routine quality control but these activities expanded into research work. The committee characterised this as a trend from 'a more passive to a more active attitude'.[26]

The links between DSM's works laboratories and of the Central Laboratory indeed go beyond organisational links. Research at the SBB's works laboratory in particular played an important role in the establishment of Central Laboratory. The new research organisation completed DSM's build-up of technological capabilities in the chemical industry.

Diversification: Alcohol

Berkhoff's role in the establishment of the Central Laboratory shows the strategic role he developed. Before he and Pieters wrote the proposal to centralise research, Berkhoff had put the issue of diversification on the agenda. In October 1932 he wrote a report in which he outlined the position of the SBB. Berkhoff expected that the price of fertilisers, ammonium sulphate in particular, would drop further, and that diversification was therefore necessary. He listed possible fertilisers but also pointed to other products.[27] The SBB's works laboratory was already working on one possible diversification outside fertilisers: the production of alcohol.

Research on alcohol started in 1931. Goris, who had been transferred to the SBB's works laboratory together with Berkhoff, conducted the crucial work on this project. Research started with a review of the available literature. It was known that alcohol could be manufactured from ethylene, using concentrated sulphuric acid. Several companies used this route in the 1920s, but DSM would use ethylene from coke oven gas, and moreover on a large scale. That was a departure from established practice. In the manufacture of hydrogen in the coke oven gas separation section of the ammonia plant, a fraction was released that contained ethylene. It was used to fire equipment but production of alcohol promised to be a more profitable use.

As the route to alcohol was known, research focused on process development and engineering. In 1935 a pilot plant was constructed and the decision to build an industrial plant was taken in December of that year. Research continued, however, and in 1938 construction of the plant started. In 1940 it was in regular production. It was the first plant in the world that produced alcohol on the basis of ethylene from coke oven gas, a real breakthrough.

During the construction of the alcohol plant, DSM hired several equipment manufacturers for specialist tasks, but the alcohol plant primarily relied on in-house work. Innovation strategy was offensive. The development of the alcohol process shows that research at the SBB's works laboratory enabled a diversification shortly after DSM had entered the chemical industry. Capabilities were being built fast.

Diversification, and research that led to diversification, were feedstock-driven. Again, DSM simply assumed there was a market. For the sale of its product the company struck a deal with the central sales office of the other alcohol producers in the Netherlands in 1939.[28]

Diversification in Fertilisers: The Start of Mixed Fertiliser Production
Around the time when the SBB started production of alcohol, it also started producing mixed fertilisers. Straight fertilisers such as ammonium sulphate contained only one of the three plant nutrients (nitrogen, phosphate, potassium) while mixed fertilisers contained two or all three. They could be manufactured by chemical processes or by dry-mixing several straight products. Mixed fertilisers were typically produced in a wide variety of formulations.

In 1937, Berkhoff put the possibility of mixed fertiliser production on the map. He argued that mixed fertilisers were attractive to DSM from a commercial point of view, given the demand for them and the price level. Berkhoff also expected that, in the long term, fertilisers with a high content of plant nutrients would dominate the fertiliser market. Mixed fertilisers presented an option to adapt to this trend because they contained little else beside plant nutrients. Calcium ammonium nitrate, for instance, contained marl.

In his report, Berkhoff reviewed the available options to start mixed fertiliser production. He considered that DSM should produce only one grade and should not aim at product diversity. This implied that he focused on chemical processes, in which there were two basic options. To obtain a product with phosphate, the necessary ingredient was phosphate rock, which was mined in several places around the world. Phosphate rock could be treated with sulphuric acid, a practice commonly used in the well-established manufacture of superphosphate, the main straight phosphate fertiliser. Treating superphosphate with ammonia led to ammonium phosphates, a mixed fertiliser with nitrogen and phosphate.

Another route to mixed fertilisers treated phosphate rock with nitric acid. This process also led to products with nitrogen and phosphate but these were called nitro phosphates. Several companies had investigated this route in the 1920s, but with mixed success as product quality was poor. In 1928, the Norwegian company Odda Smelteverk developed a nitro phosphate process that promised to lead to marketable mixed fertilisers with calcium nitrate, a straight fertiliser, as a by-product.

Berkhoff expected that Odda's process would give the SBB a strong position in the production of mixed fertilisers. He felt that the costs of treating phosphate rock with nitric acid instead of sulphuric acid would be lower, and that the SBB would therefore be able to meet the competition of the superphosphate industry. Packaging and transportation costs were low when calculated on the basis of plant nutrients because the content of plant nutrients was high. This gave farmers the opportunity to save on fertilisers. For this reason, Berkhoff expected mixed fertilisers to have a promising future.

Odda, however, had taken out patents on its process, but had not developed the process on an industrial scale. Buying a plant from an engineering contractor was not possible, simply because they had not developed the necessary technology. Establishing mixed fertiliser production therefore imposed higher demands on the SBB's internal capabilities than the entry into the fertiliser business in the late 1920s. Berkhoff did not consider this a problem. At the end of 1937, DSM established contact with Odda. Berkhoff was present at the first meeting with the Norwegian company. At this meeting it became clear that DSM could obtain a license on Odda's patents. Odda valued the involvement of DSM and hinted at the possibility of further technology sales when DSM had developed the process. Negotiations continued for several years, but were hindered because IG Farben had taken over an option on Odda's German patents and also tried to patent its variant of the Norwegian process in the Netherlands. DSM prevented this by opposing IG Farben's patent application, but could now only buy Odda's Dutch patents. Odda and DSM struck an agreement in principle in 1939. Two years later, just before the plant was to go on stream, DSM finally bought the patents.

Alongside the negotiations with Odda, research on the mixed fertiliser process had started. Jean Plusjé, who had just graduated from Delft Technical College, was hired for this project in 1937. In the following year he developed the Odda process on laboratory scale, without making major changes to the Norwegian technology. Development work started in 1938 and two pilot plants, a small one and a larger one, were built in that year.

In June 1938, only six months after the first contacts with Odda, DSM's top management decided to build a mixed fertiliser plant. It was part of a larger expansion programme that boosted the production of ammonia, nitric acid and calcium ammonium nitrate as well. In 1941 the production of mixed fertilisers started, but it had to be stopped a year later because of a shortage of phosphate rock, the basic raw material of mixed fertiliser production. After the war, however, mixed fertiliser production was taken up again and expanded to become an important product for the SBB.[29]

As in the case of the alcohol process, the SBB's works laboratory initiated and enabled diversification in mixed fertilisers. Odda's patents provided a springboard into this field, but the Norwegian process had to be developed into an industrial process. Besides development, some process research was also necessary. In-house research work complemented external technology in this way. Innovation strategy was defensive. In the case of alcohol, DSM pursued a more offensive innovation strategy and external technology played no role. In other words, the role of external technology varied according to DSM's innovation strategy.

Incremental Innovation: The Improvement of the Ammonium Sulphate Process
The SBB's works laboratory not only initiated and enabled diversification. After Berkhoff had been transferred to the works laboratory, the improvement of the SBB's ammonium sulphate was one of the first projects he was involved in. It was also a project in which he performed the role of researcher.

Ammonium sulphate was the SBB's only product until the calcium ammonium nitrate plant went on stream. Competition came from the Dutch town gas industry and from foreign manufacturers, particularly from BASF, the leading company in the fertiliser industry at that time. Ammonium sulphate was the main nitrogen fertiliser, but in the late 1920s and early 1930s many other operators of coke oven plants had started manufacturing fertilisers with ammonium sulphate on a large scale. The market was oversupplied and prices were dropping. (See also graph 2.2.) BASF, moreover, had succeeded in improving the quality of its ammonium sulphate. Nitrogen fertilisers had a tendency to cake: they attracted water, making the particles stick to each other and form one solid mass. Another unwanted feature was the formation of dust (small particles) in fertiliser bags. BASF had succeeded in reducing caking and dust formation in its ammonium sulphate. The German company exported large amounts of fertilisers to the Netherlands and to several other markets in which the SBB was also active.

Berkhoff started working on ammonium sulphate in 1931. This fertiliser was manufactured with ammonia and sulphuric acid through a crystallisation process in saturators, basically vessels made from a material that could withstand the corroding effect of the acid. Berkhoff investigated how crystallisation worked and whether it could be modified to improve product quality. Berkhoff's research led to changes in operating procedure and to changes in the design of the plant. The SBB's staff engineered the plant modifications and altered the installation while production continued. By September 1933 they finished this work.

Berkhoff also investigated the influence of sulphuric acid. He found that certain impurities led to small crystals, and worked out a procedure to bind the impurities and prevent the formation of small crystals. Finally, the SBB introduced a coating, a common procedure in the fertiliser industry to prevent or reduce caking by adding a compound to the fertilisers. In this case, some gas oil covered the ammonium sulphate crystals and reduced the product's tendency to cake.

With the improved ammonium sulphate process the SBB innovated for the first time, only a short time after large-scale fertiliser manufacture had started. Product quality improved crucially through Berkhoff's research at the works laboratory, enabling the SBB to meet the competition. Similar improvements were made to other acquired plants as well. Van Aken modified the production of calcium ammonium nitrate for instance; these modifications were put on stream in March 1935.[30] In the improvement of the ammonium sulphate process, research meant development work but some engineering had to be done as well.

Research at the SBB in the 1930s
The research performed at the SBB's works laboratory played an important role in the development of DSM's chemical businesses in the 1930s. In the first place, it enabled DSM to defend existing market positions. The quality of the SBB's ammonium sulphate had to be improved to remain competitive. Berkhoff's research played a crucial role here. In the second place, research led to diversification. The SBB's works laboratory initiated diversification in mixed fertilisers and alcohol. Its research also enabled these two projects.

Berkhoff was the crucial figure at the SBB's works laboratory. Hired for production support in the ammonia plant in 1929, his research formed the basis of the improvement of ammonium sulphate. At the SBB's works laboratory, Berkhoff developed a strategic role. He wrote a report on diversification in 1932 and, with Pieters, put the issue of a dedicated research organisation on the agenda three years later. Berkhoff also initiated the mixed fertiliser project. Berkhoff's appointment as the Central Laboratory's head in 1940 clearly indicates how much his role had changed in the eleven years he had worked for DSM.

Berkhoff's work on ammonium sulphate also shows the continuity in subjects researched at the SBB's works laboratory and the Central Laboratory. Research on crystallisation started when Berkhoff investigated the ammonium sulphate production process, and was included in the Central Laboratory's research programme in 1938. Similarly, Zelders had started research on corrosion while he was at the SBB's works laboratory, and he set up this research at the Central Laboratory in 1941. Plusjé and Goris also transferred to the Central Laboratory. Plusjé moved to the Central Laboratory in 1940 to work at the Physical Chemistry department. In 1943 he became head of the Inorganic Chemistry department. Goris had become head of the Organic Chemistry department a year earlier. People and projects formed the bridge between the SBB's works laboratory and the Central Laboratory.

Research by Pieters' works laboratory also influenced the Central Laboratory's research programme. This explains why, for example, the Central Laboratory continued to do research on coke oven gas purification. Other projects included pyridine, a fine chemical that could be produced from coal tar, a by-product of town gas and coke manufacture. Pieters' laboratory had started limited research on pyridine at the end of the 1920s; this research was related to coke oven gas purification. Pieters and a colleague aimed to remove the small amounts of pyridine, and also phenol, by changing the process by which benzene was removed from coke oven gas.[31]

In 1935, Pieters' laboratory had also started work on phthalic anhydride, a compound that was used in paints and that could be manufactured from naphthalene, a by-product of the coking operations. Research on this compound continued after the establishment of the Central Laboratory. A small pilot plant was started in May 1941, but operated for a short time only due to the German occupation of the Netherlands. After the war, the Dutch paint industry urgently needed phthalic anhydride. Although research had continued, it would still take time before a plant could be built. Engineering contractors offered industrial processes, however, and DSM decided to buy a plant from the American contractor Foster Wheeler to save time. DSM started producing phthalic anhydride in 1951 but it did not become an important product for the company. Production ceased in 1963.[32]

Research at Pieters' works laboratory related primarily to the coke oven plants, reflecting the origins and location of this facility. Its role in the SBB's main research-based diversifications was small, although the work on phthalic anhydride provided a foundation for the acquisition of external technology.

The Establishment of the Central Laboratory

Diversification at DSM was feedstock-driven in the 1920s and 1930s: coal-mining led to the manufacture of coke; coke oven gas led to ammonia and fertilisers. Another driver of diversification, besides the availability of feedstocks, was the availability of technology. Engineering contractors built two large coke oven plants in the 1910s and 1920s; ASED and Uhde built a large fertiliser works between 1928 and 1932 with plants for the production of ammonia, nitric acid, ammonium sulphate and calcium ammonium nitrate.

DSM rapidly built capabilities in the chemical industry. The SBB hired capable engineers and chemists and built a works laboratory. Pieters' works laboratory and DSM's central coal-related technological organisation further added to these capabilities. The SBB's works laboratory played a crucial role in the alcohol and mixed fertiliser diversifications and in the improvement of ammonium sulphate product quality. Research at DSM in the 1930s initiated and enabled diversifications, and also improved existing technologies. Research, too, was feedstock-driven. The availability of ethylene led to research on alcohol, and nitric acid linked the mixed fertiliser project to existing businesses.

In the 1930s, research at DSM was done without a formal, dedicated research organisation. Nevertheless, this research built a foundation for the establishment of the Central Laboratory, the centralised research department that grew out of the decentralised research organisation of the 1930s. Pieters and Berkhoff put centralised research on the map at DSM and both were transferred to the Central Laboratory. Several other researchers from DSM's works laboratories were also reassigned to the new research organisation.

Berkhoff personifies the road to the Central Laboratory. Hired for production support in ammonia, he became head of the SBB's works laboratory. He worked on ammonium sulphate but soon developed a strategic role. In his strategic role, Berkhoff initiated diversifications and, together with Pieters, wrote the proposal to centralise research. His appointment as head of the Central Laboratory completed his development in the 1930s.

Besides Berkhoff and Pieters, Van Iterson and Ross van Lennep were important in the development of research and the SBB in the 1930s. As head of DSM's chemical sector, Ross van Lennep translated Van Iterson's vision into operational practice. Van Iterson was the driving force behind DSM's diversifications into coke and large-scale fertiliser manufacture. He also decided that the SBB should not remain dependent on engineering contractors, and hired several engineers and chemists to give fertiliser production a foundation of technological know-how. From this perspective it is clear that Van Iterson embraced the issue of research. The SBB did not confront a specific commercial or technological threat like the R&D pioneers had done. DSM decided to establish the Central Laboratory in 1938, after the difficult period in fertilisers had been overcome. According to Van Iterson, research was necessary to keep up and remain competitive.

People and projects built continuity and laid a foundation for the establishment of the Central Laboratory. Histories of research at DSM have somewhat neglected this foundation, particularly in relation to the research work at the SBB's works laboratory in the 1930s.[33] The Central Laboratory grew out of the research organisation and the research work of the 1930s. After the Second World War, DSM embarked on a process of expansion and diversification in its chemical businesses, and the Central Laboratory similarly grew in size and scope.

Notes

1   This chapter draws on: A. van Rooij (2003). Aangekochte technologie en industriële research bij het Stikstofbindingsbedrijf van de Staatsmijnen in de jaren 1930. *NEHA Jaarboek* 66, 263-286. A. van Rooij (2004). *Building Plants: Markets for Technology and Internal Capabilities in DSM's Fertiliser Business, 1925-1970.* Amsterdam: Aksant. Dissertation Eindhoven University of Technology. Chapters 3 and 4. The case studies in particular draw on these studies.

2   For an overview see: W. Buschmann, Ed. (1993). *Koks, Gas, Kohlechemie: Geschichte und gegenständliche Überlieferung der Kohleveredlung.* Essen: Klartext Verlag.

3   See Van Rooij 2004, op. cit. chapter 3 for a more extensive analysis of the reasons to acquire technology.

4   E. Homburg, with contributions by A. van Rooij (2004). *Groeien door kunstmest: DSM Agro 1929-2004.* Hilversum: Verloren, 59-62, 65-68. The history of the fertiliser cartel of the 1930s is well-documented. See for instance: H. G. Schröter (1991). Privatwirtschaftliche Marktregulierung und Staatliche Interessenpolitik. Das internationale Stickstoffkartell 1929-1939. H. G. Schröter & C. A. Wurm, Eds. *Politik, Wirtschaft und internationale Beziehungen: Studien zu ihrem Verhältnis in der Zeit zwischen den Weltkriegen.* Mainz: Philipp von Zabern, 117-137.

5   Homburg 2004, op. cit. 76-79.

6   F. A. M. Messing (1988). *Geschiedenis van de mijnsluiting in Limburg: Noodzaak en lotgevallen van een regionale herstructurering 1955-1975.* Leiden: Martinus Nijhof, 99. For the Dutch postal, telegraph and telephone service see: M. Davids (1999). *Weg naar zelfstandigheid: de voorgeschiedenis van de verzelfstandiging van de PTT in 1989.* Hilversum: Verloren. Dissertation Erasmus University Rotterdam.

7   RAL, 17.26/ 36A inv. no. 2: Verslag van het Centraal Laboratorium der Staatsmijnen op 1 januari 1929. CL, Pieters, 20 January 1929. H. A. J. Pieters (1929). Het Centraal Laboratorium der Staatsmijnen. *Chemisch Weekblad* 26(23), 318-321.

8   H. J. Merx (1955a). *Chronologisch overzicht van de geschiedenis van de Cokesfabrieken en het Gasdistributiebedrijf 1912-1952*. Heerlen: Archief van de Staatsmijnen in Limburg, 31. Afscheid van dr. ir. H. A. J. Pieters. *Nieuws van de Staatsmijnen* 1962, 11(2), 8.

9   Pieters 1929, op. cit. 318. J. G. de Voogd (1937). Verslag van de 65ste algemene vergadering van gasfabrikanten in Nederland. *Chemisch Weekblad* 34(37), 589-592, in particular H. A. J. Pieters. Het procédé der Staatsmijnen voor de zoogenaamde natte gaszuivering, 591-592

10 *Staatsmijnen 1902-1952: Gedenkboek bij gelegenheid van het vijftigjarig bestaan*. Heerlen: Staatsmijnen, 245-246.

11 B. Gales (2000). Houwen en stof bijten? Maakbaarheid in een mijnstreek. *Studies over de sociaal-economische geschiedenis van Limburg* XLV, 27-64.

12 RAL, 17.26/ 06A inv. no. 17: letter from top management to Mijnraad, 7 March 1930.

13 RAL, 17.26/ 36A inv. no. 2: Verslag van het Centraal Laboratorium der Staatsmijnen op 1 januari 1929. CL, Pieters, 20 January 1929.

14 RAL, 36A inv. no. 268: letter from top management to the Minister of Transport and Public Works (*waterstaat*), 17 December 1928.

15 Letter from Pieters and Berkhoff to Ross van Lennep, 9 November 1935. Original document printed in *Gouden research: DSM Research 50 jaar: 1940-1990*. (1990). DSM Corporate Public Relations, 4-5.

16 E. van Royen (2000). Steenkolenveredeling en industriële research bij Staatsmijnen. H. Lintsen, Ed. *Research tussen vetkool en zoetstof: zestig jaar DSM Research 1940-2000*. Eindhoven/Zutphen: Stichting Historie der Techniek/Walburg Pers, 12-29, in particular 23.

17 RAL, 17.26/ 36A inv. no. 1: Reorganisatie der technische en natuurwetenschappelijke onderzoekinswerkzaamheden bij Staatsmijnen. Undated, probably from 1938. Quote by Berkhoff translated from: G. F. te Roller (1990). *Een halve eeuw Centraal Laboratorium: Een serie gesprekken met oud-researchdirecteuren van DSM*. Heerlen: DSM Corporate Public Relations. Unpublished manuscript. 3.

18 RAL, 17.26/ 21A, inv. no. 46: Reorganisatie der technische en natuurwetenschappelijke onderzoekwerkzaamheden bij Staatsmijnen, 17 March 1938.

19 E. Homburg (2003). *Speuren op de tast: Een historische kijk op industriële en universitaire research*. Maastricht: Universiteit Maastricht. Inaugural lecture 31 October 2003, 27.

20 J. Selman (1952). Over de ontwikkeling van het researchwerk. M. Kemp, Ed. *Mijn en Spoor in goud*. Maastricht: Publiciteitsbureau Veldeke, 73-89, in particular 83. P. F. G. Vincken (2000). *Van Staatsmijnen in Limburg tot DSM Chemie*. Unpublished manuscript, 54.

21 F.W.R. Röthig (1966). *Chronologisch overzicht van het ontstaan en de organisatie van het Centraal Laboratorium van de Staatsmijnen, Geleen*. Heerlen: Staatsmijnen, Centraal Laboratorium, 2, appendix.

22 Röthig 1966, op. cit. 2, appendix.

23 RAL, 17.26/ 36A inv. no. 1: De centrale technische onderzoekingsdienst (CTO). CL, 27 April 1942. Probably written by Berkhoff. Röthig 1966, op. cit. 2.

24 *Gouden research* 1990, op. cit. 6-7. For the processing of DSM's synthetic rubber see: A. van Rooij (1998). *"De rest kunt u vergeten. Op de band komt het aan!" Een onderzoek naar het beeld van de fietsband tussen 1900 en 1960 als bijdrage tot de materiaalgeschiedenis van rubber*. Maastricht: Faculteit der Cultuurwetenschappen. Master thesis, 12-16.

25 Van Royen 2000, op. cit. 24. E. Homburg (2003). *Speuren op de tast: Een historische kijk op industriële en universitaire research*. Maastricht: Universiteit Maastricht. Inaugural lecture 31 October 2003, 36-37.

26 RAL, 17.26/ 36A inv. no. 1: Reorganisatie der technische en natuurwetenschappelijke onder-
   zoekingswerkzaamheden bij Staatsmijnen. Undated, probably from 1938. Berkhoff later
   published a similar argument: G. Berkhoff (1947). Research in bedrijven. *De Ingenieur*
   59(43), A371-A373. See also Selman 1952, op. cit.

27 RAL, 17.26/ 34 inv. no. 4: Stikstofbindingsbedrijf der Staatsmijnen. Enkele economische
   opmerkingen. Berkhoff, October 1932.

28 Vincken 2000, op. cit. 49.

29 See Van Rooij 2004 op. cit. chapter 8.

30 H. J. Merx (1955b). *Chronologisch overzicht van de geschiedenis van het Stikstofbindingsbedrijf
   1925-1952*. Heerlen: Archief van de Staatsmijnen in Limburg. 19.

31 H. A. J. Pieters & M. J. Mannens (1929). Winning van pyridine en van phenol uit ruwe
   benzol. *Chemisch Weekblad* 26(20), 286-290.

32 Merx 1955a, op. cit. 51. Merx 1955b, op. cit. 35, 46, 63. Vincken 2000, op. cit. 103-104.

33 *Gouden research* 1990, op. cit. Van Royen 2000, op. cit.

3

Expansion and Diversification: R&D after the Second World War

In the 1930s, Frits van Iterson had set DSM on the chemical industry track, and his successors extended this track. DSM developed into a diversified chemical company by expanding its existing chemical businesses, by diversifying into new fields and, from the late 1950s onwards, also by tapping other feedstocks besides coke oven gas. Top management invested heavily in research as they strongly believed it was a necessity. Research management emphasised the importance of 'science' and claimed freedom to explore subjects that interested them. The importance of fundamental research, research not aimed at immediate industrial application, increased.

Research increased in scale and scope, which meant that it could effectively defend existing market positions, and that diversifications increasingly rested on in-house research. Research also shifted DSM's technology base: enabling the company to branch out from fertilisers into other sectors of the chemical industry. (Table 3.1 summarises the role of research in diversification.)

In the 1920s and 1930s, most companies in industries like chemicals and electronics had become convinced of the necessity of doing industrial research. After the Second World War they expanded their research operations to an unprecedented scale, placing emphasis on scientific and fundamental research as well as long-range research in a broader sense. At some companies, however, the industrial research department drifted away from production and marketing functions and became isolated.[1] This divergence has led students of research management to pass a harsh judgement on the practices of the 1950s and 1960s.[2]

At DSM, research was independent but not isolated. The Central Laboratory developed its own views of the interests of the company and took initiatives, but this did not mean that research diverged from production, marketing or business strategy. Business management expected research to take initiatives and structures were in place to link research to business.

The role of research and the convergence with business also becomes clear from the three main cases analysed in this chapter: urea, a fertiliser; caprolactam, an intermediate for nylon; and lysine, an amino acid. The example of urea shows the increased scale of technological development after

Table 3.1. The role of research in DSM's major diversifications, 1930-1970.

Product	Start of Production	Area of application
Ammonium sulphate	1930; stop: 1966	Fertilisers
Calcium ammonium nitrate	1932	Fertilisers
Alcohol	1940; stop: 1960	Industrial uses
Mixed fertilisers	1941	Fertilisers
NPKs	1949	Fertilisers
Phthalic anhydride	1951, stop: 1963	Paints
Urea	1952	Fertilisers
Caprolactam	1952	Fibre intermediates
Polyethylene	1959 (LDPE, ICI process)	Plastics
Formaldehyde	1961; stop: 1967	Resins
Polyethylene	1962 (HDPE, Ziegler process)	Plastics
Melamine	1967	Resins
EPDM rubber	1967	Rubbers
Lysine	1968; stop: 1969	Food/ feed additives
Acrylonitrile	1969	Fibre intermediates

Legend:

	External technology	Importance of research	Initiated by research
-	No important role for external technology.	No role for research work.	No or small role for research.
+	Technology acquired in the form of a process or research work starting from process competitor.	Small-scale research project/large role for external technology.	Important role for research.
++	Plant acquired.	Research work crucial for establishment of production.	Crucial role for research.

Important elements of technology base	Role of external technology	Importance of research for diversification	Diversification initiated by research?
Not applicable	++	-	-
Not applicable	++	-	-
Process technology Organic chemistry	-	++	++
Process technology Inorganic chemistry	+	++	++
Process technology	-	+	+
Not applicable	++	-	-
Process technology Inorganic chemistry	+ to -	+ to ++	-
Organic chemistry Process technology	+	++	+
Organic chemistry Process technology Application research	+	+	+
Not applicable	++	-	-
Organic chemistry Process technology Application research	+	++	++
Organic chemistry Process technology Application research	+	++	++
Organic chemistry Process technology Application research	+	++	++
Amino acids Organic chemistry Process technology Application research	-	++	++
	++	-	-

Sources: table 3.1, text and E. Homburg (2004). *Groeien door kunstmest: DSM Agro 1929-2004.* Hilversum: Verloren. 312. P. F. G. Vincken (2000). *Van Staatsmijnen in Limburg tot DSM Chemie.* Unpublished manuscript. 194-195, 219-220.

Note: end of production is included when it falls in the period until 1990.

the Second World War, and the increasing importance of research. The example of caprolactam shows the increased scope of research and how this increased scope mattered for projects. The case of lysine shows how the capabilities acquired through caprolactam research built a new technology base and how this enabled the lysine project. DSM built a lysine plant but closed it soon after start-up. Finding a market proved to be difficult.

Together, the cases of urea, caprolactam and lysine show the expansion and diversification of DSM's chemical businesses and its research. However, in its development from a fertiliser producer to a diversified chemical company, DSM also started producing polyethylene, EPDM synthetic rubber and melamine. In this chapter, some of the main characteristics of R&D in these products are reviewed as well. Polyethylene and EPDM are less standardised products than urea and caprolactam, necessitating application research and extensive product development.

The Growth of DSM's Chemical Businesses after the Second World War

"I see the further expansion of our coal upgrading industry as an attractive task lying before us," Daan Ross van Lennep said on the occasion of his official appointment to DSM's top management on 14 February 1947. During the war, Van Iterson had retired and Ross van Lennep had taken his place. Ross van Lennep's speech shows that he intended to continue the work of Van Iterson and broaden the company's base. DSM took this course after the Second World War. The company expanded its existing businesses and diversified into new fields. In the late 1950s, however, DSM was to start loosening the ties between coal and chemicals.[3]

Upgrading Coal

When Ross van Lennep delivered his speech in 1947, expansion was being targeted at existing products and diversification, but the direction diversification should take was still unclear. Ross van Lennep mentioned resins, dyestuffs and paints as attractive areas for diversification. These products suited DSM's feedstock position and the Central Laboratory had done some work on them during the 1930s and 1940s. Through research work, however, leading companies like Du Pont, ICI and IG Farben had opened up the field of plastics and synthetic fibres. These dynamic and innovative sectors attracted a lot of attention and showed high growth rates. World production of plastics, for instance, grew by 1330% between 1945 and 1964. The Central Laboratory had also conducted preliminary research in these areas during the Second World War and shortly after. This research focused on intermediates for synthetic fibres and resins, to be manufactured on the basis of benzene and naphthalene from coal tar, a by-product of the coke oven plants. Some work had also been done on ethylene and polyethylene, the latter being a plastic developed by ICI in the 1930s.[4]

It soon became clear what course DSM would steer. The company chose to enter the plastics industry. This industry was easier to enter than the dyestuffs industry, which had been the cradle of the large-scale German chemical industry at the end of the nineteenth century. Plastics also suited DSM's structure because they were manufactured in bulk. Besides plastics, the company entered the field of fibre intermediates with caprolactam, and also diversified further in fertilisers.[5] Production of mixed fertilisers with nitrogen, phosphate and potassium, so-called NPKs, started in 1949. The Central Laboratory developed a process for the production of NPKs on the basis of the nitro phosphate process. A urea plant went on stream three years later. In the late 1960s, finally, DSM started production of several products that were closely linked to earlier diversifications. The Central Laboratory developed a melamine process that used urea as feedstock, instead of calcium cyanamide, and developed a lysine process that used caprolactam as feedstock. Its research work on polyethylene was important for the start of EPDM synthetic rubber production.[6] (Table 3.2 lists DSM's most important diversifications.)

Although chemicals increased in importance for DSM, it still relied on coal for its feedstocks. The links were either direct, through the coke oven plants, or indirect, through utilisation of an intermediate or product manufactured from coal-based feedstocks. (See table 3.2.) In this way, diversification continued to be feedstock-driven.

Coal and Chemicals Diverge

Ross van Lennep died in 1949, shortly after his appointment to DSM's top management. Jan van Aken succeeded him. Van Aken was one of the engineers hired for troubleshooting in the ammonia plant, but he moved into management positions in the 1930s. Van Aken was chosen as head of the chemical sector in 1947 when Ross van Lennep became one of DSM's top managers.[7] After Van Aken's appointment to top management, Jef van Waes became head of the chemical sector. In the 1930s Van Waes had worked for the Compagnie Neérlandaise de l'Azote (CNA), another Dutch manufacturer of nitrogen fertilisers.[8]

Towards the end of the 1950s, Van Aken, Van Waes, and others in the chemical sector increasingly saw the strong feedstock connections between coal and chemicals as a constraint. Underlying this view was an analysis of DSM's position in the chemical industry. Dynamic markets for caprolactam and plastics, and competition from research-intensive companies, called for major investments by DSM to keep its current position, which management nevertheless considered strong. Expansion became the key word for Van Aken and his close colleagues. DSM would have to diversify, build large plants and secure a supply of cheap feedstocks. A presence outside Limburg, elsewhere in the Netherlands or abroad, would also have to be established.

Table 3.2. DSM's expansion in chemicals: its most important diversifications and feedstocks, 1945-1970.

Product	Start of Production	Area of application	Feedstocks	Feedstock source
NPKs	1949	Fertilisers	Phosphate rock	Bought externally
			Nitric acid	Nitric acid plant
Urea	1952	Fertilisers	Ammonia, carbon dioxide	Ammonia plant
Capro-lactam	1952	Fibre inter-mediates	Phenol: benzene	Coke oven plants
			Phenol: toluene	Bought externally
			Sulphur dioxide	Sulphuric acid plant
			Ammonia, carbon dioxide	Ammonia plant
Polyeth-ylene	1959	LDPE[i] Plastics	Ethylene	Coke oven plants Steam cracker (1961)[iii]
	1962	HDPE[ii] Plastics	Ethylene	Idem
Melamine	1967	Resins	Urea	Urea plant
EPDM rubber	1967	Rubbers	Ethylene, propylene	Steam cracker
Lysine	1968	stop: 1969 Food, feed additives	Caprolactam	Caprolactam plant

Sources: P. Tans (1977). Van Staatsmijnen tot DSM: Hoofdlijnen van de ontwikkeling. *Land van Herle* 27(3), 87-103, in particular 96-98. T. van Helvoort (2000). Staatsmijnen gaat polymeriseren, 1945-1970. H. Lintsen, Ed. *Research tussen vetkool en zoetstof: zestig jaar DSM Research 1940-2000*. Eindhoven/Zutphen: Stichting Historie der Techniek/Walburg Pers, 44-59, in particular 49, 53. P. F. G. Vincken (2000). *Van Staatsmijnen in Limburg tot DSM Chemie*. Unpublished manuscript. 104-105, 172, 191, 198-199.

Notes:
[i] LDPE = Low Density Polyethylene, manufactured with the ICI process.
[ii] HDPE = High Density Polyethylene, manufactured with the Ziegler process. The ICI and Ziegler processes made it possible to produce a variety of polyethylene types with different characteristics.
[iii] This plant went on stream in 1961 and cracked naphtha.

The caprolactam plant in 1952. Caprolactam was DSM's first major step outside fertilisers, a step that was initiated and enabled by the Central Laboratory. R&D played an important role in many of DSM's diversifications in the 1950s and 1960s.

Securing cheap feedstocks meant that chemicals and coal would no longer be tightly connected. After the Second World War, natural gas and petroleum feedstocks became available for European chemical companies at low prices, enabling them to follow the example of the American chemical industry that was already manufacturing products on the basis of these feedstocks. DSM, however, also manufactured coal and coke, making a switch to natural gas and petroleum feedstocks difficult. The plans developed in the chemical sector disturbed the management of DSM's coal sector and several of Van Aken's colleagues in top management, causing tensions in the company. Van Waes and Gé Berkhoff left in 1961; their departure meant the removal of the management layer just under the top.

Graph 3.1. Operating profit from chemicals and other activities, 1935, 1955 and 1965.

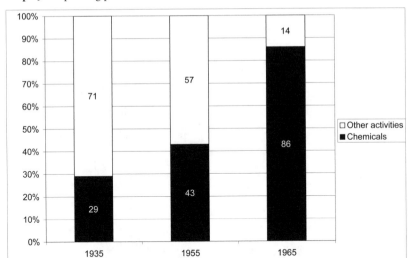

Sources: DSM annual report 1935. RAL, 17.26/34 inv. no. 12: Waarom hebben Staatsmijnen Chemische Bedrijven gesticht, 11 May 1946. RAL, 17.26/ 18C inv. no. 176: Bedrijfseconomisch Verslag 1955, 1965.

Graph 3.2. Turnover profile of DSM's chemical businesses in 1955 and 1965.

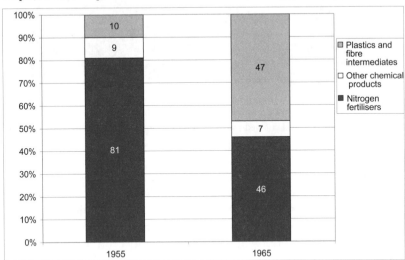

Sources: RAL, 17.26/ 18C inv. no. 176: Bedrijfseconomisch Verslag 1955, 1965.
Note: similar breakdowns for operating profit are unfortunately not given in the sources.

Van Waes went back to CNA, while Berkhoff accepted an invitation to become the first rector of the newly established Twente Technical College (Netherlands, now University of Twente).[9]

Despite the different opinions and tensions, DSM's management took an expansive course for the chemical sector, building large plants, switching to natural gas for fertiliser production and petroleum feedstocks for other chemical products. The company also established joint ventures. Expansion of the chemical sector meant that DSM increasingly relied on its chemical businesses. The share of chemicals in the company's operating profit increased from 29% in 1935, to 43% in 1955, and further to 86% in 1965 (Graph 3.1.). The profile of DSM's chemical businesses also changed. Plastics and fibre intermediates grew from 10% of chemical turnover in 1955 to 47% ten years later (Graph 3.2). For research, expansion in chemicals would mean increased room to take initiatives for diversifications and further develop existing products and processes.

The Organisation and Management of Research

After the Second World War, many companies increased their research expenditure. In the history of industrial research, the 1950s and 1960s in particular seem to be marked by an emphasis on fundamental research, and by a divergence between research on the one hand and production and marketing functions on the other. At Philips, for instance, relations between research and production divisions were difficult and research drifted away from the rest of the company. Other histories have shown the same pattern. Margaret Graham argues that research became a 'corporate counterculture': an island of fundamental research.[10]

The experience of these companies has had a strong influence on the literature on the management of R&D. Philip Roussel, Kamal Saad and Tamara Erickson characterise research management in the 1950s and 1960s as first-generation R&D. Companies hired talented people, provided excellent facilities, and hoped for results. The intuitions of R&D managers determined the course of research without the involvement of business managers, and R&D was not integrated within overall business strategy. Roussel et al. argue that first-generation R&D is a 'strategy of hope' as companies failed to integrate research and business. Roli Varma similarly argues that industrial research in the 1950s and 1960s was 'autonomous'. R&D managers controlled research, while business managers accepted research uncritically. According to Varma, the R&D function generated ideas and then turned them over to business managers for further development.[11]

Like other companies, DSM invested heavily in research after the Second World War. The number of researchers working at the Central Laboratory increased to over a thousand in the 1960s, and research expenditure increased from 3.9% of chemical turnover in 1949 to 6.8% in 1969. (See, in the appendix, graph A1 for personnel figures and A2 for research expenditures.) This expansion had consequences for the organisation and management of research. The case of DSM shows a different pattern, however, than the companies typically studied by historians of industrial research.

Research Becomes Corporate

Central Laboratory was part of CTO, which in turn was part of DSM's chemical sector that also included the SBB and the coke oven plants. The coal-mining operations formed DSM's other main sector. Auxiliary departments for sales, economics and personnel complemented the coal and chemical sectors (Figure 3.1.).

DSM's technological organisation in chemicals further expanded after the war. In 1945, DSM established Chemiebouw as the central engineering department. Chemiebouw oversaw the work of engineering contractors, or engineered the plants itself, and sold some licenses on DSM's chemical technology. A licensing subsidiary, called Stamicarbon, complemented the central research and engineering departments. DSM established Stamicarbon in 1947 to exploit some of the company's coal-related technologies, but Stamicarbon took over chemical licensing from Chemiebouw in 1952. Stamicarbon mostly licensed DSM's fertiliser technologies, but from the late 1960s onwards other processes as well.[12] (See graph A3 in the appendix).

In October 1945, researchers from the Central Experimental Station proposed a new organisation for CTO. They argued that the nature of the work of CTO differed fundamentally from that of other parts of DSM,

Figure 3.1. DSM's organisational structure until 1949.

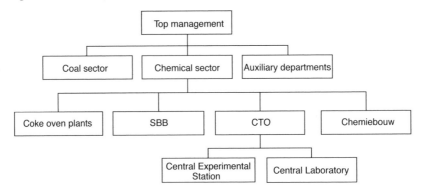

Note: a specification of the coal sector and the auxiliary departments has been excluded from this diagram. The patent department has also been excluded.

THE COMPANY THAT CHANGED ITSELF

and that CTO should therefore become a 'totally independent unit' whose head should report directly to top management. In other words, research should become a corporate activity. The report these researchers wrote, however, left the Central Laboratory out of the picture. Their plan for a new organisation and the operational plans for research included only coal-related research as conducted by the Central Experimental Station.[13]

As a result of the report of October 1945, the Central Experimental Station moved to one of DSM's central auxiliary departments in November of that year. The station was removed from CTO but did not become a corporate unit. The reorganisation had caused some unease at the Central Laboratory, but CTO remained in place.[14] In 1948, however, top management decided to abolish CTO and to restructure the Central Laboratory's management. Berkhoff remained the highest manager of research, reporting to the head of DSM's chemical sector. Berkhoff's task became a strategic one and was concentrated on the broader research picture. He was responsible for the coordination of research with the production function in DSM's chemical sector. Berkhoff also coordinated external contacts, including contacts with possible licensors.[15]

The responsibility for day-to-day management of research at the Central Laboratory moved from Berkhoff to Dick van Krevelen. Van Krevelen had studied chemistry at Leiden University and had followed courses at Delft Technical College (now Delft University of Technology) to familiarise himself with subjects related to the chemical industry. He had worked as an assistant to Hein Waterman, a professor at Delft who had many contacts in industry, on projects sponsored by Royal Dutch/Shell. Due to the war he could not find employment there, and went to DSM instead. He was stationed at the General Chemistry department of the Central Laboratory, and from 1943 onwards at the Physical Chemistry department, where he worked on various subjects.[16] In his position as research director, Van Krevelen reported to Berkhoff.

In 1948, Pieters was appointed to head a new safety department of the chemical sector. At the Central Laboratory, Jan Selman took over responsibility for the laboratory's administration and support functions. Selman had joined DSM in 1946 to work at the patent department. Like Van Krevelen, he reported to Berkhoff.

The changes in management structure signalled that the Central Laboratory would grow in the years to come. Strategy, research management and operational issues were separated. In 1949, moreover, the chemical sector was reorganised when Van Waes succeeded Van Aken. The division of responsibilities between Berkhoff, Van Krevelen and Selman remained the same but the Central Laboratory became a corporate unit. Berkhoff now directly reported to Van Aken in top management. The chemical sector became mainly involved in production, although Chemiebouw continued

Figure 3.2. DSM's organisational structure after 1949.

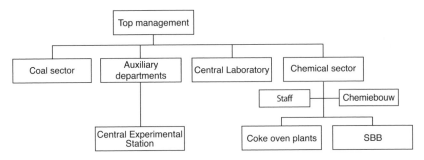

Note: a specification of the coal sector and a further specification of the auxiliary departments has been excluded from this diagram. The patent department has also been excluded.

to be part of it. Van Waes also had a staff at his disposal that played a central role in preparing investment proposals (Figure 3.2).[17]

In several steps, DSM arrived at an organisation in 1949 that made research a corporate activity. Before that year, research had been part of the company's chemical sector. Like the reorganisation of 1948, it showed the importance attached to research.

The Internal Organisation of Research

The Central Laboratory remained a corporate department after 1949. The laboratory's internal organisation continued to change, however. With the extra money and the extra people that became available for research after the Second World War, Van Krevelen set to work to expand the Central Laboratory's organisation. The laboratory expanded, not only in scale but also in scope. For instance, the analysis department expanded, specialised and invested in new methods such as mass spectrometry. In 1951, Johan Goris started building a Semi-Technical department that aimed to do research on equipment and work on problems as an intermediary step between laboratory scale and pilot plant scale.[18]

The pilot plant organisation also expanded and specialised, among other things in Inorganic Pilot Plants (for fertilisers) and Organic Pilot Plants (for caprolactam for instance). Responsibility for the pilot plants was split. Personnel was on the payroll of the SBB, but reported to Berkhoff. In 1949, Jean Plusjé became responsible for the Inorganic Pilot Plants besides his job at the Central Laboratory as head of the Inorganic Chemistry department. Plusjé moved full time to the SBB in 1953 and became director of the nitric acid and calcium ammonium nitrate plants. The fertiliser pilot plants remained the responsibility of his successor at the Central Laboratory. In 1955, moreover, Willem van Loon was appointed as director of all pilot plants under Berkhoff. Van Loon had worked on a new coal gasifica-

Figure 3.3. Outline of the Central Laboratory's organisation after 1955.

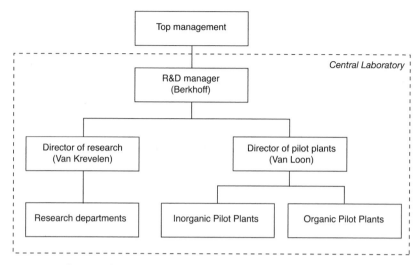

Note: a specification of all the research departments has been excluded from this diagram.

tion process and had headed the Central Laboratory's main department involved in that research.[19]

In 1955, Selman transferred to the personnel department at DSM's headquarters and his responsibilities were taken over by Van Krevelen. Van Krevelen's tasks now included both the day-to-day research process and the support functions. In outline, Berkhoff managed research strategically and supervised a director of research (Van Krevelen) and a director of pilot plants (Van Loon) (Figure 3.3).[20]

Van Loon accepted an invitation to become professor at Eindhoven Technical College (Netherlands, now Eindhoven University of Technology) and left at the end of 1956. His departure coincided with a reorganisation of the Central Laboratory. In 1957, the Product Development, Analysis and Testing, and Fundamental Research sectors were established. Each sector held several functionally-organised departments. The term 'sector' came from the SBB, where groups of related plants had already been organised into sectors and placed under the responsibility of a single manager. The nature of the various research activities determined their grouping into sectors. The Product Development sector conducted product and process research that was focused on applications in existing plants or on diversification, and organised pilot plant work. In this sector, the Inorganic Chemistry department mainly concentrated on fertilisers, while the Organic Chemistry department conducted research on caprolactam, for instance. Research on plastics like polyethylene was concentrated in a Plastics department established in 1958 (Figure 3.4).[21]

Figure 3.4. Outline of the Central Laboratory's organisation after 1957.

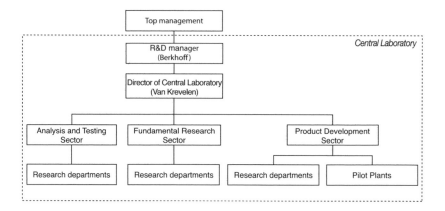

Note: a specification of the research departments has been excluded from this diagram.

Through a process of expansion and specialisation, the number of research departments increased. The organisation of sectors encompassing several departments counterbalanced the increased specialisation. The pilot plants were also integrated with the remainder of the Central Laboratory's organisation with the introduction of sectors. The full range of R&D activities, from fundamental research to development and service research, was now part of a single organisation.

In 1963, the sector organisation was changed, to bring it more into line with the main branches DSM operated in: the Feedstocks and Inorganic Products Research and Development sector focused on fertilisers and coke oven gas, and increasingly on oil; the Polymers Research and Development sector focused on plastics; Organic Products Research and Development focused on caprolactam and other organic products; and finally the Basic and Fundamental Research sector focused on generic issues and conducting fundamental research.[22]

Freedom and Constraints: The Management of Research
Van Krevelen managed the expanding research organisation with an emphasis on 'science'. He believed that the Central Laboratory should have a good standing in the academic community and that researchers should be free to explore subjects of interest. On the other hand, Van Krevelen knew very well that the context of a production company imposed certain constraints on research. In his opinion, managing research entailed finding a balance between the freedom dictated by research and the constraints imposed by the context of a production company. Van Krevelen devised many organisational schemes to tie research to production. These schemes

THE COMPANY THAT CHANGED ITSELF

included not only the organisation of sectors but also the organisation of projects, for instance, which changed continuously.[23]

Van Krevelen also invested in fundamental research and supportive generic research, and tried to nurture exploratory research aimed at new activities. The Central Laboratory had started conducting fundamental research during the Second World War. The Physical Chemistry department investigated catalysis, the backbone of the production of ammonia, which in turn was the backbone of fertiliser production.

After the war, a debate arose at DSM and other companies about the way in which fundamental research should be organised. The importance of fundamental research was not questioned. In June 1947, Henk de Bruijn, head of the Physical Chemistry department, visited BASF's main site in Ludwigshafen, Germany, as a member of the allied inspection teams. He was impressed with the organisation and scope of BASF's research, and a year later proposed to establish a separate organisation for fundamental research alongside the Central Laboratory. Berkhoff agreed, but Van Krevelen did not. Van Krevelen attached somewhat less importance to fundamental research than De Bruijn, and in his opinion DSM should not copy BASF's example. Van Krevelen won the debate and spread fundamental research over several departments, in close contact with other research activities. In 1957, however, fundamental research was concentrated in a sector.[24]

Many other companies increased their fundamental research expenditure. Du Pont and IG Farben had started this trend in the chemical industry in the 1920s; Philips started it in the Netherlands after the war. Philips and its head of research, Gilles Holst, exerted a powerful influence, not only through their policies but also through their people. Cor van Heerden for instance had worked at the research laboratories of Philips during the war, but in 1947 switched over to DSM. He became head of the fundamental research sector ten years later.[25]

The increased fundamental research effort illustrates the increased room for research. DSM's chemical sector management believed that research in general would pay off, and this belief rested on an analysis of the chemical industry. Industrial research is of paramount importance in a dynamic industry, where the life cycles of products and processes are short but where it takes a long time to develop a new product or process. In a capital-intensive industry such as the chemical industry, moreover, developing the wrong product or process has disastrous consequences. Stagnation means decline. DSM had to keep up, otherwise it would be overtaken by competitors. As a consequence, research strategy closely followed business strategy.[26]

Van Krevelen, Berkhoff and Van Aken fundamentally agreed on the importance of industrial research, but were also aware of the high cost of research. In addition, they believed that the chances of accurately predict-

Figure 3.5. Outline of the Central Laboratory's organisation after 1963.

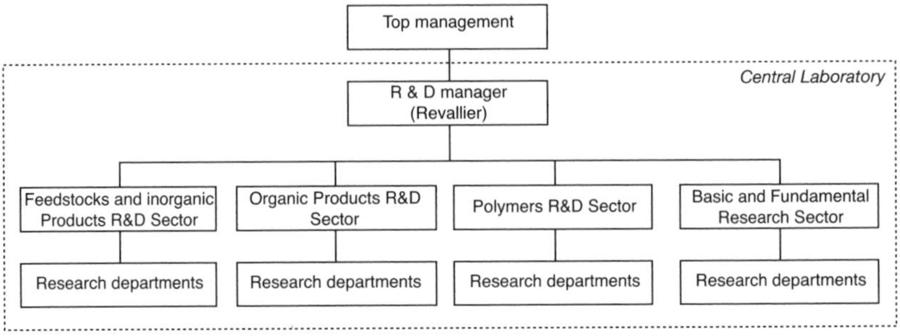

Note: a specification of the research departments has been excluded from this diagram.

ing research results were slim, and that it was inevitable that many projects would fail. In a conference lecture in 1968, Van Aken quoted the Dutch saying that costs come before results (*de kost gaat voor de baat uit*). The patience to wait for results, and the faith that results would come in some way or another, became crucial in the management of research.[27]

The arguments that Van Krevelen used to show that research mattered for the company were mainly qualitative. In a report of July 1955, he explained his two-track policy of freedom and constraint, and argued that it is difficult to express the value of research in terms of money. According to Van Krevelen, research produces results only indirectly. A new plant based on a new process, for instance, is as much the result of the work of engineers and others as it is the result of the work of researchers. Moreover, some research results, for instance an improved understanding of a problem, are hard to quantify. With the results that could be measured, Van Krevelen tried to show the value of research: he calculated that the costs of doing research were lower than the amount of money DSM saved through rationalisation and other improvements in relation to existing business-es.[28]

In 1959 Van Krevelen left to become director of research in the top management of the Dutch company AKU, a large producer of synthetic fibres. Van Krevelen's departure (a few years before that of Berkhoff and Van Waes) occurred in a climate of rising tensions between DSM's chemical and coal sectors. No major changes in research philosophy occurred in the 1960s, however. Frits Sixma, who had worked as an advisor in organic chemistry for DSM since 1956 and had been a professor in the same field at the University of Amsterdam since 1957, replaced Van Krevelen. Sixma also took over Berkhoff's tasks in 1961, unifying the operational and strategic management of research. When Sixma died in 1963, Leen Revallier replaced him (see also figure 3.5). Revallier had studied in Delft and in

THE COMPANY THAT CHANGED ITSELF

1949 went to the Central Laboratory where he worked on fertilisers at the Inorganic Chemistry department under Plusjé. Four years later Revallier headed the department, and in 1957 he was appointed as head of the Product Development sector. A more elaborate policy committee structure was put in place to coordinate research, production and top management, but in outline both Sixma and Revallier continued the policies of Van Krevelen and Berkhoff.[29]

In terms of the emphasis on science and fundamental research, increasing investments in R&D and an expanding organisation, the history of the Central Laboratory may seem to be comparable to the histories of other industrial research laboratories. However, the example of DSM is different in several respects. In the first place, Van Krevelen emphasised the importance of 'science' but at the same time devised many structures to make research and business converge. At the Central Laboratory, moreover, all types of research, from fundamental to service research, were tightly integrated. Secondly, Berkhoff, Van Krevelen's superior, bridged research and production in his contacts with Van Aken and Van Waes. After Berkhoff, Van Krevelen and Van Waes had left the company, a more elaborate committee structure was put in place to manage research, but the communication lines between top management, research and production remained short. Finally, business management believed that research should take initiatives and gave research the freedom to do so. They did not accept research uncritically, but accepted the uncertainty of research work, and hoped and trusted that results would come. This was a strategy of hope, but not of blind hope. At DSM, research and business did not diverge. In the second part of this chapter, three cases are analysed to show how research took initiatives and how research, marketing and production related to each other.

Expansion: Urea

Expansion characterised DSM's chemical sector after the Second World War, and expansion characterised the development of processes for the manufacture of urea, a compound made from carbon dioxide and ammonia. With its relatively high nitrogen content, urea is an excellent fertiliser, but it can also be used for the production of plastics and resins. In 1964, DSM had the second largest urea site in the world and stood on the brink of expanding its capacity further. This new plant used a new process, effectively making DSM the technology leader in urea. The Central Laboratory played a central role in the development of this new process, but DSM's involvement with urea began in 1946, when Chemiebouw, DSM's engineering department, started evaluating the possibilities of urea production. Research only gradually came to occupy a central position in urea.[30]

Research and Urea Production

DSM entered the urea field relatively late. BASF had put the world's first urea plant on stream in 1922. Du Pont, ICI and Montecatini followed the German company in the 1930s, while other firms developed urea processes after the Second World War. In developing a process and establishing production, two problems had to be solved. In the first place, the synthesis of urea took place in two steps, in the first of which an intermediate formed that was highly corrosive, leading to problems relating to equipment design as well as operations. Moreover, urea production led to substantial amounts of off-gases that had to be processed into by-products (once-through processes) or recycled in some way or another (recycle or recirculation processes).

At the time Chemiebouw began its study in 1946, no companies were offering technology, so this route of entry was blocked. In the 1930s, Van Waes had worked on urea synthesis when he worked at CNA, another Dutch manufacturer of nitrogen fertilisers. CNA operated a pilot plant, where in 1938 Van Waes found that addition of some oxygen could reduce corrosion during synthesis. It was an important discovery, but Van Waes feared that someone at CNA headquarters in Brussels or at Montecatini would take credit for his work. Therefore, Van Waes did not tell his superiors of his discovery.[31]

After he moved to DSM, Van Waes resumed his work on urea, as head of the then new engineering department Chemiebouw. Engineers used the addition of oxygen in the process they worked on but still confronted many other problems, making the road to an industrial plant a long one. At the end of 1946, DSM approached ASED, the engineering contractor that had built the ammonia plant and that had close relations with CNA, and asked ASED to engineer and construct a urea plant. Because both companies had not finished their research, they decided to join forces. DSM and ASED would develop a urea process together, using the CNA pilot plant that would be shipped to DSM. A formal contract, signed in April 1947, formed the basis for the cooperation.

The pilot plant arrived in May 1947 and was put into operation in January of the following year. As early as the end of 1948, DSM decided to build a plant with a capacity of 15 tons per day. The pilot plant worked as a once-through unit. In 1949, the Central Laboratory's Inorganic Chemistry department, the core of DSM's fertiliser research, investigated the possibilities of recycling the off-gases. The SBB's staff proposed using a once-through process, however, because the amount of by-products would be low at the capacity the plant would have and because a plant using a recycle process would require a larger investment. After this decision had been taken, the pilot plant stopped in October 1949. Chemiebouw started to work on the engineering of the 15-ton once-through plant. Construction started in 1950, and two years later the plant could be put on stream, producing ammonium sulphate from the off-gases. Production staff had to tackle many initial problems, however, and researchers from the Inorganic Chemistry department assisted in solving them.

Through the work of ASED/CNA and Van Waes, DSM could enter the field of urea quickly. Internal engineering work complemented inputs from the other companies; Chemiebouw was therefore at the heart of DSM's entry in urea, and the Central Laboratory to a far lesser extent.

Recycle Processes

DSM entered the urea field quickly, but late, and with a once-through process. This developed into a problem in 1953, when planning started for a second urea plant with a capacity of 150 tons per day. Recycling at least some of the off-gases became necessary because the volume of by-products would otherwise be too large.

Part of the laboratory of the Corrosion Research department in 1956. Research into the causes and prevention of corrosion played a crucial role in the urea sector.

By the time DSM started its first once-through plant, other companies had already advanced to recycle processes. Montecatini led the field, and also offered licenses on its technology. In August 1953, Van Aken and Van Waes, now head of DSM's chemical sector, travelled to Italy to talk to Giacomo Fauser, Montecatini's top engineer, and tour the urea plant at Novara. Van Aken, Van Waes and their staffs thoroughly evaluated the possibility of acquiring technology but rejected it in December 1953. Van Waes's oxygen addition gave DSM a small, but crucial, advantage over its competitors in combating corrosion in urea synthesis. In addition, the work that had been done was evaluated positively, and confidence was high that DSM would be able to develop the necessary technology in-house.

DSM pushed ahead with the development of recycle processes, a partial recycle process at first, where part of the off-gases was processed into by-products, and later a full recycle process. Plants were built in anticipation of the development of recycle technology and first operated as once-through units. The Inorganic Chemistry department started doing systematic research on urea, assisted by the Semi-Technical department and the specialised Corrosion department. Herman Zelders had built up a great deal of knowledge on the causes and prevention of corrosion, and that knowledge was vital in urea. The work of the Central Laboratory increasingly became crucial while Chemiebouw focused on its core task, the engineering and construction of plants.

In 1955, the Inorganic Chemistry department also started fundamentally-oriented research, aimed at understanding the processes of urea synthesis. It built on theoretical insights (relating to phase rules) first applied at DSM in research on the nitro phosphate process. Fundamentally-oriented research on urea paid off quickly when in 1960 Piet Kaasenbrood developed a new approach to recycling the off-gases of urea production. The off-gases were expelled with carbon dioxide, one of the reactants, in a stripper: a bundle of tall tubes. The full spectrum of the Central Laboratory's process research got involved to develop the process, called the stripping process. In 1965, DSM decided to build a plant, which went on stream two years later.

In 1968, a year after DSM's plant had been started, Revallier proposed that Kaasenbrood be awarded a substantial bonus. Revallier called the stripping process 'one of the most important technological contributions to the fertiliser industry'.[32] Compared to full recycle processes, stripping technology reduced energy consumption and simplified mechanical design. Moreover, less equipment was needed. The advantages of the process resulted in reduced production and investment costs. Stripping technology was a breakthrough and gave DSM a leading position in urea technology. Stamicarbon, DSM's licensing subsidiary, sold nine stripping plants

The pilot plant for the urea stripping process, started up in 1964. The stripping process resulted from fundamental research into urea synthesis. It represented a considerable improvement compared with conventional processes and put DSM in a leading position in urea technology.

even in 1967 and continued to sell many licenses in the following years. (See graph A3 in the appendix.) Stamicarbon in this way profited from the development of the stripping process. In turn, DSM could learn from Stamicarbon. The first two licensed stripping plants had units that were about 100 tons larger than DSM's own plant, and in this way provided an opportunity to learn how to scale up stripping units.

From a late entrant in the 1940s, DSM developed into a leading player in the 1960s. Chemiebouw had enabled the company's entry, but the Central Laboratory gradually took the lead. DSM initially followed a defensive innovation strategy, aimed at entering the field and at catching up, but developed an offensive strategy as the company caught up with the leaders. Crucial factors were the decision not to buy technology from Montecatini but to rely on in-house capabilities, and the decision to start fundamental research on urea.

Research and the Marketing of Urea

DSM expanded rapidly in urea. In the course of seventeen years, the company decided to build three plants (the once-through, recycle and stripping units) and these installations were almost continuously expanded. Production rose from 8 tons per day in 1952 to 500 tons in 1970, a spectacular increase.[33]

This spectacular growth indicates a booming market for urea. When Chemiebouw started working on a urea process, DSM targeted plastics and resins as outlets for its plant. In 1953, a market scan showed that this market was small in the Netherlands and that urea resins production by DSM might offend the two existing Dutch manufacturers. DSM consequently chose to concentrate on the fertiliser market.

This switch from resins to fertilisers had important consequences for research. Dutch manufacturers of nitrogen fertilisers sold their products through the CSV, a central sales office. Urea customers were mainly located abroad, in India, China and, to a lesser extent, the United States. DSM increasingly relied on export as the production of urea increased. In Asia, urea consumption grew fast, but the Indian and Chinese governments bought all the fertilisers they needed through central offices. These organisations had tremendous power on the fertiliser market and kept prices low, forcing urea manufacturers to stay focused on low cost even as demand grew.

For the Central Laboratory, the crucial consequences of the switch from plastics and resins to fertilisers related to product quality. Urea was the same compound no matter what the market was, but different markets valued different properties. Urea for the manufacture of plastics and resins had to be as pure as possible. Fertiliser-grade urea should not cake during transportation and storage, should not be dispersed by the wind, and farmers should be able to apply it easily. Initially, the same white powder that was sold to plastics and resins firms was marketed as fertiliser, but it caked and was dispersed by the wind during application. These problems confronted all manufacturers and hardly any firm marketed fertiliser grade urea of fine quality.

At the end of 1952, DSM started to work on the improvement of the quality of urea fertiliser when the Central Laboratory's Inorganic Chemistry department conducted tests with so-called prilling. In this procedure, molten urea was sprayed from the top of a tower. Little drops formed, and as these drops fell, they solidified into evenly shaped little balls called prills. In two years' time, a process was developed and a prilling tower could be built near the second urea plant. The prills DSM manufactured were excellent. Other companies developed prilling as well but needed additional drying and/or coating, while DSM's prills could be marketed directly. Research had been done on coating, some of this work was done at the SBB's works laboratory, but coating proved to be unnecessary.

Besides the shape of fertiliser grade urea, the amount of biuret in the product also developed into a problem after DSM chose the fertiliser market as its main outlet. Biuret had a damaging effect on some plants and caused caking, both of which were unwanted. Agricultural research set the maximum level of biuret at 2%, but DSM aimed at 1% because its competitors could manufacture urea with that amount of biuret and were actively marketing their products as such. The Inorganic Chemistry department worked on the biuret problem and found that the unwanted chemical formed particularly during prilling. In 1956, researchers found a solution and the product-finishing section of urea manufacture was modified. Two years later, competitive pressure again forced the Central Laboratory to find ways of decreasing the biuret content further, this time to 0.3%. Again the product-finishing section was modified.

Although the SBB's works laboratory also conducted some research on coating, the Central Laboratory played a central role in product quality research. This type of research was crucial for the marketing of fertiliser-grade urea and enabled DSM to switch markets from resins and plastics to fertilisers. Prilling was developed pro-actively, while pressure from competitors was the driving force behind research on ways to decrease the amount of biuret.

Expansion
DSM entered the urea field through engineering work, but the subsequent development of processes and the work done on product quality shows the increasing importance of research after the Second World War. The addition of oxygen during synthesis as a way to combat corrosion gave DSM a small lead over its competitors. Further research extended this lead and gradually DSM developed an offensive innovation strategy. Consequently, research overtook engineering and became vital in urea, enabling DSM to build a leading position technologically and contributing to DSM's commercial success in urea.

Within the Central Laboratory, in the case of urea the Inorganic Chemistry department played a central role, assisted by researchers from other departments if necessary. The majority of the research work in relation to urea focused on industrial application and proceeded in close contact with production management, the engineering department and the licensing operation. Van Krevelen's emphasis on 'science' in the management of research did not mean that the interests of research and production diverged.

Stamicarbon sold many stripping plants and a large portion of urea capacity in the world became based on DSM technology. The development of the stripping process propelled DSM into a position of technological leadership in urea. Fundamental research laid the foundation for the stripping process. This example shows that fundamental research can have a large commercial pay-off, both directly for DSM's own production and through Stamicarbon. The case of urea also shows that fundamental research originated in a desire to understand the processes fully and in a desire to design simpler and cheaper plants. The incentive to start this research came from industrial practice.

Diversification: Caprolactam

"Very interesting! Every large chemical company should make intermediates for synthetic fibres," Van Iterson wrote in the margin of a technical report on synthetic fibres of November 1939.[34] The report and Van Iterson's reaction put synthetic fibre intermediates on the map at DSM, but the outbreak of the Second World War prevented the company from taking up research in this field. After the war, intermediates for synthetic fibres were again taken up. DSM focused on caprolactam, an intermediate for nylon, and initiated large-scale research to develop a process. While urea illustrates the expansion in scale of research at DSM in the 1950s and 1960s, caprolactam illustrates a process of diversification, both in research and in business.

The World of Synthetic Fibres
Again DSM entered relatively late. In 1935, Wallace Carrothers of Du Pont had succeeded in producing a polyamide fibre from adipic acid and hexamethylene diamine (HMD), which reacted to form nylon salt, which in turn was polymerised by polycondensation and spun into fibres. Du Pont named the new fibre 'nylon', invested heavily in its development, and started production in 1938. At IG Farbenindustrie in Germany, Paul Schlack also succeeded in producing a polyamide fibre. He started from caprolactam, which was polymerised and spun into fibres. Not long after Du Pont started production, IG Farben followed; but the German product (nylon 6 with the trade name Perlon) had properties that were somewhat different from those of the American product (nylon 6.6). In May 1939, Du Pont licensed its nylon spinning technology to IG Farben, excluding

the German company from the American market at the same time.[35]

At DSM, the report of November 1939, written by Tom Niks, at that time working at the SBB under Goris, initiated research into fibres. Niks proposed a route to HMD starting from phenol, a chemical made from benzene, which, in turn, was available from coke oven gas. Profitability of benzene sales had declined in the late 1930s and DSM was looking for other outlets. Phenol promised to be one of these outlets, to be used in the manufacture of resins, but Niks' report also put the intermediates for nylon 6.6 on the map. Feedstocks again dominated thinking at DSM.

DSM was not the only Dutch company investigating nylon. The Algemene Kunstzijde Unie (AKU), created by a merger of the German Vereinigte Glanzstoff-Fabriken (VGF) and the Dutch ENKA in 1929 and one of the largest synthetic fibre producers in the world, started research into nylon in May 1939. AKU concentrated on nylon 6.6, Du Pont's product, and investigated adipic acid, HMD and nylon salt. In February 1940, the first meeting of representatives of AKU and DSM took place. Only three months later, German forces invaded the Netherlands, ending the contacts between the two companies. Both AKU and DSM, however, continued their research and in 1942 AKU once again tried to enter into a partnership with DSM but Ross van Lennep did not want to take a decision until after the war.

The Central Laboratory investigated the feasibility and possible technical problems of nylon intermediates production on a small scale after November 1939. In 1941, more substantial research started on HMD, adipic acid and nylon salt, but the war put a damper on these efforts. The phenol plans initially gained more momentum as in 1940 DSM reached agreement with the German company Rütgerswerke for a license on their phenol process. The plans included the construction of a phenol plant of 2,000 tons per year, aimed at the resins market, but this had to be cancelled in 1941, again due to the war.[36]

The Establishment of Caprolactam Production
In 1946, DSM re-established contact with AKU and this time both companies quickly reached an agreement: DSM would focus on the intermediates, while AKU would focus on the spinning process – a division of labour that suited the capabilities and market positions of both companies. Polymerisation was of interest to both AKU and DSM, but AKU was ahead in its research and secured this step as well.

In the meantime, AKU had also negotiated with Du Pont, but Du Pont would not license its nylon technologies to AKU, one of its main European competitors. On the other hand, the Dutch authorities confiscated the Dutch patents of IG Farben and made them available to DSM and AKU. Through the VGF, AKU also had some knowledge of German

Figure 3.6. Outline of caprolactam synthesis.

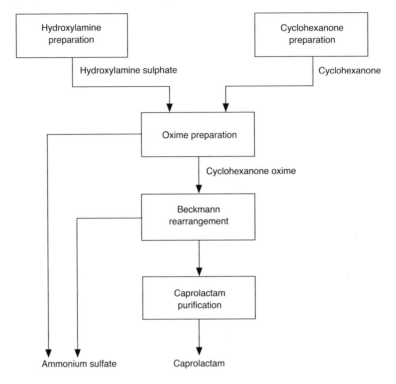

Based on: J. J. McKetta (1976-1999). *Encyclopedia of Chemical Processing and Design.* New York & Basel: Marcel Dekker. 68 volumes, vol. 6, 1978. Figure 2, 76.

developments in caprolactam, although unwilling VGF managers limited the extent of the transfer. Reports of Allied technical inspection teams also became available. For these reasons, AKU directed DSM towards caprolactam in 1947. DSM stopped research on intermediates for nylon 6.6. Representatives of AKU and DSM visited Germany to inspect caprolactam and nylon 6 plants to gather information.

At the Central Laboratory, researchers soon established the outline of the caprolactam process through information on German nylon developments. The process started from hydroxylamine and cyclohexanone, and proceeded via cyclohexanone oxime to caprolactam (Figure 3.6.). Hydroxylamine sulphate could be produced by reacting ammonium nitrite with sulphur dioxide. Sulphur dioxide was available from the sulphuric acid plants, while DSM chose to use the off-gases from the nitric acid plants to produce ammonium nitrite[37] (Figure 3.7.).

For cyclohexanone, DSM selected the IG Farben route: a process that started from phenol and proceeded via cyclohexanol to cyclohexanone.[38]

Figure 3.7. Hydroxylamine preparation.

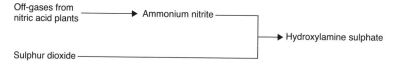

Figure 3.8. Cyclohexanone preparation.

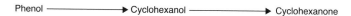

Note: these figures fall into the cyclohexanone preparation box of figure 3.6.

(Figure 3.8.) The starting point for phenol could be benzene, a compound DSM could obtain from its coke oven plants. With phenol, moreover, DSM could also enter the resins market as shortly after the war the company had not yet made a strategic choice between fibre intermediates and resins. The choice to base cyclohexanone on phenol in this way gave an extra impetus to the Central Laboratory's research on this compound. In 1946, Berkhoff visited a number of American phenol producers to investigate the possibilities of acquiring technology, but not many options presented themselves. In 1947, however, Daniel Tyrer, an American, licensed his phenol process to DSM. The process needed to be developed to industrial scale, a task the Central Laboratory took upon itself in the following years. In 1949, a pilot plant was built and four years later industrial phenol production started. Tyrer, impressed with the process worked out at the Central Laboratory, granted DSM the right to exploit the process worldwide, with the exception of the United States. However, major problems arose after DSM started the phenol plant. Although the plant had been designed with a capacity of 6,000 tons per year, only 500 tons could be produced in the first year. Major changes had to be made to the plant in 1954 but production costs remained too high and the installation remained unreliable. The Central Laboratory failed to solve the technological problems. In 1955, the phenol plant closed and DSM decided to buy phenol.[39]

In the route to caprolactam, phenol had to be converted to cyclohexanone, which proceeded via cyclohexanol (Figure 3.8.). Researchers intended to work out these processes themselves, but in 1950 ran out of time. AKU progressed more quickly than DSM and aimed to start an industrial plant for nylon in 1952. To speed up, DSM decided to acquire know-how for the steps phenol – cyclohexanol – cyclohexanone. Chemiebouw contacted a number of firms that had this know-how and, together with the Central Laboratory, selected Montecatini in 1950. The Italian company

Semi-technical installation for research on cyclohexanone, May 1951. Cyclohexanone was an important intermediate in the production of caprolactam. The semi-technical department of the Central Laboratory had been created a short time before this photograph was taken. It investigated processes on a scale between the laboratory bench and the pilot plant. Cylohexanone research was one of the first – and most important – projects of the new department.

operated a phenol – cyclohexanol process in an industrial plant but was still working on the following step. Montecatini did not want to sell know-how for this step until the process had run in a pilot plant for a number of months, and until its catalyst had been tested. The Central Laboratory in the meantime also continued its research, and late in 1950 developed a catalyst that had promising characteristics and seemed to work better than the Montecatini catalyst. DSM changed the licensing agreement with Montecatini accordingly, and the Semi-Technical department developed the process for the conversion of cyclohexanol to cylohexanone further. Goris, who had worked on caprolactam in previous years, set up this department in 1951 and the cyclohexanol – cyclohexanone process initially took up much of the Semi-Technical department's time.[40]

The other steps in the production of caprolactam also required extensive research. In 1949, the Organic Chemistry department of the Central Laboratory developed a continuous process for the preparation of cyclohexanone oxime. Two years later, in cooperation with the Organic Chemistry department, the Aerodynamics department, a department of mainly physicists that had roots in coal-related research, adapted DSM's cyclone for use in the rearrangement of cyclohexanone oxime to caprolactam. DSM's cyclone had been developed at the end of the 1930s for the separation of coal from the stones that were inevitably mined with coal. According to Van Krevelen, who had been involved himself, the cyclone gave DSM's caprolactam process its own 'special character'.[41]

DSM built a pilot plant for caprolactam in 1948/49 on the basis of its research, and on the basis of a design supplied by AKU in 1947. In 1949, the work of both DSM and AKU had progressed to the extent that the planning for industrial plants could start. The research cooperation was formalised in a contract, signed in February 1950. In October 1949, AKU had succeeded in landing a non-exclusive license on Du Pont's nylon patents, but without any technical assistance. The choice of caprolactam and nylon 6 strengthened AKU's position and Du Pont had also come under the scrutiny of the American anti-trust authorities, forcing it to license more than before. In 1952, DSM started industrial production of caprolactam in a plant with a capacity of 3,600 tons per year.

In establishing nylon production in the Netherlands, AKU and DSM could profit from German know-how; but in-house research was crucial to solve the many problems that remained and to develop a process on an industrial scale. Catalysis and process research capabilities, built in relation to fertilisers, had enabled DSM to start the caprolactam project, but as the project progressed it boosted these capabilities further and also crucially strengthened capabilities in organic chemistry, a field in which DSM had gained a foothold through the alcohol process of the 1930s. Nevertheless, the leading role of AKU in DSM's research is striking. AKU put DSM on the track of caprolactam, and AKU was in fact the market for DSM's product. In the early years, DSM exported a few tons of caprolactam but these amounts were small.

Figure 3.9. Ammonium nitrite and hydroxylamine preparation.

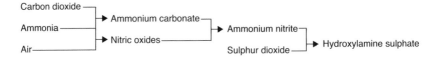

Note: this figure falls into the hydroxylamine preparation box of figure 3.6 above.

Improving the Process

After the plant had come on stream in 1952, research on caprolactam continued and concerned all steps of the process. For instance, the production of ammonium nitrite from the off-gases of the nitric acid plants had a low efficiency. Research on possible alternatives that had been started at the Organic Chemistry department in 1949 had yielded few results. In July 1950, Niks, who was now in charge of developing the production of caprolactam and other organic products at the SBB, visited Hermann Zorn from the Swiss company Holzverzuckerungs AG. Zorn, a former IG Farben expert on caprolactam, had continued his work in Switzerland. Through Inventa, the Holzverzuckerungs AG sold much of his technology. Zorn put Niks on the track of another route to ammonium nitrite: from ammonia and carbon dioxide, ammonium carbonate could be made, which in turn could be reacted with nitric oxides to form ammonium nitrite (Figure 3.9.). This promised to be a highly efficient route and Niks, Berkhoff and others considered buying this process. Instead, when the off-gases of nitric acid production no longer provided enough ammonium nitrite, Zorn's route became a subject for research. Under the umbrella of fertiliser research, a process was developed quickly and a pilot plant built in 1953. A year later, a commercial installation started at one of the nitric acid plants.[42]

Zorn not only informed Niks on ammonium nitrite, but also on the purification of caprolactam. Again, several researchers suggested buying Zorn's method, but research continued as well. AKU had little faith in Zorn's know-how and preliminary research at the Central Laboratory failed to reproduce Zorn's claims. A number of strict criteria had to be met in the production of caprolactam because contaminations interfered with the polymerisation and spinning processes. Research on the purification of caprolactam started in full around the time the commercial plant was under construction. The Analysis department of the Central Laboratory worked on the identification of contaminations in caprolactam from the plant and developed methods for this identification. The SBB's works laboratory also worked on this, and AKU suggested polymerising caprolactam from the plant on laboratory scale as a quality test. Researchers from the Organic Chemistry department in particular worked on processes to purify caprolactam, together with other Central Laboratory departments and Leo Kretzers, one of the caprolactam plant's staff engineers. In 1958, a new method of caprolactam purification was implemented in the plant, but purification and contaminations remained a subject for research in the following years.[43]

Research on purification and ammonium nitrite are just two examples of research aimed at improving the processes used in the caprolactam plants. These processes were also changed and improved on other points, and almost continuously. The importance of such research can hardly be overestimated. Purity in particular was crucial, again giving AKU a central role in DSM's research. The effects of Niks' visit to the Holzverzuckerungs AG similarly show that the research process in relation to caprolactam was more or less open, and at least partly directed by outside incentives.

Feedstocks: The Cyclohexane Oxidation Process and another Phenol Plant
After the closure of the phenol plant, DSM manufactured caprolactam from acquired phenol. Benzene could be processed into cyclohexane, which in turn could be oxidised to cyclohexanone and cylohexanol. This presented a route which would again base caprolactam production on internally available feedstocks. With increasing petroleum-refining capacity after the Second World War, moreover, cyclohexane became available at low prices and presented a long-term threat to phenol-based caprolactam production. For both reasons, the Organic Chemistry department started researching cyclohexane oxidation in 1952. Cyclohexane oxidation, however, was only used industrially for the production of adipic acid and the initial results of the Central Laboratory's research were poor: the process had a low efficiency and adipic acid was an unavoidable by-product. Researchers branded the process uneconomical.[44]

Two years later, however, research on the oxidation of cyclohexane started again, triggered in particular by the expected availability of cyclohexane from the petroleum industry. Finding suitable equipment and a suitable method for the processing of the oxidation product into cyclohexanol and cylohexanone posed problems, but in 1956 a semi-technical oxidation unit was built. In the same year, Spencer Chemical, an American chemical company, showed an interest in licensing DSM's caprolactam process. Spencer's starting point would be cyclohexane, not phenol, and this stimulated research. In 1959, the Central Laboratory had progressed to the stage where the preparations for an industrial plant could start. In 1961, DSM decided to build a plant which came on stream a year later. Spencer eventually did not acquire DSM know-how as they decided not to set up caprolactam production when their projected price offered to a potential client was undercut by a competitor.[45]

Graph 3.3. Cost prices and market prices for caprolactam at DSM, 1952-1966.

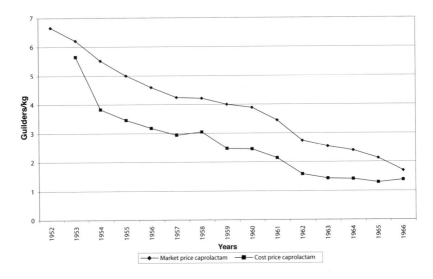

Source: RAL, 17.26/ 34 inv. no. 789: Verloop productie, kostprijs en opbrengst caprolactam 1952-1966. Bedrijfseconomische afdeling, Kikken, 26 May 1967.

Graph 3.4. Expansion of caprolactam capacity at DSM, 1952-1966.

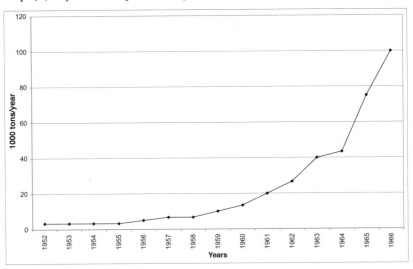

Source: RAL, 17.26/ 34 inv. no. 789: Verloop productie, kostprijs en opbrengst caprolactam 1952-1966. Bedrijfseconomische afdeling, Kikken, 26 May 1967.

THE COMPANY THAT CHANGED ITSELF

Stamicarbon profited from the cyclohexane oxidation process because most of its licensees preferred cyclohexane over phenol as starting point for caprolactam. At DSM's site in Geleen (Netherlands), only a relatively small unit was built. At the Central Laboratory, moreover, research by the Catalysis department led to a shortcut in the phenol-to-cyclohexanone process and an industrial unit started at about the same time as the cyclohexane plant.[46]

Finally, alongside research, production staff evaluated the possibilities of restarting phenol production. As caprolactam production was being expanded continuously, production of feedstocks had to keep up. In 1958, production staff decided that developing the cyclohexane oxidation process would take too long to cover immediate feedstock demands, and they started talks with Durez Plastics and Dow Chemical, both American companies. Dow had plans to build a phenol plant in Rotterdam (Netherlands) based on its own process, starting from toluene and proceeding via benzoic acid to phenol. Dow's researchers were still working on the development of the process, and initial cost calculations showed that it might be more expensive than conventional routes. DSM still chose to cooperate with Dow. It considered Dow an attractive partner and also expected the price of toluene to fall because the petroleum industry made increasing amounts available from its refining operations. DSM also managed to make Dow financially responsible for all the technological risks. DSM and Dow joined forces by establishing a joint venture, later named the *Chemische Industrie Rijnmond* (CIR).[47]

Construction of the phenol plant began in Rotterdam in 1962, and two years later it could be started up. At that time, phenol prices dropped and Dow lost its interest in the project, selling its stake in CIR to DSM in 1964. The phenol plant had many teething problems that led to poor financial results and required substantial research. The Dow process generated tar alongside phenol, and research focused on reducing the amount of tar and also tried to find ways to process it into a useful product. The Central Laboratory got the phenol plant going, but its competitive position remained weak.[48]

Despite the problems with the plant, DSM remained committed to CIR and to phenol as a starting point for caprolactam. Because of developments in phenol, the role of the cyclohexane oxidation process at DSM's own production site remained somewhat marginal. It does show the long-term view of researchers as the process did not solve any immediate problems. It also shows that research took initiatives, and was able to take such initiatives relatively independently of production management in DSM's chemical sector. Moreover, DSM started research on cyclohexane oxidation without being prompted by AKU. In matters of feedstocks and process research, DSM had accumulated much experience over the years and took decisions on its own.

The cyclohexane oxidation process represents research with a broader scope than the research on purification, for instance, as it presented an alternative to the route in operation. Both types of research for existing businesses were undertaken in an attempt to maintain profitability. Prices for bulk chemicals typically declined over time, and with declining prices, profit margins also declined.[49] Caprolactam prices followed this pattern, but DSM tried to combat these falling prices through expansion and research and succeeded in maintaining a profit margin, albeit a declining one (Graph 3.3.). It is difficult to assess the relative importance of expansion and research in the maintenance of profitability because DSM expanded caprolactam capacity almost continuously (Graph 3.4), reaching the milestone of 100,000 tons per year in 1966. Graph 3.3 indicates, however, that DSM went through a steep learning curve right after the plant went on stream.

Threats and Research
Although capacity reached 100,000 tons per year in 1966, only approximately 73,000 tons were sold in that year. A year earlier, production had also remained well below capacity. Market prices were also dropping fast, narrowing the gap with cost prices (Graph 3.3). The poor results of phenol manufacture also strained profitability.[50]

This first hitch in the development of caprolactam turned out to be temporary, but influenced research. In 1966, Revallier, DSM's R&D manager, wrote in his notes to the annual report for top management that 'change' characterised caprolactam technology and the market for fibre intermediates. Revallier noted that BASF and Bayer were planning major expansions of their caprolactam capacities in Antwerp, and that ICI and Du Pont were planning expansions of their nylon 6.6 capacities on the mainland of Europe. The extensive technical sales services of ICI and Du Pont inspired respect as well. Revallier also expected increased competition between nylon 6, nylon 6.6 and polyester due to improvements in the spinning process of the latter two fibres. Finally, other companies had new routes to caprolactam under development that particularly promised to lower the amount of ammonium sulphate. This by-product had a heavy influence on the economics of caprolactam production. The market for ammonium sulphate was mainly located in the Far East and had a cyclical character. The expansion of caprolactam production had led to increasing amounts of ammonium sulphate which, from time to time, were hard to sell. The promise of the development of ammonium sulphate-free caprolactam processes also meant that the link between fibres and fertilisers could be loosened, opening the door to fibre intermediates for companies that did not have fertiliser activities.[51]

Revallier noted a number of ways in which research was responding

THE COMPANY THAT CHANGED ITSELF

to these developments. In the first place, the research on the process used in the production plant broadened to include alternative processes. DSM set up its own sales service department and investigated the possibilities of manufacturing other fibre intermediates. These research lines characterise DSM's caprolactam research from the late 1950s onwards.

The central Laboratory had already investigated alternative processes in the early 1950s, but this research gained momentum after about 1960. The 1960s saw many activities in caprolactam and fibre intermediates generally, and patents of other companies typically motivated the start of research at the Central Laboratory. A substantial number of these projects started, but by 1965 one had become the most important: the route to caprolactam via caprolactone. Patented by the American company Union Carbide, the process omitted the preparation of cyclohexanone oxime and proceeded via cyclohexanone to caprolactone, and in turn to caprolactam. In 1961, the Organic Chemistry department started research on this process, but had trouble inventing around the patents of Union Carbide. In 1966, re-searchers found a route via the co-oxidation of cyclohexahone with benzal-dehyde, a chemical available through the Dow phenol process. The capro-lactone process could be integrated with the phenol process, resulting in an almost closed process with no ammonium sulphate by-product and lower investment costs. (Figure 3.10.) The processing of the co-oxidation product proved to be difficult, however. Research continued for a number of years, but the caprolactone process did not get off the ground. Union Carbide built a plant in the 1960s but closed it down a number of years later.[52]

As in the case of the cyclohexane oxidation process, the Central Labor-atory had taken the initiative to start research on the caprolactone process and had taken a long-term view of DSM's interests. From the perspective of research it was desirable to at least reduce the production of ammonium sulphate, and the caprolactone project was one way of achieving this goal. Other projects on alternative processes also failed to produce results. Incre-mental improvements to the existing plant proved to be an effective way of remaining competitive.

Another way of remaining competitive was by providing service: solv-ing problems that customers were confronted with in processing. An ex-pected increase in competition, as well as DSM's gradually broadening customer base, made such service important. The technical sales service of competitors served as examples for the Central Laboratory's own serv-ice department, which was initially called Spinning House (*Spinhuis*), but soon afterwards Fibre Intermediates. The department was established in 1960 with Goris as its first head. Emile de Roy van Zuydewijn was engaged as an advisor. De Roy van Zuydewijn investigated plastics and fibres at Eindhoven Technical College, and had been research director of Nyma, a

Figure 3.10. The DSM caprolactone process.

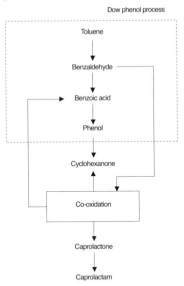

Based on: Central Laboratory Research Programme 1965.

small Dutch rayon producer. Zimmer, a German engineering contractor specialised in the field of polymerisation and spinning technology, built the necessary installations. Fibre Intermediates worked on solving problems of customers but, for example, also tried to stimulate caprolactam sales by developing Reaction Injection Moulding (RIM), a technique to polymerise caprolactam in a mould in the presence of a catalyst and other additives. Several companies showed interest in DSM's RIM know-how and conducted tests, but these contacts did not develop into substantial sales. Shortly after the establishment of Fibre Intermediates, the Central Laboratory started service and application research in plastics as well.[53]

Fibre Intermediates built a base of fibre know-how concerning caprolactam and nylon 6 and other fibres. The competition between nylon 6 and other fibres, or fear of this competition, repeatedly led to research. Intermediates for nylon 6.6, polyester, the growth fibre of the 1950s and 1960s, and acrylic fibres, another class of fibres that emerged after the Second World War, appeared on the agenda of the Central Laboratory from time to time. In 1954, Van Krevelen and his colleagues in the management of the Central Laboratory sketched the dilemma for DSM in the research programme: there were many potentially interesting routes to many potentially interesting products, but researchers had to cover the whole field because no choices could be made; the company had to rely on a partner.[54]

A machine for drawing and twisting yarn at the Fibre Intermediates department of the Central Laboratory in 1965. The department was equipped with the machines that DSM's caprolactam customers used to manufacture nylon. It helped solve customer problems and worked on product development. The Central Laboratory had similar departments to support DSM's plastics business.

This mechanism is clear, for example, in DSM's research on nylon salt, the intermediate for nylon 6.6, in the late 1950s.[55] In April 1955, AKU told DSM of its intention to build a nylon 6.6 pilot plant. AKU manufactured large amounts of nylon 6 as well as rayon, a fibre based on cellulose, and thought that nylon 6 would replace rayon for use in tyre cords, the fibres used to reinforce the carcass of car tyres. Amerenka, its American subsidiary that manufactured rayon tyre cord, already planned to make a switch to nylon 6. Major American tyre companies, stimulated by Du Pont and Chemstrand, the two major American manufactures of nylon 6.6, considered nylon 6.6 more attractive than nylon 6, however. AKU wanted to follow but did not want to manufacture nylon salt, the necessary intermediate, in-house. Only BASF marketed this compound, and AKU turned to DSM as a second supplier. DSM committed itself to producing the intermediates. After it had become clear that the know-how for the process could not be bought, the Central Laboratory's Organic Chemistry department, the Semi-Technical department and the Organic Pilot Plants rushed to get to the pilot plant stage. The project also involved: Chemiebouw; DSM's business economists; Niks, at that time head of SBB's sector

Figure 3.11. The nylon salt, cyclohexane oxidation and caprolactam processes.

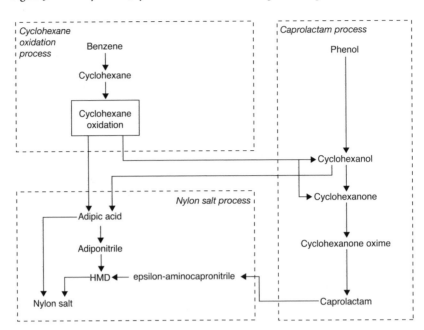

Based on: Central Laboratory Annual Report 1956.

that included caprolactam; and Kretzers, one of the staff engineers of the caproalactam plant, who was to be appointed as its head in December 1956. DSM took the development of a nylon salt process very seriously.[56]

By 1955 it was no secret that production of nylon salt revolved around hexamethylene diamine (HMD) and adipic acid. (Figure 3.11.) For adipic acid, European companies used a route that started from phenol and proceeded via cyclohexanol to adipic acid. The Central Laboratory reworked this process on the basis of data from technical literature, with most of the data originating from ICI. At the time nylon salt came into the picture, the Central Laboratory also worked on its cyclohexane oxidation process that resulted in adipic acid as a by-product. Integrated production of caprolactam and nylon salt therefore became inevitable but also spurred research on cyclohexane oxidation. The integrated route became the focus of research and, as early as 1955, pilot production of cyclohexane and adipic acid started. With HMD bought from other companies, a first batch of nylon salt was produced.

The known route to HMD proceeded from adipic acid via adiponitrile. Researchers found the step from adipic acid to adiponitrile difficult and also hired an Italian advisor for the step to HMD.[57] Researchers also found an alternative route to HMD, however, proceeding from caprolactam via epsilon-aminocapronitrile. This route had been found and patented in 1950 by TNO, the Dutch semi-public organisation for applied research, but these patents had expired and did not hinder DSM's research. Production staff also evaluated the available options and considered the route starting from caprolactam the most attractive as it gave DSM an option to develop a process that was not already being used by another company.

Finally, two options existed for the production of nylon salt: HMD could be neutralised with adipic acid in the presence of water or alcohol. In 1955, the Central Laboratory focused on the alcohol route because the nylon salt produced with the water route was hard to purify and therefore required very pure HMD and adipic acid. In July 1956, however, AKU formulated preliminary standards of quality for nylon salt that were hard to meet with the alcohol route. Work on the water route resumed and research started on purification methods.

In 1956, only a year after research had started, the Organic Pilot Plants had a full nylon salt process in operation on pilot plant scale. A year later, researchers cut the ties between caprolactam and nylon salt production when they found a way to process the cyclohexane oxidation product to cylohexanol and cyclohexanone without adipic acid, or vice versa, to produce mainly adipic acid.

In a short time, the Central Laboratory achieved pilot production of nylon salt. The evaluation of several routes to a desired end product or intermediate was typical of research in organic chemistry. In the case of urea, basically one chemical route existed and the emphasis of the research was on the technology needed to realise this route on an industrial scale. The short time it took to reach the pilot plant stage with nylon salt shows the extent to which organic chemistry capabilities had grown after the Second World War. The development of the alcohol process in the 1930s had laid a small foundation for these capabilities but they were greatly expanded through caprolactam research. Through caprolactam, DSM developed a new technology base.

Negotiations with AKU over sales of nylon salt went less smoothly than research. AKU was also negotiating with BASF and used this to put pressure on DSM. In 1957, after a year of pilot plant operations at DSM, AKU radically readjusted its expectations of nylon 6.6. AKU had aimed at tyre cords for car tyres. Tyres with cords made from nylon 6.6 suffered from so-called flat-spotting: they became less round after a car had stood at the same spot for a while. Improvements in conventional tyre cords, moreover, cut off nylon 6.6's entry. The Central Laboratory's research and the pilot plant stopped immediately. In 1958 and 1959, the pilot plant made occasional production runs when AKU had managed to secure orders for nylon 6.6, but in 1959 the pilot plant was dismantled.[58]

AKU started DSM's research on nylon salt and cancelled it. The unforeseen cancellation gave researchers a hangover, but shows that DSM relied heavily on AKU. DSM could not choose between potentially interesting fibre intermediates on its own. DSM had contact with the market for synthetic fibres only through AKU. In contrast, when AKU had put DSM on the track of nylon salt, the Central Laboratory could choose between alternative routes to HMD, for instance. In process research on caprolactam, and in the related fields of organic chemistry and catalysis, the Central Laboratory accumulated a lot of experience in a relatively short period of time and did not need a partner to direct research.

Diversification

The Central Laboratory researched caprolactam extensively, with AKU providing help at crucial crossroads. The establishment of production, the improvement of the production process, alternative processes and alternative products all received attention. Research took initiatives and started projects out of concern about the long-range prospects of caprolactam production. Production management hardly interfered with that kind of research. The caprolactam research shows the faith management had in research, and the room it gave to research; it also shows that these parameters of research management not only applied to fundamental research.

At the Central Laboratory, caprolactam cut across the inorganic/organic divide in the organisation. The Inorganic Chemistry department also conducted some research on caprolactam; the Analytical department performed crucial work on purification; and the Semi-Technical department solved many equipment problems. In general, caprolactam relied more on the increased scope of the Central Laboratory's organisation than urea; Van Krevelen's scope-building paid off in caprolactam. Process research, catalysis and organic chemistry developed into strongholds and were crucial for the establishment and maintenance of caprolactam production. Research played a central role in caprolactam production, even though AKU took crucial decisions for DSM. The Central Laboratory's work laid the vital link in the chain toward industrial production and enabled DSM to take advantage of the fast growing market for nylon 6 and its intermediates.

Like urea, the caprolactam project fitted DSM's expansive business strategy in chemicals. Also like urea, DSM entered caprolactam relatively late and aimed to catch up with the leading companies in the field. Both projects were primarily technology-push. In urea, DSM knew the fertiliser market; in caprolactam, AKU provided DSM with a link to the market and, in the early years, in fact was DSM's market. The markets for urea and caprolactam, moreover, grew fast. Entering known and fast growing markets with a technology push posed few difficulties.

More Diversifications: Polyethylene, EPDM and Melamine

Caprolactam represented a major step outside the field of fertilisers, but DSM diversified further in the 1950s and 1960s. Production of, and demand for, synthetic fibres grew fast after the Second World War but plastics boomed as well. DSM entered this field through polyethylene. Technological links led to the development of EPDM synthetic rubber. Finally, feedstock links led from urea to melamine, a product that could be used in the manufacture of thermoset resins. As in the case of caprolactam, the Central Laboratory played an important role in these diversifications.

ICI and Ziegler: DSM's Entry into Polyethylene

Like nylon, polyethylene was a new material from the 1930s. Eric Fawcett and Reginald Gibson, researchers from ICI, discovered polyethylene in 1933. They polymerised ethylene under very high pressure. ICI had a production plant in operation by 1939 and during the Second World War the new material found ample use but mainly as cable insulation.[59]

The discovery of polyethylene followed from ICI's research program on high-pressure chemistry. The British firm had close contacts with the Dutch professor Teun Michels, who was an authority in the field. The outbreak of the war prevented further contacts between ICI and Michels. Ross van Lennep, however, asked Michels in 1942 to become an advisor for the Central Laboratory's research on ammonia synthesis. Like ICI's polyethylene process, ammonia synthesis proceeded at high pressure.[60] In October of the following year, and with Michels' help, the Central Laboratory also started to research the purification of ethylene with the ultimate goal of polymerising this compound. Ethylene was available from the coke oven gas separation section and DSM was already manufacturing alcohol from this compound[61] (See chapter 2.).

In 1946, just after the end of the Second World War, a section of DSM's coal sales office made a quick market scan and contacted several potential Dutch customers. This scan showed interest in polyethylene, but DSM needed a license on ICI's patents before it could manufacture this plastic. DSM approached ICI in 1946, but the British company did not want to license its technology. By being persistent, DSM eventually got a license and secured access to the know-how necessary to build a plant and introduce the product. ICI and DSM signed the contracts on 1 April 1957.

In the meantime, the landscape had changed dramatically. Late in 1953, Karl Ziegler of the *Max Planck Institut für Kohlenforschung* discovered a catalyst that could polymerise ethylene at atmospheric pressure. The resulting polyethylene differed from ICI's product. The Ziegler catalyst led to products with a high density that were more rigid and stiff than ICI's low density, more flexible products. Because of its different characteristics, high-density polyethylene (HDPE) promised applications that differed from those of low-density polyethylene (LDPE).[62] Comparable discoveries were made at Du Pont, Standard Oil of Indiana (later Amoco) and Phillips Petroleum. Ziegler had no production interests and decided to license freely. He licensed his catalyst only, and not a process. Ziegler's licensees had to develop a process.[63]

Berkhoff and Van Krevelen attended a lecture by Ziegler at an industry fair in Frankfurt, shortly after Ziegler had made his discoveries. Berkhoff and Van Krevelen quickly recognised the importance of the new catalyst and called Ziegler on the way back to Limburg to inquire about the possibilities of a license.[64] In parallel, Berkhoff and Van Krevelen formed a small group of researchers from coal research and the Organic Chemistry department in March 1955. The research of this group was aimed at understanding the polymerisation of ethylene with a Ziegler catalyst.[65] Research was limited to fundamental investigations because DSM had not yet obtained a license. In April 1955, the company made an official request for this license. Negotiations did not take long and DSM obtained a license in November that year.

Ziegler's work and his willingness to license unexpectedly opened a second option to enter polyethylene. DSM took this opportunity and mobilised its resources quickly, but at the same time negotiations with ICI continued. Early in 1957, top management decided to go for both ICI and Ziegler. The products were complementary and competitors were moving in the same direction as DSM. Top management gave priority to LDPE, however, because an established market existed for this product and because ICI had proven technology.

While research on the Ziegler process continued, Chemiebouw started working on the engineering of an LDPE plant. They used drawings and specifications supplied by ICI. The British firm also helped DSM train its future operators. The licensing contract stipulated further that ICI would help DSM with know-how relating to the processing and applications of LDPE. In September 1957 DSM signed a similar contract with the American company Spencer Chemical. This company made a request to buy DSM's caprolactam technology in 1954. After the decision had been taken to build an ICI polyethylene plant, Spencer and DSM agreed on an exchange of know-how. In return for DSM's knowledge concerning caprolactam and nylon salt, Spencer provided DSM with its knowledge of low-density polyethylene. Spencer had licensed the ICI process in 1952, but had improved this technology and had experience with it. The exchange of know-how proceeded more to the advantage of DSM when Spencer decided to call off its plan for caprolactam and nylon salt production.[66] Finally, in March 1958 DSM signed a contract with the TNO Plastics Institute that had much experience in application research on plastics. DSM contracted TNO for application research on polyethylene and gained the opportunity to take over researchers from TNO that had worked on assignments from DSM.

Application know-how was crucial in plastics. Converters needed information on the properties of a material, on how it would behave in the machines they used, and on the characteristics of the end product; manufacturers of plastics typically supplied this information. The Central Laboratory had to organise application research in plastics. The Materials Research and Semi-Technical departments did this research before 1958. Materials Research worked on quality control and testing of materials like concrete and alloys that were used by the company. In 1958, two new departments were organised: Plastics Technology, where application research was done with plastics processing machines; and Plastics Research, where testing methods were developed and properties of materials were investigated. These departments were combined in a sector named R&D Polymers in 1963, together with a department that conducted process research on HDPE (called Polymer Development).[67]

In 1959, DSM started its LDPE plant. It had a capacity of 10,000 tons per year but soon proved too small. DSM continuously expanded this installation in the 1960s. The market for polyethylene was booming and grew fast. Through the development of new types, the application area expanded to include packaging of all sorts, toys, pipes, household goods, etc.[68] In 1958, DSM established a sales office for plastics (*Verenigd Plastic Verkoopkantoor*, VPV) together with AKU, which marketed certain nylon types for use in the plastics industry.

The VPV built a service and troubleshooting laboratory as well, enabling the Central Laboratory to concentrate its application research on product development and improvement. This would become an important task for the Central Laboratory in the 1960s. Competition came from other producers of polyethylene and other materials. Product improvement and expansion of the number of types was crucial to keep up and improve market positions. The Central Laboratory also worked on improvements of the LDPE process to make it safer and more reliable, and to cut costs. As production capacity increased, prices fell and DSM had to cut its production costs to remain competitive.[69]

DSM entered polyethylene by licensing the ICI process. The main challenge for the Central Laboratory was to build up application research in relation to both the processing and analysis of polyethylene. This was a crucial addition to DSM's technological capabilities, as caprolactam and fertilisers were much more standardised products than polyethylene. By 1961 DSM manufactured no fewer than 185 types of LDPE.

DSM needed ethylene to produce polyethylene and also to produce alcohol. Initially, enough ethylene could be made available from coke oven gas. In 1957, when DSM decided to diversify into both LDPE and HDPE,

Table 3.3. DSM's naphtha crackers.

Installation	Start	Stop	Capacity
			tons of ethylene/ year
1	1961	1971	30,000
2	1967	1975 (explosion)	135,000
3	1971		350,000
4	1979		450,000

Sources: DSM annual reports 1967, 1971, 1975. Naftakraker wordt in bedrijf gesteld. *Nieuws van de Staatsmijnen 1961*, 10(15), NAK 4 in bedrijf. *DSM Limburg Nieuws 1979*, 29(5), 1.

it became clear that not enough could be produced from this source. Production staff had already started exploring other possible methods to manufacture ethylene, including those starting from hydrocarbon feedstocks that were already widely used in the United States and that were increasingly being used in Western Europe. DSM hired Stone & Webster, one of the leading engineering contractors in the field, to build a naphtha cracker. This installation started in 1961 (table 3.3) and marked the first time that DSM did not use coal-based feedstocks. A second, much larger, cracker soon followed and the alcohol plant was also closed in 1960, freeing additional ethylene for plastics manufacture. Finally, DSM was connected to a pipeline network between several companies in the Benelux and Germany.[70]

The Central Laboratory evaluated different routes to ethylene in the 1950s and investigated hydrocarbon-based ethylene production in an attempt to optimise the process. The field was dominated by engineering contractors and DSM, like most other companies, relied on these companies for the engineering and construction of its crackers.[71]

Development of a Ziegler Process
As in the case of LDPE, DSM tried to acquire process know-how alongside the catalyst. Ziegler and his institute did not provide such knowledge, but many other companies were working on industrial processes. The German chemical firm Hibernia had already built a pilot plant by April 1955. Van Waes and Berkhoff visited this installation that month and tried to come to an agreement. Hibernia, however, had tied itself to *Chemische Werke Hüls*.

In September 1955, the vice-president of Koppers Company visited DSM. This American conglomerate had also acquired a Ziegler license and offered DSM its process know-how. In October and November 1955, Berkhoff and Van Waes travelled through the United States and visited not only Koppers, but also Phillips Petroleum and other firms. Koppers made a very good impression. Berkhoff and Van Waes thought that Koppers had already developed a process. Koppers preferred joint research with the Central Laboratory and both companies signed an agreement to that end in February 1956. In May of that year, the American company Brea Chemicals, a subsidiary of Union Oil Company of California, was included.

In 1956, the Central Laboratory shifted into high gear and engaged its full spectrum of research capabilities to develop a process. The Organic Chemistry department, which also investigated caprolactam, played an important role. The Central Laboratory also expanded its scope for polyethylene when it started systematic fundamental polymer research in 1956. The Central Laboratory's catalysis group and the department for fundamental coal research took up this work. Van Krevelen had initiated research into the constitution of coal to maintain coke quality. In relation to polymers, fundamental research was aimed at building a scientific foundation for the future production of plastics. Research included work on catalysis, developing analysis methods and studies of molecular weight distribution. Research into the latter subject was aimed at gaining a better understanding of the relationship between the production process, the catalyst and the product's characteristics. In this way, industrial interests played an important role in fundamental polymer research. Moreover, universities were doing little in the field of polymers at that time. In 1957, the Central Laboratory created a dedicated department, called Fundamental Polymer Research, under the umbrella of the Basic and Fundamental Research sector.[72]

In January 1956, several researchers, including the small group that had been formed in 1955, visited Ziegler's Max Planck institute for the first time and got full insight into the work that had been done up to that point. Soon afterwards, the first information from Koppers also became available. This made it clear that many technological problems remained. Because of these problems, polymer yields in Koppers' process were too low. The product also proved corrosive for processing equipment and this problem threatened a successful introduction of DSM's HDPE. In June 1956, researchers visited Ziegler to discuss this problem, but other licensees had not met a corrosion problem.

The Central Laboratory soon moved to the pilot plant stage, aiming primarily at process development. Researchers started from a design supplied by Koppers. Construction of the pilot plant started in June 1956. In September of the following year, the installation could be started with a batch operation. Research soon started to make the process continuous. The Central Laboratory also maintained the study of catalyst composition and behaviour. Product quality, and consequently the areas of application, were tightly connected to the catalyst used, and variations in that catalyst.

Table 3.4. Ziegler licensees up to 1955.

Licensee	Country	Contract	Start of royalties payment	Interval
				Years
Petrochemicals Ltd.[i]	UK	1952	1957	5
Montecatini	Italy	1953	1957	4
Hoechst	Germany	1954	1957	3
Ruhrchemie	Germany	1954	1957	3
Hercules Powder Co.	USA	1954	1958	4
Ameripol (Goodrich, Gulf Oil)	USA	1954	1961	7
Koppers	USA	1954	1963	9
Dow Chemical	USA	1954	1961	7
Union Carbide	USA	1954	1957	3
Hibernia/ Hüls	Germany	1955	1957	2
Monsanto	USA	1955	1963	8
Mitsui Chemicals Co.	Japan	1955	1958	3
Esso	USA	1955	1960	5
Pechiney (Naphthachimie)	France	1955	1958	3
Houilleres	France	1955	1960	5
DSM	Netherlands	1955	1963	8
Average				5

Source: H. Martin (2002). *Polymere und Patente: Karl Ziegler, das Team, 1953-1998. Zur wirtschaftlichen Verwertung akademischer Forschung.* Weinheim: Wiley-VCH, 151-153.[ii]
Note:
[i] Shell Chemicals UK bought Petrochemicals Ltd. in the mid 1950s. F. McMillan (1979). *The Chain Straighteners. Fruitful Innovation: The Discovery of Linear and Stereoregular Synthetic Polymers.* London: The MacMillan Press, 135. McMillan does not date this takeover more specifically.

[ii] Du Pont (with contract year 1955 and start of royalties in 1966) has been excluded from Martin's list as they had comparable in-house technology and licensed only to get a look at Ziegler's work and avoid patent litigation. (See: D. A. Hounshell & J. K. Smith (1988). *Science and Corporate Strategy: Du Pont R&D, 1902-1980.* Cambridge: Cambridge University Press, 491-497, particularly 493-494). For the average interval this makes little difference.

Process development, product development and research on the catalyst proceeded hand-in-hand. This was one of the defining characteristics of the research on HDPE.

In 1959, the Central Laboratory finished research in the pilot plant. The next year, DSM decided to build a plant with a capacity of 7,000 tons per year. This installation started in 1962 but suffered from several teething problems. The Central Laboratory had to solve these problems and also worked on further improvements. Product development also continued to find new applications and improve product quality for existing applications.

The development of a Ziegler process was one of the main research projects in the second half of the 1950s. Combined with the research on caprolactam and fertilisers, it shows the expansive drive to diversify the company and the crucial role the Central Laboratory played in this. Polyethylene, both LDPE and HDPE, caprolactam and urea were researched in parallel.

The Central Laboratory tracked the option Ziegler provided, and its capabilities were crucial in the establishment of HDPE production. These capabilities included organic chemistry, catalysis and process research. The Central Laboratory provided the absorptive capacity necessary to diversify. DSM built a technology base in plastics that not only overlapped with caprolactam and fertilisers (process research and catalysis), but also included new capabilities (application research and fundamental polymer research). These new capabilities were built for LDPE and HDPE at the same time.

To construct a rough indication of R&D performance, table 3.4 lists all of Ziegler's licensees up to 1955. These licensees were the first wave of companies that picked up Ziegler's work and started to develop a process. Table 3.4 also lists when the licensing contract was awarded and when the first royalties were paid. This gives an indication of the start of research and the start of commercial production, and therefore of the time it took companies to develop a Ziegler process and build an industrial plant. Table 3.4 shows that some licensees were very fast, including Hoechst and Ruhrchemie from Germany, but that others were slower. DSM is in the tail of the group of licensees with companies like Monsanto and Union Carbide. DSM started by investigating the Ziegler process in a fundamental manner and tried to obtain a license first, as well as process know-how from another company. Only in 1956 did the Central Laboratory start process development and it took almost two years before a pilot plant was built. Ruhrchemie, by contrast, quickly ensured access to Ziegler's work. After a decision by the company's managing board in January 1954, the research department started a pilot plant in April of that same year. DSM was a somewhat slower pioneer, picking up the work of Ziegler early but taking a relatively long time to develop an industrial process.[73]

EPDM and Polypropylene

If HDPE in itself was not enough, Ziegler-type catalysts opened a road to other products as well. Ziegler had limited his patent claim to polyethylene but Giulio Natta, and soon others as well, found that Ziegler-type catalysts could be used for the manufacture of polypropylene, another type of plastic, as well as synthetic rubbers. Natta worked for the Milan Polytechnic but had close ties with Montecatini. This Italian company fortified its position with many patents.[74]

In June 1955, the Central Laboratory cautiously started to explore the production of polypropylene and synthetic rubbers with the Ziegler catalyst. The starting point for polypropylene is propylene, a compound available from coke oven gas and from naphtha cracking. The catalyst needs to be selective and order the chain of molecules to a high degree (leading to so-called isotactic polypropylene). The Central Laboratory needed to find such a catalyst, one that did not infringe on the patent position of other companies, in particular Montecatini. Montecatini had claimed patents for polypropylene early, and negotiated a patent pool contract with Ziegler in 1955 that effectively gave the Italian company the right to sell or refuse licenses for polypropylene production. Montecatini set tough terms, but its patents were also challenged by other companies. For both reasons, the Italian firm sold relatively few polypropylene licenses.[75]

In September 1959, the HPDE pilot plant switched from polyethylene to polypropylene. Systematic research stopped in 1960 as it seemed unlikely that the Central Laboratory could build an independent position in the field. DSM tried to obtain a license from the Italian firm but failed. In 1963, the polypropylene plant of the *Rotterdamse Polyolefinen Maatschappij* started production. Royal Dutch/Shell and Montecatini had established this company for the production of polypropylene, and Montecatini had given it an exclusive license. The Central Laboratory investigated polypropylene again in 1962 and 1964, but on a very limited scale and without solving the problem of patents.[76]

The Central Laboratory's work on synthetic rubbers would prove more successful than its work on polypropylene. In 1954, Ziegler and his co-workers experimented with the copolymerisation of ethylene and propylene using his recently developed catalyst. Natta did the same in 1955. They both got a rubber-like product, later called EPM rubber.[77] Many companies picked up these developments and started with experiments. The Central Laboratory included copolymers of ethylene and propylene in its research on the application of Ziegler-type catalysts outside polyethylene in 1955. These products fell under the Ziegler license agreement.[78]

In 1959, laboratory research at the Organic Chemistry department on EPM rubber intensified. Researchers soon found that these products could be manufactured with almost all Ziegler-type catalysts and tried to find an optimal system. In 1960, the HDPE pilot plant switched from polypropylene to ethylene-propylene copolymers. With the product from the pilot plant, Plastics Technology started application research in the same year. They worked together with the TNO Rubber Institute because the Plastics Technology department did not yet have the necessary equipment.[79]

The market for synthetic rubbers generally grew after the Second World War. In the Netherlands, 1965 was the first year in which synthetic rubber usage exceeded natural rubber usage. The rubber market consisted of two major segments. On the one hand, so-called general-purpose rubbers had a large volume, but car tyres were the dominant application. Both natural and synthetic rubber were used. The second market segment consisted of special-purpose rubbers. Market volume was smaller than in general-purpose rubbers but prices were typically higher. Products in this segment included technical goods like cable insulation and all sorts of rubber products used in cars. Special-purpose rubbers have one or more defining characteristics that give them an advantage over general-purpose rubbers.[80]

In 1960, DSM's production staff tried to chart a course for synthetic rubbers. They aimed for the general-purpose market because of its volume. Early results of application research on EPM in car tyres showed promising results. However, major rubber companies like Dunlop and B.F. Goodrich produced both synthetic rubber and car tyres, and such close connections made the general-purpose market hard to enter. [81]

In 1961, Enjay Chemical (Standard Oil of New Jersey, now Exxon Chemical) started the first commercial plant for EPM rubbers.[82] That year the Central Laboratory found, as other companies also had found, that EPM rubber could not be vulcanised with sulphur. This was a problem, particularly in the general-purpose market. Rubber processors added a range of chemicals to both synthetic and natural rubber to improve or steer the properties of products, a procedure called compounding. They also added sulphur and heated the product to improve its mechanical properties, a procedure called vulcanisation. EPM rubber required the use of a peroxide, but that increased costs, caused a bad smell during vulcanisation and made it impossible to use other common additives. Addition of a third monomer alongside ethylene and propylene, leading to products called EPDM rubber, could circumvent these problems. However, the patents of other companies seemed to be major obstacles. DSM could acquire a license for the use of dicyclopentadiene (DCPD) from the British company Dunlop in 1962. The Polymers Development department found a variant of this compound, but nevertheless chose DCPD as it was clear who had patented this compound. Dunlop's patent, moreover, covered a wide range of compounds that could be used alongside ethylene and propylene.[83]

In October 1962, the pilot plant made the first EPDM rubbers. In the following year, research focused completely on these products. Application research showed that EPDM was comparable to general-purpose rubbers but had a better weather and ozone resistance. Rubber ages (cracks and loses its colour) through the impact of the weather and ozone in particular. EPDM ages much less quickly than other rubbers. Application research still targeted car tyres, but also belts and cable insulation, for instance. The Plastics Technology department cooperated with the major Dutch car tyre manufacturer Vredestein to develop EPDM compounding for use in car tyres and test these tyres in practice. Several types of rubbers, metal cords and fibres were used in car tyre manufacture. EPDM did not adhere very well to other types of rubber and other materials; its so-called 'tack' was insufficient for car tyre production. Plastics Technology worked for several years to reach a satisfactory solution to this problem.[84]

Alongside application research, the Central Laboratory also advanced with process development. This research moved from the Organic Chemistry department to Polymer Development in 1961. The catalyst system had to be optimised and a special reactor had to be developed. EPDM, and also EPM, manufacture led to thick and sticky solutions which complicated reactor design. Researchers tried reactors from Crawford & Russell, an American engineering contractor with much experience in polymers, but rejected them and worked out a new design. Extensive pilot plant and semi-technical research proved necessary.[85]

EPDM with DCPD had a relatively long vulcanisation time. This would reduce the production capacity of rubber processors as products would remain longer in the vulcanisation machines. Increased vulcanisation time, in turn, led to the problem of 'marching modulus': the stiffness of products did not reach an end point, but kept increasing with vulcanisation time, reducing the elasticity of the product. To circumvent these problems, Plastics Technology started working on EPDM with ethylidene norbornene (ENB) as the third monomer. Union Carbide had developed a route to ENB and the Polymer Development department tried to find a different route.[86]

Du Pont and Montecatini started EPDM production in 1963.[87] Two years later, DSM decided to build an EPDM plant with a capacity of 12,000 tons per year. The plant was started up in 1967. It had some teething problems, but capacity soon ran at 15,000 tons. In 1968, DSM decided to build a second plant with the same capacity as the first. This plant went into operation in 1970. These plants initially used DCPD, instead of ENB, as the third monomer because DCPD had advantages from a process technology point of view.[88]

As in the case of polypropylene, Montecatini arranged a patent pool agreement with Ziegler for EPM, EPDM and other synthetic rubbers in 1958. Six years later, this agreement was replaced with a second one that also included Dunlop technology. Montecatini had bought the patents of the British firm to strengthen its position further. Neither Ziegler nor Montecatini directly informed DSM, but the company got wind of these developments anyway. Montecatini offered DSM a license to start manufacture of EPDM in 1965, but tried to exclude DSM from markets other than the Benelux. DSM refused. According to the patent department, the company did not need a license from Montecatini at all. They argued that Ziegler's original patent, for which DSM had a license, also included ethylene-propylene copolymers. In the second place, DSM used DCPD and had obtained a license from Dunlop before Montecatini bought the patents of the British firm. Montecatini threatened, however, to file suit against DSM in all countries where it sold its rubber. Even if the Italian firm lost, it still would hinder DSM severely. DSM and Montecatini reached a compromise in 1968. DSM got an exclusive production license for the Benelux and remained free to export (with only a few exceptions).[89]

The fights over patents and licenses shows the importance the chemical industry attached to these products. In EPDM, a tough line from the patent department helped secure a favourable license from Montecatini. DSM's position, with its Ziegler and Dunlop licenses, was stronger than in polypropylene, where the independence of the Central Laboratory's work from Montecatini patents remained doubtful. The EPDM and polypropylene projects, however, built on the same technology base: the capabilities that had been developed for HDPE. Application research was also vital. These capabilities were not exclusively related to polyethylene but quickly branched out into related fields.

Melamine
In its drive for expansion and diversification, DSM had entered plastics and synthetic fibre intermediates. Resins were to develop into the third leg of the company's second transformation.[90] In this field, around 1950 the Central Laboratory was working on phenol, formaldehyde and urea. However, DSM switched its urea activities to the fertiliser market in 1953 and the phenol plant had to be shut down in 1955. Phenol, moreover, became a feedstock for caprolactam. DSM and the Central Laboratory remained interested in resins. Van Krevelen had heard of a patent claiming a process for the manufacture of melamine from urea. Melamine in turn could be reacted with formaldehyde and urea to manufacture resins. A feedstock drive thus led from urea to melamine, like coke oven gas had led to ammonia and fertilisers in the late 1920s. The Inorganic Chemistry department started research on melamine in 1956.[91]

Thermoset resins were an established field by the time the Central Laboratory started research on melamine. Bakelite, manufactured from phenol and formaldehyde, was the first product in the field, followed by urea-formaldehyde resins in the 1920s. Urea, at that time, was produced from calcium cyanamide. Urea-formaldehyde resins had the advantage that end products could be manufactured in many colours instead of just black or brown as was the case with Bakelite. Around 1935, the Swiss company *Gesellschaft für Chemische Industrie Basel* (CIBA), American Cyanamid and other companies found that melamine could be used for the manufacture of resins. These products were first used for the manufacture of unbreakable tableware, and in 1938 Formica started using melamine formaldehyde resins for the top two layers of their laminates for table and counter tops. The field of application later expanded to include the manufacture of plywood and chipboard as well as certain types of paints, for instance.[92]

In 1936, CIBA started producing melamine, soon followed by American Cyanamid and others. In 1949, *Süddeutsche Kalkstickstoff-Werke AG* (SKW) started a melamine plant and this German company developed into a major producer in Europe. SKW, like CIBA and American Cyanamid, used a batch process that started from calcium cyanamide, at that time a common nitrogen fertiliser, and proceeded via dicyandiamide to melamine. American Cyanamid produced large amounts of calcium cyanamide for fertiliser purposes. In 1943, the company also patented a pro—cess for the production of melamine that started from urea. Research continued, and ten years later a patent on a silica gel catalyst for this process followed. American Cyanamid did not develop this process to industrial scale. Urea-based melamine production led to ammonia and carbon dioxide off-gases that had to be recycled to urea production in order for melamine production to be economical. In the 1940s, however, urea synthesis from ammonia and carbon dioxide was still in its infancy.[93]

At the Central Laboratory, Jan Steggerda at the Inorganic Chemistry department started melamine research on the basis of the patents of American Cyanamid. He established that the process could work, and also found that it could work at, or near, atmospheric pressure instead of the 300 to 400 atmospheres mentioned in the patents of American Cyanamid. This company had also claimed the use of silica gel catalysts, but Steggerda soon found that other materials could be effective as well.[94]

In 1959, Steggerda established a two-step process. First, urea was sprayed into a fluid bed reactor. In this type of reactor, solids can behave as if they are liquids. In this case, ammonia fluidised the catalyst. In a second, fixed bed reactor, the reaction product of the first step was further converted into melamine, again in the presence of the catalyst. Using two reactors was necessary to reach a satisfactory yield. Finally, melamine, which was in the gas phase, had to be separated and converted into a solid product for further use in resin fabrication. This process departed from American Cyanamid's work on several points, and DSM applied for a patent in 1959, which was awarded six years later.[95]

Figure 3.12. DSM's melamine process.

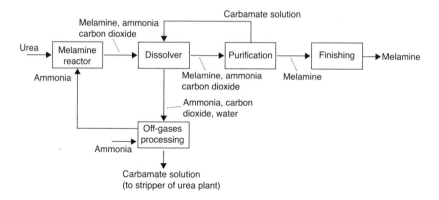

Source: P. Ellwood (1968). Melamine Process Uses Low-Pressure Reactor to Achieve Low Costs. *Chemical Engineering* (20 May 1968), 124-126.

In 1959, work on equipment for the two-step process started and a year later the Semi-Technical department built a small-scale installation. Fluidised beds are hard to study on laboratory scale. The main problems related to the handling of urea and melamine, which, together with the temperature regulation of the catalyst, also necessitated research on a larger scale than was possible at the laboratory bench. In March 1961, a pilot plant with a capacity of 100 kg of melamine per day was started up.[96]

In 1962, work on a semi-technical scale revealed that increasing the operating pressure had a positive effect on the yield of the process. Researchers at the Semi-Technical department also experimented with process configurations and tried one fluid bed reactor, and two of these reactors in series. This department built a small installation for these experiments in 1963 and quickly found that using one fluid bed reactor and a pressure of 7 atmospheres increased yield substantially over the two-step process. The outline of the process was now established (see figure 3.12) but research continued on the design of the equipment, particularly the fluid bed reactors, and also on methods to extract melamine from the reaction product.[97]

The Central Laboratory started from American Cyanamid's patents, but found different catalysts and developed a process that worked at lower pressures than the American process. The claims Cyanamid laid down in its patents varied per country. Cyanamid's process worked at high pressure, but its Dutch basic patent claimed low pressure as well. Its catalyst patent in the Netherlands was limited to silica gel but broader in other countries.[98]

At the end of 1958, DSM contacted American Cyanamid. The company said it had nothing to license; its R&D had failed. The company also did not want to license its patents only. A year later, DSM found to its surprise that American Cyanamid had granted a license to CIBA. Berkhoff and Van Waes, assisted by the head of the patent department, opened negotiations with the Swiss firm. CIBA was the largest processor of melamine in Europe and its main concern was to buy melamine cheaply, well below prevailing market prices. CIBA also wanted to keep DSM out of resin production.[99]

Cyanamid's patent on the urea-based melamine process would expire in 1966; the patent on the silica gel catalyst in 1975. DSM could wait or use a different catalyst. The Central Laboratory had other catalysts available, but these proved to be less attractive than silica gel. Moreover, DSM wanted CIBA as a customer. Production in the United States also counted as a serious option as DSM's process did not infringe on American Cyanamid's patents in that country. Together with Spencer Chemical, DSM investigated joint production of urea, melamine and formaldehyde.[100] Spencer retreated in 1962, however, because they no longer expected a profitable business.

After further negotiations, CIBA and DSM signed an agreement in 1963. CIBA granted a license on American Cyanamid's patents to DSM and would buy at least 80% of the melamine it needed from DSM. In return, DSM promised not to start manufacture of resins. CIBA could retreat from the sales agreement, and did so because it did not want to become dependent on one external supplier. As stipulated in the contract, DSM would now have to pay a royalty only and was free to enter resins if it wanted to.[101]

In 1963, with the licensing negotiations and research entering a final phase, top management decided to build a melamine plant with a capacity of 10,000 tons per year. Cost price calculations showed that melamine produced with the process developed by Central Laboratory would be at least 17% cheaper than melamine from calcium cyanamide. In 1964, Chemiebouw started with the engineering, assisted by the Central Laboratory. Additional research proved necessary to improve melamine extraction and purification, but in 1967 the plant went on stream. The off-gases, consisting of carbon dioxide and ammonia, were recycled to the urea stripping plant in the form of ammonium carbamate.

In the case of melamine, the main challenge for the Central Laboratory was to develop an industrial scale process, which entailed process research at laboratory, semi-technical and pilot plant scales. Where American Cyanamid had failed, the Central Laboratory succeeded. DSM's plant was one of the first plants in the world to produce melamine from urea on an industrial scale. Allied Chemical brought a urea-based melamine plant on stream in 1962. The *Österreichische Stickstoffwerke* (OSW, later Chemie

Linz) followed two years later, but with a small plant. BASF and Monte-catini followed in the late 1960s, at about the same time as DSM.[102]

Alongside process development, the Central Laboratory also conducted some application research. In 1958, the Inorganic Chemistry department initiated tests of melamine as a fertiliser because the product contained a high percentage of nitrogen. These tests showed that melamine poisoned plants. In 1961, the same department started to explore the reaction of melamine and formaldehyde, the crucial reaction for the production of resins, and investigated whether DSM could start manufacture of so-called pre-condensates, an intermediate product that would be sold directly to end product manufacturers. The market for these products proved to be small, however.[103]

In 1965, the Central Laboratory established a new department for application research on melamine-based resins. This department, called Thermosetting Resins, aimed to stimulate sales of melamine by investigating applications such as laminates and paints. In the late 1960s, the Thermosetting Resins department also worked on glues for the manufacture

Figure 3.13 Projects developed by DSM, 1950-1975.

Project developed by DSM

Commercialized projects		costs R & D (million guilders)	Non-commercialized projects	costs R & D (million guilders)
1950-'60	Slagging generator	1.8	Calcium carbide	5.0
	Nitrophosphate	3.0	Ferrosilicium	0.5
	Nitric acid Urea-1	0.8	Nylon salt 6,6	14.1
	Cyclohexane oxidation	2.6	Phenol (Tyrer)	0.5
	Hydranon	0.2	Synthracite 1	2.6
	Synthracite 2	6.5		
1960-'70	NPK-fertilizers	2.5	Acetic acid	1.7
	Dow-phenol 1	2.0	Lysine 1	18.8
	Benzene hydrogenation	0.1	Methionine	10.7
	Urea-2	5.6	Polybutadiene	2.1
	HDPE-1	14.0	Nylon 12	1.7
	EPDM	20.3	Single Cell Protein	1.5
	Melamine 1	7.1	Polypropylene 1	7.3
			Hydrocracking process	3.7
1970-'75	Dow phenol	2.3	Acetone	8.2
	HDPE-2 (compact process)	14.2	Lysine-2	6.6
	Hyam (HPO)	11.3	Urea-3	2.5
	Waste water treatment	5.3	Polypropylene 2	8.5
	Melamine-2	6.5	HDPE-2 (USP)	11.0
	Korlin (expanded gravel)	0.5		
	Special products	4.0		
	Total	112	Total	117

profit of Stamcarbon 1950-1974   fl 166 million
Sales of DSM based on own processes in 1974   fl 1300 million (= 25 % of total sales of DSM group, not including sales of natural gas)

Source: Personal papers Dr L.J. Revallier: Projects developed by DSM. Undated, but from approximately 1975. Note: adding the numbers mentioned in the table leads to total expenditure for commercialised projects of NLG 110.6 million and for non-commercialised projects of NLG 107.0 million.

of chipboard. This department developed recipes for specific applications in close contact with customers. Analytical work was also conducted to investigate the characteristics of melamine-based resins and to investigate how these characteristics influenced the processing of these products.[104]

By 1967, DSM had built a melamine plant and established another chemical business, alongside fertilisers, caprolactam, polyethylene and EPDM. With the latter three products, melamine represents DSM's second transformation from a fertiliser producer to a diversified chemical company. The establishment of melamine production shows some typical characteristics of this transformation. Feedstock links led the Central Laboratory to initiate research on melamine. Its work was the key to the development of an industrial scale process. Process research and development in particular were important. Application research played a less prominent role than in the case of polyethylene but was nevertheless important to find and maintain a market.

Towards a Diversified Chemical Business
The 1950s and '60s were a busy period for the Central Laboratory as it worked on several large projects more or less in parallel. It was also a productive period. In urea, caprolactam, HPDE, EPDM and melamine, DSM built on R&D and gradually broadened the base of its chemical business.

Not all research projects succeeded, however. The caprolactone project failed, for instance, as did the polypropylene project. In 1975, Revallier compared the costs of commercialised projects and projects that had not been commercialised. He only included projects that had reached the development stage and therefore counted the costs incurred during semi-technical and pilot plant research. (Figure 3.13.) The costs of commercialised and failed projects were almost even: a success rate of 50% in other words![105] Moreover, failures did not shake management's faith in research: R&D results were unpredictable and failures were inevitable. One failure was to prove a traumatic experience, however: the failure of the lysine project.

A Failed Diversification: Lysine

In 1961, Berkhoff and Hans Ottenheym, a researcher from the Central Laboratory, told their audience at a symposium on the application of amino acids in food that 'all foodstuffs can be improved'.[106] They particularly thought that foodstuffs could be improved by adding amino acids, the building blocks of proteins, necessary for growth and health in humans and animals. Most amino acids can be synthesised by the body but some, the essential amino acids, have to be provided through the diet. Lysine is one of these essential amino acids, supplied to humans and animals mostly by animal protein because vegetables, with the exception of soy and beans, contain little lysine. In the late 1950s, the Central Laboratory took the initiative to start working on the synthesis of lysine.[107]

Developing a Process

Lysine was a known compound and, like other amino acids, could be manufactured in various ways. Merck and some other companies extracted lysine from hydrolysed soybeans, fishmeal or other materials. In Japan, Kyowa Fermentation Industries developed a method to make lysine by fermentation in 1958. Merck licensed this process in 1959. Other companies, for instance Ajinomoto in Japan and Pfizer in the United States, developed fermentation processes as well and used them to manufacture lysine. In the 1950s, Du Pont in the United States and Degussa in Germany, among others, worked on lysine synthesis processes. Du Pont manufactured lysine on a small scale, but Degussa abandoned its effort before production could start because it considered prices too low. Synthesis processes were developed for other amino acids as well. For methionine, another amino acid, *Alimentation Équilibrée* (a French company which was later renamed *AEC Société Chimique Organique et Biologique* and in 1971 was bought by the French chemical conglomerate *Rhône-Poulenc*) developed a synthesis process in 1947. The company later also started making lysine in a fermentation process. Degussa also succeeded in developing a methionine synthesis process and built a plant.[108]

In the 1950s, lysine found use mainly in pharmaceuticals, but Merck also marketed lysine for application in high-protein bread and cereals while Kyowa introduced lysine as an addition to animal feeds in 1965. AEC and Degussa dominated the methionine market. Methionine was used mainly in poultry feeds and some amounts were also added to pig feeds. Production was small scale but rising, with AEC producing 80 tons in 1955 but as much as 13,000 tons in 1960.[109]

In 1957, the Central Laboratory started working on a synthesis process for lysine, a project pulled by Ottenheym. The starting point for the process was caprolactam, a route that had been explored before by researchers from outside DSM. Caprolactam was a natural starting point as the company produced this compound industrially. Similarities between caprolactam and lysine molecules also prompted research on lysine. The project, in other words, was feedstock driven and technology push. Ottenheym at first worked under the umbrella of caprolactam research at the Organic Chemistry department of the Central Laboratory. This department split in two in 1960 with Ottenheym becoming the leader of the group focusing on lysine.[110]

Ottenheym and his group started by mapping possible routes to lysine from caprolactam. In 1958, the most promising option, a multi-step process, was patented and development work started. This work rested crucially on the organic chemistry capabilities of the Central Laboratory, built through research on caprolactam. The Inorganic Chemistry department and the Catalysis department also did some research on part of the lysine process. At the end of 1958, the Organic Pilot Plants department started working on a design for a lysine pilot plant, in cooperation with Chemiebouw. The pilot plant was intended to develop the process further and to determine what the production costs would be, while the output would be used for market development work. In 1959, designs were made for a pilot plant with a capacity of 200 to 300 kg of lysine per day. The Semi-Technical department investigated possible equipment.[111]

The pilot plant started in 1960. The Semi Technical and Organic Pilot Plants departments coordinated the necessary troubleshooting. The Corrosion department advised on some unexpected problems, while the Organic Analysis group started to develop specific analytical procedures for the lysine project. Research by Ottenheym's group also continued, which means that the full spectrum of the Central Laboratory's capabilities were engaged in the lysine project.[112]

In the pilot plant many problems were confronted, but initial problems concerning corrosion, contamination and low efficiency could be overcome. However, low efficiency remained a problem in the process step where D- and L-lysine were separated from each other. All amino acids occur in two forms, a natural L-configuration and the D-configuration that is a molecular mirror image of the L-configuration. The DSM process led to D,L-lysine while only L-lysine was desired. Initially there were also concerns about the safety of D-lysine. It had to be separated and recycled, a persistent problem that was investigated on laboratory, semi-technical and pilot plant scale. After the pilot plant had started, it was soon clear that the separation of D-lysine and its recycling was the most expensive step in the process, in terms of both production costs and investments.[113]

Market Development in the Late 1950s
When the decision was taken in 1959 to build a pilot plant, it was expected that production costs would be low, regardless of the costs incurred in the separation and recycling steps, and that with low costs, a market could be found. One of the first ideas that emerged was to add lysine to bread and so improve the nutritional value of this common food in the Netherlands. Ottenheym and Berkhoff used the contacts of the Agricultural Research Bureau of the CSV (*Landbouwkundig Bureau CSV*) to probe the feasibility of this idea. In 1958, TNO started investigating the possibilities of lysine addition to bread. TNO consisted of several institutes, and for lysine the CIVO (*Centraal Instituut voor Voedingsonderzoek*, central institute for dietary research) was of particular importance; this institute investigated the

THE COMPANY THAT CHANGED ITSELF

nutritional value of lysine-enriched bread. Berkhoff and Van Waes, head of DSM's chemical sector, signed the order for conducting these tests. The Dutch government had to approve the marketing of lysine-enriched bread, a decision that the responsible minister delegated to an advisory body of civil servants and scientific experts. The type of research DSM ordered from TNO had to convince these experts.[114]

The preliminary results of the research on lysine-enriched bread seemed promising. Nutritional value increased and lysine could be added to bread without necessitating modifications to the procedures of baking. In 1959, Berkhoff tried to establish contact with Matthieu Dols, who, as a part-time professor, employee of the Ministry of Agriculture, member of the advisory body and member of the FAO and WHO, was a crucial figure in the Dutch agricultural and food sectors with many international contacts. The Agricultural Research Bureau of the CSV again facilitated the establishment of this contact. Dols showed interest in the lysine project, but believed that addition to food for humans in the Netherlands did not have priority. Other experts of the advisory body were even more sceptical, fearing a price increase in bread at a time when the government was prioritising stable prices and wages. DSM's attempts to get lysine accepted as an addition to bread thus failed.[115]

In 1957, when research on lysine started, Ottenheym had the idea that lysine could be used to increase the nutritional value of feed for pigs and chickens. These were the largest feed markets in the Netherlands in the 1950s, with production in 1960 at a level of about 1.8 million tons each. The Dutch feed industry consisted of several large cooperative manufacturers, some large and fairly large private companies, and numerous small local mixers. Feed companies used bulk components like cereals, peas, and fishmeal for instance, but also added other compounds such as vitamins, antibiotics, and amino acids. Specialised companies manufactured and packaged these additional compounds in so-called pre-mixes that feed companies added to their products. Ottenheym thought that lysine could substitute animal protein sources like bonemeal and fishmeal, which he considered to be too expensive.[116]

In 1958, the CIVO conducted some preliminary tests on lysine-enriched feed that showed promising results. On the basis of these results, Dols also concluded that lysine-enriched feeds might offer a good market for DSM. Through fertiliser production, DSM had contacts with the co-operatives, and the Agricultural Research Bureau opened doors for the Central Laboratory to probe the possibilities of lysine in feeds. *Handel-maatschappij Trouw*, a company that manufactured pre-mixes, also sought contact with DSM. Both companies agreed on a division of labour, with DSM targeting a number of large feed companies, including the cooperatives, and Trouw targeting its own customers.[117]

DSM also built a network of relationships with companies abroad. In 1961, contact was established with the British branch of Unilever that commanded a large share of the feed market in the United Kingdom. Unilever showed considerable interest in using lysine in its products and in cooperating with DSM. DSM considered Unilever an attractive partner.[118]

As in the case of bread, the effectiveness of addition of lysine to feeds had to be demonstrated. In 1960, DSM took the initiative to establish a study committee with people from universities and agricultural research stations, and chaired by Dols, in order to coordinate several tests on the effects of lysine addition to feed for pigs. In 1962, Sixma, spurred by Dols, proposed conducting internal application research, hiring researchers and an advisor, and building the necessary facilities. Alfred van Loen joined DSM. Willem Hirschfeld, director of the Zootechnical Institute of Utrecht University, was engaged as an advisor, as was Dols in 1967, after his retirement. Van Loen worked on a proposal to build a Biological Experimental Station, but research at other institutes continued as well. In 1963, *Landbouwbelang*, one of the large cooperatives, conducted a test with lysine-enriched feed for pigs. In May of that year, *Koninklijke Nederlandse Gist- & Spiritusfabriek* (NGSF, later Gist-brocades, which in 1998 was taken over by DSM), offered DSM the facilities of their research unit ILOB at Wageningen in the Netherlands (*Instituut voor Landbouwkundig Onderzoek van Biochemische Producten*, institute for agricultural research of biochemical products). Research at the CIVO also continued.[119]

Alongside bread and feed, the Central Laboratory probed other possible markets for lysine as well. In 1958, contact was established with the Dutch food company Nutricia to investigate the possibilities to add lysine to baby food. These possibilities were limited, but Nutricia saw an opportunity for lysine-enriched food in developing countries. Nutricia received a sample that it tested in the hospital of one of its advisors but concluded, for reasons it did mention in its correspondence with DSM, that the possibilities of using lysine were slim.[120]

In 1960, Revallier and Ottenheym visited Pfizer in the United States. Pfizer had much experience with fermentation processes, for instance for the production of citric acid and penicillin, and also manufactured lysine with a fermentation process for use in pharmaceuticals. DSM's process interested Pfizer, and the American company seemed to be willing to come to some sort of cooperation with DSM. Alongside Unilever, DSM considered Pfizer the best possible partner, opening the door to the pharmaceutical market.[121]

Around 1960, DSM's efforts to build a network of contacts with potentially interesting partners, customers, government agencies and research institutes had resulted in several ideas for possible markets. Lysine addition to bread had failed, but feed and pharmaceuticals promised to be attractive

The lysine plant in May 1968, just before it was completed and started up. Lysine was a major and prestigious research project but failed. Its technological spin-offs, however, laid the foundation for DSM's fine chemical business in the 1970s.

markets. The (potential) size of these markets was unclear, and clear ideas for products were also lacking. The work on feed concentrated on pigs, but that focus had never been debated. DSM's network provided the company with numerous ideas for products but not with the tools to select the most promising ones. Besides the examples mentioned above, CIVO for instance came up with the ideas of adding lysine to the sweet potato that formed the main part of the diet in New Guinea, at that time still a Dutch colony; adding lysine to 'school milk', milk handed out to schoolchildren in the Netherlands at low prices to further their growth and health; and using lysine in the improvement of pig meat, all in 1959. Two years later, Unilever thought that lysine-enriched peanut butter could be interesting and again tried to put lysine addition to bread on the agenda.[122]

Building a Plant

Although unfocused and spread out over many segments, market development together with work in the pilot plant gave the lysine project momentum. In 1961, Berkhoff and Ottenheym again visited Pfizer in the United States after attending a congress in Washington, and this trip convinced Berkhoff that a market could be opened for a plant with a capacity of 10 tons per day. He also thought that lysine presented a springboard to other activities in the broad field of food and feed chemicals. Methionine and sorbic acid, a preservative, had been topics for research since 1959, for instance.[123]

Others in the company shared Berkhoff's optimism. In 1963, Sixma, Berkhoff's successor, and Jan van Steenis, head of the Commercial Affairs department, made a proposal to top management to build a commercial lysine plant with a capacity of 3,000 tons per year. It was a joint proposal, showing that lysine was not only a research project but was broadly supported in the company. Sixma and Van Steenis were optimistic and convinced that DSM could compete with other synthetic lysine processes. How DSM's position measured up to fermentation processes was unclear, however. Early in 1963, NGSF, which rented out its stables in Wageningen to DSM and a company with much experience in fermentation, made a cost-price calculation on the basis of patents for Japanese processes that were considered state-of-the-art. NGSF concluded that the Japanese processes led to a higher cost price than DSM's synthesis process, but the reliability of these calculations was unclear.[124]

In their proposal, Sixma and Van Steenis seized the only market that was in reach: animal feeds. Pharmaceuticals could not absorb a capacity of 3,000 tons per year, while Sixma and Van Steenis considered the addition of lysine to food for humans in developing countries an option only for the long term. They wrote to top management that lysine in feed could replace expensive animal protein such as fishmeal and bonemeal. To introduce lysine to the feed industry, application research and service research, the latter after market introduction, was necessary. Sixma and Van Steenis proposed internalising this research and establishing a Biological Experimental Station under the umbrella of the Central Laboratory. Van Loen argued that the facilities of institutes such as the ILOB were not perfectly suited to lysine research, that such institutes often had other priorities, and that it was difficult to follow and control the experiments. Commercial Affairs thought that the Biological Experimental Station was necessary to break the 'conservatism' it saw ruling the feed industry. In the fertiliser sector, supporting sales by scientific research was a well-established and very successful practice. Experimental farms and agricultural research were used to show how farmers could profit from using fertilisers.[125]

Top management agreed with the proposal of Sixma and Van Steenis to build a lysine plant and a Biological Experimental Station. In their letter to the Minister of Economic Affairs, who had to approve investments because DSM was still fully state-owned at that time, top management emphasised that lysine production built on caprolactam, that the process had been developed in-house, and that large scale and low costs would open a market. Lysine, in other words, was a typical DSM project, technology push and feedstock driven, but DSM also tried to build on its existing competence to enter a new market.

In 1964, a start was made on the engineering of the lysine plant. In November of the same year, the pilot plant closed and DSM bought the lysine it needed for market development from Kyowa and other companies. Research work continued though, and in 1965 the process was modified on several points, including the separation method. In June of 1965 it became clear that more money was needed to build the plant than initially foreseen. There were also major delays during construction. In November 1968, the lysine plant came on stream, but there were many mechanical problems and the plant operated at a low overall efficiency.[126]

Market Development in the 1960s

The Biological Experimental Station became operational as an organisational unit in 1963. Facilities were soon built at the Central Laboratory to conduct experiments with small animals and the first in-house experiment with pigs started in September 1963. Van Loen also drew up a plan to conduct tests with pigs, chickens and poultry, calves, and rats, in new accommodations that would cover in total more than two hectares of land. He argued that research should be conducted under circumstances prevailing in practice as far as possible to demonstrate the usefulness of lysine-enriched feeds. Commercial Affairs organised tests at potential buyers with the same goal in mind, and as a consequence the ambitions of the Biological Experimental Station were scaled down in 1966 to understanding the addition of lysine under experimental conditions. The cooperation between the Central Laboratory and Commercial Affairs was close, so close that Van Loen transferred to Commercial Affairs in September 1965. He became part of the specialised lysine group that was established there around that time.[127]

DSM continued investigating the possibilities of enriching animal feeds with lysine, but to reinforce its commercial position Commercial Affairs proposed acquiring a premix company in 1967. This only resulted in a cooperation with one feed manufacturer, and in expected sales of only 45 tons.[128] DSM's contacts with Unilever also failed to take concrete shape.

DSM continued talking to other companies as well to find possible outlets for lysine, and to gather information on the size of the potential market. A wide range of possible products was discussed. In 1965, Revallier and a researcher from the Central Laboratory visited the British company

Protein Co. and heard representatives of that company talk about a future in which food would be supplied by industry through well-balanced packages of nutrients. They suggested that DSM produce proteins from grass and add lysine to those proteins. Expectations about the potential market for lysine also varied widely. For instance, in 1966, Standard Oil of Ohio (Sohio) seized upon a recent development of corn with two times the usual amount of lysine to argue that there would be no market for lysine at all. A year later, Allied Chemical told Revallier that it expected a market volume of 1.5 million tons in ten years' time. Both these American companies were working on lysine processes as well. Sohio started from acrylonitrile, an intermediate for acrylic fibres for which Sohio had developed a process.[129]

DSM also tried to gain a better understanding of Japanese amino acid production. Commercial Affairs attempted to gather information through the Dutch embassy in Japan and talked directly to Ajinomoto and Kyowa in 1965 and 1967, respectively. Commercial Affairs wanted a stable market, but Kyowa could not be interested in making deals. Ajinomoto, too, had little interest in DSM's lysine process.[130]

The human food market also came into the picture again. Nutricia had already pointed to the underdeveloped countries of the world as a possible market for lysine, but in 1963 Sixma and Van Steenis had branded this an option for the long term. In September of that year, however, Van Loen and a representative of Commercial Affairs visited Rome to talk to representatives of the FAO and the United Nations World Food Program Division, an organisation focused on animal feeds. It became clear that these organisations were altogether sceptical of the addition of amino acids to food and feed, and that they concluded from research that methionine addition to the human diet was more important than lysine addition. The developing countries remained a target for DSM, however, with Van Loen giving a lecture for the Dutch agricultural attachés in 1964, for instance. In a paper from 1966, he clarified the line of reasoning. Van Loen argued that the malnutrition problem in the world was due to a shortage of protein. Essential proteins could only be supplied by meat, but the growth of meat production would never be able to keep up with the growth of the world's population. According to Van Loen, substitution of animal protein by vegetable proteins with lysine was inevitable.[131]

In 1967, consultations with Theo Bot, the Dutch minister responsible for foreign aid, led to the establishment of a committee of civil servants from several departments and representatives from DSM that was to draw up plans for research in developing countries. Talks were also held with other Dutch companies interested in improving foods for developing countries and with the *Productschap Zuivel*, an organisation of the dairy industry that considered enriching milk powder with lysine interesting.[132]

In the mean time, the date of the commissioning of the lysine plant drew nearer. In 1967, researchers of the Biological Experimental Station evaluated the results of the experiments with lysine addition to pig feed. They concluded that soy and fishmeal could replace animal protein in pig feeds at lower costs than lysine: addition of lysine was an 'illusion', as it was put in the 1967 annual report of the Central Laboratory.[133] Experiments with the addition of lysine to feeds for other animals also failed to yield clear-cut results. Feeds with lysine were as good as feeds with animal protein or with soy or fishmeal. An evaluation of the whole lysine project in 1967, moreover, showed that production costs would be higher than initially expected while the revenues turned out to be lower. Finding an entry in the animal feed market would be difficult. It became clear that feed companies used protein norms that did not make it attractive to add lysine. Mixing-in of soy was enough, and this was far cheaper than using lysine. Prices of fishmeal and other animal products rose, and they lost part of the market, but soy was used as a replacement, not synthetic lysine.

With regard to the potential market in the developing countries, much depended on the willingness of the Dutch government to stimulate sales of lysine through aid programmes. Developing countries themselves lacked the funds or were unwilling to commit them. At the end of 1968, however, it became clear that the Dutch government would not commit itself to lysine, and around the same time it also became clear that international organisations such as the FAO did not support lysine either. Like the animal feed market, the market for human food in developing countries was out of reach.[134]

DSM had built a plant that had many teething problems and that produced a product for which there was no market. Large losses seemed inevitable and in 1969, after six months of production, the plant closed.

The work on other food and feed additives also failed to produce concrete results. Researchers considered sorbic acid an attractive preservative because it was non-toxic, but soon doubted if there would be a market for it and stopped research in 1963. In the same year, semi-technical work on methionine started. A synthesis process starting from acrolein had been worked out on laboratory scale. A so-called mini plant was built in 1964, at a scale in between semi-technical work and a full pilot plant, with the expectation that an expensive pilot plant would not have to be built. Chemiebouw got involved at this stage, and in 1966 started working on a first design for an industrial plant with a capacity in the range of 3,000 to 6,000 tons per year, comparable to the lysine plant.[135]

Application research on methionine started in 1962 but on a small scale. In 1967, DSM entered into a contract with the Japanese company Mitsui, a manufacturer of methionine, which enabled DSM to sell methionine from Mitsui in a number of countries. By that year, the Central Laboratory had started research on the separation of D- and L-methionine, overlapping with research on the separation of D- and L-lysine. It was expected that L-methionine might be more valuable than D,L-methionine, although both AEC and Degussa were marketing D,L-methionine. In 1968, an evaluation of the project showed that investment costs had risen to the extent that a methionine plant could only be viable at a capacity of 6,000 tons per year, and not less, because cost prices would then become too high. At two-thirds of world methionine use in 1965, that capacity would make DSM one of the largest methionine producers in the world, but market development work cast doubt on the probability that such an amount could be sold. Profitability seemed doubtful at best. In 1968, Revallier and Van Steenis proposed that research be scaled down, but after the failure of the lysine project, the methionine project stopped altogether.[136]

All Foodstuffs Can Be Improved? The Failure of the Lysine Project

The closure of the lysine plant was a traumatic experience: a big, prestigious and expensive project had failed. Up to 1965, almost 26 million guilders had been spent on research, contrasting with almost 7 million for the melamine project and 14.5 million for the EPDM synthetic rubber project. Between 1948 and 1955, roughly the period in which production had been established, almost 2.6 million guilders had been spent on caprolactam research (including the work on phenol). In the case of urea, DSM spent 7.2 million guilders on pilot plant work and semi-technical research between 1950 and 1970, the period covering the tail of the development of the once-through process and the development of recycle processes and the stripping process.[137] The lysine plant, built opposite the Central Laboratory's main building, became a highly visible reminder of a failed project.

Lysine was a new technology for DSM. Capabilities built in organic chemistry through caprolactam were crucial for the Central Laboratory's research in amino acids. However, the separation of D- from L-lysine and its recycling remained a bottleneck in the process. The Central Laboratory and Commercial Affairs also had to build expertise on the application of food and feed additives to investigate and demonstrate the usefulness of lysine. DSM's focus on large scale to achieve low costs, a strategy that had proven successful in caprolactam and urea, had not been appropriate in the case of lysine where markets were, at best, small. The intended capacity of the methionine plant was inevitable from a cost price point of view but, at two-thirds of world use in 1965, extremely large.

Lysine was also a new market for DSM. The company had no experience with the markets for food and feed additives. DSM tried to market lysine the way it marketed fertilisers: with a focus on scientific research to demonstrate the usefulness of the product, and an emphasis on large scale and low costs to persuade feed and food companies to use it. A crucial problem was finding a market, or a segment of a market, where lysine could compete. David Hounshell argues that in the case of nylon, Du Pont's focus on one market, women's hosiery, was one of the factors explaining the success of this project. Focusing on one market made it possible to commercialise nylon fast and to do so without spending large amounts of money.[138] DSM, on the other hand, struggled to identify a market for lysine. Marketing efforts were unfocused and spread out over many possible markets or market segments, simply because it was unclear where the main effort had to be concentrated. This in turn meant that research could not be directed towards market-oriented work.

The case of lysine clearly shows how difficult it is to find and develop a market. Top management, however, decided to build a lysine plant before any market development work had yielded results. The lysine project was technology push, even though marketing and production were involved in the project. Urea and caprolactam had also been technology-push projects, but turned out to be successes. In the case of urea, the target market was clear, as were the demands set by customers. This was also true for caprolactam, where AKU was in fact the market for DSM's product and played a leading role in DSM's research. A technology push complemented with technology-oriented marketing worked very well here. In the case of lysine, a market needed to be found. DSM, Commercial Affairs in particular, but also the Central Laboratory and the production organisation, had little experience with this kind of work and had no partner to help them.

Urea, caprolactam and lysine show that DSM was a technology-oriented company, and its research was technology push, but also that this was not necessarily a negative characteristic. With existing and growing markets this orientation worked very well, but the company ran into trouble when it had to find a market by itself. In the case of lysine, DSM failed in its offensive innovation strategy because it failed to build a strong interface between research and marketing.

Through a mismatch of markets and technologies, and a cost price that was too high compared to competitive routes, a big research project came to an unsuccessful end. It was to be a major influence on research in the 1970s, but there were also important technological spin offs from lysine research in that decade. Although the project failed, it meant that DSM had established some capabilities in fine chemicals. In the long run, this was to have far-reaching consequences.

R&D in the 1950s and 1960s

Industrial research played a crucial role in the development of DSM in the 1950s and 1960s. The case of urea shows that engineering, and the engineering department, also played a role, but that research was increasingly at the core of DSM's development. The successful establishment of caprolactam production rested on research, as did most other diversifications in the 1950s and 1960s (see table 3.1). In this way, the Central Laboratory contributed in a crucial way to the expansion of DSM's chemical sector. The research organisation grew and expanded in scope, but the different types of research work remained closely integrated. The Central Laboratory conducted not only fundamental research but also process research, development work and service research. Combined with Chemiebouw's engineering capabilities, this provided an effective organisation for innovation.

The Central Laboratory contributed crucially to the expansion of DSM's chemical businesses, but sometimes other companies and their know-how played an important role. In urea, the importance of external knowledge and technology declined, while in the case of caprolactam, external stimuli related to the market for synthetic fibres. In the case of caprolactam, too, process development was internally driven. AKU provided DSM with a bridge to the market.

From table 3.1, a number of shifts in technology base can be seen. DSM's markets broadened from fertilisers to fibre intermediates and plastics. The core fertiliser technology base consisted of process research and engineering capabilities, complemented with chemistry competences. In the case of urea, much work had to be put into finding efficient industrial designs. This work was backed by thorough investigation of the reactions involved in urea synthesis, but the route to this product was fixed. In the case of caprolactam, by contrast, a major part of the projects consisted of selecting reactions and finding suitable routes to end products and/or intermediates. Finding efficient industrial designs via process research and engineering was of course also important, but followed from chemistry research.

Caprolactam, moreover, built on a different branch of chemistry compared with fertilisers: organic versus inorganic chemistry. The alcohol process of the 1930s involved some organic chemistry, but on a small scale, and built particularly on process research and engineering capabilities, that is, the fertiliser technology base. The build-up of organic chemistry capabilities through caprolactam research was crucial for the lysine project. The diversifications in the field of plastics also built on this base, but complemented it with application research. The Fibre Intermediates department did some work on the properties and applications of nylon 6, but this type of work was much more important in the marketing of plastics as they were produced in many varieties that suited many different applications. Research was necessary to introduce a specific plastic variety in a specific field.[139]

Although the lysine project built on the caprolactam technology base in organic chemistry, matching technologies and markets proved difficult. Like other diversification projects, lysine was feedstock driven and technology push. In the case of urea, the market was well-known, while in the case of caprolactam, AKU safeguarded the market. Moreover, the markets for both fertilisers and fibre intermediates grew fast. In the case of lysine, DSM was on its own; without a partner in a market it could not find, and in a field of technology it did not know very well.

The lysine project was a very visible failure, but the caprolactone project had also failed, for instance. From Revallier's calculation, DSM spent almost as much on projects that were not commercialised as on projects that were. Revallier pointed to the profits of Stamicarbon, however. Van Krevelen showed that research costs were covered by savings in production. Not only research management, but also DSM's top management and management in production and marketing, considered failures part and parcel of industrial research. They all had great faith in the productivity and creativity of research but little faith in the possibility of predicting this accurately. Research was relatively free to initiate projects, but this free initiating role did not mean that research diverged from production and marketing. Researchers took their own view of what was in the interest of the company and took a long-term view of those interests.

This freedom enabled the R&D organisation to take initiatives. The Central Laboratory often started research that presented the company with an option for diversification (see table 3.1). The same freedom also enabled researchers to conduct fundamental research: to get to the bottom of a reaction, problem or phenomenon without immediately having to think of applications. The example of the work on urea shows, however, that such 'fundamental' research could pay off and was started because of its industrial relevance. The same is true of catalysis research, which was started in relation to ammonia but was relevant to a range of research projects including caprolactam, for instance. Subjects for fundamental research came from industrial practice, not from science.

The historical and management literature on industrial research underlines the central position of fundamental research, and shows examples of companies where this led to an isolated position of research. Fundamental research was a striking feature of industrial research in the 1950s and 1960s, but that does not mean that other types of research did not take place. Typically, histories of industrial research concern large, leading companies and emphasise management. These companies usually operated research on both a central, corporate level, and a decentralised, divisional, level. Graham, in her counterculture argument, focuses on corporate research and neglects the divisional level, where research for existing businesses is much more likely to be conducted, probably in close cooperation with production. This leads to an incomplete picture at best and attaches too much importance to corporate, fundamental, and long-range research.[140]

At DSM, the Central Laboratory was independent and independent-minded, but not isolated. The example of DSM also shows that a heavy emphasis on science did not mean a neglect of less glamorous research for existing businesses. Even Van Krevelen had been involved in this kind of research when he helped to introduce the cyclone in the caprolactam plant. Histories of industrial research at DSM have also neglected Berkhoff's role, which spanned research and business.[141]

The freedom to do research was accompanied by a high level of productivity. Research was technology push but closely geared to production. As Van Heerden, director of the Central Laboratory's fundamental research, put it: "(…) in much of the work the interests of the company come first, and in all work they are at least clearly present in the background; the interests of the company are felt, not as an externally imposed force, but as the essential motive of the research institute itself."[142]

Notes

1   For instance: M. B. W. Graham (1985a). Industrial Research in the Age of Big Science. *Research on Technological Innovation: Management and Policy* 2, 47-79. M. B. W. Graham (1985b). Corporate Research and Development: The Latest Transformation. *Technology in Society* 7, 179-195. K. Boersma & M. de Vries (2003). De veranderende rol van het Natuurkundig Laboratorium van het Philipsconcern gedurende de periode 1914-1994. *NEHA Jaarboek* 66, 287-313.

2   P. A. Roussel, K. N. Saad & T. J. Erickson (1991). *Third Generation R&D - Managing the Link to Corporate Strategy.* Boston: Harvard Business School Press. 6-8, 25-29. R. Varma (1995). Restructuring Corporate R&D: From Autonomous to Linkage Model. *Technology Analysis and Strategic Management* 7(2), 231-247.

3   Author's translation. RAL, 17.26/ 36A inv. no. 183: Speech by Dr Ross van Lennep, undated but from 1947. The remainder of this section draws on E. Homburg (2000). Epiloog. DSM Research op weg naar de 21e eeuw. H. Lintsen, Ed. *Research tussen vetkool en zoetstof: zestig jaar DSM Research 1940-2000.* Eindhoven/Zutphen: Stichting Historie der Techniek/Walburg Pers, 118-135, in particular 118-120. Manuscript for this chapter, July 2000, 2-7. A. van Rooij (2004). *Building Plants: Markets for Technology and Internal Capabilities in DSM's Fertiliser Business, 1925-1970.* Amsterdam: Aksant. Dissertation Eindhoven University of Technology. 123-129.

4   A. E. Schouten & A. K. van der Vegt (1966). *Plastics: Hoofdlijnen van de huidige kennis en toepassing van synthetische macromoleculaire materialen.* Utrecht & Antwerpen: Prisma-Boeken. 228. P. F. G. Vincken (2000). *Van Staatsmijnen in Limburg tot DSM Chemie.* Unpublished manuscript. 105-110.

5   Central Laboratory Annual Report 1948.

6   For melamine see: T. van Helvoort & F. Veraart (2000). Grondstoffen voor kunststoffen, 1945-1970. H. Lintsen, Ed. *Research tussen vetkool en zoetstof.* Eindhoven/Zutphen: Stichting Historie der Techniek/Walburg Pers, 30-43, in particular 35-36. For EPDM: T. van Helvoort (2000). Staatsmijnen gaat polymeriseren, 1945-1970. H. Lintsen, Ed. *Research tussen vetkool en zoetstof: zestig jaar DSM Research 1940-2000.* Eindhoven/Zutphen: Stichting Historie der Techniek/Walburg Pers, 44-59, in particular 53-57.

7   H. J. Merx (1955). *Chronologisch overzicht van de geschiedenis van het Stikstofbindingsbedrijf 1925-1952.* Heerlen: Archief van de Staatsmijnen in Limburg. 44, 53. Vincken 2000, op. cit. 6.

8   Merx 1955, op. cit. 53. Interviews with J.P.M. van Waes by E. Homburg and the author, 4 April and 17 May 2000. CNA would later change its name to Nederlandse Stikstof Maatschappij, NSM, and become part of Norsk Hydro's fertiliser division. This division is now an independent company, called Yara. For Yara see: http://www.yara.com/en/about/index. html Accessed 29 April 2005.

9   CADH minutes top management meetings 29 September and 16 October 1961. *Gouden research, DSM Research 50 jaar: 1940-1990.* (1990). DSM Corporate Public Relations. 30.

10 E. Homburg (2003). *Speuren op de tast: Een historische kijk op industriële en universitaire research.* Maastricht: Universiteit Maastricht. Inaugural lecture 31 October 2003. 39. Boersma & De Vries 2003, op. cit. 300-306 and 304 in particular. Graham 1985a, op. cit. 49. For RCA and Alcoa see Graham 1985a and 1985b, op. cit.

11 Roussel et al. 1995, op. cit. Varma 1995, op. cit.

12 Van Rooij 2004, op. cit. 131-133.

13 RAL, 17.26/ 36A inv. no. 1: Over de organisatie van de Centrale Technische Onderzoekingsdient van de Staatsmijnen. CTO, De Braaf, Dijkstra, Van Ebbenhorst Tenbergen, Fontein, Krijgsman, Tummers, 22 October 1945.

14 RAL, 17.26/ 36A inv. no. 1: Letter Van Krevelen to Groothoff, 20 November 1945. F.W.R. Röthig (1966). *Chronologisch overzicht van het ontstaan en de organisatie van het Centraal Laboratorium van de Staatsmijnen, Geleen.* Heerlen: Staatsmijnen, Centraal Laboratorium, unpublished manuscript. 3.

15 RAL, 17.26/ 36A inv. no. 1: Bekendmaking van de mutaties bij de Chemische Bedrijven. CL, 17 January 1948. Röthig 1966, op. cit. 4. The distribution of responsibilities at the Central Laboratory as described in the next two paragraphs is also based on these sources.

16 D. W. van Krevelen (1993). Vijftig jaar activiteit in de chemische technologie. *Werken aan scheikunde: 24 memoires van hen die de Nederlandse chemie deze eeuw groot hebben gemaakt.* Delft: Delftse Universitaire Pers, 243-263.

17 CADH, minutes of top management meeting, 2 November 1949.

18 Röthig 1966, op. cit. 5.

19 Central Laboratory annual report 1949. Röthig 1966, op. cit. 7.

20 *Gouden Research* 1990, op. cit. 29.

21 RAL, 17.26/ 21C inv. no. 264: letter from Berkhoff to Van Aken, 7 December 1956. Röthig 1966, op. cit. 7-9.

22 Röthig 1966, op. cit. 17-18.

23 Central Laboratory Annual Report 1949. D. W. van Krevelen (1958). Het Centraal Laboratorium, chemisch research centrum van de Staatsmijnen in Limburg. *De Ingenieur* 70(39), Ch 79-87. D. W. van Krevelen (1980). Bij het scheiden der wegen. Voordracht bij het afscheid van het Centraal Laboratorium der Staatsmijnen, te Geleen op 25 augustus 1959. *In retrospect: Een keuze uit de voordrachten.* Amsterdam: Meulenhoff, 43-47, in particular 45-46.

24 Homburg 2003, op. cit. 38-39.

25 Homburg 2003, op. cit. 28-39.

26 Central Laboratory Annual Report 1949. D. W. van Krevelen (1950). Chemische industrie en research. *De Zakenwereld*, 108-111, in particular 109. J. S. A. J. M. van Aken (1960). Management's View on Research in Chemical Industry. *TVF* 31, 57-64

27 Dr. van Aken: kracht putten uit research en samenwerking. *Chemisch Weekblad* 1968, 44, 17-19, in particular 19. Also: C. van Heerden (1966). Research in de chemische industrie. *Chemisch Weekblad* 66, 290-296, in particular 292.

28 Personal papers of Dr S. E. Schaafsma: Het Centraal Laboratorium in de periode 1948 tot en met 1954. Een poging tot waardering van kosten en baten. Van Krevelen, 20 July 1955. For Van Krevelen's argument about qualitative and quantitative assessments of R&D, compare: J. B. Quinn (1959). *Yardsticks for Industrial Research: The Evaluation of Research and Development Output.* New York: The Ronald Press Company. 1-44. DSM had Quinn's book in its library. That copy is now part of the collection of the library of Maastricht University.

29 Van Krevelen 1993, op. cit. 257-258. *Gouden Research* 1990, op. cit. 30-31.

30 This section draws on Van Rooij 2004, op. cit. chapter 7.

31 Interviews with J.P.M. van Waes by E. Homburg and the author, 4 April and 17 May 2000. Van Rooij 2004, op. cit. 142.

32 Quoted in: E. Homburg, with contributions by A. van Rooij (2004a). *Groeien door kunstmest: DSM Agro 1929-2004.* Hilversum: Verloren. 168. Quote translated from Dutch by the author.

33 *Ureumnieuws* May 1974, 7.

34 RAL, 17.26/ 36A inv. no. 71: Phenol in verband met de Nylon-vezel. SBB, Niks, 21 November 1939.

35 In general, the first two subsections are based on: E. Homburg & A. van Rooij (2004). Die Vor- und Nachteile enger Nachbarschaft. Der Transfer deutscher chemischer Technologie die Niederlande bis 1952. R. Petri, Ed. *Technologietransfer aus der deutschen Chemieindustrie (1925-1960).* Berlin: Duncker & Humblot, 201-251, in particular 234-243. I want to thank Ernst Homburg for permission to use his archival research on the establishment of caprolactam at DSM.

36 Merx 1955, op. cit. 34.

37 Central Laboratory Annual Report 1949. Merx 1955, op. cit. 68.

38 Central Laboratory Annual Report 1949. C. G. M. van de Moesdijk (1979). *The Catalytic Reduction of Nitrate and Nitric Oxide to Hydroxylamine: Kinetics and Mechanism.* Eindhoven: Dissertation Eindhoven Technical College. 13.

39 F. Veraart. *Fenol* (1939-1964). Veldman & Van Royen Report C. 1-3. H. Strijkers (1992). *Veertig jaar caprolactam bij DSM.* DSM. 6.

40 F. W. R. Röthig (1959). *Archiefdocumentatie betreffende de algemene gang van zaken bij de ontwikkeling van de projecten "Fenol - Caprolactam - Nylonzout" van de Staatsmijnen in Limburg van 1937 t/m 1959 (oktober).* Heerlen: Staatsmijnen, Bureau Secretariaat en Correspondentie. 91-97. Röthig 1966, op. cit. 5. Van de Moesdijk 1979, op. cit. 13-14. Vincken 2000, op. cit. 117.

41 Central Laboratory Annual Reports 1949, 1951. Central Laboratory research programme 1951.

42 Central Laboratory Annual Reports 1953, 1954. RAL, 17.26/ 35A inv. no. 42: Verslag van de bespreking met Dr. Zorn, Holzverzuckerungs A.G. op 20 juli 1950 te Lorrach, betreffende de bereiding van caprolactaam en de verwerking daarvan tot vezels en garen. SBB, Niks, 24 July 1950. Beschouwingen naar aanleiding van de bespreking van Staatsmijnen met Holzverzuckerungs A.G. over het caprolactaamproject. CL, Zeegers, 26 July 1950.

43 Central Laboratory Annual Reports 1951-1958. RAL, 17.26/ 35A inv. no. 42: Verslag van de bespreking AKU - SM naar aanleiding van het bezoek van BI Niks en ir. Hoek aan Dr Zorn over caprolactaam. CL, Zeegers, 9 August 1950.

44 Central Laboratory Annual Reports 1952, 1954.

45 RAL, 17.26/ 36B inv. no. 48: Bezoek van Spencer aan de Sector Research en Development van de Staatsmijnen in oktober 1957 i.v.m. de bespreking over cyclohexaanoxidatie en bereiding van nylonzout. Kaarsemaker, undated. Verslag van een telefoongesrpek tussen ir. Van

THE COMPANY THAT CHANGED ITSELF

Waes en Mr Thomas general vice president van Spencer Chemical Company d.d. 26-8-1958. Staf Chemische Bedrijven, 2 September 1958 CADH, DV 1961/ 112: Nota inzake de plannen met betrekking tot de bouw van een installatie voor de productie van cyclohexanon op basis van cyclohexaan. Staf Chemische Bedrijven, 21 April 1961. Central Laboratory Annual Reports 1954-1959. *Stamicarbon Reference List*, 1 February 1985. Strijkers 1992, op. cit. 9.

46 Central Laboratory Annual Reports 1959-1962. Van de Moesdijk 1979, op. cit. 14. Strijkers 1992, op. cit. 10.

47 Veraart, op. cit. 4-6. For the Dow process see: W. W. Kaeding (1964). How Dow Makes Phenol From Toluene. *Hydrocarbon Processing* 43(11), 173-176.

48 Veraart, op. cit. 7-8. Central Laboratory research programmes and annual reports of the 1960s.

49 R. Stobaugh & P. Townsend (1975). Price Forecasting and Strategic Planning: The Case of Petrochemicals. *Journal of Marketing Research* 12, 19-29. P. M. E. M. van der Grinten (1984). Vergrijzing en verjonging in de chemische industrie. *Chemisch Magazine* (November 1984), 677-680.

50 CADH, DV 1967/ 429: Vervaardiging van caprolactam bij DSM, aan de raad van commissarissen, 9 November 1967.

51 Letter Revallier to top management, 8 February 1966; supplement to the Central Laboratory annual report 1966.

52 Central Laboratory annual reports and research programmes 1961-1969. A. M. Brownstein (1976). *Trends in Petrochemical Technology: The Impact of the Energy Crisis.* Tulsa: Petroleum Publishing Co. Table 6.21, 248.

53 Central Laboratory annual reports and research programmes 1960-1971. RAL, 17.26/ 35A inv. no. 222: Voorstel voor een onderzoek naar de fabricage van garens en vezels uit caprolactam. CL, Revallier, November 1959. RAL, 17.26/ 36C inv. no. 2: Letter Berkhoff to top management via Van Aken, 7 May 1960.

54 Central Laboratory research programme 1954.

55 In general this paragraph and the next five are based on Central Laboratory annual reports and research programmes 1955-1957, Röthig 1959 op. cit. 103-120.

56 RAL, 17.26/ 35A inv. no. 224: Bespreking op 5 april 1955 met AKU te Arnhem. CL, Berkhoff, 18 April 1955. Strijkers 1992, op. cit. 8.

57 RAL, 17.26/ 36B inv. no. 52: letter from Berkhoff to Dr F. Codignola, 8 June 1956.

58 RAL, 17.26/ 35A inv. no. 224: Verslag van de bespreking in de managementcommissie op 12 october 1955 te Geleen. Staf Chemische Bedrijven, Lak, 27 October 1955. RAL, 17.26/ 35A inv. no. 224: Agendapunten Staatsmijnen voor de bespreking op 29 november 1956, undated. RAL, 17.26/ 36B inv. no. 50: Van Waes and Berkhoff to top management, 13 November 1959.

59 W. J. Reader (1970-1975). *Imperial Chemical Industries: A History.* London: Oxford University Press. Two volumes. Vol. 2, 1975, 349-362. D. G. H. Ballard (1986). The Discovery of Polyethylene and its Effect on the Evolution of Polymer Science. R. B. Seymour & T. Cheng, Eds. *History of Polyolefins. The World's Most Widely Used Polymers.* Dordrecht: D. Reidel Publishing Company, 9-53, in particular 9-15.

60 P. Baggen, J. Faber & E. Homburg (2003). Opkomst van een kennismaatschappij. J. W. Shot et al., Ed. Techniek in Nederland in de Twintigste Eeuw. Eindhoven/Zutphen: Stichting Historie der Techniek/Walburg Pers. Vol. 7, 141-173, in particular 161. Homburg 2004a, op. cit. 151.

61 In general, this section is based on: F. W. R. Röthig (1960). *De algemene gang van zaken bij de ontwikkeling van het polyolefinen-project van de Staatsmijnen in Limburg van 1935 t/m 1959.*

Deel II: polyethyleen - algemeen en hogedruk-polyethyleen. Heerlen: Staatsmijnen, Bureau Secretariaat en Correspondentie. F. W. R. Röthig (1960). *De algemene gang van zaken bij de ontwikkeling van het polyolefinen-project van de Staatsmijnen in Limburg van 1935 t/m 1959. Deel III: lagedruk-polyetheen.* Heerlen: Staatsmijnen, Bureau Secretariaat en Correspondentie. T. van Helvoort (2000). Staatsmijnen gaat polymeriseren, 1945-1970. H. Lintsen, Ed. *Research tussen vetkool en zoetstof: zestig jaar DSM Research 1940-2000.* Eindhoven/Zutphen: Stichting Historie der Techniek/Walburg Pers, 44-59.

62 Only the modern names HPDE and LDPE are used here. Low-pressure polyethylene and high pressure polyethylene were also used for HDPE (Ziegler) and LDPE (ICI) respectively.

63 F. McMillan (1979). *The Chain Straighteners. Fruitful Innovation: The Discovery of Linear and Stereoregular Synthetic Polymers.* London: The MacMillan Press. R. Landau (1998). The Process of Innovation in the Chemical Industry. A. Arora, R. Landau & N. Rosenberg, Eds. *Chemicals and Long-Term Economic Growth: Insights from the Chemical Industry.* New York: John Wiley & Sons, 139-180, in particular 164-165. H. Martin (2002). *Polymere und Patente: Karl Ziegler, das Team, 1953-1998. Zur wirtschaftlichen Verwertung akademischer Forschung.* Weinheim: Wiley-VCH. *Kirk-Othmer Encyclopedia of Chemical Technology.* Online version, 2005: Polyethylene, High Density. For Du Pont see: D. A. Hounshell & J. K. Smith (1988). *Science and Corporate Strategy: Du Pont R&D, 1902-1980.* Cambridge: Cambridge University Press. 491-497.

64 G. F. te Roller (1990). *Een halve eeuw Centraal Laboratorium: Een serie gesprekken met oud-researchdirecteuren van DSM.* Heerlen: DSM Corporate Public Relations. Unpublished manuscript. 5.

65 See also Central Laboratory annual report 1955.

66 RAL, 17.26/ 36B inv. no. 48: Notitie naar aanleiding van het bezoek van de heer Thomas van Spencer Chemical op 12 en 13 mei 1955. Staf Chemische Bedrijven, 14 May 1955. Voorstel wat betreft de inhoud van de "letter of intent", 8 July 1957. RAL, 17.26/ 21C inv. no. 241: Inleiding voor de Hoofddirectie over enige plannen met betrekking tot een verdere uitbreiding van de Chemische Bedrijven van de Staatsmijnen te houden op 9 december 1960. Staf Chemische Bedrijven, 7 December 1960. F. Aftalion (2001). *A History of the International Chemical Industry: From the "Early Days" to 2000.* Philadelphia: Chemical Heritage Foundation. Second Edition. 224.

67 Toespraak van Dir. D.H.E. Tom voor de gepensioneerde medewerkers van het CL tijdens de "Open Dag" op 13 juni 1981. Röthig 1966, op. cit. 5, 17-18, 21-22.

68 Schouten & van der Vegt, op cit. 201-239.

69 Central Laboratory annual reports 1958-1970.

70 F. W. R. Röthig (1960). *De algemene gang van zaken bij de ontwikkeling van het polyolefinen-project van de Staatsmijnen in Limburg van 1935 t/m 1959. Deel I: ethyleen.* Heerlen: Staatsmijnen, Bureau Secretariaat en Correspondentie. E. Homburg, A. van Selm & P. Vincken (2000). Industrialisatie en industriecomplexen. De chemische industrie tussen overheid, technologie en markt. J. W. Schot et al., Eds. *Techniek in Nederland in de twintigste eeuw.* Eindhoven/Zutphen: Stichting Historie der Techniek/Walburg Pers. Vol. 2, 377-401, in particular 384-385.

71 Röthig 1960, op. cit. part 1, 7, 18, 24, 54-56, 63.

72 Central Laboratory annual report and research programme 1956. Röthig 1966, op. cit. 9. Te Roller 1990, op. cit. 14-15.

73 Martin 2002, op. cit. passim, particularly 21, 104-106. B. Cornils & M. Rasch (1997). *Geschichte der Forschung der Ruhrchemie AG und des Werkes Ruhrchemie (1927-1997).* Frankfurt/M.: Hoechst AG; unpublished manuscript. 13.

74 Landau 1998, op. cit. 165-166.
75 Interview with Dr G. Evens, 26 July 2005. Central Laboratory annual reports 1958, 1959. Röthig 1960, op. cit. part 3, 40. R. B. Seymour (1986). Introduction to the History of Polyolefins. R. B. Seymour & T. Cheng, Eds. *History of Polyolefins: The World's Most Widely Used Polymers.* Dordrecht: D. Reidel Publishing Company, 1-7, in particular 4. J. P. Hogan & R. L. Banks (1986). History of Crystalline Polypropylene. R. B. Seymour & T. Cheng, Eds. *History of Polyolefins. The World's Most Widely Used Polymers.* Dordrecht: D. Reidel Publishing Company, 103-115, in particular 105-106. Martin 2002, op. cit. 83, 156-158.
76 Central Laboratory annual reports 1959, 1960, 1962, 1964. Röthig 1960, op. cit. part 3, 77. Homburg et al. 2000, op. cit. 388. Martin 2002, op. cit. 165-166.
77 E. G. M. Tornqvist (1986). Polyolefin Elastomers - Fifty Years of Progress. R. B. Seymour & T. Cheng, Eds. *History of Polyolefins: The World's Most Widely Used Polymers.* Dordrecht: D. Reidel Publishing Company, 143-161, in particular 153-154. Note that only the modern names are used here. Initially, ethylene-propylene copolymers were called EPR, while the terpolymers were called EPT, instead of EPM and EPDM respectively.
78 Röthig 1960, op. cit. part 3, 10-11.
79 Central Laboratory annual reports 1959-1960. Röthig 1960, op. cit. part 3, 77.
80 RAL, 17.26/46 inv. no. 110: Eigenschappen en toepassingen van EPT. Van 't Wout & Van Gorcum, undated. T. C. N. Belgraver (1970). *70 jaar Nederlandse Rubberindustrie: Uitgave ter gelegenheid van het 50-jarig jubileum van de Nederlandse Vereniging van Rubberfabrikanten 29 oktober 1970.* Appendix 3, across from 88.
81 T. van Helvoort. *Synthetische rubbers: de verlokkingen van een enorme markt.* Veldman & Van Royen report G. 1
82 http://www.exxonmobilchemical.com/Public_Products/EEB/EP_D_M/Worldwide/ Description_and_Background/Vis_Desc_HistoryInfo_1961_1970.asp. Accessed 4 August 2005.
83 Central Laboratory annual reports 1961-1963. Van Helvoort, op. cit. 2.
84 Central Laboratory annual reports 1962, 1963, 1965. RAL, 17.26/46 inv. no. 110: Rubberonderzoek. Eigenschappen van de in oktober 1962 gemaakte partijen terpolymeer. Centraal Laboratorium, afdeling Kunststoftechnologie, Van 't Wout, 16 February 1963.
85 Central Laboratory annual reports 1960-1965.
86 Central Laboratory annual reports 1966, 1967.
87 Seymour 1986, op. cit. 5. *Kirk-Othmer Encyclopedia of Chemical Technology.* Online edition, 2005. Olefin Polymers.
88 Interview with Dr B. C. Roest, 29 July 2005. Central Laboratory annual report 1965. DSM Annual Reports 1967, 1968, 1970. Belangrijke uitbreiding KELTAN-productie in Beek. *Nieuws DSM Limburg* 1981, 31(17), 1, 4.
89 Martin 2002, op. cit. 160-165, 185 (note 33). RAL, 17.26/46 inv. no. 111: Octrooisituatie EP en EPT. Octrooiafdeling, Van Leeuwen, 16 March 1967. RAL, DSM 17.26/46 inv. no. 112: Voorstel tot voortzetting van de onderhandelingen met Montecatini-Edison S.p.A. volgens haar aanbod van 15/3/1968 inzake EPT. Muller, V.d. Kar en Van Daelen, 21 March 1968. Uit verslag van de 9e bespreking van de hoofddirectie d.d. 25-3-1968. EP Rubber Patent License Agreement between Montecatini Edision S.p.A. and N.V. Nederlandse Staatsmijnen, August 1968.
90 In general this section is based on: H. Strijkers. *DSM en melamine.* Unpublished and undated manuscript. 1-14. F. Veraart. *Melamine uit ureum (1958-1969).* Veldman & Van Royen rapport E.
91 Interview with professor J. J. Steggerda on 8 August 2005. Central Laboratory annual report 1956.

92   *Ullmanns Encyklopädie der technischen Chemie.* München: Urban & Schwarzenberg. Third edition, 19 volumes, 1951-1970. Vol. 12, 1960, 279. J. L. Meikle (1991). Plastics. S. G. Lewin, Ed. *Formica & Design: From the Table Top to High Art.* New York: Rizzoli International Publications, 39-57, in particular 49-51. J. L. Meikle (1995). *American Plastic: A Cultural History.* New Brunswick, New Jersey: Rutgers University Press. 74-78.

93   *Ullmann,* third edition, op. cit. 282. *Ullmanns Encyklopädie der technischen Chemie.* Weinheim: Verlag Chemie. Fourth edition, 25 volumes, 1972-1984. Vol. 16, 1978, 508. http://www. degussa.com/en/unternehmen/history/skw.content.html. Accessed 21 June 2002.

94   Interview with prof. dr. ir. J. J. Steggerda 8 August 2005. Central Laboratory annual report 1958.

95   Central Laboratory annual report 1959.

96   Central Laboratory annual reports 1959-1961.

97   Central Laboratory annual reports 1962-1967.

98   RAL, 17.26/35A inv. no. 129: De positie van het S.M. Melamine-proces t.o.v. de octrooien van American Cyanamid Co.. Staf Chemische Bedrijven, Steggerda, 8 April 1959. RAL, 17.26/34 inv. no. 826: Stand van zaken met betrekking tot het melamineproject 4 april 1962. Sector Nieuwe Ontwikkelingen, Wolfs, 4 April 1962.

99   This paragraph and the next two are based on: F.W.R. Röthig (1965). *De contacten van de Staatsmijnen met derden op het gebied van melamine, melamine-harsen, en melamine-perspoeders.* Heerlen: Staatsmijnen, Centraal Archief. 2-47.

100 RAL, 17.26/ 36B inv. no. 48: letter from Spencer Chemical to Berkhoff, 6 May 1958. RAL, 17.26/ 21C inv. no. 241: Inleiding voor de Hoofddirectie over enige plannen met betrekking tot een verdere uitbreiding van de Chemische Bedrijven van de Staatsmijnen te houden op 9 december 1960. Staf Chemische Bedrijven, 7 December 1960.

101 RAL, DSM 17.26/34 inv. no. 826: Melamineproject. Bijlage 2: achtergronden van het contract met CIBA. Octrooiafdeling, Muller, undated but probably from January 1963.

102 RAL, 17.26/34 inv. no. 826: Samenvatting van de voornaamste punten van bespreking met CIBA op 14 juni te Bazel. Muller, 15 June 1966. A. Schmidt (1966). Herstellung von Melamin aus Harnstoff bei Atmosphärendruck. *Chemie-Ingenieur-Technik* 38(11), 1140-1143, in particular 1140. Röthig 1965, op. cit. 55.

103 Central Laboratory annual reports 1958, 1961, 1962.

104 Central Laboratory annual reports and research programmes 1965-1970.

105 Comparable figures for Revallier's data are difficult to obtain. Böning reports several wide-ranging estimates of success rates from several general studies of R&D: from 5% of all research projects to 90%. The periods these rates apply to are unclear. At Du Pont, 95% of projects started are reported to have failed. Again, the period this applies to is unclear. In contrast, Böning reports that in 1966, no less than 70% of all products manufactured by BASF came out of in-house research since 1952. Böning uses these figures to argue that R&D is risky, although it remains unclear how risky. See: D.-J. Böning (1969). *Bestimmungsfaktoren der Intensität industrieller Forschung und Entwicklung.* Clausthal-Zellerfeld: Bönecke. 28-29, 73.

106 G. Berkhoff & J. H. Ottenheym (1961). Verbetering van de voedingswaarde van eiwitten door toevoeging van lysine en methionine. *Voeding* 22(7), 292-306, in particular 292.

107 In general this section draws on: F. Veraart. *Lysine (1957-1969).* Veldman & Van Royen report H. H. Lintsen, F. Veraart & P. Vincken (2000). De onvervulde belofte: Lysine. H. Lintsen, Ed. *Research tussen vetkool en zoetstof: zestig jaar DSM Research 1940-2000.* Eindhoven/Zutphen: Stichting Historie der Techniek/Walburg Pers, 70-81. Additional research is reported in the following notes.

108 Lysine Prospects Brighten. *Chemical & Engineering News* (20 April 1959), 25. *Kirk-Othmer*

Encyclopedia of Chemical Technology. London: Wiley-Interscience. Second edition, 22 volumes, 1963-1977. Vol. 2, 1963, 166. F. W. R. Röthig (1968). *Toepassing lysine voor menselijke voeding en als therapeuticum: Contacten CL/DSM met derden.* Heerlen: Staatsmijnen, Centraal Laboratorium. 26. M. Wolf (1993). *Im Zeichen von Sonne und Mond: von der Frankfurter Muenzscheiderei zum Weltunternehmen Degussa AG.* Frankfurt am Main: Degussa. 247, 250. F. Gambrelle (ca. 1995). *Innovating for Life: Rhône-Poulenc 1895-1995.* Paris: Éditions Public Historie Albin Michel. 80-81. http://www.kyowa.co.jp/eng/prtext/history.htm. Accessed 12 March 2004.

109 See previous note and: J. J. McKetta (1976-1999). *Encyclopedia of Chemical Processing Design.* Basel: Dekker. Vol. 3, 1977, 209-211, 221-228.

110 Central Laboratory annual reports 1957-1960.

111 RAL, 17.26/ 40 inv. no. 3: minutes of Mijnraad, 6 May 1959. Central Laboratory annual reports and research programmes 1951, 1958-1960.

112 Central Laboratory annual report 1960.

113 Central Laboratory annual reports and research programmes 1960-1969

114 RAL, 17.26/ 35A inv. no. 125: Lysinesuppletie aan brood. Verslag van een bespreking op 13 februari 1958 in het TNO-Instituut voor Graan, Meel en Brood (GMB) te Wageningen. CL, Ottenheym, 28 February 1958. RAL, 17.26/ 35A inv. no. 126: Van Waes and Berkhoff to Bertram (director TNO instituut voor Graan, Meel en Brood) and to Engel (director CIVO), 25 July 1958. Röthig 1968, op. cit. 1.

115 Röthig 1968, op. cit. 3, 7-9.

116 RAL, 17.26/ 36C inv. no. 48: drs. G.K. (sic) to Van Os and Van Waes. Staf Commerciële Zaken, 14 September 1961. I. de Boer, Ed. (1974). *Boer en markt. Ontwikkeling van de Nederlandse land- en tuinbouw en de Cebeco-Handelsraad organisatie in de periode 1949-1974: Een uitgave van Cebeco-Handelsraad ter gelegenheid van zijn 75-jarig bestaan.* Graph 7, 306; table 19, 311.

117 Central Laboratory annual reports 1958, 1959. RAL, 17.26/ 36B inv. no. 83: Handelmaatschappij Trouw & Co. NV to top management DSM, 23 January 1959. RAL, 17.26/ 36C inv. no. 48: top management to Trouw (Suurenbroek), 9 December 1961.

118 RAL, 17.26/ 36C inv. no. 57: Verslag van een bespreking met vertegenwoordigers van Unilever Ltd. op donderdag 23 november 1961 te Heerlen. Ter Veer, 30 November 1961. RAL, 17.26/ 38 inv. no. 5: Verslag van de 5e bespreking op 14 december 1961 te Geleen inzake lysine en elastomeren. Staf Chemische Bedrijven, 19 December 1961. Röthig 1968, op. cit. 20.

119 Central Laboratory annual reports 1960, 1963. CADH, DV 1962/ 60: Sixma to top management, 2 March 1962. DV 1967/ 155: Van Steenis (director Commerciële Zaken) to top management, 12 May 1967. Minutes of top management meetings on 12 March 1962, 16 May 1967. RAL, 17.26/ 38 inv. no. 65: Varkensproef in samenwerking met Landbouwbelang. CL, Van Loen, 21 December 1962. Verslag van de 18e vergadering van de werkgroep chemie, gehouden op 7 mei 1963 te Geleen. Staf Chemische Bedrijven, 21 May 1963.

120 Röthig 1968, op. cit. 19. RAL, 17.26/ 36B inv. no. 84: J.C. Beunder (director Nutricia) to Revallier, 27 February 1959. Letter Nutricia (G. Schipper) to Revallier, 29 May 1959. RAL, 17.26/ 35A inv. no. 125: Toepassing van lysine. Verslag van besprekingen op 10 en 11 april te Beekbergen, Rijksinstituut voor pluimveeteelt, Hoogland, de Schothorst, proefboerderij, Zoetermeer, Nutrica. CL, Ottenheym, 21 April 1959.

121 Röthig 1968, op. cit. 26. RAL, 17.26/ 36C inv. no. 53: Gee to Jan, 13 September 1960. RAL, 17.26/ 38 inv. no. 5: Verslag van de 5e bespreking op 14 december 1961 te Geleen inzake lysine en elastomeren. Staf Chemische Bedrijven, 19 December 1961.

122 Röthig 1968, op. cit. 6-7, 20.

123 Annual Reports 1959, 1960.

124 CADH, DV 1963/ 85: Verslag van de 14e bespreking van de werkgroep chemie, gehouden op 14 februari 1963. Staf Chemische Bedrijven, 7 March 1963.

125 Central Laboratory annual report 1963. RAL, 17.26/ 38 inv. no. 15: De commerciële aspecten van het lysine project. Staf Commerciële Zaken, Van Steenis & Ter Veer, 21 January 1963. For fertilisers see Homburg 2004, op. cit. 85-97.

126 See technical reports: RAL, 17.26/ 38 inv. no. 87.

127 Central Laboratory annual reports 1963, 1965-1967. Central Laboratory research programme 1967. RAL, 17.26/ 38 inv. no. 65: Aantekeningen bij het programma van onderzoek. CL, Van Loen, 28 May 1964.

128 CADH, DV 1967/ 59: Nota inzake de wenselijkheid van verticale integratie in het gebied van de premix- en mengvoederindustrie en mogelijkheid tot concrete realisatie. Verkoopgroep Landbouw- en Voedingschemicaliën, Ter Veer, 2 March 1967. Huidige stand van zaken van het lysineproject. Ter Veer (CZ), Steeman (OF), Van de Kar (BEA), 8 May 1968.

129 Röthig 1968, op. cit. 35, 37, 38.

130 RAL, 17.26/ 38 inv. no. 1: Verslag van de besprekingen met het Directoraat-Generaal voor de Buitenlandse Betrekkingen (Economische Zaken) op donderdag 27 augustus 1964 te Den Haag. Afdeling handelspolitiek en Europese integratie. Claus, 1 September 1964. RAL, 17.26/ 38 inv. no. 9: Verslag van de bespreking met dr. Wakaki van de firma Kyowa op 15 oktober 1965 te 's-Hertogenbosch. Ter Veer, 18 October 1965. Röthig 1968, op. cit. 39.

131 Central Laboratory annual report 1964. Röthig 1968, op. cit. 31. A. van Loen (1966). *De betekenis van lysinesuppletie als directe benadering van het proteinmalnutrition-probleem in de wereld.* Heerlen: Staatsmijnen/DSM.

132 Röthig 1968, op. cit. 15, 18, 23.

133 Central Laboratory annual report 1967.

134 RAL, 17.26/ 38 inv. no. 4: Ter Veer to Beleidsgroep Lysine, 7 November 1968. RAL, 17.26/ 38 inv. no. 8: Lysine, 6 February 1969.

135 Central Laboratory annual reports and research programmes 1963-1966.

136 Central Laboratory annual report and research programme 1967. RAL, 17.26/ 38 inv. no. 14: RAL, 17.26/ 34 inv. no. 14: Letter from DSM (Agricultural and Food Division, sic, Ter Veer & Von Balluseck) to Mitsui & Co. GmbH, 13 June 1967. Sales agency contract Mitsui-DSM, undated. RAL, 17.26/ 38 inv. no. 102: Afzetmogelijkheden methionine. Staf commerciële zaken, Zaaijer, September 1966. RAL, 17.26/ 34 inv. no. 829: Revallier and Van Steenis to Beleidsgroep Chemie, 26 August 1968.

137 Personal papers dr. ir. L.J. Revallier: Vergelijking van de kosten van research en ontwikkeling van een nieuw proces versus de kosten van aankoop (licentiekosten). BEAC/C, V.d. Kar, 17 February 1966. Projects developed by DSM. Undated but from approximately 1975. Personal papers dr. S.E. Schaafsma: Het Centraal Laboratorium in de periode 1948 tot en met 1954. Een poging tot waardering van kosten en baten. Van Krevelen, 20 July 1955.

138 D. A. Hounshell (1992). Du Pont and the Management of Large-Scale Research and Development. P. Galison & B. Hevly, Eds. *Big Science: The Growth of Large-Scale Research.* Stanford: Stanford University Press, 236-261, in particular 238-245.

139 For plastics and rubbers at DSM see: Van Helvoort 2000, op. cit.

140 Particularly Graham 1985a and 1985b, op. cit.

141 H. Lintsen, Ed. (2000). *Research tussen vetkool en zoetstof: zestig jaar DSM Research 1940-2000: zestig jaar DSM Research 1940-2000.* Eindhoven/Zutphen: Stichting Historie der Techniek/Walburg Pers.

142 Van Heerden 1966, op. cit. 291. Author's translation.

4

The Large Leap Forward: Redefining the Role of R&D in the 1970s

Although Van Heerden had claimed that in much of the Central Laboratory's work the interests of the company came first, in the 1970s this claim came under intense scrutiny from both inside and outside research.[1] The failure of the lysine project dealt a blow to the self-confidence that had been nurtured. At the same time, DSM embarked on a programme of expansion and diversification, closed its mines and created divisions. Research reorganised to adapt to these changes, and business management gained a strong say in the direction of research. In the 1950s and 1960s, the Central Laboratory had played a central role in diversification; but in the 1970s, top management placed more emphasis on technology acquisitions and take-overs as means to diversify, and it stressed that markets, rather than technologies and research, should drive diversification. Diversification was initiated outside the Central Laboratory. Research played a dependent role, aimed at facilitating the process of buying technology and companies.

DSM's reorientation fits into a pattern of change in industrial research around 1970. After a period of strong faith in research, generous funding, and an emphasis on fundamental research and long-term research in general, came a period in which companies cut R&D spending, particularly spending on fundamental research, and emphasised the role of market needs in directing their research.[2] Margaret Graham and Bettye Pruitt also note, in their R&D history of Alcoa, how stronger involvement of divisional management led to a neglect of long-term research.[3] At DSM, the involvement of divisional management similarly pushed research to care more for short-term than for long-term interests.

With its reorientation of research, DSM also responded to a changing business climate. In the 1950s and 1960s, growth on many chemical markets had been spectacular, but after 1970 growth slowed down and in some markets saturation seemed imminent. Two oil shocks raised energy and feedstock prices dramatically and made it attractive for oil-producing countries to enter the chemical industry, and particularly the plastics and fertiliser industries, where feedstock price was a crucial factor in competition. Increasing labour costs, environmental consciousness and environmental regulation meant that companies had to invest considerable amounts of money in facilities to reduce pollution and increase safety. Chemical companies in Western Europe, Japan and the United States, the traditional bastions of the industry, suffered from strained profitability in the 1970s, particularly in bulk chemicals.[4]

External changes (a worsening business climate) and internal changes (expansion and diversification, establishment of divisions and reduced self-confidence in research for diversification) occurred in parallel and combined to redefine the role and position of research in the 1970s. This chapter is about this redefinition, but also analyses DSM's entry – initiated and enabled by the Central Laboratory – into fine chemicals, a field where the company profited from lysine research.

The Final Step Towards DSM's Transformation into a Chemical Company

After the Second World War, the importance of DSM's chemical businesses increased significantly as a result of diversification and expansion of production capacities for existing products. Coal, coke and chemicals were closely related from a feedstock point of view, but were organisationally separated. The Central Laboratory was part of DSM's chemical sector and conducted research for this part of the company. The Central Experimental Station, on the other hand, belonged to coal-mining activities and conducted research in that field. Manufacturing and marketing functions were organised in the same way. DSM had a functional organisation within the two broad areas of chemicals on the one hand and coal and coke on the other.[5]

In 1965, the Central Laboratory and the Central Experimental Station merged, signalling an important change. The production of coal, coke and coke oven gas went into decline in the 1960s, and in 1962, losses were incurred for the first time. Three years later, on 14 December 1965, the Dutch government announced the end of coal-mining in the Netherlands. Not only DSM's pits would be closed but also those of private companies. The government made a restructuring plan to create jobs for the miners.[6]

The end of the coal and coke activities in the foreseeable future meant that DSM had to consider a new course of action. Moreover, from the late 1950s, the policy of Van Aken and his close colleagues had been aimed at expansion to reinforce the company's position. Merging DSM's chemical businesses with another Dutch company, particularly AKU, DSM's main customer for caprolactam, also counted as a serious possibility. Merger attempts failed, however, and AKU merged with KZO to form AKZO in 1969.

The failed merger with AKU left DSM on its own, with a coal business that would soon be shut down and a set of chemical businesses that it considered too small. At this crossroads, top management decided to take up the challenge. The company should make a 'Large Leap Forward' on the foundation of the chemical businesses DSM had built in the 1950s and 1960s. The chemical businesses would be expanded considerably, manufacture of new products would be taken up and the organisation of the company revised. The Large Leap Forward aimed to secure the company's survival and its revitalisation at the same time.

The production of coke and coke oven gas ended in December 1968. Five years later, DSM's last pit closed.[7] The Large Leap Forward consisted of several routes to replace the company's coal related activities. In the first place, DSM attempted backward integration to secure the necessary feedstocks for the production of chemical products. DSM already had a stake in the exploitation and distribution of natural gas in the Netherlands. The company made plans to build a refinery in Limburg together with Royal Dutch/Shell, but when these plans failed in 1971, DSM decided to participate in the exploitation of oil and natural gas fields in the North Sea. These moves were business-driven and were of little consequence for research as the Central Laboratory did not work in this field.

From oil and natural gas, DSM mainly manufactured intermediates that other companies used to manufacture end products. DSM wanted to get closer to those markets: forward integration was the second part of the Large Leap programme. In 1967, DSM bought Curver, a manufacturer of plastic products, and four years later it acquired a majority interest in the textile firm *Macintosh Confectie*. In the early 1970s, DSM also bought several construction firms. The company mainly targeted plastics, textiles and construction in its efforts to integrate forwards but acquired other interests as well. In 1967, for instance, DSM helped the Dutch manufacturer of trucks and cars, DAF, to establish a plant in Limburg in an attempt to create new jobs in the region. DSM also acquired chemical companies and bought Synres, a Dutch manufacturer of resins, in 1970. Acquisitions were a sign of the times, although DSM was somewhat slower than other Dutch companies to pick up on this trend.[8] For DSM, buying companies was a new way to enter new markets and to generate growth.

Besides forward integration, DSM diversified horizontally and took up the manufacture of additional plastics and fibre intermediates. The company started production of acrylonitrile, an intermediate for acrylic fibres, as well as the production of the plastics PVC, polypropylene and ABS, for all of which it had the necessary feedstocks. These products were well-suited to reach a large scale as they were established products for which there was a large market. DSM in fact had no choice but to build large plants, because smaller plants would be a cost disadvantage compared with established manufacturers. This pushed the company towards buying technology, because these processes were proven on a large scale. Finally, DSM wanted to diversify fast. The Central Laboratory did not have the time or the resources to quickly enable all these diversifications. The acrylonitrile, PVC, polypropylene and ABS plants were all built with external technology.

DSM also expanded capacity of existing products. In the late 1960s, DSM boosted urea and melamine production substantially. The company also hired engineering contractors to build a second, very large ammonia plant and a third cracker for the production of ethylene with a similarly large capacity. DSM strove for large-scale operation in new and established products alike.

The Large Leap Forward meant that DSM expanded in all directions. This 'aggressive' expansion programme, as it was called by Ton Rottier, chairman of DSM's top management from 1962 to 1973, was complemented with a major revision of the company's organisation. According to Rottier, the transformation from coal and coke to chemicals not only entailed new products and new markets but also a different way of working. Top management considered decentralisation necessary, and in three steps DSM arrived at a divisional structure in April 1975. Production, marketing, accountancy and personnel matters became the responsibility of the divisions, but research remained centralised and became a so-called group service (*Concerndienst*), a department directly under the responsibility of DSM's top management. Knight Wegenstein, a Swiss consultancy firm, helped DSM complete its divisional design. In 1970, this consultancy firm had briefly considered the possibility of decentralising research (which would give each division its own research organisation and would make the divisions responsible for research management and funding), as well as the possibility of including research with the corporate planning department and Stamicarbon in a separate division. Both these options were rejected quickly because central research was considered to be more flexible and more creative.[9]

Six divisions were established in 1975: Chemical Products (caprolactam among others), Industrial Chemicals (which included Synres), Plastics (polyethylene among others), Plastics Processing (Curver and similar firms), Construction (which bundled DSM's participations in several construction companies), and Energy (DSM's activities in the exploration and exploitation of oil and natural gas, as well as other energy-related activities). In 1972, DSM's fertiliser activities had been merged with VKF, a Dutch fertiliser company, to form UKF (*Unie van Kunstmestfabrieken*), with DSM attaining a majority share. The Chemical Products division governed DSM's interests in UKF, but in January 1979 the fertiliser activities became an independent division and later that year DSM became the sole owner of UKF.[10]

Wim Bogers succeeded Rottier as chairman of DSM's top management in 1973 and energetically continued DSM's expansion and diversification. The Leap Forward was the final push in DSM's transformation from coal and coke to chemicals. Turnover from chemical activities jumped from 0.7 billion guilders in 1970 to 7.9 billion ten years later! Growth in several chemical markets slowed down after the 1970s, however. Many other companies also expanded, leading to overcapacity and strained profitability in the chemical industry. DSM's profits declined significantly after 1974, forcing the company to cut costs and economise.[11]

Re-Aligning Research and Business

The first half of the 1970s was a turbulent period: DSM changed internally, expanded on a major scale and faced a changed business climate. These changes also affected the Central Laboratory: it had to adapt its organisation to the company's emerging divisional structure, to cuts in the research budget, and to a different view of the role of research in diversification.

Organising Research in the 1970s

Although the Central Laboratory remained a corporate entity, the Large Leap Forward and the emerging divisional structure prompted the Central Laboratory to change its organisation. In 1972, the departmental structure was changed for the first time in order to align it with changes taking place in the company. Alongside the patent department, two main departments were created in which research was concentrated on chemical products (that is, fibre intermediates and fertilisers) and plastics, respectively. These two departments also became responsible for fundamental research, but generic research like analysis remained a separate department (Figure 4.1). Both research management and DSM's top management preferred this product-based organisation of research because they considered that it provided a better link between research, manufacturing and marketing than the old structure of the Central Laboratory. The new organisation also ended the existence of split groups. Catalysis, for instance, had been investigated in two Catalysis departments: one focused on applied work while the other conducted fundamental research. In practice, such borders proved fuzzy and caused confusion.[12]

In the reorganisation of 1972, the management and funding mechanisms of research remained unchanged. In 1968, Leo Kretzers took over the duties of Van Aken, who retired in that year, and became responsible for research. Kretzers had worked in caprolactam and had headed DSM's plastics production before being appointed to DSM's top management in 1967. He drew up the research programme together with Leen Revallier, DSM's R&D manager, and the heads of the central commercial and finan-

Figure 4.1. The Central Laboratory's organisation in 1972.

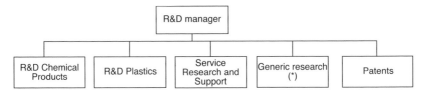

Source: Reorganisatie Sector Research en Octrooien. *DSM Nieuws* 1972, 21(5), 8.
(*): generic research included the analysis and process control groups, for instance.

cial departments. In principle, service research and process and product improvement work were paid by DSM's production units while all other research work was funded centrally. When the first steps in the direction of a divisional structure were taken, top managers of the divisions replaced the managers of the marketing and financial groups in the periodic meeting on research led by Kretzers. The exact distribution of responsibilities for research projects and their funding were repeatedly debated as divisional managers, particularly from the Plastics division, tended to focus research on marketing and production issues and hesitated to fund other research. In the structure DSM was implementing in the early 1970s, divisions became responsible for marketing and production, but not directly for research. The fundamental problem the company faced was how to preserve the link between centralised research and decentralised marketing and production.[13]

In the light of this problem, the organisation of the Central Laboratory was discussed again in 1974. Revallier, helped by DSM's corporate organisational efficiency department, organised a series of meetings with the heads of the divisions and units within the divisions, as well as with his own researchers. The divisions and the Central Laboratory rejected decentralisation of research, as they considered the scale of both research and manufacturing too small to make such an organisation work. Researchers saw little need to adjust the organisation again, but felt that more uniform communication with the divisions was necessary. The Central Laboratory worked with several internal coordinating mechanisms: the heads of departments or a project coordinator organised research's communication, depending on the scale and scope of the project. Within DSM's production organisation, the multiple coordination mechanism caused confusion about who acted as focal point and who was in charge, while the organisation also argued that these unclear lines of communication made research's input less effective. The Plastics division had decentralised much responsibility in units organised around one product and headed by a plant manager and a marketing manager. This left a void for input from

THE COMPANY THAT CHANGED ITSELF

research, and the Plastics division suggested appointing research managers that would participate in the management of its units. The Construction division already worked with a coordinator who also participated in the division's management meetings. This mechanism became the example for the creation of so-called directors of research (*werkgebiedmanagers*), whose job was to organise projects and communicate with the divisions. Together with divisional management, they determined the research budget and research programme for a division. They controlled these budgets, supervised the execution of projects and set priorities if necessary.[14]

Top management emphasised the importance of input from the directors of research in the management of the divisions and DSM's subsidiaries. They argued that six directors of research should be appointed: for fertilisers, organic products, plastics, plastics processing, construction and industrial chemicals. This corresponded to DSM's divisional structure. Only the Energy division was not represented, simply because no research was conducted in this area, while the UKF got its own director of research even though it was at that time still part of the Chemical Products division. Top management also argued that, to ensure their leverage inside research, the directors of research should be placed directly under Revallier and be part of the management of the Central Laboratory. Not every division funded the same amount of work, however, and only the Plastics division felt an immediate need for the introduction of directors of research. Revallier and top management agreed to appoint three directors of research directly under Revallier. Each director combined two of the six areas (fertilisers, now combined with organic products; construction, combined with industrial chemicals; and plastics, combined with plastics processing).[15]

In addition to the introduction of directors of research, the Central

Figure 4.2. Central Laboratory's organisation after implementation of the matrix.

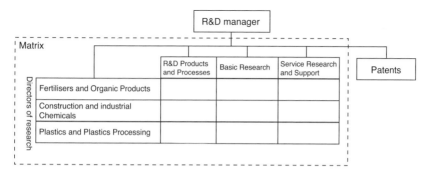

Source: Reorganisatie in fasen van de Concerndienst Research en Octrooien. Geleidelijke invoering van matrix-organisatie. *Nieuws DSM Limburg* 1976, 26(4), 6.

Laboratory's departmental structure also changed. The divisions positively evaluated research's effectiveness, but argued that it could be further improved. In their view, the heads of the Central Laboratory's departments focused too much on the performance of their own department. The Central Laboratory decided to separate research from control responsibilities. This principle, in combination with the newly-introduced directors of research, resulted in a matrix organisation. The directors of research formed the vertical axis of this matrix, while the horizontal axis was formed by two new departments oriented on the type of research work: a department for Product and Process Research and Development, which included research on both plastics and organic products; and a department for Basic Research, which included both fundamental and generic research[16] (Figure 4.2).

DSM's Corporate Planning department added another ingredient to the reorganisation: following the principle of decentralisation that had guided the decision to establish divisions, they argued that research management, broadly conceived to include patenting policies and issues of external research and buying technology, should be the primary responsibility of the divisions. With Revallier, they agreed upon a distribution of responsibilities. Outside the sphere of interest of each division, the Central Laboratory held responsibility for fundamental and generic research, and for long-range research aimed at diversification. This work would be funded at corporate level, but this funding would not exceed a third of the total research budget. Within the sphere of interest of each division, research would try to get approval for projects. This 'contract research' would include process and product improvement and service research, as well as diversification research when the goals of this research had crystallised out and the time horizons had shortened. In this way, a clear distribution of responsibility for research projects and their funding was agreed.[17]

The matrix organisation and the new funding structure were implemented in 1975 and 1976. The Central Laboratory also changed its name to CRO (*Concerndienst Research en Octrooien*, corporate research and patent department).[18] Research remained centralised, but CRO was not a corporate laboratory like Philips and RCA had, for instance. These companies had a centrally-funded corporate research laboratory, while divisions also operated and funded their own laboratories. In such organisations, the corporate laboratories often concentrated on long-range and/or fundamental research, while the divisional laboratories concentrated on short-term research and development work.[19] At DSM, CRO was a corporate department, but it was for a large part funded by the divisions. Moreover, CRO worked on the full range of the R&D spectrum. DSM's divisions had no R&D laboratories of their own.

The first evaluations of the matrix organisation and the directors of research in late 1977 and early 1978 were positive. According to divisional management, research had become less fragmented and budget estimates were more accurate. The structure of CRO's organisation was left unchanged in the second half of the 1970s. In 1978, however, Dick Tom was appointed head of CRO alongside Revallier. Tom had joined the Central Laboratory in 1953 and worked in the Organic Chemistry department. He started with application research in the Semi-Technical department in 1957 and became the head of the Plastics Technology department when it was formed in 1958. Tom had also led the polymer R&D sector from 1963 until 1969, when he was appointed head of DSM's Corporate Planning department. After Revallier's retirement in 1980, Tom became CRO's sole manager.[20]

Research and Diversification

Alongside the Central Laboratory's internal reorganisation, top management kept up the pressure to keep costs down throughout the 1970s. As early as 1971, the first economising programme started, focusing on personnel reduction as salaries made up most of the research costs. In two years' time the number of researchers declined from approximately 1,200 to 1,000 (see graph A1 in the appendix). Research expenditure as a percentage of turnover also declined sharply as DSM's turnover grew much faster than research expenditures in the 1970s (see graph A2 in the appendix).[21]

After 1970, the rapid growth of the Central Laboratory ended. The number of researchers declined and the research budget no longer kept up with the growth of DSM's turnover. Top management took a more critical view towards R&D in the 1970s than in the 1950s and 1960s. Their main aim was to make DSM market-driven, which translated into a preference for business-driven diversification realised through the acquisition of technology or companies. Revallier attempted to show in 1975 that research was more effective than acquisition by comparing the cost incurred in semi-technical and pilot plant work in projects that had, and had not, been commercialised in the period between 1950 and 1975 (Figure 3.13). He showed that DSM had spent slightly more on projects that had not been commercialised, but that the success rate of research was about 50%. Moreover, Revallier pointed to the profits of Stamicarbon, which covered roughly 72% of the costs of all projects. His figures also showed that DSM's sales from products manufactured with internally-developed processes ran up to 25% of the company's total sales. According to Revallier, this was a significant share that showed the importance of research.[22]

Revallier's analysis was to no avail. Top management focused on failed projects, not on successful ones, and emphasised that DSM had to expand immediately. This created time pressure that pushed the company further towards acquisitions of technology and companies.

There was yet another reason for the change of direction of DSM's research policy. In June 1970, a draft long-range plan for the Central Laboratory had been presented to Kretzers. Cees Bokhoven, who had worked in the field of catalysis and generic research for a long time but was appointed head of the support department in 1968, was part of the group who had written this draft. The long-term plan focused on research that should lead to new businesses. According to Bokhoven, many projects with this aim had failed in the preceding ten years. There were marketing problems, and the Central Laboratory had perhaps not acted in accord with DSM's business strategy; but Bokhoven also argued that improving externally-bought technology was the strong point of DSM's technological capabilities. He pointed out that urea and caprolactam had become successes while lysine and methionine had not.[23]

The failure of the lysine project had a significant effect on research aimed at diversification. Bokhoven was far from alone in his views. The presumed lack of marketing capabilities and the detachment of research from business strategy were recurring themes in policy discussions: research had been technology push and the lysine case had proven the fallacies of that approach. Opinions differed as to whether research had really diverged from business strategy before 1970, however. Some, including Kretzers, placed emphasis on the absence of a clearly formulated long-term company plan. The decreased effectiveness of research aimed at diversification was a shared view, and consequently buying plants or buying companies became an interesting option. The reduced risk and the better grip on construction costs were emphasised. Acquiring companies led to fast market entry and appropriation of marketing knowledge that could then be used to improve products and processes. Kretzers and divisional managers became the main voice of this policy.[24]

Compared to the research policies of the 1950s and 1960s, a somewhat more pessimistic view of the role of research in diversification developed in the 1970s. In the 1950s and 1960s, the Central Laboratory had played an initiating role as researchers were supposed to come up with ideas for innovation and diversification. Research had an independent position. In the 1970s, research was supposed to be market-oriented and closely aligned to the company's businesses. Diversification was initiated from outside the Central Laboratory. Research played a dependent role.

Research and Technology Acquisitions
Although the view of the role of research in diversification changed after 1970, research could still facilitate diversifications based on external technology. The Central Laboratory's role in the acquisition of technology was small, however. Researchers sometimes provided advice, for instance on the height of the stack for the acrylonitrile plant, but Chemiebouw and

Acrylonitrile plants, 1972. In the 1970s DSM bought technology to diversify and expand. The process used in DSM's acrylonitrile plants had been developed by the American company Sohio. Acrylonitrile is an intermediate for acrylic fibres but the compound, and the by-products released during its production, also stimulated fine chemicals research and production. The Central Laboratory also worked on improvements to the Sohio process.

the staff technologists of the production plants were crucial in the process of buying plants. Chemiebouw's name changed to Nieuwbouw at the end of 1967, but its tasks remained unchanged.[25]

For several of the plants that were based on external technology, process research was done. The Central Laboratory worked on boosting capacity of the acrylonitrile plants, for instance. DSM had built two plants with a design capacity of 90,000 tons in total. The Central Laboratory helped boost capacity to 140,000 tons, leading to a significant cost advantage. In the early 1970s, researchers developed a new catalyst for acrylonitrile manufacture as well. The initial results were promising, but DSM did not have a test reactor to investigate the new catalyst on a sufficiently large scale. Cooperation was sought with Sohio, the licensor of the process, and the Dutch chemical company Ketjen, which had the necessary test facilities, but neither of these firms were interested. The project was therefore stopped and in 1973 DSM bought the improved catalyst Sohio had developed.[26]

The development of a new catalyst for acrylonitrile manufacture was stopped, but this example does show that technology acquisitions and research are not mutually exclusive. Buying technology and subsequently trying to improve it by in-house industrial research had been established practice at DSM as early as the 1930s.[27] In acrylonitrile, the Central Laboratory was able to pick up research on the catalyst because it had much experience in this field. In-house research provided a crucial part of the absorptive capacity necessary to track, acquire and integrate external technologies.

A Redefinition of the Central Laboratory's Role
The 1970s were a period in which research and business interests had to be re-balanced in light of DSM's internal changes and in light of a changed business climate. DSM's expansion programme and the establishment of the divisions, as well as a slowdown of growth and intensified competition in the chemical industry, triggered a redirection of research. In the 1950s and 1960s, DSM's head of chemical production had not had a decisive say in the direction of research but in the early 1970s the balance of power shifted towards divisional management. The coordination of research through the triangle consisting of top management – head of production – head of the Central Laboratory was replaced by a structure that included the heads of the divisions. Given the circumstances they were facing and given the wish to expand rapidly, they pushed research towards a more dependent role. The changed funding mechanism further strengthened the position of the divisions. Finally, the failure of the lysine project led to reduced confidence in the powers of research to innovate and particularly in the powers of research to enable diversification.

In summary, economics, organisational change and diminished self-confidence resulted in a dependent role for research. These internal and external changes occurred roughly between 1969, when the lysine plant closed, and 1975, when both the divisions and the matrix organisation in research were established. The changes occurred fast, and more or less at the same time. Strategic reorientation entailed the expansion of existing businesses and the establishment of new businesses. In parallel, the structure of the company was changed, the role of R&D renegotiated, and the Central Laboratory reorganised.

The debate on the role and importance of industrial research was not unique to DSM. Many other companies were struggling with the same issue and many also cut their research budgets.[28] A combination of unfavourable economic circumstances and the idea that industrial research was becoming less effective in diversification are important factors that caused this shift. Basil Achilladelis, Albert Schwarzkopf and Martin Cines come to the same conclusion in a macro study of innovation in the chemical

industry. David Hounshell argues that the failure of many research programmes to come up with marketable products was an important cause
of the decline in research budgets in the United States in the 1970s.[29] At
DSM, organisational change further reinforced the change in research
policies, in line with what Graham and Pruitt have shown for Alcoa.[30]

DSM's Entry into Fine Chemicals

While DSM was expanding its chemical businesses, established divisions
and redefined the role of research, the Central Laboratory initiated a diversification that was to have crucial long-term effects on the company's
development. In contrast to research's dependent role, the Central Laboratory pushed DSM's entry into fine chemicals. DSM also took over a
company, but research played an important role in establishing a foothold
in this business. Lysine research, moreover, proved important for several
fine chemical products.

The Fine Chemicals Industry in the 1970s

DSM was not alone in selecting fine chemicals as an attractive business.
In contrast to the high volumes and low margins associated with bulk
chemicals, fine chemicals are high value-added products manufactured in
low volume. Like bulk chemicals, fine chemicals are specification products
and customers buy them because they have a certain chemical composition. Food additives, pharmaceuticals and agrochemicals are important
outlets for fine chemicals. Specialties, on the other hand, are performance
products that solve specific problems or address specific needs. Like fine
chemicals, they are often manufactured in low volume but with high margins and they are not very sensitive to cyclical highs and lows.[31]

Although the differences between the various types of chemical products are gradual, manufacturing and marketing fine chemicals and specialties and manufacturing bulk and pseudo-bulk chemicals are different
businesses. Plants for the manufacture of bulk chemicals are large, capital
intensive and dedicated (they typically produce only one product). Producers mainly compete on price, leading to a strong focus on cutting production costs through process improvements. Specialties, on the other hand,
are typically manufactured in small, less capital-intensive plants that may
produce a range of products (so-called multi-product or multi-purpose
plants). Extensive knowledge of customer needs and practical know-how
about the application of products is essential. Finally, fine chemicals are
somewhere between the extremes of bulk chemicals and specialties. Plants
have a low volume and can be continuous, but are often batch-operated
and sometimes several products can be manufactured with the same installation. Process technology is important, but so is knowledge of customer
needs and of applications.[32]

Despite the differences, the high margins of fine chemicals and special-ties attracted many bulk-oriented firms to these businesses. Like DSM, many companies suffered from strained profitability and many chose fine chemicals as part of their response. Unlike DSM, however, other chemi-cal companies often preferred to enter by acquiring specialised firms, a trend that continued well into the 1980s regardless of the problems many companies faced in integrating these companies and in maintaining their profitability.[33]

The Start of Special Products

In the late 1960s, several ideas for fine chemicals had been born at the Central Laboratory. Questions from other companies, and compounds that were used in the production of bulk chemicals, had provided oppor-tunities for the production of what was called 'kleine producten' (literally: small products). For instance, during the research on the separation of D- and L-lysine, a method had been worked out that used L-pyrrolidone carboxylic acid. Unilever was interested in using this compound as a food additive, and they approached DSM. Unilever bought 3.6 tons in 1968, indeed a small amount when compared to DSM's other businesses, but Unilever expected substantial growth.[34]

A group of researchers were of the opinion that fine chemicals got too little priority. In January 1969, they published a report with the aim of putting fine chemicals on the map. The report asked the question of whether the fine chemical activities were a 'hobby or a pillar' of the com-pany, and called for a systematic commitment and for the establishment of a separate group to initiate fine chemicals projects. The report took up DSM's Large Leap Forward strategy of expansion and diversification, arguing that fine chemicals could counterbalance the typical downward trend of market prices and cost prices in bulk chemicals and that a pas-sive attitude, focused on fine chemical compounds for captive use and on responding to occasional questions from other companies, would not provide the means to set up a fine chemicals business to the extent that it would contribute substantially to DSM's results.[35]

In April 1969, top management decided to devote 2.5 million guilders over two years to a new group for fine chemicals manufacture, taking over the name that the Central Laboratory had given to these activities: Small Products. The group started in October 1969 and operated from the facili-ties of the Organic Pilot Plant department of the Central Laboratory to obtain the necessary flexibility in production. Ruud Selman, and from 1971 Hans Bigot, managed the new group.[36] Selman, a son of Jan Selman, who had been operational director of the Central Laboratory, had joined DSM in 1963 to work in the caprolactam plant, and moved to Stamicarbon two years later. In 1971 he became general manager of Nypro, DSM's British caprolactam joint venture, and was succeeded as head of Special Products by Bigot, a researcher who had worked for the Central Laboratory since 1958 on caprolactam and on polymers, and who had research management experience.[37]

Top management intended to give the head of the sales office for coal and coke and the coordinator of chemical sales final responsibility for Small Products, but with the instruction to give the group much room to operate independently. Apparently top management saw fine chemicals as an experiment. The allocated budget was also small by DSM's standards.[38]

Besides the budget of 2.5 million guilders for two years, Small Products got permission to use equipment from the shut-down lysine plant and facilities from another plant that was not being used. Production staff also sold part of these plants as scrap to get some extra money. Utilities were tapped from the neighbouring caprolactam plant. Backed-up by recipe development at the Central Laboratory, Small Products started production. Among the first products were two proprietary catalysts, one for the production of cyclohexanone and another for polyethylene, which had been developed by the Central Laboratory and had also been manufactured by the research organisation on a semi-technical scale. The installation used to produce the catalyst for polyethylene manufacture was later adapted for the production of a number of oximes, used in agrochemicals amongst others, which became a substantial business in the 1970s.[39]

In 1971, Small Products was renamed Special Products and got permission to initiate dedicated investments. The group shared the personnel and some support services with the Organic Products group but remained independent. In 1975, Special Products became part of the Industrial Chemicals division.[40]

The Central Laboratory was very active in fine chemicals in the 1970s, as is reflected in the number of patent applications from that decade (Graph 4.1). Research played an important role in a number of major early fine chemicals diversifications. In the Dow phenol process, the oxidation of toluene to phenol proceeded via benzoic acid, but the oxidation product also contained benzaldehyde. Dow had pointed to the possibility of removing these compounds and built an installation for benzaldehyde extraction near its phenol operation in Kalama (Washington) in 1970.[41] Benzoic acid was mainly used in preservatives, with world production at about 30,000 tons by 1968, while benzaldehyde's applications included flavours, the largest market, and pharmaceutical products.[42]

At the Central Laboratory in 1962 and 1963, Bigot and a colleague studied the possibility of using benzoic acid as a starting point for a plasticiser for PVC. Contrary to initial tests at TNO, however, they found that their product could not match conventional plasticisers. In 1964, the Central Laboratory developed a method to purify benzoic acid from phenol pro-

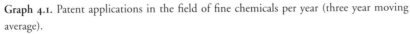

Data compiled by Wim Hoogstraten. Counted are so-called premier depots: the first patent application for a specific invention.

duction, starting from a patent by Dow. Marketing purified benzoic acid was not easy, however. The main market was in preservatives, and companies that manufactured these products often made their own benzoic acid. In 1965, CIR, DSM's Rotterdam phenol subsidiary, started to sell crude benzoic acid to the Dutch chemical company *Chemische Fabriek Naarden*, which processed it into preservatives and an additive for anti-freeze mixtures. CIR initially shipped about 2,000 tons of benzoic acid per year, increasing to almost 4,000 tons in 1981 with a share of the European market of almost 60%.[43]

With regard to benzaldehyde, CIR's production staff argued that recycling this compound was necessary to keep the oxidation reaction going, but research data showed that removal of most of the benzaldehyde in the recycle toluene stream did not have a negative effect on benzoic acid production. Special Products proposed extracting benzaldehyde and purifying it at DSM's main site in Geleen (Netherlands). Benzaldehyde could be produced more cheaply in this way than in conventional routes, and the project had a short pay-out time. Top management approved the construction of plants at CIR and at Special Products with a capacity of 1,500 tons of benzaldehyde per year. Production started around 1972 and sales volumes quickly rose to 4,656 tons in 1981, with a market share in Europe running up to 60%. Benzaldehyde showed the viability of Special Products and gave the group more leverage to deploy new activities.[44]

Besides research, other methods were also used to build up activities in fine chemicals. Selman studied import statistics and made visits to users of fine chemicals to see which products could be attractive. He visited Andeno for instance, a Dutch company active in the fine chemicals sector. Andeno manufactured intermediates for penicillin from phenylglycine among others, and this compound could be produced from ammonia, hydrocyanic acid and benzaldehyde, which were chemicals DSM had available. Hydrocyanic acid was a by-product from acrylonitrile production. The manufacture of phenylglycine was taken up in this way around 1972. Sales volumes rose to 728 tons in 1981, with a share of the world market running up to 40%.[45]

Through the initiative of the Central Laboratory, and supported by research in crucial ways, DSM entered fine chemicals. This role contrasts sharply with the Central Laboratory's dependent role in the 1970s, but production of benzaldehyde, phenylglycine and other fine chemicals was relatively small-scale. Special Products' activities were mostly spin-offs from the manufacture of bulk chemicals: either technologically, as in the case of benzoic acid and benzaldehyde; or commercially, as in the case of phenylglycine, where the availability of chemicals from bulk manufacture enabled Special Products to start production.

Lysine, Phenylglycine and Amino Acids

DSM's first forays into fine chemicals had been the lysine and methionine projects and, more generally, research into food and feed additives. These initial activities had not been successful, with the closure of the lysine plant as the most visible and most costly failure. Production of lysine by chemical synthesis was reconsidered several times in the first half of the 1970s when market prices rose. DSM talked with Allied Chemical in the United States and Degussa in Germany about possible cooperation.[46]

Research on lysine continued even after the closure of the lysine plant. In 1966, the Central Laboratory had started working on a route to lysine starting from acrylonitrile, a route on which Sohio, the company that licensed its acrylonitrile process to DSM, had done some research. Three years later, the Central Laboratory found a route to lysine from acrylonitrile and acetaldehyde via gamma-cyanobutyraldehyde but as the commercial outlook remained bleak, research was cut back in 1972. The cost of lysine produced with DSM's process was too high compared to fermentation processes. Research reached the conclusion that synthesising lysine was viable only when cost prices could be reduced by a breakthrough, but that the chances of achieving such a breakthrough were small. The separation of D- and L-lysine was identified as the crucial bottleneck in the process, and pioneering research aimed at simplifying or possibly omitting this step continued. In 1975, however, research on lysine was finally stopped completely.[47]

It seemed that a major research project of the 1960s came to a quiet end in this way, but research had taken a turn in the previous years. In the late 1960s, the Central Laboratory had invested in a Biological Testing Station where application research on lysine was done and where capabilities in biology were built. At this department, fermentation processes were also investigated for lysine and other compounds such as glutamic acid, a food additive that dominated the amino acid market in volume. In 1969, after the closure of the lysine plant, application research on lysine stopped. The Biological Testing Station, renamed Biology department, started to search for ways in which their knowledge could be made useful to DSM. Fermentation research continued, but on a small scale. Researchers considered this technology to be too far removed from DSM's core. On the other hand, the Biology department saw opportunities in research on the use of enzymes in organic chemistry: they reasoned that enzymes are biological catalysts, and that catalysts are of prime importance in the chemical industry. A few other companies, research institutes and universities were already active in this field. Some processes operated commercially. In Japan, for instance, Tanabe Seiyaku Co. had operated a process for the production of several L-amino acids since 1969. The main markets and applications of enzymes, however, were in detergents and dairy products among others. DSM was among the first companies to try applications in organic chemistry.[48]

In 1972, the Biology department became part of the large Chemical Products Research and Development department. The Pioneering Research section of this department, headed by Ottenheym, gave an extra input and impetus to the idea of researching enzymes. They proposed including phenylglycine. Like lysine, phenylglycine is an amino acid, and DSM in fact manufactured D,L-phenylglycine. Special Products' main customer for phenylglycine was Andeno, which had the technology to separate the D-configuration from this mixture, which was then sold to pharmaceutical companies for the production of penicillin. Separation was necessary as only the D-configuration was active against bacteria. Andeno worked with specific and complex technology that only worked for D,L-phenylglycine.[49]

Around 1975, researchers found a way to separate D-phenylglycine from the L-configuration by using an enzyme. Novo Industri A/S (now Novo Group) manufactured the necessary enzyme in a fermentation process that Novo and DSM optimised together. Novo was one of the largest manufacturers of enzymes in the world. DSM had approached the Dutch company Gist-brocades, another large manufacturer, but in their opinion the possibilities of using enzymes in organic chemistry were slim and they declined the offer.[50]

The new process for phenylglycine was a technological success but the production costs were high. Special Products would be competing with its main customer: Andeno. Andeno's parent company Océ-Van der Grinten, whose main line of business was reprography, contacted DSM's top management when Andeno got wind of DSM's work on D-phenylglycine. Océ hinted that Special Products' sales of D,L-phenylglycine to Andeno might be endangered. Special Products would then have to sell directly to manufacturers of penicillin. This reaction from Andeno and Océ, combined with the high production costs, ended the prospect of commercialising the enzymatic process.[51]

Research on the enzymatic separation of amino acids continued, although it was not commercialised in the manufacture of phenylglycine. Research was fundamentally orientated and CRO operated with a vision that the selectivity of enzymes would become an advantage in the fields of pharmaceuticals and agrochemicals. In amino acids, often only either the D- or L-configuration was active in a product, while the other was 'ballast' or could induce unwanted, and sometimes even harmful, side effects.[52]

The process underlying the production of phenylglycine could also be used for other amino acids, and the enzymatic separation method appeared to work for a range of these compounds. In this way, DSM had a generic process for the production of D- or L-amino acids. The process was operated on bench scale only because of the small size of the market. Glutamic acid dominated the amino acid market with a production volume of approximately 220-250,000 tons in 1977, followed by methionine with 100,000 tons and lysine with 30,000 tons. Specialty amino acids had a volume of about 100 tons but grew fast and commanded high prices. In this market, enzymatic methods had to compete with chemical and fermentation processes.[53]

Research again continued, and in the early 1980s the separation method was further refined and another enzyme was found that was applicable to a different range of amino acids. In 1987, top management approved the construction of a commercial scale plant, which came on stream a year later.[54]

As a result of the continuation of centrally-funded pioneering research on the separation of D- and L-lysine, research on this product eventually paid off. Lysine research had contributed crucially to the growth of a body of knowledge that could be used in the fine chemicals sector. This body of knowledge was expanded through the initiative of researchers to start research on enzymes; this initiative, too, sprang from the failed lysine project.

Lysine, Pyridine and Alpha-picoline
Besides amino acids, lysine research provided a stepping-stone to pyridine and alpha picoline. Pharmaceuticals and agrochemicals are important outlets for so-called heterocyclics like pyridine, the picolines and the lutidines.

The alpha picoline plant in 1977. This plant was Special Products' first major investment. CRO had developed the process, using spin-offs from lysine research. DSM had learnt from the lysine project, however, and construction of the alpha picoline plant did not start until a long-term sales contract had been concluded.

In the late 1960s, ICI was by far the largest customer of pyridine. The English company used it to manufacture Paraquat and Diquat, herbicides that were more environmentally-friendly than other contemporary products. By 1980, world use of pyridine and derivatives had passed 40,000 tons a year.[55]

Pyridine had traditionally been manufactured from coal tar. The American company Reilly Tar & Chemical Corporation produced the largest amounts of pyridine and related products, while in Europe the Swiss chemical company Lonza led the field. Other companies, including DSM in the 1960s, manufactured small amounts of pyridine out of coal tar from their coking operations. Only relatively small amounts could be produced from this source, however, and several companies investigated synthetic routes to pyridine and related families of compounds. Reilly Tar developed a method starting from acetaldehyde and ammonia. Other companies followed, and this type of process became the main synthetic route to pyridine and derivatives. By varying the conditions and starting materials of the process, several products could be produced, but by-products always resulted.[56]

The closure of DSM's coke oven plants would also mean the end of pyridine production, but in 1969 the Central Laboratory started to work on two alternative approaches to the synthesis of pyridine. The route to lysine that started from acrylonitrile proceeded via gamma-cyanobutyraldehyde.

THE COMPANY THAT CHANGED ITSELF

Figure 4.3. Simplified map of the potential paths from acrylonitrile to lysine, pyridine and alpha-picoline.

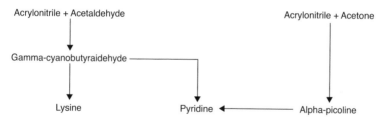

Jos Thoma, who had worked on lysine from acrylonitrile since 1966 and had been head of the Organic Chemistry department since 1969, also inspired research on finding other products from gamma-cyanobutyraldehyde, with pyridine as the main target. A second route to pyridine was investigated as well, starting from acrylonitrile and acetone and proceeding via alpha-picoline to pyridine (Figure 4.3). The main advantage of this process was the absence of by-products, and if another compound was used instead of acetone, other products could be produced by the same route. For instance, by switching from acetone to cyclohexanone, quinoline could be manufactured. This compound could be used to manufacture a decontaminant for seed for sowing. Research identified 2,3 lutidine as an interesting product; it could be used as an intermediate for nicotinic acid, a vitamin B.[57]

Research on pyridine was again technology push, a spin-off from research on the acrylonitrile lysine process. As early as 1970, however, market development work started. Special Products established contact with Lonza to explore the possibilities of selling 2,3 lutidine to the Swiss company. Lonza produced very large amounts of nicotinic acid and planned to expand capacity, but had not yet covered the supply of the necessary intermediates. Commercial Affairs estimated market volume for alpha-picoline at about 5,000 tons per year, with half of it used to manufacture a chemical that improved the bonding of tyre cords and rubber. Many firms produced both compounds and it would be difficult to gain an entry in the market for alpha-picoline because of this captive use. Commercial Affairs also probed the market for coumarin, used as an aroma in soap and perfumes, and quinoline. Special Products worked on a plan to manufacture 500 tons of quinoline, 100 to 200 tons of coumarin, and 300 tons of alpha-picoline per year in one plant. The process under development was continuous and manufacturing several products entailed switching feedstocks between production runs.[58]

Pyridine had by far the largest market volume, however. Commercial Affairs expected demand for pyridine to develop to 10,000 tons per year in the next three to five years because of ICI's growing sales of Paraquat and

Diquat. They established contact with ICI and the British company promised to evaluate DSM's pyridine process. DSM kept open the options of developing the process together with ICI or developing the process alone and then either licensing it to the British company or producing pyridine for them.[59]

Research found the route to pyridine via gamma-cyanobutyraldehyde difficult because of the instability of this intermediate. Pyridine from alpha-picoline was unattractive economically when compared to Reilly Tar's process. In 1971, ICI indicated that it did not want to switch suppliers and did not want to devote funds to developing the pyridine process together with DSM. This focused the Central Laboratory on the alpha-picoline process starting from acrylonitrile and acetone, with the possibility of manufacturing different products by replacing acetone by other compounds. As Lonza decided to enlarge in-house production of the intermediates it required, Special Products' plan to manufacture quinoline, coumarin and alpha-picoline gained momentum. Special Products probed the market for these and other compounds and made a new estimate of market volumes.[60]

The project to start manufacture of alpha-picoline and other compounds was Special Products' first major investment. Top management demanded guarantees that the output of the plant could be sold. For alpha-picoline, Special Products concluded a long-term contract with Dow, which used it in the production of agrochemicals, and top management then approved the construction of a plant in June 1973.[61]

Nieuwbouw engineered Special Products' new plant with a capacity of 3,000 tons per year. In one stroke, DSM became the third largest producer in the field of pyridine and related compounds in Europe, after Lonza and the European subsidiary of Reilly Tar.[62] By mid-March 1977, the plant was ready to be started up. This was done in phases, and the Catalysis section of the Central Laboratory assisted during start-up by testing the quality of the intermediate product for alpha-picoline. In July 1977, production of alpha-picoline started. Special Products made some 2,3 lutidine with the same plant and used it for producing pyridine 2,3-dicarboxylic acid, a compound for crop protection products. Switching feedstocks entailed cumbersome shutdown and start-up procedures, and alpha-picoline soon proved to be the most attractive product from a commercial point of view. The plant was therefore dedicated to this product. Sales of alpha-picoline rose to 2,434 tons in 1981, most of which went to Dow. Special Products had also captured 40% of the European market by that year.[63]

The relatively large scale of Special Products' entry into the production of alpha-picoline shows the fluidity between fine and bulk chemicals. Low volume at DSM meant a few thousand tons, which was low compared to the hundreds of thousands of tons of plastics and fertilisers DSM produced, but other fine chemical companies operated at lower volumes. What emerged as an alpha-picoline plant had in essence been a technology-push project like the cases of lysine and methionine. On the other hand, the research on pyridine, alpha-picoline and other compounds was a small-scale project. Market probes were conducted at an early stage in the project, and top management now wanted to see results from market development work before it committed DSM to investing in a multi-product plant. Special Projects was closely involved, securing a bridging mechanism between research and commercial interests. In this way, technology-push research could lead to commercial success.

Acquisitions: Bridging the Gap to Specialties?
Besides research, DSM tried other means to achieve the diversification it was aiming at in the 1970s. In fine chemicals, few possibilities existed to buy technology from engineering contractors or other companies, but several opportunities to acquire existing companies presented themselves. Philips Duphar, a Dutch company active in agrochemicals and pharmaceuticals, approached DSM twice with the possibility of a take-over. In 1973, top management, divisional management and Special Products agreed that Philips Duphar's profitability was poor and that it would take a major effort to match its activities with Special Products' profile. DSM therefore declined the offer. Two years later, Philips Duphar wanted to sell part of its activities in vitamins and intermediates for flavours to DSM, but was again turned down. Top management did not want to free the necessary funds, and argued that the activities that would be taken over from Philips Duphar would have to be moved to Geleen to make an optimal fit with DSM. Moving seemed impossible, however.[64]

In 1979, *Chemische Fabriek Naarden* offered its small Spanish benzoic-acid subsidiary for sale to DSM but was turned down on Bigot's advice. Instead, both companies reached an agreement by which DSM obtained *Naarden's* know-how for purifying benzoic acid and pharmaceutical-grade sodium benzoate in exchange for exclusive sales rights in a number of countries for *Naarden's* subsidiary *Jan Dekker*.[65]

Also in 1979, *Chemie Combinatie Amsterdam* CCA (now Purac), a company that made lactic acid and other sugar-based chemical products, went up for sale. CCA's parents, the Dutch sugar company CSM (*Centrale Suiker Maatschappij*) and the Dutch conglomerate HVA (*Verenigde HVA-Maatschappijen*), wanted to sell as CSM had sought other areas to diversify into, and as both owners thought that CCA's financial results were poor. CSM and HVA also expected that CCA would develop better as part of a chemical concern. CCA's parents talked to the German company *Benckiser Knapsack*, but CCA also approached DSM. Both top management and divisional management saw it as an opportunity to complement the work on enzymes and obtain industrial experience with fermentation technologies. CSM asked too much in the eyes of DSM, however, and top management expressed concerns about the profitability of CCA and the influence of European Community agricultural policies. For CCA, it mattered a great deal whether it could process sugar at world market prices or at the higher prices set by the European Community. Talks with *Benckiser Knapsack* also failed and CCA remained with CSM and HVA.[66]

In the 1970s, one acquisition attempt by DSM was successful. In 1975, contact was established with Chem-Y, a specialties company whose main line of business was surfactants and which was owned by the Dutch family De Jong. Surfactants have a broad range of possible applications, but the main markets are in consumer products in the areas of household cleaning and personal care. Surfactants (surface active agents) are added to these products to improve their characteristics. Added to shampoos, for instance, surfactants increase foaming. With 75 employees and sites in Bodegraven in the Netherlands and Emmerich in Germany, Chem-Y's turnover was about 16 million guilders in 1976. Its main market was in cosmetics, as De Jong also owned the cosmetics company Andrélon. In 1977, the possibility to buy Chem-Y took concrete shape when De Jong decided that they wanted to sell. Chem-Y had developed a plan to restructure production, closing the site in Bodegraven and expanding the installations in Emmerich.[67]

The head of the Industrial Chemicals division, of which Special Products was part, and Tom, at that time head of DSM's long range planning group, drafted a proposal to buy Chem-Y. They argued that the company had a good patent position, which illustrated its innovative capacity. They also showed that financial performance was very poor. Substantial losses were being incurred and would continue to be incurred in the years to come as Chem-Y's plants were outdated and too small, while the company's marketing function was not up to its task. Tom and the head of the division argued that Chem-Y was a 'threshold investment' DSM would have to make to enter the surfactants field. Expected growth for surfactants in several markets, increased scale and DSM's managerial expertise would lead to an improvement of Chem-Y's operations and its results. Top management agreed and also saw an opportunity to move Chem-Y to the south of Limburg. On DSM's scale, the sum involved in the acquisition and the subsequent investment in Emmerich was small, while on Special Products' scale, buying Chem-Y would boost sales volumes substantially. DSM formally acquired Chem-Y in December 1977 and grouped it under Special Products.[68]

Lack of synergy and lack of profitability had prevented the acquisition of Philips Duphar and CCA, but the same arguments did not prevent the acquisition of Chem-Y. It is also striking that, whereas companies oriented towards bulk chemicals often bought specialty companies not just to gain technical know-how of an unrelated business but also to gain marketing know-how, DSM's management considered Chem-Y's marketing inadequate. The takeover of Chem-Y was clearly a strategic move: a threshold investment necessary to enter an attractive field.

After DSM had bought Chem-Y, Nieuwbouw made a new plan for restructuring production, doubling Chem-Y's capacity. Production moved to Emmerich, but the staff department remained in Bodegraven. In 1980, the new plants were gradually started up, but they had cost more than twice the planned budget and suffered from many teething problems. Production of specialties relies on the possibilities of operators to formulate products, whereas Nieuwbouw had built a plant with a central control room, which is characteristic of bulk chemicals plants, but much less suitable for the flexible production of specialities. Moreover, Chem-Y's personnel were of poor quality and its research was limited and unrelated to DSM's research. CRO did little work for Chem-Y. The commercial synergy between Special Products' existing lines of business and Chem-Y proved to be meagre, as Chem-Y operated in very different markets.[69]

The technological and commercial problems led to poor results. In 1982, the management of Industrial Chemicals started a drastic reorganisation, focusing the company's product portfolio to improve its competitive position. Two years later, after attempts to divest Chem-Y had failed, Special Products put Chem-Y at arm's length so that it would not interfere with its own business.[70]

Lack of commercial and technological synergy and familiarity caused serious problems after Chem-Y had been taken over, but the same reasons had prevented the acquisition of Philips-Duphar and CCA several years earlier. Moreover, Nieuwbouw mismatched its own capabilities with the requirements of the Chem-Y expansion project. DSM found it difficult to adapt to the differences between bulk chemicals and specialties. In a lecture from 1984, Bigot argued that DSM's activities in fine chemicals could provide a bridge between bulk chemicals and specialties, but this turned out to be a rather optimistic view.[71]

Fine Chemicals in the 1970s: Hobby or Pillar?
The fine chemicals field was *en vogue* in the 1970s, and many bulk chemicals companies tried to improve their strained profitability by taking up activities in this sector of the chemical industry. The path DSM chose, however, is striking. In contrast to the dominant trend at DSM in the 1970s, research played an important role in the company's entry into fine chemicals. The Central Laboratory took the initiative to establish Special Products and provided the new group with several of its products. The establishment of the production of benzaldehyde and alpha-picoline, and

to a lesser extent also phenylglycine, was the result of in-house research work. The amount of research work done in the 1970s is also reflected in the number of patent applications in that period. (Graph 4.1.)

Moreover, whereas other companies relied primarily on acquisitions to enter fine chemicals, DSM relied primarily on research. The company had options for acquisitions, but did not use them, with the exception of Chem-Y – in which case, as with many of the acquisitions of specialty companies by bulk-chemicals-oriented companies, difficulties were encountered in adapting the different businesses to each other.

A striking feature of Special Products' development was that it profited from the lysine project. Not only was some equipment of the plant reused, but the knowledge accumulated through lysine research also paid off through activities of Special Products. Pisano's dual output model of R&D, where projects not only lead to immediate results but also to a build-up of knowledge and experience, is a fruitful way of looking at the lysine case. The research project failed, but contributed to the accumulation of capabilities in a particular field. Research on the separation of D- and L-lysine was broadened to phenylglycine and led to the development of a versatile process for the manufacture of several amino acids. The lysine project also provided a stepping-stone to the development of a pyridine synthesis and subsequently for the alpha-picoline process.

The failure of lysine research from a project point of view had a strong effect on the research policies of the 1970s, but the secondary effects of this research played no role in the policy debate, and they are also underestimated in the historical literature on DSM. By focusing on the project and the plant, historians have neglected the contribution of lysine to the build-up of DSM's capabilities in the fine chemicals sector.[72]

One reason why the spin-offs from the lysine project have not been noticed, and why research could play an important role in fine chemicals development at DSM in contrast to its generally dependent role in the 1970s, is that fine chemicals were of relatively minor importance for DSM as a whole. Special Products' turnover amounted to 1 million guilders in 1971 and rose to 91 million in 1981; in several products the group had large market shares. This growth was in itself spectacular, but in 1981, turnover in fine chemicals had grown to just 1% of DSM's turnover in chemicals. Special Products occupied a niche.[73]

Environmental Concerns: Research into Waste Water Treatment in the 1970s

The example of DSM's fine chemical sectors shows that research remained an important driver of the company's development. In the 1970s, moreover, it became clear that research could also be important to adapt to the changing circumstances DSM had to operate in. One of the best examples of this mechanism is environmental research. To some extent this type of research overlapped with the aims of process improvements, but an increased consciousness of environmental problems, both inside DSM and in Dutch society, was driving environmental research in the 1970s. Environmental research, moreover, overlapped with research in fine chemicals.

DSM had already been active in the field of environmental research before 1970. In 1958, a researcher from the company's safety department was assigned to research aimed at reducing air and water pollution caused by chemical plants. One of the activities was to follow water quality in the river Maas, one of the major rivers in the Netherlands and DSM's outlet for waste water. At that time, the Central Experimental Station had a department for combating pollution from DSM's mining operations. In 1964, DSM also took a so-called Pasveersloot into operation for the treatment of waste water from the company's chemical plants. Developed by TNO's engineer Aale Pasveer in the 1950s, these installations consisted of an oval-shaped ditch where bacteria broke down organic compounds. Rotors kept the water moving and supplied the bacteria with the oxygen that they needed to decompose the pollutants in the waste water. DSM built a relatively large Pasveersloot.[74]

In 1966, DSM's environmental research was concentrated in a new department of the Central Laboratory. Here the study of water quality continued, but research also started into the processes which took place in the Pasveersloot. Such activities led to a gradual increase in capacity and to a new system to supply oxygen to the bacteria.[75]

In the late 1960s, government regulations and interventions also became an incentive to do environmental research, particularly in relation to waste water from DSM's chemical plants. In 1968, Rijkswaterstaat, the government body responsible for roads and waterways, made it clear that the level of pollution in the river Maas was unacceptable. In the early 1970s, this was translated into clear objectives. The Maas, and particularly pollution by nitrogen compounds, was targeted. DSM was responsible for 25% of this pollution and was forced to reduce this level significantly.[76]

The Central Laboratory's research was an important stepping-stone in meeting the more stringent waste water pollution standards. In 1968 a four-step waste water treatment system was worked out on laboratory scale. This system broke down not only organic compounds but also nitrogen compounds. Research into the water quality of the Maas had shown that nitrogen compounds were important pollutants, but that they were not removed from waste water through processing in the Pasveersloot. This research finding, coupled to the Dutch government's actions in the early 1970s, prompted DSM to build a new, large-scale waste water treatment installation. In the late 1960s, the process was developed to semi-technical scale, an intermediary step between laboratory scale and the capacity of a dedicated pilot plant. During this phase of the research, it became clear that a three-step system might suffice. A dedicated pilot plant came on stream in September 1972. Several years of research followed, aimed at optimising the process design. In addition, tests were conducted with high levels of pollution, which might occur when there were major problems in one of the production plants. In October 1977 the first part of the new waste water treatment plant was put on stream. By July of the following year, the installation worked to full capacity and the Pasveersloot was taken out of service.[77]

The research into waste water treatment and the construction of the new plant were only part of the work done in the 1970s to reduce pollution from chemical plants. The emissions of nitrogen oxides from the nitric acid plants and from the manufacture of ammonium nitrite for the synthesis of caprolactam, which caused brown-coloured fumes from the stacks and was a very visible form of pollution, were reduced and other measures were also taken to reduce emissions from fertiliser production.[78] Near the new cracker for the production of ethylene, installations were built to remove particular compounds from the plant's effluent which caused a bad smell when the effluent was processed in the new waste water treatment plant.[79]

The Central Laboratory's environmental research was also linked with fine chemicals. In 1973, the environmental research group merged with the Biology department, where research on enzymes was done. DSM's waste water process was essentially a biological process as bacteria decomposed the pollutants. The Biology group improved the understanding of the decomposition process, research that continued after the new waste water processing installation had started. Moreover, the merger of the two groups initiated research on using enzymes to decompose urea and melamine in waste water. Processes were worked out but not commercialised. In the case of urea, the enzymatic method had advantages over chemical routes. In the case of melamine, research found an enzyme to decompose this compound, which was something new, but the enzyme proved difficult to manufacture.[80]

The primary objectives of environmental research were complemented with subjects that were important for the long-term development of DSM through the merger of the Biology group and the environmental research unit. The research on waste water treatment touched upon the burgeoning field of biotechnology and research on the separation of D- and L-amino acids with an enzyme also related to this field. By the early 1980s, the use of enzymes as catalysts in chemical processes had emerged as a spearhead of biotechnology research.

Urea: Beyond Major Process Improvements

Research efforts triggered by environmental concerns reflect the role of research in responding to threats. But the Central Laboratory also continued to work on existing products and technologies to maintain and improve DSM's position. By 1970 the urea stripping plant had been on stream for three years, but corrosion remained a problem and the stripper had to be replaced in 1973. The Central Laboratory mounted a major effort to combat the problems and focused in particular on selecting the right materials for the construction of strippers.[81]

The stripping plant had been built not only to increase production of fertiliser grade urea but also to feed DSM's production of melamine. Research on the possible integration of urea and melamine production started in 1967, and integration proved to be a viable idea. In 1970, a combined extension of melamine and urea production came on stream.[82]

Such integration was also tried between ammonia and urea. Engineering contractors such as the Italian company SNAM Progetti, which had circumvented DSM's patents on the stripping process by using ammonia instead of carbon dioxide as a stripping agent, pushed the integration of ammonia and urea processes. They hoped for reductions in costs through increased energy efficiency. The Central Laboratory took up research in 1967. Kaasenbrood thought that integrated production of ammonia and urea would become the next step in the reduction of production costs. The SBB, responsible for manufacturing urea, saw few advantages. They argued that the reduction in costs was too small and that far-reaching integration of ammonia and urea production reduced flexibility. Research was stopped in 1970 when Stamicarbon came to the conclusion that an integrated process would be hard to license to other companies.[83]

Research on urea mostly focused on issues related to operational problems in DSM's stripping plants and in the plants licensed by Stamicarbon, and as such contrasted with the work of the previous decades. What research saw as the next step in urea manufacturing, integrated production with ammonia, did not get off the ground as the manufacturing organisation and Stamicarbon were not interested.

Two factors combined to cause this shift in urea research. The efficiency of the stripping process was already quite high, limiting the effectiveness of further improvements. Technological maturity in this sense played a role but other companies continued to improve their processes. The position of DSM's fertiliser activities was also important. An overcapacity crisis in the late 1960s pushed DSM to rethink its fertiliser strategy. DSM expected the fertiliser industry to develop on a global scale as technology was freely available from many sources. New entrants in regions closer to the most important markets, and with access to cheaper feedstocks, would capture large parts of export markets. DSM focused on the European market, where calcium ammonium nitrate was the main fertiliser rather than urea, as well as other outlets for urea, including melamine. VKF made a similar analysis of its position on export markets, and initiated the merger with DSM's fertiliser activities that resulted in UKF. The new company indeed redirected its efforts to the European market, and consequently gave urea and urea research less emphasis. The problems continued for UKF in the 1970s, however, with rising costs and eroding market positions.[84]

In retrospect, the analysis made by DSM and VKF at the end of the 1960s proved to be correct in outline. The oil shocks of the 1970s prompted countries in the Middle East to start petrochemical production. They produced fertilisers from cheap and abundant supplies of natural gas and, because they lacked a home market, exported most of their production. The Middle East's share of world production remained modest in the 1970s and beyond, but because of its export orientation this region posed an increased competitive threat to Western Europe, where the traditional export-oriented fertiliser companies were located. Moreover, India, and above all China, the two largest fertiliser export markets, embarked on a programme of plant construction. China remained a net importer of fertilisers but the amounts declined significantly. For Western European companies like DSM, fertiliser export markets became much more difficult and UKF responded by focusing on the European market. Having been the growth fertiliser of the 1950s, urea got into a position of stagnation by the early 1970s. Urea research reflected this development.[85]

The Development of the HPO Caprolactam Process

The problems on the fertiliser market also had their effect on the production of caprolactam, in which substantial amounts of ammonium sulphate by-product were released. Like urea, ammonium sulphate had to be exported and this became increasingly difficult during the 1970s. Urea, moreover, competed with ammonium sulphate. Its nitrogen content was almost twice that of ammonium sulphate, which meant that transportation costs were significantly lower when calculated on the basis of the amount of nitrogen.[86]

The Central Laboratory had long recognised the threat to caprolactam of ammonium sulphate by-product. The caprolactone process was free from by-product and by 1965 was the most important alternative route to caprolactam the Central Laboratory was working on. Researchers, however, considered that the caprolactone process would be difficult to develop and therefore would take time. As a second-best option, the Central Laboratory worked on a process that later became known as the HPO process and that reduced the amount of by-product ammonium sulphate rather than eliminating it. After the failure of the caprolactone project, HPO moved to centre stage.[87]

DSM's HPO plant for the manufacture of caprolactam in 1977. The HPO process was an important technological breakthrough that reduced the amount of by-product (ammonium sulphate). It also was the first of DSM's internally developed technologies that was not used in the company's own plant first.

Ammonium Sulphate and the Central Laboratory: Research on the HPO Process

In 1956, the Central Laboratory started working on what was later to become the HPO process. Research basically focused on finding a new way to manufacture hydroxylamine. DSM's caprolactam process was essentially a variant of IG Farben's technology. Hydroxylamine sulphate was produced from ammonium nitrite and sulphur dioxide, reacted with cyclohexanone to cyclohexanone oxime, which in turn was rearranged to caprolactam with oleum (see figure 3.6). The preparation of cyclohexanone oxime and its rearrangement led to substantial amounts of ammonium sulphate (per ton of caprolactam, about 2.7 tons in the first step and approximately 1.8 tons in the second).[88]

In 1951, BASF started working on a catalytic route to hydroxylamine by reacting nitric oxide with hydrogen, the so-called nitric oxide reduction process, and in 1956 it was able to start up a plant. The American firm Spencer Chemical Company was working on a comparable process that catalytically reduced nitric acid with hydrogen to hydroxylamine nitrate. Both processes kept the rearrangement section of the conventional route

Figure 4.4. Outline of the Spencer process as worked on by the Central Laboratory.

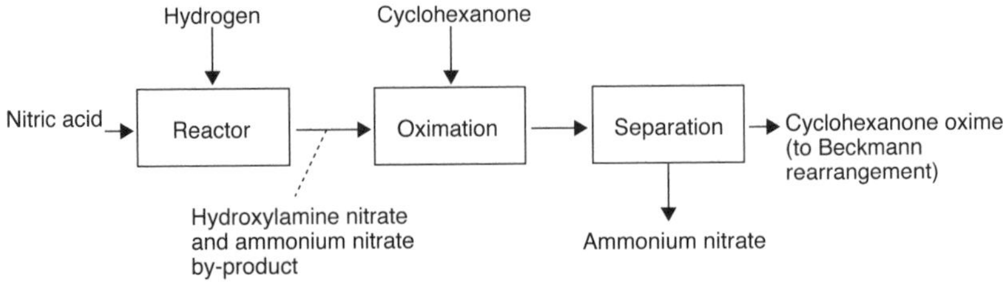

Sources: Central Laboratory annual reports 1958, 1961.

to caprolactam intact, including the by-product stream from that section. BASF's process substantially reduced the amount of by-product from hydroxylamine preparation, however. Spencer's process led to ammonium nitrate as a by-product, used as a fertiliser in the United States and an intermediate for calcium ammonium nitrate. BASF's chemistry was simpler but the company had fortified its process with many patents and followed a restrictive licensing policy.[89]

DSM and Spencer had been in contact with each other since 1954, and struck a deal for the exchange of know-how in 1957. DSM would supply Spencer with its caprolactam and nylon salt technologies, while Spencer would supply DSM with know-how related to the ICI polyethylene process (see also chapter 3). Spencer's hydroxylamine process remained outside this exchange. Nevertheless, the Central Laboratory started research on it in 1956. The Organic Products department established that the reduction of nitric acid opened the possibility to change the by-product from ammonium sulphate to ammonium nitrate (see figure 4.4 for an outline of the process the Central Laboratory worked on). In this way, Spencer's process opened up the possibility to switch from ammonium sulphate to calcium ammonium nitrate, the common nitrogen fertiliser in the Netherlands and in Europe. In other words, Spencer's process opened up the possibility to switch to a more valuable by-product than ammonium sulphate. Although there were no immediate problems with the sale of ammonium sulphate at that time, researchers expected that this would change as caprolactam production would increase, and considered the dependence on exports risky.[90]

In 1957 the project switched to the Inorganic Products department, and a year later Herman de Rooij, who had just graduated from Delft Technical College (now Delft University of Technology), was put on the project. Research stopped in 1961 when an evaluation by production staff showed that the nitric acid reduction process was too expensive compared to the conventional route and that it produced large amounts of calcium ammonium nitrate: about 1.9 tons of calcium ammonium nitrate would be produced per ton of caprolactam alongside the 1.8 tons of ammonium

Figure 4.5. Simplified scheme of the HPO process of 1963.

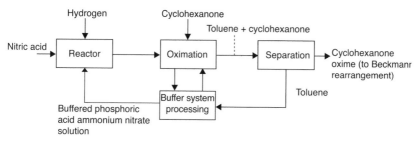

Sources: J. Damme, J. T. van Goolen & A. H. de Rooij (1972). Cyclohexanone Oxime Made Without Byproduct $(NH_4)_2SO_4$. *Chemical Engineering* (10 July 1972), 54-55. A. H. De Rooij, C. Dijkhuis & J. T. J. van Goolen (1977). A Scale-up Experience: The DSM Phosphate Caprolactam Process. *Chemtech* 7(5), 309-315. Figure 5, 311.

sulphate from the rearrangement section. Technological problems centred around the catalyst and around methods to integrate the reduction of nitric acid in the conventional route to caprolactam.[91]

After the negative evaluation by caprolactam production staff, this staff, the Central Laboratory and Chemiebouw together reached the decision to stop research on the reduction of nitric acid. They also decided, however, to formally take a license on the Spencer patents as 'an insurance' to keep open the possibility of using this process. In 1961, Van Waes initiated licensing negotiations with Spencer Chemical, and a year later top management eventually decided to formally take out a license.[92]

Although research on the Spencer process had officially been cancelled, De Rooij continued to work on it because he believed that a solution to the problems could be found. He also realised that an explosion might be possible if the concentration of nitric acid became too high, so the process was unsafe. In the summer of 1963, De Rooij made a breakthrough. He proposed making hydroxylamine and cyclohexanone oxime in a buffered system that would prevent an explosion and opened a way to solving the technological problems (Figure 4.5). Because of the buffer system, neutralisation with ammonia as in the conventional caprolactam process was not necessary but the preparation of hydroxylamine and cyclohexanone oxime would have to be integrated. This led to two recycle streams: of the buffer system, and of cyclohexanone oxime and its solvent toluene. De Rooij transformed the once-through Spencer process with ammonium nitrate by-product in a two-recycle stream process with no by-product.[93]

The main advantage of the new process was that it cut the amount of by-product from caprolactam production. In the conventional process, the 2.7 tons of ammonium sulphate formed during the preparation of cyclohexanone oxime accounted for 60% of the total amount that was produced. De Rooij's process became known as the Hydroxylamine Phosphate Oxime (HPO) process and later as the Low Sulphate Process as well. The process also had an environmental advantage: since ammonium nitrite, one of the starting materials for the production of hydroxylamine in the conventional process, was no longer necessary, the air pollution resulting from the nitric oxides released during the production of this compound was eliminated.[94]

Semi-technical research started in 1964, very soon after De Rooij's breakthrough. The Central Laboratory built a mini plant, a pilot plant at the smallest possible capacity to save costs. The recycle loops were omitted and only the preparation of hydroxylamine and cyclohexanone oxime were developed to semi-technical scale. The mini plant was operated until the end of 1969. A method had to be developed to remove the catalyst from the reaction product in which it was suspended. Activation of the catalyst also posed a problem, but this could be solved by adding germanium (a procedure later known as the 'germanium shot'). The Central Laboratory's Catalysis section played a crucial role here.[95]

The reduction reaction still gave a small amount of ammonium nitrate by-product which proved difficult to remove because of its high solubility. There were also problems with the necessary purity of the nitric acid. In 1966, De Rooij came up with the idea of supplying nitrate to the process through a conventional combustion of ammonia, commonly used for the production of nitric acid, which destroyed the by-product at the same time. With this idea, the process had taken on its definitive shape (Figure 4.6).[96]

The development of the HPO process illustrates the often far from straightforward routes research takes. Without De Rooij's unofficial continuation of research, the process would not have been developed at all. Moreover, the HPO process was at first only a medium term, temporary solution as long as the caprolactone process remained under development. After the failure of the caprolactone project, however, HPO gained in importance. Andries Sarlemijn and Marc de Vries have called this 'the piecemeal rationality of R&D', arguing that the individual steps in a process that eventually leads to an innovation may be managed rationally, but the overall innovation process often cannot. From step to step, the circumstances change, as do the targets and the problems the innovation is supposed to solve.[97]

Ammonium Sulphate and Stamicarbon: Selling the HPO Process
Around 1970, the fears that had prompted the Central Laboratory to start research on methods to reduce by-product ammonium sulphate formation became a reality. Periodically, large stocks of ammonium sulphate accumulated because of marketing problems. In 1969, a committee representing

Figure 4.6. Simplified scheme of the HPO process of 1966.

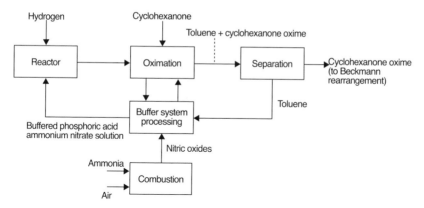

Sources: J. Damme, J. T. van Goolen & A. H. de Rooij (1972). Cyclohexanone Oxime Made Without Byproduct $(NH_4)_2SO_4$. *Chemical Engineering* (10 July 1972), 54-55. A. H. De Rooij, C. Dijkhuis & J. T. J. van Goolen (1977). A Scale-up Experience: The DSM Phosphate Caprolactam Process. *Chemtech* 7(5), 309-315, in particular figure 5, 311.

the SBB, Commercial Affairs, production staff and other departments, but not the Central Laboratory, started a study into the ammonium sulphate problem. The committee reported its conclusions in March 1970. DSM was already using ammonium sulphate in the production of nitro phosphates, but increasing production of mixed fertilisers was unattractive as DSM did not have a strong commercial position in this type of fertilisers.[98] Commercial Affairs argued that additional production would have to be exported, to the very markets where problems with ammonium sulphate were being encountered, and thereby would only shift the problem from one product to another. They also saw few opportunities to sell ammonium sulphate to companies that would blend it into their own mixed fertilisers. The committee started working when the market for ammonium sulphate was oversupplied, but they expected that this would change. They argued that if the production of ammonium sulphate had to be reduced, the HPO process would be attractive, but that the time for such a reduction had not yet come. The committee calculated the minimum earnings for ammonium sulphate below which prices had to fall before measures were needed to reduce production of this by-product: this minimum price was not yet in sight.[99]

The circumstances on the caprolactam market did not favour a rapid introduction of the HPO process either. Although production volume still grew after 1970, it grew slower than in the 1950s and 1960s (Graph 4.2). Moreover, regional shifts in production and competition between several types of fibres reshaped the industry after 1970 (Graphs 4.3 and 4.3). Price

Graph 4.2. World man-made fibre production, 1950-1990.

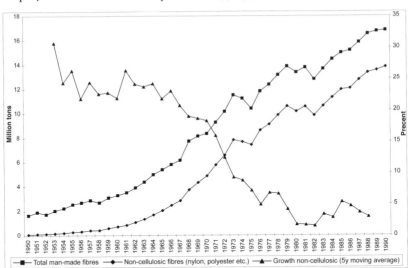

cuts of cotton and other natural fibres stiffened the competition between natural and (semi-)synthetic materials. Polyester, moreover, grew fast and increasingly took market share, while nylon grew much more slowly. Carpets and other furnishings, as well as textiles, accounted for the major share of the market for nylons. The Western textile industry suffered from low-cost competition from the developing regions of the world, and the same type of competition was also affecting fibre production. The traditional fibre-producing countries and regions, the United States, Europe and Japan, were faced with declining market shares, while the rest of Asia increasingly established itself as the region of man-made fibre production (including cellulose-based fibres such as rayon). AKZO, still DSM's major customer for caprolactam, and other European fibre producers suffered in particular from the changing structure of the fibre and fibre-consuming industries. Their plants operated below design capacity and profitability was poor.[100]

DSM felt the changes in the fibre industry indirectly. Production management, and also DSM's top management, concluded that introduction of the HPO process was not necessary. If markets were to grow, debottlenecking would provide the means to expand production.[101]

Stamicarbon, however, took a different position. In the late 1960s, the urea stripping process and other fertiliser technologies accounted for most of Stamicarbon's business (see graph A3 in the appendix) but they were looking for other opportunities as well. Besides melamine, caprolactam seemed to offer such an opportunity, and Stamicarbon actively tried to market the conventional caprolactam process and the HPO process.[102]

Stamicarbon came into contact with Montedison, the company that

Graph 4.3. World synthetic fibre production per type of fibre.

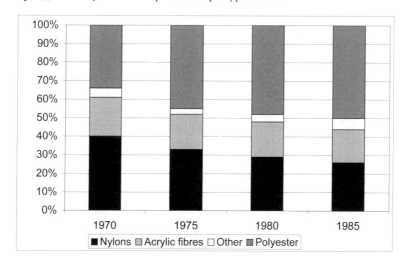

Graph 4.4. World nylon production per region.

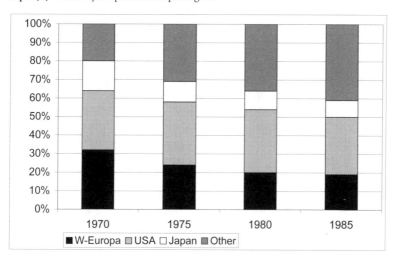

Source: B. von Schlotheim (1987). Märkte entwicklen sich auseinander. *Chemische Industrie* 39(4), 25-32, in particular table 3 (for graph 4.3) and 4 (for graph 4.4), 28.

had been formed as a result of the merger between Montecatini and Edison in 1966, who were seriously interested in licensing the HPO process, and Stamicarbon also managed to interest the Japanese company Ube. DSM's caprolactam joint ventures in the United Kingdom and the United States also showed an interest in the HPO process. These joint ventures had been set up in the late 1960s when DSM started to seek internationalisation. In the United Kingdom, Nypro, a joint venture between DSM and the British company Fisons Fertilisers, put its first caprolactam plant on stream at Flixborough in 1967. In the United States, Pittsburgh Plate Glass and DSM had established the Colombia Nitrogen Corporation at Augusta (Georgia) in 1962 for the production of nitrogen fertilisers, but started manufacturing caprolactam in June 1966 in a joint venture called Nipro. In 1970 this company became fully owned by DSM.[103]

After intensive contacts, Montedison decided not to buy the HPO process. The Italian company was working on its own technology as well and thought that this would be better than DSM's process. In 1969, Nypro decided to build an HPO plant. Fisons had a share of 24% in Nypro and held responsibility for sales of by-product ammonium sulphate. In 1968, DSM decided that it wanted to expand caprolactam capacity as the British market was still growing. Fisons refused to guarantee sales of the additional ammonium sulphate, however, making the introduction of the HPO process attractive. DSM also approached the National Coal Board (NCB), which had interests in fertiliser manufacture through its coke interests and could also provide an outlet for by-product ammonium sulphate from Nypro. The NCB also had a benzene plant and could supply feedstock for Nypro's cyclohexane oxidation plant. The NCB became a partner in the joint venture in 1969.[104]

Nypro's decision to build an HPO plant helped Nipro in the United States and Ube to reach the same decision. Ube and Nipro also faced problems with the disposal of ammonium sulphate. At DSM's production site in Limburg (the Netherlands), production staff decided in 1973 to introduce the HPO process. Although caprolactam sales were still stagnating, production management and top management expected demand to increase in the near future. The problems with selling ammonium sulphate had also worsened to the point that they could no longer be ignored. A plant would be built with a capacity of 70,000 tons of caprolactam per year, bringing total capacity to 190,000 tons. Of the capacity of the new installation, 40,000 tons represented an expansion and the other 30,000 tons a rationalisation. The cyclohexane oxidation unit, where cyclohexanone was manufactured, was closed in 1975 and all caprolactam became phenol-based. In September of the following year, the new HPO plant went on stream. Existing facilities were used for rearrangement and purification (see table 4.1. for an overview of the first HPO plants).[105]

The Central Laboratory had initiated research on Spencer's nitric acid reduction process without any commitment and participation from the production organisation. DSM had no integrated strategy in caprolactam: the Central Laboratory, Stamicarbon, production staff as well as Nypro and Nipro all developed their own views on the attractiveness of the HPO process. While research continued to push the development of new

Table 4.1. The first HPO plants.

Company	Decision	On stream	Capacity (tons/ year)
Nypro (UK)	1969	1973	50,000
Ube Industries	1970	May 1972	50,000
Nipro (US)	1970	June 1972	50,000
DSM	1973	1976	70,000
Nipro (US), 2nd unit.	1974	1977	70,000

Sources: J.T.J. van Goolen, 18 January 2005. New Construction. *Chemical & Engineering News* (8 June 1970), 21. DSM's caprolactamkennis vindt wereldwijd toepassing. *DSM Magazine* (9, September 1975), 9-10. HPO-fabriek van Groep Organische Producten in bedrijf genomen. *DSM Limburg Nieuws* 1976, 26(17), 1, 2. *Stamicarbon Reference List* 1 February 1985, 12. H. Strijkers (1992). *Veertig jaar caprolactam bij DSM*. DSM. 11, 12, 14, 15, 16.

processes, Production saw itself confronted with stagnating market growth. Rationalisation and defending existing market positions gained priority over expansion and thereby reduced the chances for the introduction of a new process; in fact the HPO extension and rationalisation programme was the only major increase in capacity in Geleen in the 1970s. In the 1950s and 1960s, markets had grown so fast that major expansions of capacity were periodically needed, which provided a chance for new technology.

The First Plants
As Stamicarbon generated interest in the new process and as the mini plant stopped, research continued. The first HPO plants had capacities of 50,000 tons a year, but in the research stage a smaller capacity had initially been foreseen. Building plants at smaller capacities was not viable, however, because the HPO process had to be integrated with existing facilities for rearrangement and purification. The new plants also had to compete with established large plants, making the prospect of a small HPO plant economically unattractive.[106]

Moreover, the reactor where hydroxylamine was formed in the mini plant was equipped with a mechanical stirrer, but for technical and economic reasons this was considered to be unattractive for the large scale of industrial plants. The Central Laboratory opted for a bubble column design, a type of reactor where the reactants are not mixed by mechanical means but by blowing bubbles in the column. Generic research was being conducted on this type of reactor at that time. Experiments were done on a model, but the scale-up factor was large. Research on an intermediary scale was too expensive, however, and confidence was high.[107]

The so-called Little Hyam, an installation built in 1970 for catalysis research in relation to the HPO process. An improved catalyst was developed here.

Similarly, the oximation section was changed. Initially it took place in a number of vessels in series but the Central Laboratory's Technology department, part of the generic research effort where researchers worked on equipment, unit operations and other generic process technology related issues, designed a custom column (the so-called pulsed-packed column), which simplified oximation. Both the bubble column and the pulsed-packed column show how generic research, a field in which the Central Laboratory invested heavily after the Second World War, played an important role in a concrete project.[108]

Finally, De Rooij had developed the idea of breaking down ammonia with nitric oxides in 1966, but the decision to use this idea in the plants was taken after the mini plant had been stopped. Although this change crucially affected the recycle streams in the process, it could not be studied on mini plant scale. Laboratory tests were done, however, as well as tests in an industrial nitric acid column at the SBB.[109]

Stamicarbon made the process design on the basis of mini plant work and additional research. Ube started the first HPO plant and soon ran into trouble. Contaminations accumulated and poisoned the catalyst. The extent and type of the contaminations had not been seen in the mini plant,

        THE COMPANY THAT CHANGED ITSELF

mainly due to the later change in the handling of by-product ammonia in the process. Frequent sampling in the mini plant had also prevented large accumulations of contaminations. The HPO process required excellent operators and operating procedures. Regular processing improved performance, but Ube's plant, followed by Nypro's and Nipro's plants, did not reach their design capacity. In 1970, the Central Laboratory had started a new, smaller, semi-technical installation to continue research on the HPO process. The Catalysis section had developed an improved catalyst to boost performance of the process. This improved catalyst was used to reach the designed capacity of the first HPO plants.[110]

In 1973, a year after initial start-up, Ube's plant made the test run, a common contractual obligation meant to show that the plant lived up to the specifications detailed in the contract. The plant completed the test run successfully. This demonstrated the viability of the HPO process and showed that the problems with the plants of Nypro and Nipro could be solved in principle. The successful test run also boosted confidence of DSM's divisional and top management and was the final push that made DSM decide to build an HPO plant in Geleen.[111]

The final step of the HPO process to industrial scale plants did not go smoothly. The changed handling of the by-product after the mini plant had been stopped, which meant that this change could not be investigated as part of the recycle loops, and this later led to problems. Also, the size of the first plants was rather large. The plants could perhaps have been built smaller, but the HPO process had to be integrated with the other steps in caprolactam production and had to compete with products from conventional plants. The minimum economic size of plants had increased, and with it the costs of building a first plant and the risks involved in scale-up, even though researchers thought it could be done. Moreover, it was not possible to build a protected niche for a new technology, given the circumstances on the market. In the 1950s, DSM could enter markets with relatively small plants, learn and research, and expand production as markets grew. This was a far more favourable climate for process innovation.

In this way innovation became more complex in the 1970s than in the previous decades. Market growth and development could no longer be taken for granted, and this significantly narrowed the window of opportunity for the introduction of new, or substantially improved, processes, and also called for a strong interface and interchange between research, marketing and production. DSM lacked this interface in the early 1970s: the Central Laboratory, production staff and Stamicarbon all had their own considerations for supporting or not supporting the HPO process. Divisional management, responsible for marketing and production, responded to the stagnation of caprolactam markets by pushing towards rationalisation and consequently towards the short term: in 1970 they considered that no measures were needed to reduce the production of ammonium sulphate, and concluded that research on this subject was not necessary either. Only a few years later, while the market of caprolactam was still difficult, did the division decide to build an HPO plant in Geleen when the problems with marketing ammonium sulphate had worsened further. In the meantime, Stamicarbon and DSM's Nypro and Nipro operations abroad had kept research going, while Ube's plant had provided an opportunity to learn and had shown the viability of the process.

Troubleshooting and Finding Markets: Melamine and EPDM in the 1970s

The Central Laboratory continued to do research not only on urea and caprolactam but also on melamine and EPDM synthetic rubbers. The problems in melamine and EPDM were similar: the first plants had initial problems that required research. In EPDM, moreover, new markets had to be found.

Melamine

The first melamine plant, which started in 1967, had several teething problems but in that same year top management decided to expand production.[112] After further market studies, the capacity of the expansion was set at 30,000 tons per year, three times as large as the first plant. Urea production had to be expanded as well to feed the new melamine plant. The Inorganic Chemistry department of the Central Laboratory had also worked on the integration of melamine and urea production since 1967. Instead of recycling a carbamate solution, the ammonia and carbon dioxide off-gases from melamine synthesis would now be fed directly into urea synthesis. The second melamine plant and the expansion of the urea plants went on stream in 1970 and had this tight integration.[113]

An important argument for top management to triple melamine production was the technological lead DSM had. Urea-based melamine production was simply cheaper than calcium cyanamide-based production. Top management expected DSM to be able to capture a large part of the melamine market from established producers. Speed was essential, because other companies, particularly Montecatini and BASF, were also working on urea-based melamine processes. Because DSM manufactured urea and ammonia, the key feedstock for melamine, on a large scale and at low costs, top management had confidence that melamine production would be profitable.[114]

Demand for melamine proved to be strong in the first half of the 1970s, and financial results were satisfactory.[115] Through information provided by Stamicarbon, however, the Central Laboratory established in 1969 that competing urea-based melamine processes were cheaper than DSM's. This prompted research to optimise the process. The second melamine plant, moreover, reached only a third of its design capacity due to problems with the reactor. The Central Laboratory helped to correct some of the problems, and by 1971 the plant reached regular production. On a yearly basis, 15 to 20% of production was still being lost due to reactor-related failures. Research to find a new design followed. In 1973, Industrial Chemicals and Stamicarbon agreed to finance the construction of a large, 5,000 tons per year, melamine test reactor tied in with the second melamine plant. In the same year, Industrial Chemicals started planning for a third melamine plant.[116]

In March 1974, maintenance crews discovered cracks in the melamine reactor of the second plant during a regular maintenance shutdown. The plant remained shut down for the remainder of the year. The problems were so severe that Industrial Chemicals raised the question of whether melamine production should continue at all. One of Stamicarbon's licensees took legal action and had to be paid a large sum in damages, compounding the problems even further.

The Central Laboratory, however, had advanced with its research on a new reactor design to the point where it was able to convince Industrial Chemicals to push on. By 1976 the new design was ready. It not only combated the production problems, but could also achieve much larger capacities in a single stream, cutting costs substantially. Industrial Chemicals scrapped the plans for a third plant and decided to equip the second plant with the new reactor. The second melamine plant restarted in 1978, debottlenecked to a capacity of 55,000 tons. The first and oldest plant was taken out of production in the same year. The new reactor design meant the final technological breakthrough of melamine at DSM.[117]

In summary, it took time before DSM learnt to operate its melamine plants. CRO played a supportive, but crucial, role in this process. A new reactor design eventually overcame the problems and put melamine production on a firm footing.

EPDM

In the 1960s, EPDM was generally believed to be the next big synthetic rubber. Ethylene and propylene were cheap feedstocks and would lead to a cheap product. The product also seemed suited for car tyre manufacture, the biggest rubber market.[118]

In 1970, DSM had two EPDM plants in production. Operating these two plants proved more difficult than anticipated, however, mainly because of the thick and sticky product that had to be processed. All producers had problems with their plants but it drove up prices. Moreover, it became clear that several disadvantages were hampering the application of EPDM in car tyres. Among other things, the tack, the adhesion of EPDM

Manufacture of Erres washing machines containing EPDM parts, March 1970. DSM found a market for its EPDM rubber in washing machines by working closely together with manufacturers. Such cooperation was important for product development for other synthetic materials as well.

to other rubbers and to materials, remained a problem. In addition, the elasticity of EPDM was too low, and tyres containing EPDM had a poor resistance to the heat that built up during driving.[119]

The Central Laboratory continued application research and tried to open up other markets. Thanks to this research together with rubber processors and manufacturers of home appliances, EPDM found its way into hoses and seals for washing machines, for instance, because it could withstand the impact of washing powders better than other materials. EPDM also found use in roofing materials that were more flexible than the common bitumen materials. EPDM roofing materials resisted the impact of ozone and aged slowly; in other words, they did not crack and remained black. The ozone resistance of EPDM also attracted the automobile industry. Window seals and other rubber parts would remain black and without cracks if they were made from EPDM. The Swedish car manufacturer Saab developed a fender with EPDM that kept its shape after a low speed collision.[120]

The automotive market became one of the major outlets of EPDM, but it took time to develop applications. These markets were also smaller than the market for synthetic rubber used in car tyres. In the meantime, the Central Laboratory had already started attempts to improve the manufacturing process in 1969. From these efforts, combined with increasing manufacturing experience, it became clear that the EPDM plants could be debottlenecked. In 1974, DSM closed the oldest plant but conserved it. At the same time, the company renovated the second plant, which boosted its capacity to 40,000 tons per year, more than twice its design capacity. This improved the economics of EPDM manufacture. Moreover, the first oil shock pushed up rubber prices, helping DSM get through the difficult period of the early 1970s.[121]

From 1979, DSM gradually restarted its oldest EPDM plant and built facilities to increase the number of EPDM types that could be manufactured. In the early 1980s, the two plants worked to full capacity. CRO investigated new catalyst systems to increase product diversity, improve product quality and cut costs. Application research also continued. Close relations between CRO, rubber processors and users of end products remained of vital importance.[122]

As in the case of melamine, it took some time for DSM to learn how to produce EPDM. The Central Laboratory had not anticipated these problems but helped solve them in the 1970s. Application research and product development were crucial for finding new markets. In the long run, EPDM developed into an important product for DSM. The company developed into one of the largest producers in the world.

Plastics in the 1970s

Plastics was one of the most expansive fields at DSM in the 1970s. Following the Large Leap Program, the Plastics division set out on an expansive course, which involved both boosting the capacities for existing products and taking up diversification. The expansion in scale was reflected in DSM's cracking operations, for instance. The Plastics division built two large crackers in the 1970s, leading to a capacity of 800,000 tons of ethylene per year by 1979 (Table 3.3). These plants were built to reinforce the company's position in bulk plastics like polyethylene. Large scale would bring down costs and enable the production of a wide range of plastics. Both top management and divisional management were of the opinion that DSM needed to increase the scale of its operations in plastics in order to survive the harsh economic climate and the fierce competition of the 1970s.[123]

In 1970, polyethylene was the only plastic manufactured by DSM, and EPDM the only synthetic rubber, but the company quickly diversified to broaden its markets (Table 4.2). By this time, processes from other companies had also become available. The Plastics division, in cooperation with

Table 4.2. Plastics diversifications in the 1970s.

Product	Start-up	Technology from
PVC	1972	Sumitomo Chemical
ABS	1974	Japan Synthetic Resins
Polypropylene	1977	Mitsubishi Petrochemical

Sources: RAL, 17.26/46 inv. no. 60: letter from top management to supervisory board, 19 August 1969. New construction. *Chemical & Engineering News* (12 January 1970), 27. Nieuwe fabriek voor lagedichtheid polyetheen. *DSM Nieuws* 1972, 22(20), 1. DSM kan krakergas 'propeen' volledig gaan benutten voor hoogwaardig eindproduct. *DSM Nieuws* 1973, 23(24), 1, 2.

CRO, Commercial Affairs and other departments, developed a policy that favoured external technology. These processes were proven and promised excellent product quality. In 1970, CRO restarted research on polypropylene for the third time, but the question of whether this process could manufacture what the market wanted remained open. This was decisive in favour of external processes. For similar reasons, DSM also bought technology for the establishment of PVC and ABS technology. Afterwards, CRO optimised production processes and built on its own application research to develop additional product types and improve product quality.[124]

In 1972, DSM once again acquired technology for LDPE production. The company manufactured this product in autoclaves but acquired know-how for the more modern tubular reactors from the Japanese company Sumitomo Chemical. With this equipment an additional range of product types came within reach. CRO, however, played an important role in scaling-up the tubular reactors. The first LDPE unit with tubular reactors started in 1975. The next unit was put on stream four years later and had almost twice the capacity of the first one.[125]

CRO also continued to work on HDPE, for which it had developed its own technology in the 1950s and 1960s. In 1968, Cees van den Berg of the Central Laboratory's Polymer Development department found a catalyst for the production of HDPE that was more active than the one in use. In conventional HDPE production, the catalyst had to be removed from the product. Because the new catalyst was more active, less was needed and it could remain in the product. An HDPE plant therefore no longer needed a catalyst removal section, which simplified the plant design and brought down costs. DSM named the new process 'the Compact process' because it was literally compact.[126]

As the Compact process shows, catalyst improvements typically pushed innovation in polyethylene and related products. Developing a substantially more active catalyst simplified production processes and cut costs. In a comparable way, more selective catalysts reduced by-product formation, made it possible to omit the by-product removal step from production processes, simplified processes and cut costs. After 1970, cutting costs increasingly became imperative for DSM to remain competitive.[127]

Early in 1969, top management decided to build a new HPDE plant using the Compact process. The plant came on stream three years later and doubled HDPE capacity. In 1970, Stamicarbon had licensed the Compact process to Sinclair-Koppers (a company Sinclair Oil and Koppers had formed in 1965 for the production of plastics). Stamicarbon's contacts showed demand for bigger capacities and for a process that could produce a wider range of HPDE types. Although the new catalyst was more active, it led to products that could not be processed into bottles and films, which were major markets. CRO attempted to expand the application area but the Plastics division stopped this research and focused the Compact process on the product range that could be manufactured with it. Such limitations were not unique. Polyethylene is a versatile product. Specific catalyst, process and product combinations existed alongside each other and have continued to do so until the present day.[128]

Research's role in plastics shifted after 1970. Following the Large Leap programme, the Plastics division expanded in scale and diversified, and to be able to do so it acquired technology. Consequently research's role in establishing diversifications declined somewhat compared to the 1950s and 1960s. Through scale-up and optimisation, however, CRO helped to cut production costs and to improve competitiveness. Such supportive work was crucial in the economic climate of the 1970s.

CRO's support of the Plastics division's market position included product development and application research. In 1970, DSM and AKZO closed down the VPV, their joint sales office for plastics. The Plastics division continued the technical service function, while CRO continued product development and improvement. This work broadened to include PVC, ABS and polypropylene, following the division's expanded product line.[129]

A Large Leap but in Which Direction? DSM and the Central Laboratory in the 1970s

In the 1970s, DSM made a large leap under difficult circumstances. The company shed its coal-related activities, expanded the capacities of existing products in big steps and took up the manufacture of several new products in a period when chemical-industry growth slowed down and competition intensified. Finally, the company replaced its functional organisation by a divisional structure. These changes occurred more or less in parallel and over a short period of time. By 1975, the company had completely renewed itself.

The Large Leap Forward had important consequences for the Central Laboratory. It realigned its organisation in response to the emerging divisional structure of the company. Directors of research provided a new bridge between research and the divisions, but the balance of power shifted towards divisional management, pushing research to the short term and initiating diversification outside the Central Laboratory. In the 1970s, research played a dependent role, which was derived from DSM's business strategy. Organisational change combined with a changed business climate and the failure of the lysine project to shift research polices in this direction.

The contrast between research policy before and after 1970 is striking. In the 1950s and 1960s, research played, and was expected to play, a crucial role in the establishment of new businesses. The Central Laboratory initiated diversification and self-confidence was high. Research, production, Stamicarbon, and later even the foreign subsidiaries to some extent, developed their own view of the company as a whole and the role of research and technology. The HPO process shows how independent the Central Laboratory was at that time: it was able to continue research on a subject it considered vital for the company without any clear commitment from Production or Stamicarbon. After 1970, DSM embarked on a journey to align these views and interests by giving primacy to the divisions. The slowdown of chemical-industry growth and the discussion as to how to give the divisions a say in the direction of centralised research pushed research towards the short term and towards a dependent role.

The example of the HPO process shows that Stamicarbon was important for the Central Laboratory and for DSM as a whole. Stamicarbon was interested in the HPO process and enabled research to be commercialised when DSM's production organisation at first did not seem interested. Similarly, research on integrated ammonia and urea processes stopped when Stamicarbon passed a negative judgement (as the division had done earlier). In the case of melamine, Stamicarbon and the Industrial Chemicals division co-financed a test reactor. Stamicarbon could provide the Central Laboratory with extra support and an extra outlet for its R&D. This outlet was highly profitable as Revallier showed in his comparison of research costs and licensing profits. DSM could learn from Stamicarbon projects, moreover, as the first HPO plants were built for other companies, for example.

An important exception to the short-term focus that dominated research work in the 1970s was the field of fine chemicals. Although Special Products was a small group, research played an important role in the entry of fine chemicals. Bulk chemicals oriented companies like DSM often preferred entry by acquisition. The failure of the lysine project had a negative impact on research policy in the 1970s, but the research done during this project led to an accumulation of knowledge and experience that proved important for other products and led to some important spin-offs. Fine chemicals, together with the work done on waste water treatment, also initiated a step into the field of biotechnology.

DSM's activities in fine chemicals built not only on knowledge accumulated during lysine research, but also on generic capabilities in process research and catalysis. These capabilities were also vital for the development of the HPO process. The scale-up of this process was no easy task but proved to be a success, while catalysis research provided the means to reach design capacity with the first plants. Application research on polyethylene and caprolactam in the 1950s and 1960s similarly built a base that enabled the Central Laboratory to guide the introduction of ABS and other plastics, as well as acrylonitrile. In this way, DSM could profit from the expansion of the Central Laboratory that had started after the Second World War.

The case of fine chemicals also shows that DSM had learnt a lesson from the lysine failure. Although research remained technology push, the crucial difference was that in the 1970s market development kept up with research and was taken into account before a decision to build a plant was taken. In the case of alpha-picoline, the creativity of the Central Laboratory caused some unexpected turns in research – research switched from lysine to pyridine and then to alpha-picoline – but an outlet for alpha-picoline had to be found before top management would approve the construction of a plant. In contrast, the lysine plant had been built before market development work had led to clear results.

In summary, DSM made a Large Leap in the 1970s, but had to realign research and the divisions in a changed business climate. R&D's role was redefined and moved away from the strong, independent role it had played in the 1950s and 1960s. The consequences of this redefinition and the Large Leap were to make themselves felt towards the end of the 1970s and in the following decade. This will be the subject of the next chapter.

Notes

1   C. van Heerden (1966). Research in de chemische industrie. *Chemisch Weekblad* 66, 290-296, in particular 291. See the end of chapter 3.
2   D. A. Hounshell (1996). The Evolution of Industrial Research in the United States. R. S. Rosenbloom & W. J. Spencer, Eds. *Engines of Innovation: U.S. Industrial Research at the End of an Era.* Boston: Harvard Business School Press, 13-85. E. Homburg (2003). *Speuren op de tast. Een historische kijk op industriële en universitaire research.* Maastricht: Universiteit Maastricht. Inaugural lecture 31 October 2003.
3   M. B. W. Graham & B. H. Pruitt (1990). *R&D for Industry: A Century of Technical*

Innovation at Alcoa. New York: Cambridge University Press. 500. Also: N. S. Argyres & B. S. Silverman (2004). R&D, Organization Structure, and the Development of Corporate Technological Knowledge. *Strategic Management Journal* 25, 929-958.

4   P. H. Spitz (1988). *Petrochemicals: The Rise of an Industry.* New York: Wiley. 462-506. J. L. van Zanden (1997). *Een klein land in de 20e eeuw: economische geschiedenis van Nederland 1914-1995.* Utrecht: Het Spectrum. 212-241. F. Aftalion (2001). *A History of the International Chemical Industry: From the "Early Days" to 2000.* Philadelphia: Chemical Heritage Foundation. Second Edition. 319-373.

5   Except where otherwise noted, this section is based on: E. Homburg (2000). Epiloog. DSM Research op weg naar de 21e eeuw. H. Lintsen, Ed. *Research tussen vetkool en zoetstof: zestig jaar DSM Research 1940-2000.* Eindhoven/Zutphen: Stichting Historie der Techniek/Walburg Pers, 118-135, in particular 122. Also the draft of this chapter, July 2000, 1, 7-9. J. Schueler. *Diversificatie en de plaats van research in de DSM-organisatie (1967-1980).* Veldman & Van Royen report I. 4-16.

6   For an analysis of the closure of the mines and the restructuring plans for Limburg see: F. A. M. Messing (1988). *Geschiedenis van de mijnsluiting in Limburg: Noodzaak en lotgevallen van een regionale herstructurering 1955-1975.* Leiden: Martinus Nijhof.

7   P. Tans (1977). Van Staatsmijnen tot DSM: Hoofdlijnen van de ontwikkeling. *Land van Herle* 27(3), 87-103, in particular 93. Messing 1988, op. cit. 348, 349.

8   K. E. Sluyterman (2003). *Kerende kansen: Het Nederlandse bedrijfsleven in de twintigste eeuw.* Amsterdam: Boom. 205-211.

9   CADH, corporate archives on research: Research. Knight Wegenstein, French, 16 December 1970. F.W.R. Röthig (1966). *Chronologisch overzicht van het ontstaan en de organisatie van het Centraal Laboratorium van de Staatsmijnen, Geleen.* Heerlen: Staatsmijnen, Centraal Laboratorium. 22. Structuur DSM wordt afgestemd op marktgerichte stijl van werken. Vraaggesprek met president-directeur dr. A. Rottier. *DSM Nieuws* 1971, 20(13), 1, 2. Eerste stap op 1 september 1971. *DSM Nieuws* 1971, 20(13), 4, 5. Organisatie van DSM in 1973. *DSM Nieuws* 1971, 20(13), 2-4. DSM-concern past per 1 april '75 zijn structuur aan. *Nieuws DSM Zuid-Limburg* 1974, 24(24), 4-5, 7.

10   H. Strijkers (1992). *DSM Chemicals: een terugblik, 1975-1991.* DSM. No page numbers. CADH, minutes of top management meeting 2 October 1979.

11   Aftalion 2001, op. cit. 319-320. H. Strijkers (2002). DSM, een koninklijke eeuwling: kroniek van de laatste 25 jaar. *Het Land van Herle* 52(3). 16.

12   Professor A. H. de Rooij, 7 February 2005. Reorganisatie Sector Research en Octrooien. 1972, *DSM Nieuws* 21(5), 8. CADH, corporate archives on research: Sector Research en Octrooien. Revallier and Zwietering, 16 November 1972.

13   CADH, corporate archives on research: Verslag van de 32ste vergadering van de beleidsgroep research en ontwikkeling, gehouden op 8 en 11 december 1970 te Geleen. DSM Directoraat Chemie, Hinskens, 27 August 1970. And other meetings of this type, early 1970s.

14   CADH, corporate archives on research: Organisatie Sector R&O. Verslag van een gesprek tussen de heren Grotens, Phielix, Revallier en v.d. Weijden op 28 mei 1974. CDOE, V.d. Weijden, 20 June 1974. Organisatie Sector R&O. Verslag van een gesprek van dr. Revallier met de chefs ROCP op 21 augustus 1974. CDOE, V.d. Weijden, 8 October 1974. Organisatie van de sector Research en Octrooien. CL, Revallier, 24 October 1974.

15   CADH, corporate archives on research: Verslag van de vergadering van de Bedrijfsleiding Concerndienst Research en Octrooien op 24 november 1975. CRO, 25 November 1975. Bespreking CRO-matrix tussen leden van de Raad van bestuur (Kretzers en Van Liemt) en Bedrijfsleiding (Revallier, Van Heerden, De Rooij, Phielix) op 7 januari 1976. CRO, ROCP, De Rooij, 9 January 1976. Reorganisatie in fasen van de Concerndienst Research

en Octrooien. Geleidelijke invoering van matrix-organisatie. *Nieuws DSM Limburg* 1976, 26(4), 6. F. J. G. Kwanten (1993). *Onderzoek bij Staatsmijnen in Limburg / DSM Centraal Laboratorium / DSM Research 1940-1990*. DSM Research Report R 89 8061 (1 September 1993). 25.

16 CADH, corporate archives on research: Organisatie van de sector Research en Octrooien. CL, Revallier, 24 October 1974. Reorganisatie in fasen van de Concerndienst Research en Octrooien. Geleidelijke invoering van matrix-organisatie. *Nieuws DSM Limburg* 1976, 26(4), 6.

17 Letter from De Quay (OPO) to Bogers and Kretzers, 18 February 1975. Letter from De Quay (OPO) to top management, 1 April 1975. Kwanten 1993, op. cit. 27. Schueler, op. cit. 28-29.

18 Kwanten 1993, op. cit. 25. 'Corporate research and patent department' is the translation used in the English version of DSM's annual report for 1975.

19 See for Philips: K. Boersma & M. de Vries (2003). De veranderende rol van het Natuurkundig Laboratorium van het Philipsconcern gedurende de periode 1914-1994. *NEHA Jaarboek* 66, 287-313. For RCA: M. B. W. Graham (1988). *The Business of Research: RCA and the VideoDisc*. London: Cambridge University Press.

20 Schueler, op. cit. 42. Drs. D.H.E. Tom, scheidend directeur Concerndienst Research en Octrooien: Uniek laboratorium in Nederland. *DSM Magazine* (67, July 1985), 7-9.

21 CADH, corporate archives on research: Letter from Revallier to Rottier and Bogers, 10 February 1971. H. Lintsen, J. Schueler & F. Veraart (2000). Naar een heroriëntatie van de research, 1970-1985. H. Lintsen, Ed. *Research tussen vetkool en zoetstof: zestig jaar DSM Research 1940-2000*. Eindhoven/Zutphen: Stichting Historie der Techniek/Walburg Pers, 82-103, in particular 87, 91-92.

22 Interview with Dr L. J. Revallier, 18 January 2005. Personal papers of Dr L.J. Revallier: Projects developed by DSM. Undated but from approximately 1975.

23 CADH, corporate archives on research: Verslag van de 28ste vergadering van de beleidsgroep research en ontwikkeling, gehouden op 9 juni 1970 om 14.30 uur in Geleen. DSM Directoraat Chemie, Hinskens, 1 June 1970. Dr. C. Bokhoven van CL 25 jaar in dienst. *Nieuws DSM Zuid-Limburg* 1974, 24(18), 2.

24 Lintsen, Schueler & Veraart 2000, op. cit. 94. Schueler, op. cit. 20, 27. See also: L. M. Kretzers (1980). Markt en technologie als drijfveer voor de Nederlandse chemische industrie. *Chemisch Magazine* (November 1980), m 701-m 705.

25 Central Laboratory Annual report 1968. A. van Rooij (2004). *Building Plants: Markets for Technology and Internal Capabilities in DSM's Fertiliser Business, 1925-1970*. Amsterdam: Aksant. Dissertation Eindhoven University of Technology, 131.

26 Dr S. E. Schaafsma, 22 January 2004. CADH, corporate archives on research: Verslag van de 29ste vergadering van de beleidsgroep research en ontwikkeling, gehouden op 11 augustus 1970 om 14.30 uur in Geleen. DSM Directoraat Chemie, Hinskens, 27 August 1970. Verslag van de 32ste vergadering van de beleidsgroep research en ontwikkeling, gehouden op 8 en 11 december 1970 te Geleen. DSM Directoraat Chemie, Hinskens, 29 December 1970. Grondstoffenbesparing en productievergroting door nieuwe katalysator in ACN. *DSM Nieuws* 1973, 23(24), 1. *Ullmann's Encyclopedia of Industrial Chemistry*. Weinheim: VCH. Fifth edition, 36 volumes, 1985-1996. Vol. A1, 1985, 177.

27 Van Rooij 2004, op. cit. chapter 10.

28 See for the chemical industry: R. Olin (1973). R&D Management Practices: Chemical Industry in Europe. *R&D Management* 3, 125-135. Particularly 126. J. R. Anchor (1985). Managerial Perceptions of Research and Development in the UK Chemicals Industry, 1955-1981. *Chemistry and Industry* (1 July 1985), 426-430, (15 July 1985), 459-464, (5 August 1985), 498-504, in particular part 1, 426-427.

29 B. Achilladelis, A. Schwarzkopf & M. Cines (1990). The Dynamics of Technological In-
    novation: The Case of the Chemical Industry. *Research Policy* 19, 1-34, in particular 29-30.
    D. A. Hounshell (1996). The Evolution of Industrial Research in the United States. R. S.
    Rosenbloom & W. J. Spencer, Eds. *Engines of Innovation: U.S. Industrial Research at the End
    of an Era.* Boston: Harvard Business School Press, 13-85, in particular 50-51.

30 Graham & Pruitt, 1990 op. cit.

31 C. H. Kline (1976). Maximising Profits in Chemicals. *Chemtech* 6 (February), 110-117, in
    particular 110-115. J. A. Bigot (1980). Heden en toekomst van de Nederlandse fijnchemie.
    Chemisch Magazine (November 1980), m 729-m 732, in particular m 729-m 730.

32 For a detailed review of the differences see: L. D. Rosenberg & C. H. Kline (1981). Should
    Management Seek More Profits Downstream? *Hydrocarbon Processing* 60(12), 158-167.

33 Rosenberg & Kline 1981, op. cit. 164-165. Aftalion 2001, op. cit. 346-348. M. Eckstut & P. H.
    Spitz (2003). Strategy Development in the Chemical Industry. P. H. Spitz, Ed. *The Chemical
    Industry at the Millennium: Maturity, Restructuring, and Globalization.* Philadelphia: Chemi-
    cal Heritage Press, 111-144, in particular 126-127.

34 Central Laboratory annual reports 1960, 1961. Personal papers of Dr S. E. Schaafsma: Kleine
    Produkten: Hobby of Hoeksteen? Een bijdrage tot de meningsvorming over het belang van
    kleine produkten voor DSM en de wijze waarop een aantrekkelijk pakket moet worden
    opgebouwd. CL, Vermijs and Van Doesburgh, 30 January 1969.

35 Personal papers of Dr S. E. Schaafsma: Kleine Produkten: Hobby of Hoeksteen? Een bij-
    drage tot de meningsvorming over het belang van kleine produkten voor DSM en de wijze
    waarop een aantrekkelijk pakket moet worden opgebouwd. CL, Vermijs and Van Does-
    burgh, 30 January 1969.

36 Interview with Dr J. A. Bigot, 8 December 2003. CADH, Minutes of top management
    meeting 14 April 1969. H. Strijkers (1994). *Van hobby naar hoeksteen: 25 jaar Speciale Produk-
    ten bij DSM.* Geleen: DSM Fine Chemical, Special Products. 2-3.

37 Ir. R.E. Selman nieuwe 'general manager' van Nypro (U.K.) Ltd. *DSM Nieuws* 1971, 20(18),
    4. Dr. J.A. Bigot chef Speciale Producten. *DSM Nieuws* 1971, 20(18), 4.

38 CADH, Minutes of top management meeting 14 April 1969.

39 Dr S. E. Schaafsma, 22 January 2004. Dr J. A. Bigot, 7 February 2005. Central Laboratory
    annual report 1969. CADH, RvB 82/249: letter from head of Industrial Chemicals (name
    illegible) to top management, 5 October 1982, in particular Strategienota Groep Speciale
    Produkten, appendix 4. Strijkers 1994, op. cit. 3-4.

40 Dr J.A. Bigot, 7 February 2005. Strijkers 1994, op. cit. 2-3, 6.

41 W. W. Kaeding (1964). How Dow Makes Phenol From Toluene. *Hydrocarbon Processing*
    43(11), 173-176, in particular 173-174. New Construction. *Chemical & Engineering News* (16
    February 1970), 24.

42 RAL, 17.26/ 19C inv. no. 55: Benzoëzuur. NVCP, afdeling marktonderzoek, Arentsen, 18
    July 1968. CADH, DV 1972/16: Benzaldehyde. CIR, Groep Speciale Produkten, 17 January
    1972.

43 Central Laboratory annual reports 1962-1964. RAL, 17.26/ 19C inv. no. 55: Letter from Van
    Steenis and Schram to Chemische Fabriek Naarden, 13 October 1965. Benzoëzuur. NVCP,
    Pieterse, 21 March 1966. CADH, RvB 82/249: letter from head of Industrial Chemicals
    (name illegible) to top management, 5 October 1982, in particular Strategienota Groep Spe-
    ciale Produkten, appendix 4.

44 Interview with Dr J. A. Bigot, 8 December 2003. CADH, Minutes of top management
    meeting 24 January 1972. CADH, DV 1972/16: Benzaldehyde. CIR, Groep Speciale Produk-
    ten, 17 January 1972. CADH, RvB 82/249: letter from head of Industrial Chemicals (name

illegible) to top management, 5 October 1982, in particular Strategienota Groep Speciale Produkten, appendix 4.

45　Interview with R. E. Selman, 27 June 2003. CADH, RvB 82/249: letter from head of Industrial Chemicals (name illegible) to top management, 5 October 1982, in particular Strategienota Groep Speciale Produkten, appendix 4. J. J. Dahlmans, W. H. J. Boesten & G. Bakker (1980). Enzymatische scheiding van D- en L-aminozuren op technologische schaal. *Chemisch Magazine* (May 1980), m 322-m 323, in particular m 322.

46　CADH, corporate archives on research: Verslag van de 32ste vergadering van de beleidsgroep research en ontwikkeling, gehouden op 8 en 11 december 1970 te Geleen. DSM Directoraat Chemie, Hinskens, 27 August 1970. F. Veraart. *Lysine (1957-1969)*. Veldman & Van Royen report H. 16, 20-21.

47　Central Laboratory annual report 1966. Verslag van de 7e E-vergadering, 7 June 1972. CADH, corporate archives on research: Verslag van de 25e Research-vergadering d.d. 1 mei 1975. Zaayer, 19 May 1975.

48　Interview with Dr H. G. Bakker, 16 March 2005. Central Laboratory annual report 1969. For overviews of enzyme technology in the early 1970s see: J. J. Dahlmans (1975). Enzymen in de organische proces-industrie. *Chemisch Weekblad* (28 November 1975), 24-26. K. J. Skinner (1975). Enzymes Technology. *Chemical & Engineering News* (18 August 1975), 23-41.

49　Interview with Dr H. G. Bakker, 16 March 2005.

50　Dr S. E. Schaafsma, 22 January 2004. Interview with Dr H. G. Bakker, 16 March 2005. Dahlmans et al. 1980, op. cit. m 322. For Novo see: *Novo Nordisk History*, undated. http://www.novonordisk.com/images/about_us/history/history_uk.pdf. Accessed 9 February 2004.

51　Dr S. E. Schaafsma, 22 January 2004. Minutes of top management meeting 7 August 1978.

52　Dr S. E. Schaafsma, 22 January 2004. Lange Termijnplan van de Concerndienst Research en Octrooien 1979-1984. E. M. Meijer (1987). *Biokatalyse en fijnchemie: grenzen en perspectieven*. Eindhoven: Eindhoven University of Technology. Inaugural lecture 15 May 1987. 5-7.

53　E. Gwinner (1978). *Wirtschaftliche Aspekte der Biochemie, Bioenergie und Biotechnologie*. Düsseldorf: Handelsblatt Verlag für Wirtschaftsinformation. 105. Voortgaan op biotechnologische weg. *DSM Magazine* (50, October 1982), 9-11, in particular 10.

54　CADH, corporate archives on research: Verslag van de 15e-COPCO vergadering op 17 november 1987. J. Kamphuis, J. A. M. van Balken, H. E. Schoemaker, E. M. Meijer & W. H. J. Boesten (1988). Biotechnologische productie van optisch actieve aminozuren. *I2-Procestechnologie* 4(9), 31-41, in particular 35-38. DSM start productie van specialty aminozuren. *DSM Limburg Nieuws* 1988, 38(21), 1.

55　*Kirk-Othmer Encyclopedia of Chemical Technology*. London: Wiley-Interscience. Second edition, 22 volumes, 1963-1977. Vol. 16, 1968, 780. A. Budzinski (1981). Pyridin hat noch Wachstumschancen. *Chemische Industrie* XXXIII(September), 529-531, in particular 529.

56　Budzinski 1981, op. cit. 529-531. C. G. M. van de Moesdijk (1986). Development of a Continuous Process for Substituted Pyridines and other Heterocycles. *Chemistry & Industry* (4), 129-134, in particular 129, 131. P. F. G. Vincken (2000). *Van Staatsmijnen in Limburg tot DSM Chemie*. Unpublished manuscript. 161.

57　Dr S. E. Schaafsma, 22 January 2004. Central Laboratory annual report 1969, 1970. De heer J.A. Thoma wordt directeur van de Groep Organische Producten. *Nieuws DSM Limburg* 1981, 31(20), 1.

58　Dr S. E. Schaafsma, 22 January 2004. Dr J.A. Bigot, 7 February 2005. Central Laboratory annual report 1970.

59 Central Laboratory annual report 1970. CADH, corporate archives on research: Verslag van de 32ste vergadering van de beleidsgroep research en ontwikkeling, gehouden op 8 en 11 december 1970 te Geleen. DSM Directoraat Chemie, Hinskens, 29 December 1970.

60 Dr S. E. Schaafsma, 22 January 2004. CADH, corporate archives on research: Verslag van de 34ste en 35ste vergadering van de beleidsgroep research en ontwikkeling, gehouden op 8 en 24 maart 1971 DSM Directoraat Chemie, 7 April 1971. Verslag van de 37ste vergadering van de beleidsgroep research en ontwikkeling, gehouden op 8 juni 1971 te Geleen. DSM Directoraat Chemie, Hinskens, 21 June 1971. Van de Moesdijk 1986, op. cit. 130. For Lonza: W. Eschenmoser (1997). 100 years of progress with Lonza. *Chimia* 51(6), 259-267, in particular 264.

61 Interview with Dr J.A. Bigot, 8 December 2003. Verslag van de 14e vergadering van de Research, gehouden op 20 juni 1973. Hinskens, 29 June 1973

62 Budzinski 1981, op. cit. table 1, 530.

63 Interview with Dr J.A. Bigot, 8 December 2003. Dr S. E. Schaafsma, 22 January 2004. E-mail by Dr S. E. Schaafsma to the author, 28 February 2005. CADH, RvB 82/249: letter from head of Industrial Chemicals (name illegible) to top management, 5 October 1982, in particular Strategienota Groep Speciale Produkten, appendix 4. SP neemt eerste eenheid van nieuwe fabriek voor hoogwaardige fijnchemicaliën in bedrijf. *DSM Limburg Nieuws* 1977, 27(14), 6. Bigot 1980, op. cit. m 731. Van de Moesdijk 1986, op. cit. 132.

64 Verslag van het bijzonder gedeelte van de 32e vergadering van de Hoofddirectie op maandag 13 augustus 1973. CADH, Minutes of top management meeting 2 June 1975.

65 Dr J. A. Bigot, 7 February 2005. CADH, Minutes of top management meeting 12 June 1979.

66 Interview with Dr J. A. Bigot, 8 December 2003. CADH, Minutes of top management meeting 20 February 1979. K. E. Sluyterman (1995). *Driekwart eeuw CSM: cash flow, strategie en mensen.* Diemen: CSM. 156, 186. See also: J. Verhoog & H. Warmerdam (1994). *Melkzuur?... natuurlijk! 25 jaar PURAC Biochem BV 1969-1994.* Noordwijk: Van Speijk. H. Benninga (1990). *A History of Lactic Acid Making: A Chapter in the History of Biotechnology.* Dordrecht: Kluwer. 335, 377-382, 417-423, 428-450.

67 Interview with Dr J. A. Bigot, 8 December 2003. CADH, Minutes of top management meetings 20 October 1975 and 31 May 1977. Chem-Y brengt nieuwe technologie in huis. *DSM Magazine* (24, April 1978), 19-21. P. L. Layman (1982). Surfactants - A Mature Market with Potential. *Chemical & Engineering News* (11 January 1982), 13-16, in particular 13.

68 Interview with Dr J. A. Bigot, 8 December 2003. CADH, Minutes of top management meeting 24 October 1977. CADH, RvB 1977/318: letter from Quanjel and Tom to top management, 20 October 1977. Strijkers 1994, op. cit. 7.

69 Interview with J. T. J. van Goolen by the author and D.J. van Waes, 5 December 2003. Dr S. E. Schaafsma, 22 January 2004. Productie-activiteiten geconcentreerd en verdubbeld in nieuw complex te Emmerich. *DSM Magazine* (38, September 1980), 8-11, in particular 8-10.

70 CADH, RvB 82/249: letter from head of Industrial Chemicals (name illegible) to top management, 5 October 1982. CADH, RvB 84/ 257: Beleidsvoorstellen met betrekking tot Chem-Y. Groep Speciale Produkten, Venderbos, 31 October 1984.

71 Personal papers of Dr J. A. Bigot: J. A. Bigot (1984). *Fine Chemicals as a Means to Bridge the Gap Between Commodities and Specialties.* Manuscript.

72 H. Lintsen, F. Veraart & P. Vincken (2000). De onvervulde belofte: Lysine. H. Lintsen, Ed. *Research tussen vetkool en zoetstof: zestig jaar DSM Research 1940-2000.* Eindhoven/Zutphen: Stichting Historie der Techniek/Walburg Pers, 70-81.

73 Excluding turnover related to energy activities. CADH, RvB 82/249: letter from head of Industrial Chemicals (name illegible) to top management, 5 October 1982, in particular Strategienota Groep Speciale Produkten, appendix 1.

74 Milieuresearch: waakzaam en beschikbaar. *DSM Magazine* (55, July 1983), 22-24, in particular 22. Industrieel erfgoed - Dankzij particulier initiatief werd in het Zeeuwse Dreischor een originele 'Pasveersloot' in oude staat hersteld. *TNO Magazine* 2003, (3), 28.

75 Röthig 1966, op. cit. 23. Afdeling Milieutechniek van Stamicarbon doet goede zaken. *DSM Nieuws* 1973, 23(20), 1, 2. P. G. Meerman (1978). Tien jaar research aan integrale afvalwaterzuivering. Van 1:100.000.000 naar 1:1. *DSM Magazine* (26, August 1978), 4-8, in particular 4.

76 Meerman 1978, op. cit. 5-6. Researchgroep ontwikkelt nieuwe centrale zuiveringsinstallatie. *DSM Nieuws Extra, Externe editie* (28 April 1972), 1, 4, in particular 1.

77 Vlotte start van proefbedrijf voor zuivering afvalwater van onze chemische bedrijven. *DSM Nieuws* 1972, 21(17), 5. Eerste straat IAZI opgestart. *DSM Limburg Nieuws* 1977, 27(17), 1. Strijkers 2002, op. cit. 28. Meerman 1978, op. cit. 4-8.

78 Interview with J. Damme by E. Homburg and the author, 23 November 2000. Research in de aanval tegen bruine pluim. *DSM Informatie* 4 (29 March 1974), 4.

79 Afvalwaterstripper NAK 3 gaat stankhinder rigoureus te lijf: Ook loogneutralisator voor zelfde doel in opstart. *DSM Limburg Nieuws* 1977, 27(14), 5.

80 Interview with Dr H. G. Bakker, 16 March 2005. Milieuresearch: veelzijdige afdeling met één gericht doel. *DSM Limburg Nieuws* 1979, 29(9), 6-7, in particular 7. Voortgaan op biotechnologische weg. *DSM Magazine* (50, October 1982), 9-11, in particular 10-11.

81 Central Laboratory annual reports 1969 and 1970. CADH, corporate archives on research: Verslag van de 34ste en 35ste vergadering van de beleidsgroep research en ontwikkeling, gehouden op 11 mei 1971. DSM Directoraat Chemie, ir. De Bruijn, 7 April 1971. E. Homburg, with contributions by A. van Rooij (2004). *Groeien door kunstmest. DSM Agro 1929-2004.* Hilversum: Verloren. 171.

82 Central Laboratory annual report 1967. Ureum capaciteit naar 450.000 ton per jaar. *Staatsmijnen Nieuws* 1968, 17(17), 1,2.

83 RAL, DSM 17.26/ 19C inv. no. 114: Visie op de toekomst van stikstofmeststoffen. Samenvatting van de vierde vergadering, gehouden op 27 maart 1969. CADH, corporate archives on research: Verslag van de 24ste vergadering van de beleidgroep research en ontwikkeling, gehouden op 18 februari 1970 om 14:30 te Geleen. DSM Directoraat Chemie, Hinskens, 25 March 1970. P. J. C. Kaasenbrood & J. D. Logemann (1969). DSM's Urea Stripping Process. *Hydrocarbon Processing* 48(4), 117-121, in particular 117, 120-121. V. Laguna & G. Schmid (1975). Snamprogetti's Newest Urea Process. *Hydrocarbon Processing* 54(7), 102-104.

84 Homburg 2004, op. cit. 210-215, 249-270.

85 K. Chapman (2000). Industry Evolution and International Dispersal: The Fertiliser Industry. *Geoforum* 31, 371-384. Particularly 376, 378-379.

86 See for an overview of the fertiliser market and DSM's position at the beginning of the 1970s: CADH, D.V. 1970/102: Bijdrage tot de formulering van het toekomstig stikstofbeleid van DSM (tweede nota). Concept. CZ: Gardeniers, Giepmans, Harten, De Bussy, Trienekens, Vlek; BEA: Claassens, Donders; 5 January 1970.

87 Central Laboratory research programme 1965. Letter from Revallier to top management, 12 January 1965; supplement to Central Laboratory annual report 1965.

88 J. Damme, J. T. van Goolen & A. H. de Rooij (1972). Cyclohexanone Oxime Made Without Byproduct (NH4)$_2$SO4. *Chemical Engineering* (10 July 1972), 54-55, in particular 54.

89 Interview with J .T .J. van Goolen by the author and D. J. van Waes, 5 December 2003. F. Hoelscher (1972). *Kautschuke, Kunststoffe, Fasern. Sechs Jahrzehnte Technische Herstullung*

synthetische Polymere. Ludwigshafen: BASF. 104-106. C. G. M. van de Moesdijk (1979). *The Catalytic Reduction of Nitrate and Nitric Oxide to Hydroxylamine: Kinetics and Mechanism*. Eindhoven: Dissertation TH Eindhoven. 15.

90 Professor A. H. de Rooij, 7 February 2005. Central Laboratory annual reports 1956, 1957.

91 Interview with Professor. A. H. de Rooij by the author and D. J. van Waes, 8 December 2003. Central Laboratory annual reports 1957-1961. Van de Moesdijk 1979, op. cit. 15.

92 RAL, 17.26/ 36C inv. no. 18: letter from N.C. Robertson (vice president research and development Spencer Chemical Company) to Van Waes, 6 January 1961, and further correspondence. RAL, 17.26/ 34 inv. no. 789: ZA in relatie tot caprolactam. Staf Chemische Bedrijven, Bedrijfsstaf OF, Roozemond, 17 September 1963.

93 Interview with Professor A. H. de Rooij by the author and D. J. van Waes, 8 December 2003. Central Laboratory annual report 1964. Damme et al. 1972, op. cit. 54-55.

94 Interview with Professor A. H. de Rooij by the author and D. J. van Waes, 8 December 2003.

95 Interview with Professor A. H. de Rooij by the author and D. J. van Waes, 8 December 2003. Annual reports Central Laboratory 1965-1970.

96 Interview with Professor A. H. de Rooij by the author and D. J. van Waes, 8 December 2003. Central Laboratory annual reports 1965-1970.

97 A. Sarlemijn & M. J. de Vries (1992). The Piecemeal Rationality of Application Oriented Research: An Analysis of the R&D History leading to the Invention of the Philips Plumbicon in the Philips Research Laboratories. P. A. Kroes & M. Bakker, Eds. *Technological Development and Science in the Industrial Age*. Dordrecht: Kluwer Academic Publishers, 99-131.

98 See for the development of this technology: Van Rooij 2004, op. cit. 178-188.

99 RAL, 17.26/ 19C inv. no. 114: Markt-studie-mengmesten: analyse en prognose van de wereldmengmestenmarkt ivm een mogelijke productie uitbreiding met monoammoniumfosfaat (MAF) of nitrofosfaten (NF) bij DSM te Geleen. Commerciële Zaken/Marktonderzoek, Anten, 23 December 1969. CADH, D.V. 1970/104: ZA-problematiek. Afd. Marktonderzoek CZ, Bedrijfsstaf OF, Staf Nitraatsector SBB, BEA, NO, 9 March 1970. CADH, D.V. 1970/104: Letter from Hamm and Quanjel to Beleidsgroep Chemie, 10 March 1970.

100 Ein Aufschwung bei Chemiefasern ist keinesweg sicher. *Chemische Industrie* 1976, XXVIII(2), 80. D. A. O'Sullivan (1977). West European Man-Made Fibre Outlook is Grim. *Chemical & Engineering News* (21 February 1977), 16-20. H. J. Kolowski (1983). Abbau der Synthesefaser-Kapazität in Westeuropa. *Kunststoffe* 73, 724-726. Aftalion 2001, op. cit. 323. http://www.fibersource.com/f-info/fiber production.html. Accessed 30 November 2004. For AKZO: Auch Holland hat jetzt einen Chemie-Großkonzern. Die Akzo und ihre Möglichkeiten. *Chemische Industrie* 1970, XXII(2), 8-85. Akzo auf dem Wege der Besserung. *Chemische Industrie* 1979, XXXI(6), 401-403.

101 CADH, corporate archives on research: Verslag van de 2e E-vergadering Research gehouden op woensdag 10 november 1971 te 14.30 uur. Hoofdkantoor, Hinskens, 17 November 1971.

102 Interview with J. T. J. van Goolen by the author and D. J. van Waes, 5 December 2003. Interview with Professor A. H. de Rooij by the author and D. J. van Waes, 8 December 2003.

103 Interview with J. T. J. van Goolen by the author and D. J. van Waes, 5 December 2003. J. T. J. van Goolen, 18 January 2005. Owners Shout "Si" to Montecatini Edison. *Chemical & Engineering News* (4 April 1966), 66-70, in particular 66. HPO-fabriek van Groep Organische Producten in bedrijf genomen. *DSM Limburg Nieuws* 1976, 26(17), 1, 2, in particular 2. Van de Moesdijk 1979, op. cit. 18, 21. Messing 1988, op. cit. 270. H. Strijkers (1992). *Veertig jaar caprolactam bij DSM*. DSM. 11, 14.

104 Interview with J. T. J. van Goolen by the author and D. J. van Waes, 5 December 2003. R. E. Selman, 19 July 2005. RAL, 17.26/19C, inv. no. 40: Verslag van de bespreking van de hoofddirectie inzake chemisch beleid gehouden op 10 juni 1968. Staf Chemische Bedrijven, 20 June 1968. Strijkers 1992, caprolactam, op. cit. 12.

105 Interview with J. T. J. van Goolen by the author and D. J. van Waes, 5 December 2003. HPO-fabriek van Groep Organische Producten in bedrijf genomen. *DSM Limburg Nieuws* 1976, 26(17), 1, 2. DSM-concern kan in rond eenzesde deel van wereldcaprolactambehoefte voorzien. *DSM Magazine* (9, September 1975), 5-8, in particular 5. Strijkers 1992, caprolactam, op. cit. 15. Homburg 2004, op. cit. 254-255.

106 Interview with J. T. J. van Goolen by the author and D. J. van Waes, 5 December 2003. J. T. J. van Goolen, 18 January 2005.

107 Professor A. H. de Rooij, 7 February 2005. L. L. van Dierendonck (1970). *Vergrotingsregels voor gasbelwassers.* Enschede: Dissertation TH Twente. J. T. J. van Goolen (1976). Development and Scaling-Up of a Three-Phase Reactor. *Chemical Reaction Engineering. Proceedings of the 4th international symposium, 6-8 April 1976, Heidelberg.* Frankfurt am Main: Dechema, 309-407.

108 Interview with Professor A. H. de Rooij by the author and D. J. van Waes, 8 December 2003. Professor A. H. de Rooij, 7 February 2005.

109 Interview with J. T. J. van Goolen by the author and D. J. van Waes, 5 December 2003. J. T. J. van Goolen, 18 January 2005. Central Laboratory annual report 1969.

110 CADH, DV 1973/ 256: letter from P. Zwietering, T. C. van Hoek and C. C. M. Dijkhuis to top management via Revallier, 27 September 1973. Central Laboratory annual reports 1969, 1970. A. H. de Rooij, C. Dijkhuis & J. T. J. van Goolen (1977). A Scale-up Experience. The DSM Phosphate Caprolactam Process. *Chemtech* 7(5), 309-315, in particular 313. Van de Moesdijk 1979, op. cit. 17.

111 J. T. J. van Goolen, 18 January 2005. CADH, DV 1973/ 256: letter from P. Zwietering, T. C. van Hoek and C. C. M. Dijkhuis to top management via Revallier, 27 September 1973.

112 In general this section is based on: H. Strijkers. *DSM en melamine.* Unpublished and undated manuscript. 15-33. Interview with Dr R. van Hardeveld, 29 August 2005. Interview with W. J. W. Vermijs, 29 August 2005.

113 CADH, minutes of top management meetings 23 October 1967 and 19 February 1968. Central Laboratory annual report 1967. P. F. G. Vincken (2000). *Van Staatsmijnen in Limburg tot DSM Chemie.* Unpublished manuscript. 189.

114 CADH, minutes of top management meeting 23 October 1967. CADH, DV 1967: letter from top management to supervisory board, 10 November 1967.

115 DSM annual reports 1970-1974.

116 Central Laboratory annual report 1969, 1970. DSM annual report 1973. RAL, DSM 17.26/34 inv. no. 826: Melamineproces BASF. Stamicarbon, Krekels, 2 May 1968.

117 Melamine glut worries Europe. *Chemical Week* (10 November 1976), 58-59, in particular 58.

118 Interview with Dr B. C. Roest, 29 July 2005. RAL, 17.26/46 inv. no. 110: Eigenschappen en toepassingen van EPT. Van 't Wout & Van Gorcum, undated. *Ullmann*, fifth edition op. cit. vol. A23, 1993, 284.

119 Interview with Dr G. Evens, 26 July 2005. Interview with Dr B. C. Roest, 29 July 2005.

120 Interview with Dr G. Evens, 26 July 2005. Keltan onderdelen in wasautomaten. *DSM Nieuws* 1971, 20(5), 4. Bouwindustrie gaat Keltan voor dakbedekking en bassinbekleding gebruiken. *DSM Nieuws* 1971, 20(5), 4. Veiligheidsbumper van kunstrubber Keltan. *DSM Nieuws* 1971, 20(21), 1.

121 Interview with Dr B. C. Roest, 29 July 2005. Central Laboratory annual report 1969. Belang-rijke uitbreiding KELTAN-productie in Beek. *Nieuws DSM Limburg* 1981, 31(17), 1, 4.

122 Interview with Dr B. C. Roest, 29 July 2005. DSM annual reports 1982, 1983. Belangrijke uitbreiding, op. cit. 1, 4.

123 Directeur Grotens van Divisie Kunststoffen: DSM heeft voor de productie van grondstoffen voor volgproducten zowel NAK 3 als NAK 4 nodig. *DSM Limburg Nieuws* 1978, 28(3), 6-7. Groepsdirecteur van Polymeren: stalen zenuwen? *DSM Limburg Nieuws* 1980, 30(2), 3.

124 Central Laboratory annual report 1970. Interview with Dr G. Evens, 26 July 2005. Interview with Dr B. C. Roest, 29 July 2005.

125 Interview with Dr G. Evens, 26 July 2005. Nieuwe fabriek voor lagedichtheid polyetheen. *DSM Nieuws* 1972, 22(20), 1. De opstart van systeem 16: nog in de jaren zeventig. *Nieuws DSM Limburg* 1980, 30(3), 1, 2.

126 Interview with Dr G. Evens, 26 July 2005. Interview with Dr B. C. Roest, 29 July 2005. Compactproces van Groep Polymeren staat op het punt product af te leveren. *DSM Nieuws* 1972, 21(6), 1, 6.

127 Interview with Dr G. Evens, 26 July 2005.

128 Interview with Dr G. Evens, 26 July 2005. Interview with Dr B. C. Roest, 29 July 2005. Central Laboratory annual report 1969. CADH, corporate archives on research: Verslag van de 24e Research-vergadering, gehouden op 18 februari 1975. Zaayer, 1 April 1975. Stamicarbon develops new high density polyethylene process. *Chemical & Engineering News* (20 April 1970), 38.

129 DSM annual report 1970. Technisch partner van polymerenafnemers. *DSM Magazine* (17, January 1977), 22-24.

5

The 1980s: Moving Away from Cyclicality and into High Value-Added Products

The second oil crisis of 1979, and the economic downturn that followed it, deeply affected the chemical industry and marked the end of DSM's Large Leap Forward. DSM's turnover grew, but profitability declined and the strategy of expansion had to be adjusted. The company consolidated its activities in bulk chemicals and sought expansion in knowledge-intensive products with high value-added.

The new twofold strategy implied an innovation drive, but its implementation was initially hampered by the company's weak results of the early 1980s. Nevertheless, DSM's strategic shift enlarged the playing field for research, as knowledge-intensive products mainly meant research-intensive products. CRO had played a smaller role in diversification in the 1970s than in previous periods but in the 1980s the number of research-based diversifications increased again (see table 5.1). CRO translated DSM's business strategy into a set of so-called corporate development programmes that aimed to help the company reach its goal of finding products with higher value-added and improving its results.

Under a new strategy, and helped by improving results, DSM found a new balance between research and business interests around 1985. After the Second World War, the tremendous growth of the chemical industry and the strong faith in research had enabled research to play a key role in DSM's expansion and diversification in the chemical industry but research, marketing, production and other functions had been independent of each other. After 1970, due to internal and external changes, business and research had to be realigned but DSM's solution pushed research towards short-term work. After 1980, research gradually got more room again. A strategic shift added emphasis to research and improving business results made a more generous research budget possible. The corporate development programmes, moreover, provided the means to coordinate the needs of medium-term to long-term oriented research with the needs of business.

Table 5.1. The role of research in DSM's major diversifications, 1970-1990.

Product	Start of Production	Area of application
Thermoset resins	1970	Resins
PVC	1972	Plastics
Methanol, formaldehyde, urea-formaldehyde	1972	Resins
Construction	1973; stop: 1983	Construction
ABS	1974	Plastics
Polypropylene	1977	
Benzaldehyde	Early 1970s	
Phenylglycine	Early 1970s	Fine chemicals (pharma)
Surfactants	1977	Specialties
Alpha-picoline	1977	Fine chemicals (agro, pharma, other)
MTBE	1981	Petrol improvement
RIM Nylon	1986	
Intermediates for penicillin	1987	Fine chemicals (pharma)
Aspartame	1988	Sweeteners
Amino acids	1988	
Controlled release fertilisers	1990	Horticulture
Fertilisers with specialty additives	1990	Horticulture
Dyneema	1990	Fibres
UHMW-PE	1990	Engineering plastics
Stanyl	1990	Fibres/engineering plastics

Sources: see text, and P. Tans (1977). Van Staatsmijnen tot DSM: Hoofdlijnen van de ontwikkeling. *Land van Herle* 27(3), 87-103, in particular 99. Schone fabriek gaat milieuvriendelijk product maken: Contract voor MTBE-installatie getekend. *DSM Limburg Nieuws* 1979, 29(12), 1. Florerende tak van DSM Agro: DSM Agro Specialties. *DSM Magazine* 1990 (98), 12-14, in particular 12. F. J. G. Kwanten (1993). *Onderzoek bij Staatsmijnen in Limburg/ DSM Centraal Laboratorium/ DSM Research 1940-1990.* DSM Research report R 89 8061. (1 September 1993). 25. H. Strijkers (2002). DSM, een koninklijke eeuwling: kroniek van de laatste 25 jaar. *Het Land van Herle* 52(3). 23, 52, 54.
Note: end of production is included when it falls in the period until 1990.

Important elements of technology base	Role of external technology	Importance of research for diversification	Diversification initiated by research?
	++ (Synres)	-	-
Application research	+	-	-
	++ (joint venture with AKZO	-	-
	++ (construction companies)	-	-
Application research	+	-	-
	+	-	-
Process technology Organic chemistry	-	++	++
Process technology Organic chemistry	-	++	+
	++ (Chem-Y)	-	-
Process technology Organic chemistry	-	++	++
	++	-	-
Fibre application research	-	+	+
	++ (Andeno)	-	-
Process technology Organic chemistry: enzymes	+	++	+
Organic chemistry: enzymes	-	++	+
Fertilisers research Resins	-	+	+
Fertilisers research	-	+	+
Fibre application research Process technology	-	++	++
Process technology	-	++	++
Process technology Organic chemistry	-	++	++

Legend:

	External technology	Importance of research	Initiated by research
-	No important role for external technology.	No role for research work.	No or small role for research.
+	Technology acquired in the form of a process or research work starting from process of competitor.	Small-scale research project/large role for external technology.	Important role for research.
++	Plant acquired.	Research work crucial for establishment of production.	Crucial role for research.

Shifting Strategies and Research Policies in the 1980s

Towards a New Business Strategy

In the economic downturn after the second oil shock of 1979, many firms found that their diversification strategy had not made them less sensitive to cyclical fluctuations. They responded by directing their attention to what they thought were their core activities. In the chemical industry, many companies had expanded their plants after 1974 and 1979, sometimes with good results in the short term, but problems became apparent in the early 1980s when slow demand brought overcapacity (particularly in bulk chemicals) accompanied by low prices and intense competition. The recession of the early 1980s cut deep into the flesh of the industry. The response was twofold. On the one hand, chemical companies concentrated on core activities and tried to rationalise their hard-hit bulk chemicals businesses through cost-cutting programmes, portfolio swaps and capacity reductions. On the other hand, companies continued to seek expansion, but this time in areas offering higher margins than bulk chemicals. Fine chemicals and specialities ranked first on the priority list of many companies. High performance polymers, ceramics and composites attracted a lot of attention as well.[1]

The expansion response was more innovation-driven and research-driven than the rationalisation response. Companies with major research departments typically chose this route. For instance, Monsanto, an American chemical company with extensive interests in bulk chemicals, targeted food, agriculture and healthcare as fields to grow in. The French chemical conglomerate Rhône-Poulenc followed a similar course and focused its expansion efforts on healthcare and agriculture, like Monsanto, but also on fine chemicals. Rhône-Poulenc belonged to the category of chemical companies that tried to diversify even more radically by taking up fields such as electronics. The American chemical company Hercules tried aerospace components, for instance. Companies chose all these fields to balance their bulk chemicals oriented portfolios and improve profitability.[2]

At DSM in the 1970s, Leen Revallier had tried to keep diversification-oriented research going within the framework of the Large Leap Forward plan but had met with only a lukewarm response from divisional and top management. In a report on research policy to DSM's supervisory board of November 1975, however, top management made a carefully-worded statement on the possibility that, in the long term, the growth of bulk chemicals could be limited by developments in the markets for these products and increasingly stringent environmental regulations. Top management suggested that DSM should perhaps change its course and initiate more research on products, instead of improvements of existing processes, and specifically products with high value-added as opposed to low-margin bulk chemicals.[3]

In the supervisory board, Evert Verwey, who had been research director at Philips from 1946 until his retirement in 1966 and who was active in science and technology policy-making in the Netherlands, took up these ideas and emphasised that DSM should break with its course of the past and start searching for high value-added products. Verwey also argued that DSM should start spending more on research. He visited DSM in August 1976 to talk to Leo Kretzers, Revallier, the head of CRO's Products and Processes department and the head of DSM's corporate planning department and again underlined his ideas. It took a further three years, however, before the search for high value-added products formally became part of CRO's long-range plan. The company's weak results caused the delay; DSM simply did not have a lot of money available to spend on research.[4]

DSM's weak results also eventually prompted top management to change course. Towards the end of the 1970s, it had become clear that expansion alone did not bring the expected improvement in results. Top management chose the twofold strategy common in the chemical industry at that time. Consolidation and rationalisation became the key objectives in bulk chemicals, while growth would have to come from new knowledge-intensive products with a high potential profitability. Ruud Selman, who, having been appointed to top management in 1979, took over responsibility for research from Kretzers and also involved himself with the Chemical Products division, emphasised that research should play an important role in the shift DSM was to make.[5]

In 1982, however, DSM made a substantial loss for the first time in its history. The loss had a tremendous impact and started another round of economising. DSM decided to retreat from the construction industry in 1983 and sold the interests it had in construction firms. The research budget was also cut and the number of researchers declined. The innovation-driven search for new businesses did not get off the ground, but in 1983, and once again in 1984 for the supervisory board, top management reaffirmed the strategic shift. Bulk chemicals would remain the core of the company, but DSM would have to push rationalisation vigorously to excel as this was the only way to maintain its position. The ceiling of growth in bulk chemicals was in sight and made it necessary to search for new businesses. When DSM recovered from the low point of 1982, this innovation-driven search could get off the ground.[6]

It took time to adjust the expansion and diversification policies of the Large Leap programmes but DSM's strategic reorientation of the first half of the 1980s was a major one. The company refocused and no longer aimed at vigorous expansion of its bulk chemicals, traditionally the core of the company. Instead, DSM tried to 'reach out' to new business activities from its base in bulk chemicals.[7]

The Corporate Development Programmes

After the course top management wanted to steer had become clear and economic circumstances had improved, CRO started to think about the implications of DSM's business strategy for itself. In the eyes of CRO, it was clear that DSM should spend more on research. The company had fallen behind its competitors and the existing work aimed at diversification would not be enough to develop knowledge-intensive products with high value-added. A first compilation of ideas within CRO resulted in a long list of possible projects. Together with DSM's corporate planning department, CRO selected the most promising ideas and classified them into two types of projects: projects that would have to be fit for commercialisation within a period of five years and projects that would have to lead to results in ten years' time (see table 5.2). The selected projects were called corporate development programmes. A committee comprising people from research, DSM's corporate planning department, and the divisions (as well as Selman) was set up to direct these programmes. This committee became an important platform for directing research and diversification. In December 1984, top management officially decided to start the corporate development programmes.[8]

Following the decision to start the programmes, DSM's research expenditure sharply increased from 1.6% of chemical turnover in 1985 to 4.2% five years later (see graph A2 in the appendix). The corporate development programmes would initially be funded at corporate level; when a project was clearly formulated and ready for commercialisation it would be transferred to the divisions. An essential element in the decision-making process was that the Ministry of Economic Affairs granted DSM a subsidy. In the 1980s, the Dutch government developed a series of measures to stimulate Dutch industry, in a response to the economic crisis and several reports by advisory committees. In this case, following the broad incentive to stimulate research in Dutch industry, the Ministry of Economic Affairs granted DSM bilateral subsidies. The total amount was quite large compared to the budget of the corporate development programmes.[9]

DSM targeted fine chemicals, with the underlying field of biotechnology, and materials as the two main growth areas (see table 5.2. items a1-3 and b1-2 for materials and a4-5 and b3 for biotechnology). The list of corporate development programmes later expanded, but the focus on materials and biotechnology remained.[10] Biotechnology and materials research generated a lot of interest in the chemical industry. Monsanto, for instance, selected food, agriculture and healthcare as businesses to grow in because biotechnology underlay all of them.[11] DSM followed the trend, but its choice also matched the profile of its technological capabilities. Through the company's business activities and research on products such as polyethylene and other plastics, capabilities had been built in the field of

Table 5.2. Corporate development programmes.

a.		Short-term programmes: commercialisation in five years
	1.	Strong polyethylene fibres
	2.	Special composites and resins using strong polyethylene fibres
	3.	High-performance plastics
	4.	Amino acids
	5.	Biological nitrogen fixation
b.		Long-term programmes: commercialisation in ten years
	1.	Conductive polymers
	2.	Silica and ceramic materials for use at high temperatures
	3.	New high pressure, electrochemical and bio-catalytic synthesis methods for chemical intermediates

Based on: H. Lintsen & F. Veraart (2000). De nieuwe bloei van research, 1985-1990. H. Lintsen, Ed. *Research tussen vetkool en zoetstof: zestig jaar DSM Research 1940-2000.* Eindhoven/Zutphen: Stichting Historie der Techniek/Walburg Pers, 104-115, in particular 109-110.

materials research. Through the work on phenylglycine, amino acids and waste water treatment, DSM had gained a foothold in the field of biotechnology. Both in biotechnology and in materials, research work of the 1970s had contributed to the corporate development programmes.

CRO translated DSM's strategic reorientation of the first half of the 1980s into corporate development programmes. In the 1970s, DSM had had difficulty in aligning research plans and business strategy but the corporate development programmes ensured a tight fit between R&D plans and strategy and ensured mutual commitment between the research organisation and the divisions. Research was again linked with diversification; innovation was an important part of DSM's readjusted business strategy. This, combined with improved profitability, resulted in more room for research in the 1980s. Towards 1990 this was to pay off in a number of research-based diversifications (see table 5.1). DSM's strategy to combat the problems in the chemical industry was not unique, nor was its emphasis on research. DSM belonged to those chemical companies that had a major research department and that deployed this department to diversify and balance their bulk chemicals oriented portfolio.

Organising Research in the 1980s
The strategic shift and the corporate development programmes also had consequences for the organisation of research. New laboratories were built and existing ones renovated. In 1985, a new name was also chosen for CRO: DSM Research. The matrix remained in place as both the divisions and re-

search were of the opinion that this organisation worked, but the divisions wanted to reinforce their control of research further. Top management responded by suggesting that the directors of research be placed under the responsibility of the divisions. DSM Research implemented this change in 1985. In the same year it changed its departmental structure to create smaller departments and more effective communication within them.[12]

Although the divisions again considered decentralisation of research unattractive, some R&D started to be done under their responsibility in the 1980s. Chem-Y's laboratory had not been integrated into CRO because of a lack of synergy, and in thermoset resins Synres operated an independent research laboratory. In 1982, DSM bought Urachem, the resins activities of Unilever. This included a research laboratory in Zwolle (the Netherlands), which remained intact. When DSM established a Resins division in 1983, this division also became responsible for its two research laboratories. The Resins division used DSM Research's central facilities in Geleen (Netherlands) alongside its own laboratories, however. The Plastics division similarly developed a pattern of both central and decentralised research. In 1986, the Applied Research and Technical Service (ARTS) laboratories were split off from DSM Research and placed under the responsibility of the Plastics division. To create close contacts with customers, the ARTS laboratories organised service research for marketing in several units centred around one product.[13]

The trend towards decentralisation of research through expansion of laboratories in divisions and business units was less pronounced at DSM than at other companies. Some divisions set up limited research laboratories but the main effort was still concentrated in DSM's centralised, corporate research laboratory. The divisions and the research department were not so large that centralised research became unmanageable.[14]

Dyneema: The Development of Strong Polyethylene Fibres

Around 1963, Albert Pennings and Ron Koningsveld of the fundamental polymer research unit needed a polyethylene solution of uniform temperature; they decided to stir the solution mechanically. It led to a surprising discovery: polyethylene crystals formed on the stirring rods. Crystallisation of polyethylene had been observed before, but only through cooling. This chance discovery triggered further research, which in turn was ultimately to lead to Dyneema, a strong and stiff fibre (a high strength-high modulus fibre).[15]

Beyond a Discovery
In 1956, the Central Laboratory had started fundamental polymer research, as had many other companies around that time. Companies primarily engaged in polymer research and universities only followed later.[16]

The Central Laboratory's new research unit at first focused on polyethylene, the polymer for which DSM was building a plant at that time. One of the subjects was fractionation: methods to make polyethylene with uniform and sharply-defined molecular weight and distribution. Commercial polyethylene was not homogeneous in this respect. Molecular weight and distribution were key parameters that influenced the characteristics of the product, and uniform polyethylene was therefore important for research aiming to understand this relationship. In the long run, it promised an improvement in product quality. In 1959, research had advanced to the stage that substantial amounts of polyethylene could be fractionated on semi-technical scale.[17]

In 1963, Pennings and Koningsveld converted their crystallisation discovery into a method to fractionate polyethylene, resulting in very homogeneous substances. Pennings and Koningsveld published their discovery and the results of their research in 1964. With a colleague, they discovered in the same year that polyethylene crystallised into a fibrous form. Further research showed a branched, so-called 'shish kebab', molecular structure. The fibres were very strong and stiff, and their appearance could vary from

Production of Dyneema strong polyethylene fibres. The idea for this product originated in fundamental polymer research but it took a long time before a market and a production process could be developed.

paper-like to down-like. In 1966, Pennings developed a method to crystallise polyethylene into a sheet which could be written upon and a patent was applied for. Revallier came up with the idea of using the new material to reinforce other plastics. The Central Laboratory's application research group investigated this idea but came to the conclusion that new equipment would have to be developed. Plastics processing companies would have to invest in this new equipment, which made introduction of the fibre to reinforce plastics unattractive.[18]

Around the middle of the 1960s, the Central Laboratory's work on polyethylene fibres still had not identified any field of application and there was no process with which polyethylene fibres could possibly be manufactured on an industrial scale.[19] Research was fundamentally oriented and was aimed at understanding the structure and properties of the crystals and how they formed. It generated little interest in DSM's manufacturing organisation.

The work of the fundamental polymer research unit on polyethylene fibres reflects the importance attached to fundamental research and research work in general in the 1950s and 1960s. There was much room to explore subjects without concern for immediate applications and research work could continue even when there was no clear interest from manufacturing. As we have seen in the previous chapter, this changed in the 1970s. The Central Laboratory's budget was cut and the divisions funded research for a large part. In particular, less importance was attached to fundamental research, and the fundamental polymer research section was consequently reduced from twenty-five to fifteen people during an economising programme in 1970. Pennings left for Groningen University (Netherlands). By contract, DSM partly funded his research.

Developing a Process

Although fewer people worked on fundamental polymer research after 1970, work on polyethylene fibres continued but on a small scale. Pennings also continued research on the subject in Groningen. In 1969, before Pennings left for Groningen, he had started research on continuous processes for the manufacture of polyethylene fibres. He had made little progress that year but in Groningen Pennings and his group developed the so-called surface growth method. Ultra high molecular weight polyethylene (UHMW-PE) was used here. A seed fibre was immersed in a vessel containing UHMW-PE, and from a rotating inner cylinder a tape-like fibre could be drawn (Figure 5.1). This fibre had the shish kebab molecular structure. The surface growth method demonstrated for the first time that high-strength, high-modulus polyethylene fibres could be made. DSM patented the process because of the funding contract.[20]

Although Pennings had shown that a fibre could be made, CRO was sceptical about the surface growth method. It was a very slow way of making a fibre, and this fibre did not have a homogeneous thickness. The process was also difficult to scale up.[21] On the other hand, other companies were investigating high-strength, high-modulus fibres as well. ICI showed an interest in the surface growth method, but nothing came of this as the company's fibre activities were in stormy weather. DSM approached AKZO, but they were not interested because they were aiming at other fibres and considered themselves specialists in the field. Although the contacts of CRO with other companies did not result in concrete partnerships, these contacts, and the activities of other companies in the field, did encourage research to continue. Revallier in particular stimulated the project: the fibre seemed unique, had been patented by DSM and was based on polyethylene, in which the company had accumulated much experience.

At the end of 1978, CRO hired Paul Smith, one of Pennings' PhD students, to work on the development of a process to make polyethylene fibres amongst other items. Together with Piet Lemstra, he came up with the idea of gel spinning, a process that dissolved polyethylene, pushed the solution through a spinneret, quenched the fibres and drew them to obtain the desired strength. (Figure 5.2).[22] All polyethylene molecules were aligned when this method was used, leading to the best possible strength and stiffness. In 1979, DSM applied for a patent on the gel spinning process. A conflict arose with Pennings as to who should get the scientific credits because Pennings argued that the gel spinning process built on his own work in crucial ways. The conflict ended the cooperation between DSM and Pennings.

Funding Research

With the gel spinning process, research took a crucial step forward: now a fibre could be manufactured in principle. Additional research needed to be funded, however, to develop the process further and commercialise products. The Plastics division, which was linked to the project through polyethylene, showed no interest. The Chemical Products division manufactured intermediates for synthetic fibres, caprolactam and acrylonitrile, but no fibres. Although CRO had know-how in the field of fibres through its Fibre Technology department (formerly Fibre Intermediates), this market remained uncharted territory for DSM. Chemical Products and Plastics did not plan to start manufacturing fibres nor did they change course because of the development of the gel spinning process.

If the polyethylene fibres project was to continue, corporate funds would have to be made available. At that time, in the early 1980s, top management was reorienting DSM's strategy towards knowledge-intensive products and from this perspective polyethylene fibres were interesting products. CRO used the possible applications of strong polyethylene fibres

Figure 5.1. Surface growth method.

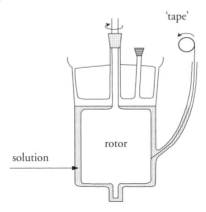

Source: M. J. N. Jacobs (1999). *Creep of Gel-Spun Polyethylene Fibres: Improvements by Impregnation and Crosslinking.* Eindhoven: Dissertation Eindhoven University of Technology. Figure 2.2, 20.

Figure 5.2. The gel spinning process.

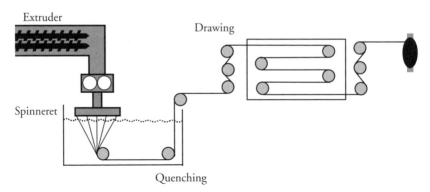

Source: M. J. N. Jacobs (1999). *Creep of Gel-Spun Polyethylene Fibres: Improvements by Impregnation and Crosslinking.* Eindhoven: Dissertation Eindhoven University of Technology. Figure 1.2, 6.

to convince Selman and top management, but economic circumstances made it difficult to fund a major research programme. Top management left the question as to whether DSM would eventually manufacture polyethylene fibres unanswered until the company's patent position was clear. In 1981, top management agreed to fund further research, in a plan to do part of the scale-up work to decide whether DSM should start fibre manufacture or should license out the technology. Because of the limited resources, CRO conducted some experiments in cooperation with the

THE COMPANY THAT CHANGED ITSELF

Eindhoven University of Technology (Netherlands) and Aachen Polytechnic (Germany). CRO also built a small installation at Fibre Technology to research the gel spinning process for polyethylene fibres and to investigate whether the process could be applied to other fibres, for instance nylon. The Chemical Products division therefore partly paid for the installation. Fibre Technology created a post for development of the gel spinning process, but combined this research with technical service work. Only through this combination could enough funding be secured.[23]

In 1982, another general round of cost cutting started because DSM had made a loss that year but the polyethylene fibre project survived, particularly because the spinning installation had just been started. Although Lemstra and Smith's gel spinning process overcame the slow production speed of the surface growth method, it proved difficult to make a homogeneous and viscous polyethylene solution. To tackle this problem, researchers developed a special twin-screw extruder.[24] Gel spinning proved to work only for polyethylene and it also became clear that the quality of the raw materials needed to make polyethylene fibres was crucial. The small spinning unit made fibres that were not as strong as expected because UHMW-PE, the raw material, was impure. The supplier could not solve the problems and CRO proposed developing a process for making the necessary UHMW-PE and securing supply of the raw material for Dyneema, as the product was now called. In doing so CRO built on its knowledge of polyethylene catalysts. UHMW-PE could also be sold as an engineering plastic.

In September 1983, after DSM had been granted a crucial patent, top management decided that licensing out the accumulated know-how concerning strong polyethylene fibres was less attractive than in-house production. On the other hand, both top management and CRO agreed that DSM lacked a lot of know-how of spinning, application development and marketing in the field of synthetic fibres, and lacked the time to develop such know-how in-house. Finding a partner became crucial. AKZO once again came into view, but once again refused. Polyethylene fibres were of interest to Allied Signal Inc. from the United States, however, and the company had been working on a gel spinning process itself. Allied tried to challenge the validity of DSM's patents, but failed, and then had to negotiate a license. Allied accepted a very high licensing fee and this convinced many people at the top of DSM that the company was onto something valuable.[25]

At the end of 1984, CRO included the strong polyethylene fibre project in the list of proposed corporate development programmes. Its acceptance by top management meant that more corporate funds became available for the project. In the same year DSM selected the Japanese company Toyobo as its partner. In 1986, the two companies established a joint venture to develop the polyethylene fibre further. DSM owned 51% of the shares. Toyobo was an attractive partner because it had extensive know-how of spinning synthetic fibres while its marketing knowledge and techniques were also valuable for DSM. Moreover, the market could be easily divided. Toyobo became responsible for the Far East, New Zealand and Australia, Allied owned the exclusive rights for the United States, and DSM could operate in the rest of the world's markets. Toyobo and DSM used Dyneema as a trade name while Allied marketed its polyethylene fibres as Spectra.[26]

Allied worked fast to introduce its new fibre on the market and tried to patent certain applications while other companies were developing comparable products as well. At the end of 1986, DSM and Toyobo agreed on a 'Hurry-Up Programme' that aimed to build pilot plants for UHMW-PE and Dyneema. In 1987 these plants came on stream. The Dyneema pilot plant was built in Japan.

In 1988, just a year after the pilot plants had been started, the decision to build industrial scale installations came into sight but Toyobo hesitated and did not want to take the risk involved. They raised doubts about the success of Dyneema in Europe and suspected that DSM could profit far more from the joint venture because it provided an entry into the Japanese market. DSM tried to solve the problems by involving the Japanese more in the engineering and construction of its Dyneema plant, but the joint venture had to be restructured. The pilot plant in Japan would be expanded under the joint venture, but the plant in the Netherlands would become the sole responsibility and property of DSM. Toyobo provided full technical assistance, however. In 1990, industrial production of Dyneema started at an industrial area in Heerlen (Netherlands) while production of UHMW-PE started in the same year.[27]

Finding a Market
In the early 1980s, it gradually became clear that a process for a polyethylene fibre could be developed. Although it was by that time clear that fibres would also be the area of application, much work needed to be done to determine which applications would be promising for the new material. Dyneema is a strong, stiff, lightweight fibre, resistant to UV radiation and many chemicals, but it has a relatively low melting point compared with aramid high-strength, high-modulus fibres like Du Pont's Kevlar. DSM aimed not so much at finding new applications for its fibre but at substituting other materials in existing applications. Dyneema competed not only with aramid fibres but also with other types of fibres and materials.[28] Du Pont tried to market Kevlar as a tyre cord but with limited success. It also developed other applications, however, such as bullet-proof vests and other protective clothing, cables and composites. In the last category of

The UHMW-PE plant in 1990. Ultra high molecular weight polyethylene (UHMW-PE) is used to manufacture Dyneema. DSM also marketed UHMW-PE as an engineering plastic.

applications, carbon fibres also competed. Strong but lightweight, carbon-fibre-based composite materials were well-suited for use in the aerospace industry and in sports equipment. Several companies were manufacturing these fibres by the early 1980s.[29]

At DSM, application research started in 1981 when the small spinning unit was installed. There were contacts with TNO (the Dutch organisation for applied research) and personal contacts with employees of AKZO. Under the corporate development programme, additional funds became available and a dedicated application research laboratory was built for Dyneema and opened in 1985. A new composites laboratory opened a year later and also engaged in application research on the new material.[30]

By 1990, application research and marketing efforts had opened three main markets. The first was ropes and cables, particularly for offshore and nautical applications. Dyneema was promoted as a material for anchoring ships and offshore drilling rigs, for instance. It floated on water, which was an advantage when a line broke. Dyneema's strength, stiffness and low weight also made it better than steel. Dyneema cables were also more durable than steel cables as they could better withstand the varying stress caused by heavy or moderate seas. The second important area of application was as a material for protection against bullets, shrapnel and other kinds of ammunition. In this field, specific applications called for specific Dyneema variants, depending on the degree of protection desired and on the type of ammunition. Dyneema competed with Kevlar and other aramid fibres in this market. Because of its relatively low melting point, Dyneema could not be used as a tyre cord. Finally, Dyneema found ample use in composites, with applications ranging from helmets to sails, tennis rackets and skis. Dyneema was well-suited for sails because of its strength and its resistance to UV radiation. Competition came from a range of materials and depended on the specific requirements in use.[31]

Introducing a New Product

From 1990 onwards, Dyneema gradually developed into a success story for DSM. The number of applications increased, as did production capacity and sales. Against the background of this commercial success, the story of the development of the polyethylene fibre may seem odd. Why was Dyneema's potential not realised sooner?

Karel Mulder argues in his dissertation that the fundamental polymer research unit was isolated, and that this position made it difficult to get DSM's manufacturing organisation interested in the discovery made by Pennings and Koningsveld; which is why it took a long time before Dyneema was commercialised.[32] In comparison to the fundamental catalysis section of the Central Laboratory, the polymer research unit does seem to have been more isolated. For catalysis, a contact group was established with members of the manufacturing organisation, researchers and also people from the SBB's works laboratory, while catalysis expertise was also frequently needed in a broad range of projects. This was not the case for fundamental polymer research, which was isolated in this sense.

The discovery made by Pennings and Koningsveld, moreover, was a long way away from any commercial product. There were several ideas, but none of them were very clear and targeted. Research aimed at finding a process started only in 1969, six years after the initial discovery had been made. In the 1960s, the project was not in a phase that it seemed likely DSM's manufacturing organisation would become interested. Only in the late 1970s did a feasible industrial process come into view, and with it, fibres as a possible field of application.

THE COMPANY THAT CHANGED ITSELF

When fibres emerged as the most promising field of application, another problem emerged. Although DSM had some technological knowledge of the spinning and processing of synthetic fibres through the work of CRO's Fibre Technology department, the gel spinning process differed from the typical processes for synthetic fibres.[33] More importantly, DSM had no knowledge of the fibre market and had no expertise in marketing fibres. This explains the divisions' reluctance to support Dyneema in the 1980s. For Chemical Products, the step toward actual fibre manufacture was large because of this lack of market knowledge. For the Plastics division the project was both a different business and a different technology. In this way, Dyneema almost naturally became a corporate project. Dyneema was a long-term project and not related to the markets and technologies the divisions were active in. The question of whether or not DSM should start manufacturing fibres was a very fundamental one and was directly related to strategy issues.

The harsh economic climate and the company's poor results in the early 1980s made it difficult to allocate a large amount of corporate funds to Dyneema. Around the middle of the 1980s this changed and, at the same time, the strategy to move away from bulk chemicals intensified. Dyneema was an interesting project from this perspective and more funds could, and were, made available. The new material was then commercialised in a relatively short period of time, with Toyobo providing the necessary know-how on manufacturing and marketing synthetic fibres.

The critical steps in the story of Dyneema were the translation of a discovery into a product and finding a market for that product. In cases like caprolactam and urea it was clear what the product was and who the potential buyers were. In the case of Dyneema, DSM had to develop an offensive strategy. As fibre manufacture was a commercial and technological mismatch, this was not easy and took time. Indeed, it was a tremendous achievement that the Dyneema project was brought to a successful conclusion. Innovations along the axis of both technology and markets often fail, as the lysine case shows for example.[34]

The case of Dyneema also shows the evolution of research policies over the years. Confidence in research was high in the 1950s and 1960s, and research played an initiating and enabling role. There was also much room for fundamental research, as the work of the Central Laboratory's fundamental polymer research section shows. Researchers could work on projects that manufacturing was not immediately interested in and, at least at first, they did not need to concern themselves with targeted product and process research.

In the 1970s, DSM shifted its research policies. Costs and effectiveness were reviewed critically and the divisions funded a large part of the research budget. Fundamental research was scaled down and, with it, research on strong polyethylene fibres. Towards the end of the 1970s, DSM decided to try to reduce its emphasis on bulk chemicals and expand in other, faster-growing and more profitable areas while research was regarded more positively as well. Top management shifted its strategy in a severe economic climate, but by the middle of the 1980s the company's results improved and research aimed at entering new markets was again on the map. The corporate development programmes ensured there was room for research and expenditures grew. The Dyneema case shows that the importance attached to industrial research varied in a wave-like pattern over time.

Dyneema was the most expensive corporate development programme. An evaluation of all the programmes in 1990 concluded that the results had been positive. The list of projects had shifted somewhat compared to the original ideas, but by 1990 only 20% of the projects had been discontinued with limited spin-offs (Table 5.3).

DSM's Expansion in Fine Chemicals

Dyneema shows the importance of materials in the search for new markets, but DSM made fine chemicals another spearhead in its expansion and diversification plans. After more than a decade, Special Products' turnover reached about 90 million guilders in 1982. The group produced twenty products but seven products, including benzoic acid, benzaldehyde, alpha-picoline and phenylglycine, generated 80% of its turnover and 60% of sales were in the intermediates for agrochemicals and pharmaceuticals markets.[35]

Special Products' turnover growth fell behind expectations, particularly after 1978 when growth started to stagnate. The managements of Special Products and the Industrial Chemicals division had different opinions on the course to be taken. From the division's perspective, activities in fine chemicals were scattered over too many areas – a view that was reinforced by the poor results of the acquisition of Chem-Y, both in financial terms and in terms of synergy with Special Products' technologies and markets. Industrial Chemicals' response also forms part of a broader backlash in Dutch industry against the emphasis put on diversification and acquisitions. Diversification had not cushioned the effects of an unfavourable economic climate, while integrating companies with unfamiliar businesses proved difficult, draining the expected results.[36]

In 1982, a new long-term strategy plan was agreed upon. Special Products would focus on its existing businesses, and on improving them through better marketing and through better management of production. Although activities had to be focused, both Special Products and Industrial Chemicals agreed on the need for further growth in fine chemicals to achieve the critical mass necessary for survival. In the revised strategy, this

Table 5.3. Evaluation of the corporate development programmes in 1990.

Projects	Expenditure (million guilders)	Share of total cost (%)
Commercialised projects		
1. Dyneema	70	22
B. Projects passed to the divisions with good prospects for commercialisation		
2. Engineered composites	27	
3. Carmat	15	
4. Plastic waste processing	3	
5. Amino acids (spin-off)	28	
Total:	73	23
C. Ongoing projects with good to acceptable chances of success		
6. S-RIM	5	
7. Strong film/ Geltrusion	19	
8. Epoxy moulding compounds/ E&E materials	3.5	
9. Biomedical applications	6	
Total:	33.5	11
D. Ongoing projects with low to minimal chances of success in the short term		
10. PVA and new high-performance fibres (including first phase of Dyneema)	31	
11. High-performance plastics/LCPs	39	
12. Biochemistry	4	
13. Conform	2	
Total:	76	24
E. Discontinued projects with limited spin-off		
14. Silica	29	
15. Ceramics	20	
16. Agro-biotechnology	2	
17. Chemical intermediates	4	
18. Enzymatic hydroxylation	5	
Total:	60	20
Total for all programmes:	313	

Source: H. Lintsen & F. Veraart (2000). De nieuwe bloei van research, 1985-1990. H. Lintsen, Ed. *Research tussen vetkool en zoetstof: zestig jaar DSM Research 1940-2000.* Eindhoven/Zutphen: Stichting Historie der Techniek/Walburg Pers, 104-115, in particular table 8.1, 112.

would be achieved through autonomous growth and by a targeted acquisition. Special Products should in ten years' time reach the level of companies like SSF Dottikon (now EMS Dottikon) and Lonza, both Swiss companies. Dottikon had been established in 1913 and had branched out into fine chemicals and custom synthesis, where it produced a specific intermediate for a customer or the customer's proprietary compound.[37] Lonza was established in 1897 as an electricity and carbide works. Lonza branched out into calcium cyanamide fertiliser in 1915, followed by ammonia synthesis in 1925 and later other bulk chemicals as well. Carbide also provided a route to acetylene, which in turn secured Lonza's entry into fine chemicals. The company developed into a conglomerate of energy, bulk chemicals and fine chemicals activities, but chose the latter as its core after 1980. Lonza pushed down the share of bulk chemicals in its turnover from 76% in 1970 to 65% in 1980 and 44% in 1985.[38]

DSM's top management confirmed the new strategy for fine chemicals in October 1982 and integrated it into DSM's overall diversification strategy in 1984.[39] Organisationally, Special Products moved to the Chemical Products division in 1983. After the acquisition of the resins division of Unilever, DSM established a new Resins division by merging the acquired activities with the existing activities of Industrial Chemicals in this field. The remaining groups of the Industrial Chemicals division became part of the Chemical Products division.[40]

A Joint Venture: Aspartame

DSM aimed to achieve growth in fine chemicals both organically and via acquisitions. Nevertheless, an opportunity presented itself to start production of aspartame, a sweetener about 200 times sweeter than sugar but low in calories.

In 1965, a chemist working at the American pharmaceutical company G.D. Searle & Co. discovered that a dipeptide from aspartic acid and L-phenylalanine tasted intensely sweet. However, it took a long time before aspartame was approved for applications in food as doubts were raised on the safety of the compound. In 1979, France was the first country to grant approval. The United States followed two years later, and in 1983 also approved the use of aspartame in soft drinks, which became a particularly important application. Because it was low on calories, aspartame could be used in diet soft drinks. Searle's aspartame business, under the trade name NutraSweet, grew fast. In 1985, Monsanto acquired Searle as part of its strategy to move into businesses that were more profitable than bulk chemicals. Searle had patented the use of aspartame in many fields, and only Ajinomoto in Japan had been granted a license. Although competing sweeteners were on the market, this patenting strategy greatly enhanced the profitability of aspartame for Searle and later Monsanto.[41]

In 1966, the lysine group at the Central Laboratory had started working on aspartame of their own accord. DSM patented an aspartame process in 1972. The reaction of aspartic acid and D,L-phenylalanine yielded a racemic mixture. Only the L-configuration tasted sweet, while the D-configuration tasted bitter and had to be removed. This removal proved difficult to achieve.[42]

In Japan, the Toyo Soda Manufacturing Co. Ltd. (which changed its name to Tosoh in 1987) had also worked on a method to synthesise aspartame, initially together with the Sagami Chemical Research Centre. In 1976 they found a way to produce only the sweet-tasting component of aspartame by using an enzyme. In the following years, they developed a process and built a pilot plant.[43]

DSM worked on a route to D,L-phenylalanine, the most expensive intermediate for aspartame. In the early 1980s, DSM's corporate planning department re-evaluated the route to aspartame the company had patented in 1972 and found it too expensive compared to Searle's route. CRO pointed to the Japanese route, however. As an evaluation showed that this process was promising, CRO and DSM's corporate planning department approached Tosoh. In 1984, the Japanese company proposed marketing aspartame in Europe together. DSM's research appealed to Tosoh and they were already working with D,L-phenylalanine manufactured by Special Products. Tosoh thought that the Japanese market was too small while the American market would be hard to enter because of Searle's application patents. Tosoh considered production in Europe necessary to prevent high transportation costs and also feared import taxes. In 1985, Tosoh and DSM reached an agreement and established Holland Sweetener Company, with both companies holding an equal part of the shares of their joint venture. In December of that year, DSM's top management approved the construction of an aspartame plant. The required investment amounted to 181 million guilders, but DSM needed to provide only half that amount and, moreover, secured government subsidies under various industrial policy programmes, reducing the necessary funds to 50 million guilders. This was still no small amount when compared to previous investments in fine chemicals, with the exception of the overrun expansion project for Chem-Y, and also when compared to projects in bulk chemicals.[44]

The Japanese engineering contractor Chiyoda engineered and constructed an aspartame plant with a capacity of 500 tons per year. Market studies initiated by Chemical Products indicated a market volume in Europe of 1,000 tons and projected that Holland Sweetener Company would be able to capture 35% of this market. Exports of 100 to 200 tons added up to a volume of about 500 tons. NutraSweet provided by far the toughest competition, but other companies were also considering entering aspartame. Searle's application patents would in most countries expire between 1986 and 1988, and in the United States in 1992. By being the first to profit from the expiration of these patents, Chemical Products expected to capture market share and deter other companies from entry. In 1988, production of aspartame started when the European market was free of Searle's patent claims. NutraSweet defended its position by lowering prices in Europe, but Holland Sweetener Company, helped by an import tariff imposed by the European Community, could establish and maintain a position in the aspartame market.[45]

Some of DSM's technological input in the joint venture with Tosoh was generic and related to the knowledge base it had built in fine chemicals and in particular to the knowledge about the use of enzymes that it had accumulated. Another part specifically related to the production of D,L-phenylalanine. In 1985, the company decided to build a plant for the production of this compound. It was a multi-purpose plant that could manufacture other products as well. DSM Research developed the routes used in the multi-purpose plant and scaled them up in the so-called small scale installation (*Kleinschalige Installatie*, KSI), started in 1980, and later in mini plant 2, started in 1989. Matthew Hall Keynes, a British engineering contractor with offices in the Netherlands, engineered and constructed the multi-purpose plant. It went on stream in 1987.[46]

The start of aspartame production built on Tosoh's enzymatic process, but the Japanese company's knowledge was complemented by DSM's work in the field of fine chemicals. DSM's know-how for the production of D,L-phenylalanine was important in this respect, as was the research that had been done on enzymes. DSM also built on its own research to overcome the initial start-up problems of the aspartame plant and also to improve the process. This pattern of complementarity is in line with the general DSM pattern of technology acquisitions. With a defensive innovation strategy, DSM acquired technology through a joint venture to enter the existing aspartame market. The company's internal research attracted Tosoh and backed up the acquisition.[47]

Acquisitions: Andeno
Tosoh presented DSM with the opportunity to start aspartame production, but Special Products also actively went looking for companies to take over after its new strategy had been drafted. Special Products, with the help of consultants, scanned the fine chemicals industry in search of attractive take-over candidates. The group targeted American companies in particular. It generated about a quarter of its turnover in the United States, but further growth was difficult to achieve from the Netherlands. Nepera, a company producing pyridine and derivatives which in terms of scale was second only to Reilly Tar, came into view for instance, as did Kalama (now Noveon Kalama), a producer of phenol and related fine chemicals, which presented an opportunity to expand and reinforce Special Products' benz-

aldehyde business. Both examples show that Special Products followed the strategy of 1982 to expand in related businesses. Nepera was not up for sale, but Special Products started talks with Kalama in 1984. The company had been a Dow phenol production site but Dow had sold it to three employees in 1971. However, the owners asked a high price when DSM approached them, while the profitability of the operations was poor. DSM's Chemical Products division, moreover, wanted to exclude Kalama's phenol production from the deal.[48]

The joint venture with Tosoh presented an opportunity to gain access to a promising technology. The attempt to buy Kalama, by contrast, was driven by an attempt to expand market access. This remained important for Special Products after the takeover of Kalama failed. The group hired Charles Kline's consultancy firm to make a new scan of possible takeover candidates in the United States. Nepera again came into view. Schering decided in 1986 to sell its fine chemicals division, of which Nepera was a

Aerial view of part Andeno's plants in Venlo (the Netherlands), 1987. Andeno manufactured pharmaceutical intermediates and was Special Products' major customer for phenylglycine. DSM bought Andeno in 1986, at a time when the company was increasingly using acquisitions as a strategic tool for achieving growth in fine chemicals.

part. Special Products, backed by divisional management, wanted to bid. Nepera's activities and technologies complemented those of Special Products and, with a turnover of about 45 million dollars, its acquisition would boost Special Products' growth substantially. However, top management refused to make a bid because it considered that Nepera had a low potential for growth and that its acquisition would contribute little to DSM's corporate business strategy.[49]

Although Schering decided to divest its fine chemicals division in 1986, the company had branded it as an attractive field only four years earlier. Schering's move reflects the trend to focus on core business. Other pharmaceutical companies similarly de-emphasised in-house fine chemicals production. In turn, this gave dedicated fine chemicals companies or fine chemicals units of larger companies a chance to become suppliers to the pharmaceutical industry, and provided opportunities for custom synthesis. In its search for companies to take over, Special Products established valuable contacts that boosted its pharmaceutical business.[50]

On the one hand, Special Products was searching for takeover candidates, but on the other hand companies were offered to DSM. Special Products considered most of these companies unattractive, but in December of 1986, Andeno, Special Products' main customer of phenylglycine, came up for sale. Océ-Van der Grinten, a Dutch company, had established Andeno in 1957 to produce the chemicals it needed in reprography, its main business. Andeno started manufacturing pharmaceutical intermediates in 1968. By 1986, its turnover amounted to 125 million guilders, which meant that its acquisition would more or less double Special Products' turnover. Moreover, Andeno's commercial and technological profile matched that of Special Products. The two companies operated in related and complementary fields. For example, they were both working on amino acids. Moreover, Andeno had worked together with Special Products in research on D,L-phenylglycine and in the development of other intermediates for antibiotics around the middle of the 1980s.[51]

DSM had already tried to acquire Andeno in the early 1980s, but at that time Océ had refused to sell. Contacts remained, however, and in December 1986 Océ communicated to DSM's top management that it wanted to divest Andeno. Océ was restructuring its businesses while Andeno was suffering from poor results. Andeno's strategic importance to DSM was clear, and discussions between top management and the division focused on the price to pay for the company. DSM and Océ quickly reached an agreement and DSM bought Andeno in April 1987.[52]

Andeno became part of Special Products. Like Chem-Y, Andeno had its own, relatively small, research department. Unlike the case of Chem-Y, for which little research was done in DSM's R&D base in Geleen, Andeno's research and businesses were closely related to those of Special Products.

DSM left Andeno's research department intact. Coordination was necessary but was not formally organised until 1990, when a research coordinator was appointed to improve coherence in research and to try to exploit synergies better.[53]

Like aspartame, the acquisition of Andeno complemented Special Products' existing businesses and technologies. These acquisitions were also more research-driven than the failed acquisitions, particularly in the case of Andeno as it presented a springboard for the extension of fine chemicals research.

Together with the aspartame project, the acquisition of Andeno boosted DSM's activities in fine chemicals to a substantially higher level. Andeno's and Special Products' turnover were comparable while the (expected) turnover from aspartame added another large lump. Aspartame and Andeno were two crucial steps in DSM's expansion in fine chemicals.

In-house Research: Amino Acids
The body of knowledge that was complemented by the aspartame and Andeno projects related to the use of enzymes in the production of fine chemicals. Research on enzymes had started in the 1970s, at first in relation to phenylglycine but later to amino acids generally, and continued in the 1980s. In 1985, amino acids became a corporate development programme. The project was well-advanced and in 1986 became the responsibility of the Chemical Products division. In July of the next year, top management decided to build a plant for amino acids.[54]

Special Products' management characterised the project as technology push: demand for specialty amino acids would arise as these products would become available. The stage for the project had been set in 1985 when, under the corporate development programme structure, the American consultancy firm Arthur D. Little studied the technology's potential and the market's opportunities. They considered phenylglycine, phenylalanine and valine to be the most important products to be produced in the new plant. The idea was to market D-phenylglycine without hurting the existing manufacturers of this compound, and particularly Andeno of course, but the attractiveness of using the new plant for D-phenyglycine declined when DSM bought Andeno. Tosoh bought phenylalanine, which the Japanese company used in the pilot production of aspartame. There was no need to separate D- and L-phenylalanine in the Japanese aspartame process. All this meant that of the three initial amino acids which were branded as the most attractive products, only D- and L-valine remained. In 1984, Zoëcon had approached DSM for the production of D-valine, a compound it needed for the production of its insecticide, Arsenal. A specific enzyme was selected so that D-valine could be produced and this enzyme opened up a new range of products.[55]

Of the three crucial products the new amino acid plant was to make, only one remained when the installation was started in 1988. There were also some initial problems with the plant, and process improvements were needed to bring down costs. It also took some time before marketers found customers for amino acids that could be made by DSM with the enzyme discovered in the 1970s and the enzyme used for the production of valine. Andeno's marketing expertise and experience with the pharmaceutical industry proved of great value here.[56]

Networks in Biotechnology
One of the enzymes DSM needed to manufacture amino acids was supplied by the Danish firm Novo Industri, which had developed a fermentation process for the production of this enzyme. DSM and Novo did some research together in this field as well. In 1986, when the outlook for amino acid production was still bright, both firms considered the possibility of establishing a joint venture together to build on this research. DSM had gained some experience with screening and selecting enzymes, but did not have the knowledge necessary to produce on a larger scale and secure supply. For Novo, a joint venture would reduce the risks of research because it would be assured of a customer for its product. The Danish company also sought new markets to supplement its traditional outlets such as detergents, which showed some signs of saturation.[57]

Together with the Dutch company Gist-brocades, Novo was a leading company in the field of enzymes. DSM had considered Gist-brocades and other companies for cooperation as well, but Gist-brocades refused. DSM chose Novo because of its good relations with the Danish company and the quality of their research. In 1987 the joint venture plans were cancelled, but a year later a research agreement was signed, which focused on the development of improved enzymes. A market was not found, however, and the research cooperation with Novo was stopped in 1990.[58]

The agreement with Novo is just one example of a long list of projects in which DSM conducted research together with other companies, research institutes and universities. In the 1980s, companies generally made more use of outside sources of research than they had done before. Historians have tried to explain this trend by pointing to the decline in companies' research expenditure. Above all, less money was spent on fundamental and/or basic research and this was compensated for by using outside research. Historians also point to increased internationalisation.[59]

Economic explanations for the increase in the use of outside research in the 1980s centre around the increased cost, complexity and risk of doing R&D. Such explanations are based on a rather linear view of technological change, but there are also economic studies that underline the importance of government policies and argue that scouting for long-term opportunities is sometimes done through collaborative research.[60]

THE COMPANY THAT CHANGED ITSELF

At DSM, many collaborative projects related to biotechnology. Jos Schakenraad and John Hagendoorn counted twenty-one instances where DSM collaborated with other organisations in biotechnology research until 1988. Most of these were focused on fine chemicals and agro chemicals while other segments were neglected, a pattern that reflects DSM's technological and business positions. Other companies (in the Netherlands mainly large companies) also networked extensively in biotechnology. AKZO's collaborative research showed a pattern comparable to DSM's, but Royal/Dutch Shell and Gist-brocades spread their activities over more fields.[61]

In biotechnology, DSM focused on enzymes in particular and they were also a topic for collaborative research. In 1986, DSM started research on the fungus *Aspergillus niger* together with TNO and Wageningen Agricultural University. These institutes had been researching fungi for a period of ten years. The aim of the project with DSM was to try to find ways in which *Aspergillus niger* could produce enzymes, which in turn could be used for the production of a specific class of compounds. The project was fundamentally oriented and only loosely aimed at possible applications, as was the case with many collaborative research projects.[62]

Besides enzymes, DSM also ran other biotechnology projects. One was biological nitrogen fixation, which was part of the corporate development programme. Some microorganisms can make nitrogen from the air available to plants and can in principle replace nitrogen fertilisers. DSM thought that biological nitrogen fixation could lead to a new line of business for UKF, its fertiliser division, and had the opportunity to participate in a project of the American company Biotechnology General Inc. The potential rewards would be great but the effects of the microorganism under study were as yet unproven. DSM would participate in the project of Biotechnology General by funding research at Wageningen Agricultural University through the IOP-b programme, thereby minimising the company's exposure. The IOP-b was the first fully-fledged Innovation Oriented Research Programme (*Innovatiegerichte Onderzoeksprogramma's*, IOP), developed by the Ministry of Economic Affairs and aimed at stimulating research and innovation in areas that were considered to offer attractive growth possibilities for Dutch business (so-called *aandachtsgebieden*). DSM and Wageningen could not reach agreement, however, as the university claimed royalties and rights to publication that DSM regarded as excessive. Cooperation with other Dutch research institutes was considered, but agreement could not be reached and research on biological nitrogen fixation did not get off the ground.[63]

The Ministry of Economic Affairs had developed the IOP-b programme with the explicit aim of reinforcing cooperation between universities. To this end, advisory councils with members from science and industry were put in place for universities and research institutes to give advice on the projects they should undertake. DSM Research also participated in several of these councils.[64]

Besides the IOP-b, the Dutch government also established other frameworks for stimulating Dutch industry, and the European Economic Community also offered subsidies. DSM tried to use these programmes as much as possible, and to this end set up a special unit at the corporate planning department in the 1980s. In general, the national programmes were used more than the European ones. DSM found applications for European subsidies difficult to organise and funds for the chemical industry proved to be limited in practice.[65]

Although the number of collaborative research projects increased in the 1980s and although many of these projects were subsidised, using outside research was nothing new in the sense that DSM had had many relations with other companies and academic research before 1980. DSM had worked with advisors from universities, some researchers were professors by special appointment and DSM funded graduate work, for instance. The company also participated in several industry research institutes, which mostly focused on generic subjects like distillation and were funded by companies from several countries. Research collaboration with other firms was rare, but ASED and DSM had worked on the development of a once-through urea process shortly after the Second World War, for instance.

A major change in relation to outside research was that collaboration and building relationships with universities and other research institutes became an explicit goal of research policies in the 1980s. CRO felt that the company was becoming more and more diversified and built on an increasingly wide range of knowledge fields. Funds for research were strained in the early 1980s, however, making it difficult to be active in all these fields. CRO argued that external research, in many forms, could complement DSM's own research very well.[66]

An increase in the use of outside research in general, and outside research in relation to biotechnology in particular, is considered to be a feature of industrial research in the 1980s. The DSM pattern is not that different, although perhaps the trend towards internationalisation of research was less pronounced than in other companies, but the shift in research policies in relation to outside research is striking. DSM also used external research to scout for long-term opportunities. Moreover, as much of the company's collaborative research work was subsidised, the risks for the company were minimal. If something came out of the collaborative projects, DSM was in a position to utilise it, but if not, the losses were minimal. The short-term effect of collaborative research was, on the other hand, rather minimal as no new businesses developed from the many cooperative research projects in biotechnology.

Fine Chemicals in the 1980s

The 1980s were a crucial decade for DSM's fine chemicals activities. In the early 1980s growth had still fallen short of expectations, but around 1985 expansion gained momentum through the aspartame project and the acquisition of Andeno. Both acquisitions boosted turnover and were related to Special Products' existing commercial and technological profile. The lesson from Chem-Y had been learnt and formally implemented into Special Products' business strategy in 1982: in-house research complemented acquisitions.

The long-term view taken at CRO in the 1970s on the utility of enzymes proved its worth in the 1980s, and enabled research to continue to play an important role in fine chemicals. The work on enzymes and amino acids provided the base that enabled DSM to take up aspartame production together with Tosoh, to acquire Andeno, and to establish the amino acid business. The partnership with Novo provided the crucial know-how of how to manufacture enzymes, while networking with external research institutes provided the means to reinforce DSM's base in biotechnology and scout for long-term opportunities. Again the pattern is complementary, this time between in-house and external research.

Research and Bulk Chemicals in the 1980s

Dyneema, amino acids and aspartame are examples of products in areas DSM considered attractive, but the company was still manufacturing bulk chemicals and did not intend to discard these businesses. Graph 5.1 shows that research on existing products, combined with customer support and plant service, accounted for roughly 80 to 90% of the research budget between 1980 and 1990.

Caprolactam

In 1979, DSM manufactured its two millionth ton of caprolactam. The company had grown into one of the largest manufacturers of caprolactam in the world, and remained in that position throughout the 1980s (Table 5.4). Annual growth of caprolactam demand was only about 2% per year, however. The European market grew little, while the manufacture of synthetic fibres increasingly moved to the Far East and developing countries (Graph 5.2). DSM gained a foothold in these markets through exports and built a position in Latin America by minority participations in licensed caprolactam plants. New customers and markets had to be found, the more so since AKZO, DSM's long-time major customer, no longer bought caprolactam exclusively from DSM and closed its British subsidiary British Enkalon. Courtaulds decided around the same time to end nylon production in the United Kingdom. Nypro, DSM's British caprolactam operation at Flixborough, lost its customers. The plant had been rebuilt after the

Graph 5.1. Research expenditure by category.

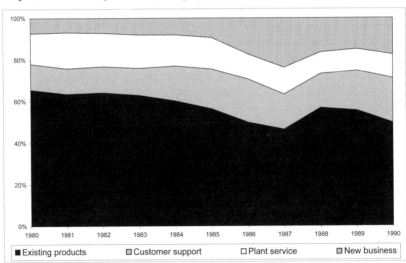

Source: Data compiled by Siep Schaafsma.

explosion of 1974, but closed permanently in 1980. Production of capro-lactam at Nipro, DSM's American subsidiary, also fell in the early 1980s.[67]

DSM continued to invest in caprolactam production in Geleen, though. In 1982, the rearrangement section was renovated. Control rooms were centralised and digitised, while the pneumatic control devices in the plant were replaced by electronic ones. Production and maintenance costs could be cut and product quality could be improved as well. In 1983 and the following year, the purification section was revamped. Between 1984 and 1986, the capacity of the HPO plant could be increased from approximately 70,000 tons to about 100,000 tons through small modifications. The increased scale meant reduced costs per ton, and this was attractive regardless of the development of the market for caprolactam. The capacity boost meant the definitive breakthrough of HPO technology.[68]

Increasing energy efficiency was a very important theme in caprolactam at the beginning of the 1980s. DSM embarked on a company-wide pro-gramme of reducing the use of energy and feedstocks by good housekeep-ing. Without making major investments, DSM aimed to keep consump-tion of raw materials and utilities to a minimum by stimulating awareness among plant personnel and by keeping track of consumption figures. Such measures saved millions of guilders.[69]

CRO played a relatively limited role in these measures, but it did carry out research on increasing energy efficiency and reducing consumption of raw materials. Specifically in relation to caprolactam, research tried to im-prove the phenol process, for instance. In 1978, a second phenol plant was

THE COMPANY THAT CHANGED ITSELF

Graph 5.2. World caprolactam production by region, 1980-1990.

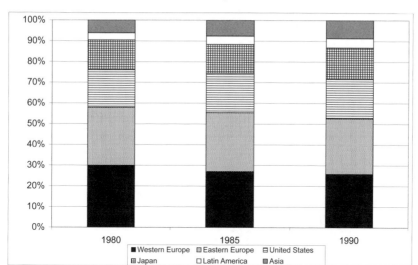

Source: *Kirk-Othmer Encyclopedia of Chemical Technology.* London: Wiley-Interscience. Fourth edition, 16 volumes, 1991-1996. Vol. 4, 1992, table 3, 834.

started up at CIR, DSM's subsidiary located in the harbour region of Rotterdam (Netherlands). CRO started research on possible improvements to the phenol process, but in 1979 reached the conclusion that DSM's toluene-based phenol process was in principle more expensive than a competitive route that started from cumene, a compound made from benzene. In an attempt to make the DSM phenol process more attractive, research tried to improve the first two steps of the process (the oxidation of toluene and the subsequent oxidation of benzoic acid) and also tried to increase production of the by-products of phenol manufacture (benzoic acid and benzaldehyde). The by-products in DSM's phenol process contributed significantly to the viability of phenol manufacture at CIR. The position of DSM's phenol process remained difficult, however. Buying phenol on the market instead of manufacturing it at CIR would substantially cut the costs of caprolactam production in Geleen. CIR closed the oldest plant in Rotterdam in the early 1980s. Additional phenol, needed to manufacture caprolactam, was bought from other firms.[70]

The improvement of the process for the oxidation of cyclohexane was also a project that aimed at reducing the amounts of energy and raw materials used in the production of caprolactam. Oxidation of cyclohexane was part of the route to cyclohexanone that started from benzene. DSM's process oxidised cyclohexane in a cascade of five reactors. Efficiency was relatively low, but could be increased substantially by leaving out the cata-

Company	Country	1980		1985		1990	
		Capacity 1000 t/ y	Rank	Capacity 1000 t/ y	Rank	Capacity 1000 t/ y	Rank
Techmashimport[i]	Russia	550	1	550	1	550	1
BASF	Germany	440	2	440	2	460	2
DSM	Netherlands	435	3	380	3	390	3
Allied Signal	USA	220	4	250	4	300	4
SNIA/					5		6
Montedipe	Italy	170		170		195	5
Ube Industries	Japan	160	6	160	5	180	6
Bayer	Germany	150	7	150	7	110	8
Toray Industries	Japan	130	8	130	8	145	7
Polimex	Poland	110	9	110	9	110	9
Chung Tai	Taiwan	90	10	100	10	110	10

Source: *Kirk-Othmer Encyclopedia of Chemical Technology.* London: Wiley-Interscience. Fourth edition, 16 volumes, 1991-1996. Vol. 4, 1992, table 3, 834.

[i] Sic. This was the Soviet agency responsible for technological imports, but it did not run the actual plants.

lyst in the first three reactors. Although the cyclohexane oxidation unit in Geleen had closed in 1975, CRO continued research on the improvement of the process as Nipro, DSM's American caprolactam subsidiary, would profit from this research. Stamicarbon could also profit from an improved cyclohexane oxidation process since licensed caprolactam plants, with a few exceptions, all started from benzene instead of toluene. In 1979, Nipro converted two of its three cyclohexane oxidation units to the improved process, followed by its third unit in 1981. There were several initial problems but the consumption of cyclohexane per ton of cyclohexanone could be reduced. Research continued on this subject throughout the 1980s and the efficiency of cyclohexane oxidation was further improved.[71]

Research that aimed to remove or reduce the by-product stream of ammonium sulphate also continued. Ammonium sulphate had a great influence on the economics of caprolactam production and often the price of the ammonia contained in the sulphate could not be recouped. Researchers tried several options to reduce or even get rid of this by-product, but the most viable one proved to be the optimisation of the rearrangement section. This did not remove by-product manufacture completely, but at least minimised the amounts. Research also developed a two-step rearrangement to reduce the amount of by-product ammonium sulphate further. Research on by-product reduction was an ongoing process and the results were continuously being applied in the plants.[72]

Management of the Chemical Products division pursued a two-track strategy in relation to ammonium sulphate. On the one hand, the volume of the by-product stream should be minimised as much as possible, but on the other hand Chemical Products initiated research with the aim of improving the production of ammonium sulphate as such. The energy efficiency of the sulphate plants was improved, leading to lower production costs. In 1982, CRO started to research the possibilities of making larger granules, which would make by-product ammonium sulphate suitable for use in mixed fertilisers, fertilisers which contained two or all three plant nutrients. DSM manufactured mixed fertilisers by chemical processes, but these products could also be made by dry-mixing several individual fertilisers. CRO succeeded in doubling the size of the ammonium sulphate granules, making them suitable for use in dry-mixed fertilisers. Improved product quality also made it possible to sell ammonium sulphate outside the fertiliser market, for instance for use in fire extinguishers.[73]

By minimising the amount of ammonium sulphate and by improving its quality at the same time, the influence of the by-product stream on the economics of caprolactam production was combated. Such rationalisation measures were important in the 1980s to maintain competitiveness. DSM's production capacity at Geleen increased only modestly in the 1980s.[74] Technological modifications were relatively small and innovations were incremental, but this work was nevertheless crucial.

Research beyond incremental improvements was also performed, however. Stamicarbon licensed caprolactam technology, and in 1980 they competed for a project in Mexico. BASF's offer caused some concern to CRO as the projected use of feedstocks and energy were low. Even though Stamicarbon had built in more reserves in its tender than BASF, the Mexican project triggered a study into possible improvements of the HPO process. CRO worked on this study and soon concluded that BASF's nitric oxide reduction process was in principle more attractive than DSM's HPO process. The use of nitric oxide meant that only half of the hydrogen was needed and this cut costs substantially. CRO investigated the use of nitric oxide in the HPO process and called it the HPNO process. Using nitric oxide would cut costs, but was a disadvantage at the same time. Nitric oxide had to be produced by oxidising ammonia with pure oxygen instead of with air, which was the route to nitrous gases in the HPO process and a method widely used for the production of nitric acid. The use of oxygen made the process expensive and the necessary investments would not pay. Moreover, at about the same time that research was being done on the HPNO process, the capacity of the HPO plant was being boosted substantially through debottlenecking. This reduced the costs of existing caprolactam production plants and in turn reduced the attractiveness of converting the existing plant to the HPNO process. Therefore, the project was stopped in 1984.[75]

DSM continued probing possible alternatives for its technologies. In 1988, divisional management and CRO initiated the ALTAM project ('alternative caprolactam'). Demand for caprolactam grew only slowly. Polyester, and synthetic fibres made from cheaper feedstocks in general, threatened caprolactam, while major reductions in costs were considered to be unachievable with the existing caprolactam technology. In the ALTAM project, CRO investigated the possibilities of a route to caprolactam starting from butadiene, a compound available from steam crackers. Butadiene was cheaper than phenol, but the ALTAM process also reduced energy consumption and would be cheaper to build, adding up to a major cost advantage over existing technologies. The ALTAM process was complex, however, consisting of four steps. In 1992, cooperation was sought with Du Pont, and DSM and the American company built a pilot plant together. The ALTAM process has as yet not been commercialised, however. No major capacity expansions have been necessary because the slow growth of caprolactam demand could be met through debottlenecking and through small modifications. The necessity to build a new plant has not arisen, making it unattractive to commercialise the ALTAM process.[76]

The HPNO and ALTAM projects were both major projects and reflected an increased confidence in the necessity of research for maintaining and improving market positions. Neither of them was commercialised, however. An important reason for this was that the market for synthetic fibres, and particularly nylon, was growing much more slowly in the 1970s and 1980s than in the 1960s. Major expansions of capacity were less frequently needed, if at all. Moreover, plants had become large scale. A new plant with a new process would have to be built large or otherwise it would not be economically viable. This not only increased the risks of process research, but also the investments that were needed to commercialise new technologies. In addition, the plants built in the 1960s and 1970s were not at the end of their life yet. In bulk chemicals, replacing existing plants with a new plant incorporating new technology pays off only in exceptional cases. Even the ALTAM process was not such an exceptional case. Moreover, existing plants could also be improved by incremental innovations and debottlenecking. The HPNO process lost its attractiveness when it became clear that the capacity of the existing HPO plant could be boosted without any major changes.[77]

The HPNO and ALTAM projects, as well as the projects that were closely related to existing technologies, were all focused on the consolidation of caprolactam, but diversification on the basis of caprolactam also remained a subject. A big project concerned the development of nylon 4.6, Stanyl, related to caprolactam through knowledge and experience that had been accumulated in application research.

In the 1970s, CRO worked on nylon 4 as a replacement for cotton, together with the American company Chevron. Textile products made of nylon 4, however, were very flammable and CRO stopped the project. With the knowledge that had been developed, nylon 4.6 also seemed in reach. Reinoud Gaymans from Twente Technical College (now University of Twente) had also approached DSM. Gaymans and his colleagues were working on nylon 4.6 and had established the principle of a two-step process for the manufacture of this compound. This type of nylon could withstand high temperatures and later proved to be impact-resistant as well. After a market study showed considerable potential for nylon 4.6, in 1982 the Chemical Products division gave a high priority to this research and targeted tyre cord in particular. The high melting point would be an advantage to tyre producers as they would be able to produce more tyres with the same equipment. The engineering plastics market was also targeted, which meant that the Plastics division co-sponsored the project. Stanyl did not become a corporate development programme because of the more advanced stage of the project. In 1986 a pilot plant was started up, followed by commercial production four years later. Applications as engineering plastic, particularly in computer equipment, proved to be the most important for Stanyl.[78]

Stanyl reflects DSM's strategy to seek opportunities in businesses that seemed more profitable than its activities in bulk chemicals, and the emphasis on materials in this search. In this way, Stanyl contributed to the company's search for products with high value-added. Nevertheless, the most important aim of research directly relating to caprolactam was consolidation. In the first place, this entailed making small modifications to the plant and incremental innovation to maintain competitiveness. Increasing energy and feedstock efficiencies, as well as the work done on ammonium sulphate, are examples of this type of research work. In the second place, consolidation research meant that the possibilities of alternative processes were probed, but these projects were difficult to commercialise. In summary, work on caprolactam reflects DSM's business strategy of the 1980s. The development of the market was recognised and a strategy was developed that aimed at maintaining the company's position.

Urea

Another bulk chemical DSM manufactured was urea. When a new long-range plan was drafted for CRO in 1979, DSM's know-how in urea, and fertilisers generally, was considered to be outdated. Competitors had advanced in the 1970s, mainly in relation to product finishing techniques and in reducing energy consumption of manufacturing processes. With regard to urea, Stamicarbon and CRO feared competition from other licensors on the market for technology and above all from Snam Progetti, whose marketing techniques CRO and Stamicarbon characterised as 'aggressive'. Moreover, the patents on the carbon dioxide stripping process would expire in the 1980s. Snam, which had already developed an ammonia stripping process, Ammonia Casale, Montedison and Toyo Engineering all developed variants of DSM's carbon dioxide stripping process. Stamicarbon could no longer rely on technological leadership. The high numbers of urea licenses sold in the 1960s and early 1970s declined, and Stamicarbon's market share and profitability became strained (see graph A3 in the appendix for the number of licenses).[79]

DSM intensified research on urea. The integrated production of ammonia and urea was again considered, as competitors had developed such processes in the 1970s, but once again nothing came of this. In addition, the first attempts were made to develop a next generation of stripping technology. It would have to be a low-energy process with low investment costs. CRO meanwhile made attempts to regain a strong patent position. The processes of competitors were evaluated and researchers also came up with several alternatives. Montedison's method of stripping with both ammonia and carbon dioxide in two subsequent strippers was considered. DSM acquired a patent from an engineering contractor that described such a process. High pressure stripping was also investigated, as were several variants of the construction of the stripper. A pilot plant was built in 1981 and came on stream in November of the following year. One of the aims of research in this plant was to improve the understanding of stripping efficiencies under circumstances that differed from those in the traditional DSM process.[80]

In 1984, pilot plant research was stopped and the results obtained were evaluated. Stamicarbon reached the conclusion that no significant improvement of the carbon dioxide stripping process seemed viable, and therefore research ended. Stamicarbon changed its marketing strategy and placed emphasis on factors such as experience instead of technological superiority, and attempted to include services such as renovations and debottlenecking of existing plants (revamps). The work done on the new stripping process could also be used in these areas and Stamicarbon positively evaluated the research effort for this reason.[81]

It was Stamicarbon that pushed research on the urea stripping process, not UKF, DSM's fertiliser division. Fertilisers still occupied an important place in DSM's portfolio at that time. In 1979, DSM became the sole owner of UKF. Urea, however, was not the most attractive product because it was sold primarily on export markets. Feedstock prices, ultimately the prices of natural gas, were vital for the cost price of fertilisers, particularly in export markets where competition was fierce. The policy of the Dutch government had been to stimulate industry by keeping natural gas prices low, but in the 1970s these prices gradually became linked to the (rising) prices of petroleum, leading to a structural disadvantage for UKF.[82]

DSM's competitors not only worked on improving urea production but also improved the quality of their fertilisers. The ability to produce coarse-grain fertilisers gained in importance as products were increasingly shipped in bulk and were no longer bagged. Coarse-grain fertilisers caked less and this was an advantage with bulk transportation. In addition, farming increased in scale and in the rate of mechanisation, further increasing demand for coarse-grain fertilisers. In Geleen, UKF prilled urea. Granulation, making fertiliser grains in revolving pans or drums, made it possible to manufacture larger particles than in prilling towers. NSM, UKF's Dutch competitor, actively developed urea granulation and succeeded in putting a plant on stream in July 1979.[83]

Not surprisingly, CRO also targeted granulation in the long-range research plan of 1979. The SBB switched production of calcium ammonium nitrate from prilling to granulation in 1979 and substantial research was done in this field in the 1980s to improve granulation processes and to develop coatings. Most of this work was of a practical nature and focused on the problems of production, but some fundamental research was also done.[84]

CRO started research on the granulation of urea at the end of the 1970s. Researchers attempted a fluidised-bed technique and developed special equipment. In 1983, a process was developed that did not infringe on NSM's patents, but UKF was not interested. In 1983, CRO started research to decrease the height of prilling towers, but again UKF did not commercialise it. In the late 1970s, production staff had made small modifications to the prilling process so that larger prills could be made with the existing installations. Moreover, the works laboratory of the SBB had found a coating that also improved product quality. All this research was not in vain: Stamicarbon later offered granulation processes to its customers.[85]

In the second half of the 1980s, the growth of European fertiliser markets stagnated and competition intensified. Some companies retreated from the industry while others intensified their efforts and increased their scale.[86] DSM tried to maintain its strategy of consolidation and expansion for DSM Agro, the new name chosen for UKF in 1986. CRO worked on several projects, including specialty fertilisers and biological nitrogen fixation, which were aimed at renewing the division's businesses. In 1990, DSM Agro introduced these specialty fertilisers but it sold these businesses only one year later.[87]

The strategy of consolidation and expansion became increasingly difficult to maintain as Agro's results were poor. In 1989, the division spent 0.6% of its turnover on research. In relation to the R&D spend of competitors, which was in the range of 1 to 2%, CRO considered this budget adequate, but in absolute terms the difference was substantial because of the high turnover of the fertilisers division. Of the total research budget, CRO allocated 75% to existing businesses and the remaining 25% to new activities. CRO aimed to minimise research in relation to existing products and processes to keep working on new activities as much as possible. It dissolved the specialised group of researchers who worked on urea in 1988 as any improvements that might still be realised would not outweigh the costs of continued research. At CRO, cuts in the budget for research aimed at new activities caused more concern than cuts in research aimed at improving existing processes.[88]

In 1989, the management of Chemical Products prevented Stamicarbon from selling DSM's entire urea know-how to a consortium of three engineering contractors, mainly because of the close relationship between urea and melamine. The division bought the know-how and also stimulated Stamicarbon to develop the stripping process further. In two steps, Stamicarbon simplified the necessary equipment, resulting in lower investments for a new plant. A fertiliser company in Bangladesh built the first plant incorporating the first phase of the improvements and started production in 1994. DSM's new urea plant, which started in March 1998, was the first to utilise the second phase of the improvements.[89]

The changes Stamicabon made to the urea process involved only engineering and no research. Although they were often relatively minor, they showed that 'mature' technologies could still be improved. In the late 1980s, research on urea, and fertilisers in general, followed from a specific choice: work on existing products and processes was scaled down to a level that was considered the bare minimum, but research that could renew the fertiliser division's businesses was kept up. Cuts in this type of research caused concern at DSM Research, which felt that it would no longer be able to help the division establish new activities.[90]

Consolidation and Selective Expansion: Caprolactam and Urea Research in the 1980s

The cases of urea and caprolactam show that there was more room for research in the 1980s than in the 1970s. Consolidation did not mean less research, but meant work on improving energy and feedstock efficiencies. Expansion was also sought, but selectively in segments that looked attractive. The focus of the corporate development programmes also played a role here. Stanyl reflects the emphasis on materials, while the biological nitrogen fixation project was related to biotechnology. Through consolidation and selective expansion, caprolactam and urea research followed DSM's business strategy of the 1980s.

In research on urea, and to a lesser extent on fertilisers in general, Stamicarbon played an important role in the 1980s. Stamicarbon stimulated research out of a concern for its own position on the market for technology. Although it had to be prevented from selling DSM's urea know-how altogether, Stamicarbon showed in the 1990s that the stripping process could be further improved.

In the 1980s, there was also room for researchers to explore possible alternative processes but both in urea and in caprolactam this line of research did not lead to results. In the case of urea, the conclusion was reached that the carbon dioxide stripping process could not be significantly improved. The examples of the HPNO and ALTAM process, on the other hand, show that it had become very difficult to introduce new processes. Slow market growth, the large scale at which plants became economical, and incremental innovation in existing technologies and plants were important factors. There were still options available to take big steps in improving processes, but these opportunities were hard to seize.

The case of urea also shows that business strategy and research policy were important. It may have been that the urea stripping process was mature and highly optimised, but a project like ALTAM was never set up for urea. Fertilisers drifted away from DSM's core during the 1980s and particularly after 1985. Stamicarbon was able to adapt the stripping process to the changing requirements of its market. Research policy was not shifted similarly in the late 1980s when the fertiliser division was scaled down and when the research budget consequently declined. As a renewal of the fertiliser division seemed unlikely, focusing research on existing processes would have been more probable than minimising this type of research. In the case of urea, slow growth in the marketplace worked hand-in-hand with business strategy and research policies.

Plastics in the 1980s

Consolidation and selective expansion also characterised plastics R&D in the 1980s. Consolidation had the upper hand in the early years of that decade. DSM's Plastics division expanded and diversified in the 1970s, but with disappointing financial results. The division incurred losses in several years in the 1970s and early 1980s. The Western European plastics industry faced overcapacity as companies had continued to expand while demand growth slowed down. The minimum economical scale of ethylene plants and plastics units had increased in the 1950s and 1960s, which meant that companies expanded in very big jumps. Markets continued to grow but it took time before they could take up the extra capacity. Moreover, there were many companies producing plastics, making the industry highly competitive.[91]

Over the years, DSM had built a highly integrated complex of crackers and production plants in the belief that this would lead to high efficiency and low production costs. The interconnectedness of the complex, however, narrowed the room to manoeuvre in the early 1980s. Closing down a relatively weak product line would worsen the performance of the crackers. The Plastics division calculated that closing down a cracker in combination with product plants would not improve its performance either. The Plastics division believed a shake-out to be inevitable and argued it could survive this phase because its plants were modern and large, and because it manufactured products of high quality. After the shake-out, profitability would return. In the meantime, cutting costs and improving product quality became vital.[92]

For CRO, DSM's strategy in bulk plastics meant optimising processes to drive down costs and improve product quality. Optimisation became a defining characteristic of DSM's research in plastics. For instance, CRO

DSM's fourth naphtha cracker in 1982. The fourth cracker started production in 1979 with a nameplate capacity of 450,000 tons, underlining the expansion in scale the company's plastics business had gone through in the 1970s. Expansion alone, however, failed to bring the expected results and the Plastics division changed its course in the early 1980s.

THE COMPANY THAT CHANGED ITSELF

went to such lengths to optimise PVC that Sumitomo, which had licensed its technology to DSM, got interested in buying back know-how from DSM. CRO also worked on improving the HDPE, LDPE, polypropylene and ABS processes. To aid process improvement, CRO opened a new mini plant complex for research on HDPE and polypropylene in 1980.[93]

Application research and associated process research continued as well and was aimed at developing new product types for new applications. Together with a Finnish shipyard, CRO developed an ABS type specifically suited for pleasure boats, for instance. CRO also developed a type of polyethylene suited for making fuel tanks for cars. This type of work proceeded in close contact with (potential) customers and consumed a large part of the plastics R&D budget.[94]

Application research and product development provided springboards for the development of products with higher value-added than bulk plastics. Following the strategic change initiated by top management, the Plastics division and CRO increasingly aimed at such products in the 1980s. The anticipated shake-out did not occur, although companies rationalised their plastics production and shut down some capacity. However, demand for plastics improved and the results of the Plastics division improved with it. The division got more room to sponsor the development of products with high value-added.[95]

These products were mainly to be found in areas that imposed specific demands (resistance to high temperatures, chemicals, etcetera). Such high-performance materials got a prominent place in the corporate development programme of 1985. Besides Dyneema, blends of different polymers, composites and ceramics were included. CRO's work on blends led to Stapron, a combination of styrene – maleic anhydride and other polymers. DSM built a plant in 1993, but closed it down only six years later.[96] Stanyl and Dyneema were more successful, however, as was UHMW-PE for the engineering plastics market.

As in the case of fertilisers and synthetic fibre intermediates, DSM developed a strategy of consolidation and selective expansion in plastics. Research not only optimised production processes but also worked on broadening the product portfolio. Diversification and product development built on the same technology base that had fuelled the bulk plastics business.

Searching for Products with High Value-Added

In the 1980s, DSM chose a common twofold strategy to combat the problems in the chemical industry and improve its results. This strategy left more room for research than in the 1970s, both in bulk chemicals and in diversification projects and strategic spearheads such as fine chemicals.

The balancing of research and business interests was more successful than in the 1970s, particularly through the corporate development programmes. Towards 1990, the increased room for research paid off in a number of research-based diversifications (see also table 5.1).

Although confidence in research did not reach the levels of the 1950s and 1960s, it did increase in the 1980s. Confidence in research varied in a wave-like pattern, as the case of Dyneema shows in a nutshell. The increased productivity of research in diversification towards 1990 shows that at least some independence is necessary. In order to be productive in renewing the company's lines of business, research needs room to develop its own view of what is in the interest of the company and room to act on this view.[97]

DSM increased its research spending in the 1980s, but did not reach the levels of the 1950s and 1960s. The level of spending was adequate, however, to allow research to reclaim its importance in diversification. The major difference between the 1980s and the period before 1970 was the much stronger integration of research and business strategy, and the stronger organisational integration of research, production, marketing and other company functions. In the 1950s and 1960s, research took initiatives and management responded, leading to a rather loose interplay between research and DSM's production organisation. In the 1980s, by contrast, research took initiatives within a clearly-defined strategic framework that enabled a closer coordination between research and business needs. Compared to the 1970s, during the 1980s DSM found a better way to involve the divisions in research. The corporate development programmes were funded centrally and subsidised by the Dutch government, but the divisions monitored progress and took over well-defined projects. This provided the means to involve the divisions, but without testing their patience and confidence with the many turns and unexpected results that are characteristic of research.

Research's role in the 1980s built on its accumulated technological capabilities. The work on urea and caprolactam shows research's ability to help DSM maintain its market positions and to evaluate the attractiveness of variants of technology used in plants. The corporate development programmes also built on previous research work and accumulated technological capabilities. Dyneema's long development finally gained momentum with the development of an industrial process. Existing knowledge of fibre processing, although not very extensive, enabled the absorption of Toyobo's input.

Similarly, the expansion in fine chemicals and the research work in this field had started in the 1970s, but gained momentum in the 1980s. The work on enzymes provided a stepping-stone to the establishment of amino acid production and to engaging in the joint venture with Tosoh for aspartame production. The acquisition of Andeno complemented Special Products' business as well as the technological capabilities and research built in fine chemicals. Through research and complementary acquisitions, fine chemicals made its breakthrough and developed from a niche in 1970 to a strategic spearhead by 1985.

After DSM's shift from coal to fertilisers, and from fertilisers to bulk chemicals, DSM embarked on a third shift after 1980. Fine chemicals had started as a niche in the 1970s, but DSM started to emphasise this field after 1980. At that time, the company was developing new materials as well. This trend continued after 1990 and was to transform DSM into a fine chemicals and materials company. Research laid a crucial foundation for this transformation in the 1980s.

Notes

1   C. H. Kline (1984). Breaking Through to New Technologies. *Chemtech* 14(3), 148-151. Particularly table 3, 150. K. E. Sluyterman (2003). *Kerende kansen: Het Nederlandse bedrijfsleven in de twintigste eeuw.* Amsterdam: Boom. 240, 246-247, 262. P. H. Spitz (2003). Restructuring: The First Wave. P. H. Spitz, Ed. *The Chemical Industry at the Millennium: Maturity, Restructuring, and Globalization.* Philadelphia: Chemical Heritage Press, 9-50.

2   Monsanto: M. Fransman (1992). *Biotechnology: Generation, Diffusion and Policy.* UNU/INTECH working paper #1. 29-34 and particularly 30. Rhône-Poulenc: F. Gambrelle (ca. 1995). *Innovating for Life: Rhône-Poulenc 1895-1995.* Paris: Éditions Public Historie Albin Michel. 106-109. Hercules: P. H. Spitz (1988). *Petrochemicals: The Rise of an Industry.* New York: Wiley. 526.

3   CADH, corporate archives on research: De Research bij DSM. Nota ten behoeve van de Raad van Commissarissen/NV DSM. Heerlen, November 1975. Accenten bij industriële research zullen geleidelijk aan anders worden gelegd. *DSM Magazine* (8 July 1975), 4-7.

4   CADH, corporate archives on research: Uit: Verslag van de 61e Vergadering van de Raad van Commissarissen van de Naamloze Vennootschap DSM gehouden d.d. 8 januari 1976. Verslag van de bespreking met dr. E.J.W. Verwey over algemene aspecten van het researchbeleid van DSM, op 18.8.1976 op het Centraal Laboratorium. CRO, Afd. Res. en Ontw. Prod. en Processen, De Rooij, 19 August 1976. For Verwey see: H.A.M. Snelders. Verweij, Evert Johannes Willem (1905-1981). *Biografisch Woordenboek van Nederland.* http://www.inghist.nl/Onderzoek/Projecten/BWN/lemmata/bwn3/verweij Last update: 5 September 2003. Accessed 10 March 2005.

5   Werkverdeling Raad van Bestuur per 1 januari 1979. *DSM Magazine* (29, February 1979), 3. E. Homburg (2000). Epiloog: DSM Research op weg naar de 21e eeuw. H. Lintsen, Ed. *Research tussen vetkool en zoetstof: zestig jaar DSM Research 1940-2000.* Eindhoven/Zutphen: Stichting Historie der Techniek/Walburg Pers, 118-135, in particular 124-125. J. Schueler. *Diversificatie en de plaats van research in de DSM-organisatie (1967-1980).* Veldman & Van Royen rapport I. 36-38, 41.

6   CADH, corporate archives on research: Het lange termijn plan van de naamloze vennootschap DSM voor de jaren 1982-1987. 2e concept, August 1982. Concept ondernemingsplan 1983-1988. Staf LTP, May 1983. De ontwikkeling van DSM in het komend decennium. Discussie-nota over het diversificatiebeleid voor de Raad van Commissarissen. Undated but probably from 1984. DSM annual report 1982. H. Lintsen & F. Veraart (2000). De nieuwe bloei van research, 1985-1990. H. Lintsen, Ed. *Research tussen vetkool en zoetstof: zestig jaar*

DSM Research 1940-2000. Eindhoven/Zutphen: Stichting Historie der Techniek/Walburg Pers, 104-115, in particular 106-107.

7   C. H. Kline (1983). Surviving the Petrochemical Collapse. *Hydrocarbon Processing* 62(2), 84-A-H, in particular 84-B.

8   Personal papers of Dr S.E. Schaafsma: Ontwikkeling van de DSM-Research tot 1990. CRO, Schaafsma, 15 March 1984. CADH, RvB 84/ 279: De Visser via Van der Grinten to top management: Voorstel concernontwikkelingsprogramma's. OPO, 27 November 1984. CADH, corporate archives on research: Organisatie Concernontwikkelingsprogramma's OP&O, 19 June 1985. CADH, minutes of top management meeting 4 December 1984.

9   Interviews with Dr S.E. Schaafsma on 27 June 2003, 21 April 2004. Letter from Ministry of Economic Affairs (H. Lelieveld) to DSM (Van Liemt), 15 September 1986.

10 Lintsen & Veraart 2000, op. cit. table 8.1, 112.

11 W. B. Duncan (1982). Lessons from the Past, Challenge and Opportunity. D. H. Sharp & T. F. West, Eds. *The Chemical Industry.* Chichester: Ellis Horwood, 15-30, in particular 22. Kline 1984, op. cit. Fransman 1992, op. cit. 30.

12 CADH, minutes of top management meeting 22 November 1983. CADH, RvB 85192: Re-organisatie CRO. Personeelszaken Topkader en Concernorganisatie, Selman, Rongen, Tom en Venderbos, 5 September 1985. F. J. G. Kwanten (1993). *Onderzoek bij Staatsmijnen in Limburg/DSM Centraal Laboratorium/DSM Research 1940-1990.* DSM Research report R 89 8061 (1 September 1993). 25, 29.

13 Niet alleen 'schouder aan schouder'. In ARTS werkt men bovendien 'arm-in-arm'. *DSM Limburg Nieuws* 1986, 36(22), 4. Ir. R.E. Selman: Ruimte voor research. *DSM Magazine* (May 1990), 4-7, in particular 6. H. Strijkers (1992). *DSM Chemicals: een terugblik, 1975-1991.* DSM. No page numbers.

14 Ir. R.E. Selman: Ruimte voor research. *DSM Magazine* (May 1990), 4-7, in particular 6. H. I. Fusfeld (1994). *Industry's Future: Changing Patterns of Industrial Research.* Washington: American Chemical Society. 78-79.

15 Except where noted otherwise, this section is based on: K. Mulder (1992). *Choosing the Corporate Future: Technology Networks and Choice Concerning the Creation of High Performance Fiber Technology.* Dissertation Rijksuniversiteit Groningen. H. Lintsen, J. Schueler & F. Veraart (2000). Naar een heroriëntatie van de research, 1970-1985. H. Lintsen, Ed. *Research tussen vetkool en zoetstof: zestig jaar DSM Research 1940-2000.* Eindhoven/Zutphen: Stichting Historie der Techniek/Walburg Pers, 82-103, in particular 98-100 Lintsen & Veraart 2000, op. cit. 112-114. These works are also primarily based on Mulder's dissertation.

16 Central Laboratory annual report 1956.

17 Central Laboratory annual reports 1956, 1957, 1959. H. Hagen & H. Domininghaus (1961). *Polyäthylen und andere Polyolefine.* Hamburg: Brunke Garrels. Second edition. 62-63, 84-86.

18 Central Laboratory annual reports 1963-1965.

19 Contrary to what Mulder suggests: Mulder 1992, op. cit. 52-53.

20 Central Laboratory annual report 1969. M. J. N. Jacobs (1999). *Creep of Gel-Spun Polyethylene Fibres: Improvements by Impregnation and Crosslinking.* Eindhoven: Dissertation Eindhoven University of Technology. 20-21.

21 Jacobs 1999, op. cit. 21.

22 Jacobs 1999, op. cit. 4-7, 21-22.

23 Dr S.E. Schaafsma, 21 April 2004. Interview with R. Kirschbaum, 7 January 2005. R. E. Selman, 19 July 2005.

24 Interview with R. Kirschbaum, 7 January 2005.

25 Interview with R. Kirschbaum, 7 January 2005. R. E. Selman, 19 July 2005. CADH, Minutes of top management meeting 17 September 1983.

26 Licht en sterk. Dyneema. *DSM Magazine* (80, October 1987), 22-24, in particular 23-24.

27 Interview with R. Kirschbaum, 7 January 2005. Een supersterk verhaal... *DSM Magazine* (89, March 1989), 8-11, in particular 9-10. Nieuwsfeiten. *Business Value* 2002, 16(5), 5, 7, 9-10, in particular 9. De 'alfabet-fabriek' en het ABC van de kunststoffen. *DSM Nieuws* 1990, 40(24), 4-5, in particular 4.

28 Licht en sterk. Dyneema. *DSM Magazine* (80, October 1987), 22-24, in particular 22-23. Een supersterk verhaal... *DSM Magazine* (89, March 1989), 8-11, in particular 10-11.

29 P. L. Layman (1982). Aramides, Unlike Other Fibers, Continue Strong. *Chemical & Engineering News* (8 February 1982), 23-24. Major Growth Ahead for Carbon Fibers. *Chemical & Engineering News* (17 May 1982), 18.

30 Nieuw 'Gel-lab' geopend. *Nieuws DSM Limburg* 1986, 36(13), 1. Nieuw lab geopend bij DSM Research: Proeftuin voor composieten. *DSM Limburg Nieuws* 1986, 36(20), 1.

31 Interview with R. Kirschbaum, 7 January 2005. Dyneema zit gebeiteld. *DSM Nieuws* 1990, 40(23), 4-5.

32 Mulder 1992, op. cit. 52-53 in particular.

33 Jacobs 1999, op. cit. 5.

34 E. Roberts & C. Berry (1985). Entering New Businesses: Selecting Strategies for Success. *Sloan Management Review* 26(3), 3-17.

35 CADH, RvB 82/249: letter from head of Industrial Chemicals division (name illegible) to top management, 5 October 1982. In this letter: Strategienota Groep Speciale Produkten.

36 CADH, RvB 82/249: letter from head of Industrial Chemicals division (name illegible) to top management, 5 October 1982. Also appendixes: Strategienota Groep Speciale Produkten; Overlevingsplan voor Chem-Y? Sluyterman 2003, op. cit. 246-248.

37 Advertisements SSF Dottikon in *Chemische Industrie* 1987, 39(4), 97 and 1987, 39(9), 55.

38 P. L. Layman (1985). European Custom Chemical Makers Shift Focus to Specialisation. *Chemical & Engineering News* (27 May 1985), 30-31, in particular 30. W. Eschenmoser (1997). 100 years of progress with Lonza. *Chimia* 51(6), 259-267.

39 CADH, minutes of top management meeting 12 October 1982. CADH, corporate archives on research: De ontwikkeling van DSM in het komend decennium. Discussie-nota over het diversificatiebeleid voor de Raad van Commissarissen. Herzien concept, undated but probably from 1984.

40 H. Strijkers (1994). *Van hobby naar hoeksteen: 25 jaar Speciale Produkten bij DSM.* Geleen: DSM Fine Chemicals, Special Products. 9

41 A. G. Nill (2000). *The History of Aspartame: Food and Drug Law/Third Year Paper, Professor Peter Hutt. Harvard Law School.* http://leda.law.harvard.edu/leda/data/244/. Accessed 14 August 2003. 8-9, 26, 28-29. Nill gives an overview of the safety controversy concerning aspartame in the United States. K. Oyama (1995). The Industrial Production of Aspartame. A. N. Collins, G. N. Sheldrake & J. Crosby, Eds. *Chirality in Industry. The Commercial Manufacture and Applications of Optically Active Compounds.* Chichester: John Wiley & Sons, 237-247, in particular 238. http://www.monsanto.com/monsanto/layout/about_us/timeline/timeline5.asp. Accessed 14 January 2004.

42 E. M. Meijer (1985). Diversificatie naar speciale chemische producten. *Biotechnologie in Nederland* 2, 98-100, in particular 98. H. Lintsen, F. Veraart & P. Vincken (2000). De onvervulde belofte: Lysine. H. Lintsen, Ed. *Research tussen vetkool en zoetstof: zestig jaar DSM Research 1940-2000.* Eindhoven/Zutphen: Stichting Historie der Techniek/Walburg Pers, 70-81, in particular 81.

43 E. M. Meijer, W. H. J. Boesten, H. E. Schoemaker & J. A. M. Van Balken (1985). Use of Biocatalysts in the Industrial Production of Specialty Chemicals. J. Tramper, H. C. van der Plas, J. A. M. van Balken & P. Linko, Eds. *Biocatalysts in Organic Synthesis. Proceedings of an International Symposium Held at Noordwijkerhout, 14-17 April 1985.* Amsterdam: Elsevier, 135-156, in particular 148. Meijer 1985, op. cit. 98. Oyama 1995, op. cit. 240-241, 245.

44 Interview with R. E. Selman, 27 June 2003. Interview with Dr H. G. Bakker, 16 March 2005. CADH, minutes of top management meetings 29 October and 3 December 1985. HSC, Holland Sweetener Company: de 'weight-watchers' van DSM. *DSM Magazine* (72, May 1986), 3-5.

45 CADH, RvB 84/204: Letter from head of Chemical Products division (Van Waes) to top management, 31 August 1984. CADH, Minutes of top management meetings 17 December 1985. Maatregelen tegen dumping aspartaam. *DSM Nieuws* 1990, 40(24), 3. Strijkers 1992, op. cit.

46 CADH, corporate archives research: Budget en werkprogramma 1984, 9 December 1983. Speciale Producten bruist. *DSM Limburg Nieuws* 1986, 36(5), 4. Eerste grote multi-purposefabriek: Bij business-eenheid Speciale Producten. *DSM Limburg Nieuws* 1987, 37(10), 1, 3. Speciale gerechten uit de 'keuken van de fijnchemie'. Miniplant 2 onmisbaar voor ontwikkeling specialties SP. *DSM Limburg Nieuws* 1989, 39(13), 5.

47 Compare A. van Rooij (2004). *Building Plants: Markets for Technology and Internal Capabilities in DSM's Fertiliser Business, 1925-1970.* Amsterdam: Aksant. Chapter 10.

48 CADH, Minutes of top management meetings 13 March 1984 and 6 November 1984. CADH, RvB 86172: letter from head of Chemical Products division (Van Waes) to top management, 3 June 1986. http://www.noveon.com/products/NoveonKalama/default.asp. Accessed 24 January 2005.

49 CADH, RvB 86175: letter from head of Chemical Products division (Van Waes) to top management, 5 June 1986. CADH, minutes of top management meeting 10 June 1986.

50 Dr J. A. Bigot, 7 February 2005. H. Siedel (1982). Feinchemikalien: bei Schering wächst ein neue Unternehmensbereich heran. *Chemische Industrie* XXXIV (July), 488.

51 Andeno: de aandrijving van de pharma. *DSM Magazine* (79, August 1987), 18-20. R. A. Sheldon (1987). Biokatalyse en fijnchemie in Nederland. *Biotechnologie in Nederland* 4(1), 18-19. Strijkers 1992, op. cit. J. F. den Hertog & E. Huizenga (2000). *The Knowledge Enterprise: Implementation of Intelligent Business Strategies.* London: Imperial College Press. 120.

52 Interview with R. E. Selman 27 June 2003. J. Zuidam, 27 July 2005. CADH, minutes of top management meetings on 16 December 1986 and 24 March 1987.

53 CADH, corporate archives on research: Budget en werkprogramma 1984, 9 December 1983. Strategische analyse van de R&D van DSM 1990, 29 May 1990.

54 CADH, corporate archives on research: COPCO Rapportage: stand van zaken COP's. P. Harten, OPO, 20 May 1986. Verslag van de 15e COPCO vergadering op 17 november 1987.

55 CADH, corporate archives on research: Verslag van de researchstrategiebespreking concern-research, gehouden op 16 januari 1984. CRO, 10 February 1984. Meijer 1985, op. cit. 98. J. Kamphuis, W. H. J. Boesten, B. Kaptein, H. F. M. Hermes, T. Sonke, Q. B. Broxterman, W. J. J. van den Tweel & H. E. Schoemaker (1995). The Production and Uses of Optically Pure Natural and Unnatural Amino Acids. A. N. Collins, G. N. Sheldrake & J. Crosby, Eds. *Chirality in Industry: The Commercial Manufacture and Applications of Optically Active Compounds.* Chichester: John Wiley & Sons, 187-208, in particular 196-197.

56 CADH, corporate archives on research: Samenvattingen COPCO-verslagen 3e kwartaal 1988. Van: H. Claassen, SP. Voortgangsverslag aminozurenproject 3e kwartaal 1988. Verslag van de 18e COPCO-vergadering d.d. 17 augustus 1988. Hoofdkantoor, Secr. RvB, M. Philippens, 2 September 1988.

57 CADH, corporate archives on research: Samenwerking DSM-Novo. OPO, Meij, 14 March 1986.

58 CADH, corporate archives on research: Verslag 4e COPCO vergadering 17 March 1986. Verslag van de 1e COPCO-vergadering gehouden op 22 februari 1990. Concern Secretariaat, 5 June 1990. H. Strijkers (2002). DSM, een koninklijke eeuwling: kroniek van de laatste 25 jaar. *Het Land van Herle* 52(3). 49.

59 R. Varma (2000). Changing Research Cultures in U.S. Industry. *Science, Technology, & Human Values* 25(4), 395-416, in particular 410. E. Homburg (2003). *Speuren op de tast: Een historische kijk op industriële en universitaire research.* Maastricht: Universiteit Maastricht. Inaugural lecture 31 October 2003. 12-13, 48.

60 J. Hagedoorn (2002). Inter-firm R&D Partnerships: An Overview of Major Trends and Patterns Since 1960. *Research Policy* 31(4), 477-492, in particular 480-487. J. Howells, A. James & K. Malik (2003). The Sourcing of Technological Knowledge: Distributed Innovation Processes and Dynamic Change. *R&D Management* 33(4), 395-409, in particular 398, 402.

61 Biotechnology - Seeking the Right Corporate Combinations. *Chemical Week* (30 September 1981), 36-40. A. C. M. Schakenraad & J. Hagedoorn (1988). Industriële R&D-samenwerking op biotechnologisch gebied. *Biotechnologie in Nederland* 5(6), 313-316. Table 2, 314.

62 DSM wil Aspergillus 'temmen'. *DSM Magazine* (65, March 1985), 26-27, in particular 26. E. M. Meijer (1987). Aspartaam en aminozuren. *Biotechnologie in Nederland* 4(1), 15-16.

63 CADH, RvB 84/279: De Visser via Van der Grinten to RvB: Voorstel concernontwikkelingsprogramma's. Appendix. OPO, 27 November 1984. CADH, corporate archives on research: Highlights Biochemicaliën, chem. intermediates en plantengroeibevorderaars (o.a. Azospirillum). 1302 OPO-O/1.1.1.-101.2, 27 May 1986. Concernontwikkelingsprogramma's. Kwartaalverslag 4e/3e kwartaal 1986. OP&O, Ondernemingsontwikkeling, Harten, 21 January 1987. R. R. van der Meer (1980). *Biotechnologie en innovatie: Advies uitgebracht aan de Minister voor Wetenschapsbeleid door het CIVI (Centraal Instituut voor Industrieontwikkeling) te 's-Gravenhage.* 's-Gravenhage: Publicatie van de Voorlichtingsdienst Wetenschapsbeleid.

64 E. M. Meijer (1987). *Biokatalyse en fijnchemie: grenzen en perspectieven.* Eindhoven: Eindhoven University of Technology. Inaugural lecture 15 May 1987. 5-6. K. F. J. Niebling, R. E. Pourier, R. A. Fisher & N. B. F. Telders, Eds. (1990). *Innovatiegericht Onderzoekprogramma Biotechnologie (IOP-b) 1985-1990.* Eindverslag. Leidschendam: Programmabureau Biotechnologie. Two volumes, vol. 2, 190-191.

65 CADH, corporate archives research: Europese Technologieprogramma's. Concernstaf Planning en Ontwikkeling, Subsidiezaken, Jochems, undated. Van den Oetelaar (Concernstaf Planning en Ontwikkeling, Subsidiezaken) aan Van der Grinten en Venderbos: Europese Technologieprogramma's.

66 CADH, corporate archives on research: DSM-CRO contactenpatroon, undated. Budget en werkprogramma 1984, 9 December 1983. Driejarig operationeel plan. Samenvatting. RES IS 975 RA, undated.

67 E-mail from D. J. van Waes to the author, 28 January 2005. CADH, corporate archives on research: Verslag van de strategiebespreking Divisie Chemische Producten d.d. 7 september 1982, undated. Letter from Van Waes to RvB: relatie AKZO/DSM inzake caprolactam. Notitie voor topgesprek AKZO/DSM op 4 juli a.s. DCP, 20 June 1984. 'Winstherstel, saneren, excelleren.' Caprolactam op breukvlak in de tijd. *Nieuws DSM Limburg* 1983, 33(22), 4. H. Strijkers (1992). *Veertig jaar caprolactam bij DSM.* DSM. 16-17. *Kirk-Othmer Encyclopedia of Chemical Technology.* London: Wiley-Interscience. Fourth edition, 16 volumes, 1991-1996. Vol. 4, 1992, 834-836.

68 Interview with J. T. J. van Goolen by the author and D. J. van Waes, 5 December 2003. E-mail from D. J. van Waes to the author, 28 January 2005. Nieuwe omlegging caprolactamfabriek. Dertig jaar oud fabriekgedeelte geheel gerenoveerd. *Nieuws DSM Limburg* 1982, 32(24), 5. Renovatie caprolactamfabrieken. *DSM Limburg Nieuws* 1984, 34(23), 1, 2, in particular 2.

69 Energierekening kan f 70 miljoen omlaag: Omvangrijke campagne volgende week van start. *Nieuws DSM Limburg* 1983, 33(5), 1. Wat is energiebewaking? *Nieuws DSM Limburg* 1983, 33(5), 3. Ruim f 200 miljoen bespaard in 3 jaar. *DSM Limburg Nieuws* 1986, 36(6), 1.

70 Interview with J. T. J. van Goolen by the author and D. J. van Waes, 5 December 2003. Verslag van de Top CRO-vergadering, gehouden op 27 juni 1979, 26 november 1980. Het lange termijn plan van de naamloze vennootschap DSM voor de jaren 1982-1987. 2e concept, augustus 1982. C. G. M. van de Moesdijk (1979). *The Catalytic Reduction of Nitrate and Nitric Oxide to Hydroxylamine: Kinetics and Mechanism.* Eindhoven: Dissertation Eindhoven Technical College. 13.

71 E-mail from Dr S. E. Schaafsma to the author, 9 March 2005. CADH, corporate archives on research: Verslag 22e researchvergadering, 23 October 1974. Verslag van de 27e Researchvergadering d.d. 23 maart 1976, 7 April 1976. Verslag van de TOP-CRO vergadering van 23 april 1980, 28 januari 1981, 1 juli 1981. Strategische analyse van de R&D van DSM 1990, 29 May 1990. J. A. de Leeuw den Bouter, L. L. van Dierendonck & W. O. Bryan (1978). Computer-Aided Development of the Cyclohexane Oxidation Process. V. W. Weekman & D. Luss, Eds. *Chemical Reaction Engineering: 5th International Symposium, Houston, Texas, March 13-15, 1978.* Washington, D.C.: American Chemical Society, 348-358.

72 Interview with Professor A. H. de Rooij by the author and D. J. van Waes, 8 December 2003. E-mail from D. J. van Waes to the author, 28 January 2005.

73 Sulfaatfabriek begeeft zich op nieuwe markten: De tweede jeugd van een 'oud product'. *DSM Limburg Nieuws* 1987, 37(1), 3.

74 *Kirk-Othmer*, op. cit. 834.

75 Interview with J. T. J. van Goolen by the author and D. J. van Waes, 5 December 2003. Interview with Professor A. H. de Rooij by the author and D. J. van Waes, 8 December 2003. CADH, corporate archives on research: Verslag van de TOP CRO vergadering van 30 januari 1980. CRO, 4 March 1980. Verslag van de TOP-CRO vergadering van 28 januari 1981, undated. Budget en werkprogramma 1985, 7 December 1984.

76 D. J. van Waes, 18 November 2003. Interview with J. T. J. van Goolen by the author and D. J. van Waes, 5 December 2003. A. Dijkgraaf (2003). Volgende caprolactamfabriek wordt goedkoper. *Chemisch2 Weekblad* (6 December 2003), 14-15.

77 Also R. B. Stobaugh (1988). *Innovation and Competition: The Global Management of Petrochemical Products.* Boston: Harvard Business School Press. Particularly 19-23.

78 Dr S. E. Schaafsma, 22 January 2004. Interview with R. Kirschbaum, 7 January 2005. CADH, corporate archives on research: Top CRO vergadering 17 February 1982. Stanyl: nieuwe nylon, product van innovatie. *DSM Magazine* (61, July 1984), 9-11. J. Schuijer (2001). Van Nylonkous tot GSM. H. van Bekkum, J. Reedijk & S. Rozendaal, Eds. *Chemie achter de dijken: Uitvindingen en uitvinders in de eeuw na van 't Hoff.* Amsterdam: Koninklijke Nederlandse Akademie van Wetenschappen (KNAW), 92-93. Strijkers 2002, op. cit. 46.

79 CADH, corporate archives on research: Verslag Top CRO-vergadering, gehouden 31 januari 1979. CRO, 12 March 1979. Verslag van de TOP CRO vergadering van 30 januari 1980. CRO, 4 March 1980. Strategienota Stamicarbon BV, 13 September 1983.

80 CADH, corporate archives on research: Tom & Revallier to RvB, 14-2-1980. Strategienota CRO. CRO, 21 April 1981. Top CRO vergadering 17-2-1982. Kanttekeningen bij budget 1983 CRO. Concerndienst Financiën en Economie, Kokkeler, 7 January 1983. Supplement: budget en werkprogramma CRO 1983. Budget en werkprogramma CRO 1984, 9 December 1983.

81 CADH, corporate archives on research: Strategienota Stamicarbon BV, 13 September 1983. Budget en werkprogramma CRO 1985, 7 December 1984.

82 CADH, corporate archives on research: Het lange termijn plan van de naamloze vennootschap DSM voor de jaren 1982-1987. 2e concept, August 1982. UKF: its origins and development. *Nitrogen* 1984, (147), 14-16, in particular 14.

83 P. Puype, G. Beauchez & M. Jongsma (1979). *Van kiem tot korrel: Nederlandse Stikstof Maatschappij N.V. 1929-1979*. Kloosterzande: Duerinck-Krachten. 142, 164, 166.

84 CADH, corporate archives on research: Kanttekeningen bij budget 1983 CRO. Concerndienst Financiën en Economie, Kokkeler, 7 January 1983. Supplement: budget en werkprogramma CRO 1983. Strategienota van de Concerndienst Research en Octrooien. Bijlage 1. CRO, 25 May 1983. Driejarig operationeel plan. Samenvatting. RES IS 975 RA, undated. KAS-Granulatiefabriek SBB maakt eerste produkt. *DSM Limburg Nieuws* 1979, 29(10), 1.

85 Interview with J. Damme by E. Homburg and the author, 23 November 2000. CADH, corporate archives research: Verslag van de TOP CRO-vergadering gehouden op 15 september 1982. CRO, 24 September 1982. Strategienota van de Concerndienst Research en Octrooien. Bijlage 1. CRO, 25 May 1983. Budget en werkprogramma 1984, 9 December 1983.

86 See for an overview: H. Heerings & W. Smit (1986). *Internationale herstrukturering in de kunstmestsector: Nederlands overheidsbeleid en de gevolgen voor ontwikkelingslanden*. Amsterdam: Stichting Onderzoek Multinationale Ondernemingen (SOMO). Particularly chapter 3.

87 Driejarig operationeel plan. Samenvatting. RES IS 975 RA, undated. Strijkers 2002, op. cit. 54, 57.

88 Interview with Dr S. E. Schaafsma, 27 June 2003. CADH, minutes of top management meeting 2 September 1986, and appendix: DSM-Agro strategy development. Background and work planning. Kick-off meeting August 20, 1986. Reprints from slide presentation. CADH, corporate archives on research: Strategische analyse van de R&D van DSM 1990, 29 May 1990.

89 Interview with J. Barendse by E. Homburg and the author, 22 September 1999. Interview with D. J. van Waes by E. Homburg and the author, 15 July 2003. CADH, corporate archives on research: Concerntop-bijeenkomst d.d. 28.08.89. H. van Baal (1996). Nieuwe technologie maakt ureumproductie goedkoper. *Chemisch Magazine* (October 1996), 416. *Stamicarbon: The Know-How People: Urea*. Geleen: Stamicarbon. Undated, probably from 1999.

90 CADH, corporate archives on research: Strategische analyse van de R&D van DSM 1990, 29 May 1990.

91 E. Homburg, A. van Selm & P. Vincken (2000). Industrialisatie en industriecomplexen. De chemische industrie tussen overheid, technologie en markt. J. W. Schot & et al., Eds. *Techniek in Nederland in de twintigste eeuw*. Eindhoven/Zutphen: Stichting Historie der Techniek/Walburg Pers. Vol. 2, 377-401, in particular 384-385. Spitz 2003, op. cit. 9-50.

92 CADH, RvB 1981: Letter from Grotens (head of Plastics division) to top management, 29 October 1981.

93 Verslag van de TOP CRO-vergadering gehouden op 15 september 1982. CRO, 24 September 1982. Nieuw miniplant-complex op CRO. *Nieuws DSM Limburg* 1980, 30(14), 1.

94 Ronfalin EST. DSM ontwikkelde nieuwe kunststof. *Nieuws DSM Limburg* 1983, 33(6), 4. DSM ontwikkelde kunststof voor fabricage van brandstoftanks. *Nieuws DSM Limburg* 1983, 33(11), 1.

95 DSM presenteerde nieuwe typen kunststoffen. *Nieuws DSM Limburg* 1983, 33(20), 1, 5.

96 DSM annual reports 1991, 1999. STAPRON in opmars. *DSM Limburg Nieuws* 1987, 37(6), 1, 4.

97 Cf. M. B. W. Graham & B. H. Pruitt (1990). *R&D for Industry: A Century of Technical Innovation at Alcoa.* New York: Cambridge University Press. 502-504.

6

Conclusion. Research and Business at DSM

Carl Bosch once predicted that the chemical industry would have to transform its foundations every fifteen years. Charles Kline, an American marketing consultant who frequently worked with chemical companies, remarked in the early 1980s that the chemical industry was a 'chameleon industry' continuously adapting itself to new circumstances.[1] Change is indeed an important feature of the chemical industry and of chemical companies. DSM is no exception, having transformed itself from a coal-mining company and coke manufacturer into a fertiliser company and then into a large and diversified chemical company focused on bulk chemicals, and then again into a firm focused on fine chemicals and high performance materials. What role did research play in these processes of change? And how was research managed?

This chapter provides an overview of these issues. Table 6.1 summarises the roles of industrial research in the cases analysed in this book and provides structure to this chapter. It shows that enabling diversification and meeting threats were important roles of research at DSM. The role of research in diversification is linked with management views on research. In several cases analysed in this book, moreover, research's role changed over time from enabling diversification to meeting threats, as improving and maintaining market and technological positions becomes important after a business has been entered. Research's absorptive capacity enabled a number of diversifications as well. Research played no role in controlling technological change. DSM followed an imitative innovation strategy in ammonia, for instance, the crucial intermediate for fertilisers. Low costs were central here. Chemiebouw and the plant's staff played crucial roles in cutting production costs and in expanding production capacity. When engineering contractors developed a new generation of ammonia processes, DSM bought a new plant incorporating this technology.[2]

Enabling Diversification: Research and New Businesses

Shifting Technology Bases
DSM developed from coal and coke to fertilisers in the 1920s, and from fertilisers to plastics and fibre intermediates in the 1950s and 1960s. DSM

Table 6.1. Roles of research and innovation strategy: products.

Role of industrial research	Innovation strategy	
	Offensive	Defensive
Enabling diversification	Alcohol (1940)	
		Mixed fertilisers (1941)
		Caprolactam (1952)
	Urea (stripping: 1967)	
	Lysine (1968)	
		Phenylglycine (early 1970s)
		Benzaldehyde (early 1970s)
		Alpha-picoline (1977)
	Specialty amino acids (1988)	Aspartame (1988)
	Dyneema (1990)	
Meeting threats		Ammonium sulphate
		Urea
		Caprolactam
Absorptive capacity		Mixed fertilisers
		Caprolactam
		Chem-Y (1977)
		Andeno (1987)
		Aspartame (1988)

Note: years between brackets refer to the year of start-up (of a plant), or the year of acquisition (in the case of Chem-Y and Andeno). See chapter 1 for the definitions of 'offensive' and 'defensive'.

became a diversified chemical company, and this enabled the company to survive the shutdown of the Dutch coal-mining industry. DSM continued to renew itself, however, and from its base in plastics and fibre intermediates sought high value-added products in fine chemicals and high performance materials after 1970 and particularly after 1980.

Technology bases shifted along with this pattern of diversification and transformation. DSM entered the chemical industry by hiring engineering contractors but soon started to build its own technological capabilities, and this process gained momentum after the Second World War. The improvement of the process for the manufacture of ammonium sulphate, as well as the development of the mixed fertiliser and alcohol processes, built a foundation of capabilities in process research, development and engineering, as well as a specific body of knowledge relating to fertilisers (product finishing techniques and later phase rule expertise in relation to mixed fertilisers). After the Second World War, the engineering capabilities were institutionalised in Chemiebouw while the Central Laboratory started to grow in scale and scope. In the case of urea, the engineering capabilities of Chemiebouw and the process research capabilities of the Central Laboratory combined to form an effective organisation for innovation. Specific fertiliser know-how was utilised in urea (phase rules) and also expanded (prilling). DSM in this way expanded the technology base it had started to build in the 1930s.[3]

After the Second World War, the Central Laboratory started to do fundamental research on a major scale. Catalysis research started in relation to ammonia, but later shifted to other products and provided a valuable input in a diverse range of projects. In the case of ammonia, catalysis research was conducted together with the works laboratory of the fertiliser business and closely coordinated with the ammonia plant's staff. Catalysis research was valuable to both research and production.[4]

In the case of urea, fundamental research even started out of direct industrial relevance: an effort to improve full recycle processes. As such, fundamental research played an important role in the development of the stripping process: DSM's breakthrough that propelled it into a position of technological leadership.

DSM also started fundamental research on polymers. It related to what was at the time a core activity and it also led to Dyneema (after some unexpected turns and detours). Both fundamental polymer research and catalysis were subjects that universities had difficulty handling within their discipline-oriented organisation. This prompted DSM and other companies to start research in these areas, alongside their industrial relevance.[5]

The fundamental research carried out at DSM after the Second World War points to the deepening and widening of the company's research effort. This can also be seen in the case of caprolactam, where the Central Laboratory greatly expanded on the small-scale research in organic chemistry of the 1930s. In urea, the route to the product was known and research focused on finding possible process configurations and on finding the most efficient, low-cost configuration. This was partly engineering work, as in the case of the once-through process, but also entailed development and process research, particularly when DSM's innovation strategy in urea developed from defensive to offensive.

Research in organic chemistry, by contrast, often entailed a substantial amount of work to find a route to a targeted product, and then the work on finding a suitable process configuration still had to be done. The caprolactam process proceeded in more steps from feedstock to end-product than urea. This was typical of organic products and could lead to unexpected turns in research. For instance, the research that led to the establishment of alpha-picoline production had targeted pyridine at first, but when this compound proved to be out of reach, it targeted alpha-picoline.

The capabilities that were built in relation to caprolactam built a new technology base alongside the technology base in fertilisers. Some elements overlapped, particularly the capabilities in relation to process research, development, engineering and catalysis, and these overlapping capabilities were pivotal in the development of a new technology base from the existing one. Through caprolactam, however, DSM acquired extensive capabilities in organic chemistry and also, although on a smaller scale, capabilities in relation to the processing of synthetic fibres. In particular, an application research capability was built in relation to polyethylene and other plastics in DSM's portfolio, where product variety and knowledge of plastics processing was vital for marketing.[6]

The caprolactam technology base was important for other products as well. Most of Special Products' initial activities were spin-offs from caprolactam production or research. For instance, the Dow phenol process was uncompetitive, and in this sense not very successful in its primary function. Nevertheless, the process provided the opportunity for producing benzaldehyde and benzoic acid. Finally, the best example of DSM's increased capabilities in organic chemistry and the importance of caprolactam research is the lysine case. DSM's attempts to synthesise lysine required an extensive base in organic chemistry. Without caprolactam, DSM would not have been able to undertake this attempt.

Although the primary objective of the lysine project failed, its secondary effects were major. The lysine project led to an accumulation of knowledge that could be applied to other products as well. The pyridine project started with an intermediate from the acrylonitrile-based process. More important for the long-term development of DSM, the knowledge of the separation of the D- and L-lysine widened when research included methionine. This knowledge could be applied to phenylglycine and, in turn, further deepened DSM's capabilities in this field. The accumulated knowledge was vital to the establishment of specialty amino acid production in the late 1980s. This body of knowledge also provided one of the incentives to acquire Andeno and was used as input into the cooperation with Tosoh that led to the production of aspartame. These acquisitions complemented DSM's capabilities and sparked further development of the fine chemicals activities.

The caprolactam technology base was also important for Dyneema and Stanyl, projects that could profit from knowledge of fibre manufacture built through application research that had been started in relation to caprolactam production, and of application research more broadly in relation to plastics. The links with plastics were pivotal in the development of a technology base in high performance materials.

In summary, DSM was able to shift its technology base through generic technological capabilities (see also figure 6.1). Generic process research, development and engineering capabilities, the extensive research DSM did on catalysis, and application research on caprolactam and plastics were pivotal in the development of a new technology base from an existing one. Fertiliser research, for instance, built process research, development and engineering capabilities that also enabled research on caprolactam. This clearly shows the importance of these types of research for diversification projects and the development of the company.

This mechanism of shifting technology bases through generic technological capabilities is what Pisano points to in his dual output model of R&D. In the case of DSM, however, the secondary effects of research projects were much broader than generic knowledge of how to improve the efficiency and effectiveness of R&D projects. Research projects, moreover, sometimes built sets of knowledge that could be transferred from project to project. The spin-offs from lysine research are examples of this mechanism. Such capabilities are specific, and deepen and extend existing technology bases but do not build new bases. The spin-offs from lysine research, for example, extended DSM's base in fine chemicals and provided a foundation for the company's business in this field, but did not build a new technology base.

Patterns and Drivers of Diversification
The shifts in technology base reflect the three transformations DSM went through over the course of its history. Its pattern of transformation emerged step by step, through a series of strategic shifts. Until 1970, DSM entered new businesses mainly because it had the necessary raw materials in-house and simply assumed that it could find a market. For instance, DSM started large-scale manufacture of nitrogen fertilisers primarily because it could extract hydrogen from its coke oven gas, not because the market for fertilisers boomed. Such feedstock-driven diversification continued after the Second World War, but the feedstock links between coke and chemicals were first loosened, and later cut, while the Central Laboratory grew in size and scope. Although feedstocks remained important, the ability to develop or otherwise obtain technology increasingly steered diversification. The shift from feedstocks to technology as a driver of diversification was gradual. Expansion became the key word, boosting capacity of existing products, taking up new lines of business and loosening, later cutting, the ties between chemicals and coal and coke.

The diversification and expansion of DSM's chemical businesses took place at a time when markets were growing fast. After 1970 growth stagnated, but DSM aimed to make a Large Leap Forward, pushing ahead with expansion and diversification to replace the coal and coke businesses.

Figure 6.1. Map of shifts in DSM's technology base.

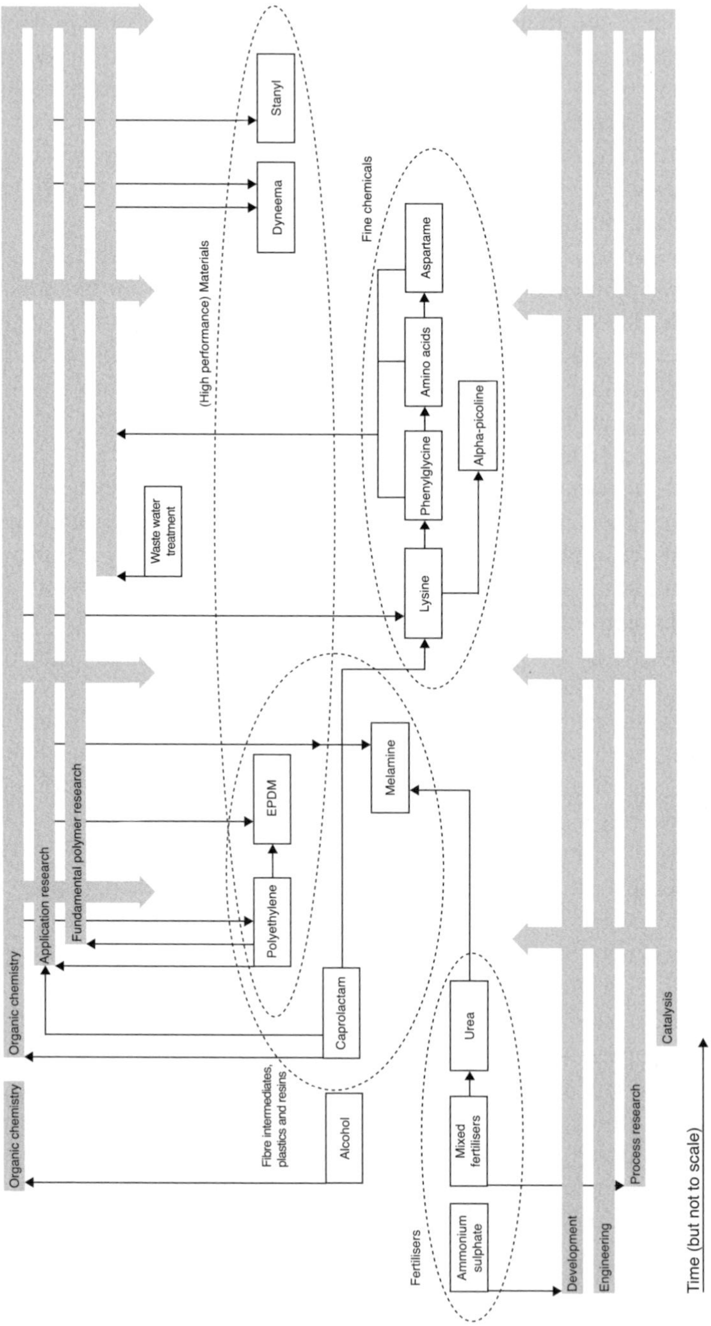

Note: boxes contain research projects, grey rectangles generic technological capabilities and the ellipses specific technology bases. Arrows indicate direct links.

The Large Leap Forward was a major break with previous patterns. Markets came into play more fully and the perceived commercial attractiveness of diversifications became a central concern. DSM also drastically reorganised and established divisions. The not-so-spectacular growth of many markets after 1970 caused headwind, however. From the late 1970s onwards, DSM tried to refocus, shifting away from its large-scale, low-profit bulk chemicals into fine chemicals and high performance materials. By the middle of the 1980s, the tide had turned and DSM focused on innovation and renewal, intensifying the move into high value-added products.

The Role of Research in Diversification
The importance of diversification increased over the course of DSM's history as the company repeatedly transformed itself. Diversification became particularly important after 1966, when DSM rid itself of its coal-related businesses and expanded in chemicals (Graph 6.1).

One quick way of showing the contribution of research to diversification is to count the number of diversifications that built on research (Graph 6.2). This shows that throughout the history of DSM, research has played an important role in establishing new lines of business. The importance of research as an enabler of diversification varied in a wave-like pattern over time, however (see also table 6.2). In the feedstocks phase, technology was acquired and internal capabilities were built. DSM hired engineering contractors to build several plants for fertiliser manufacture,

Graph 6.1. Cumulative number of diversifications.

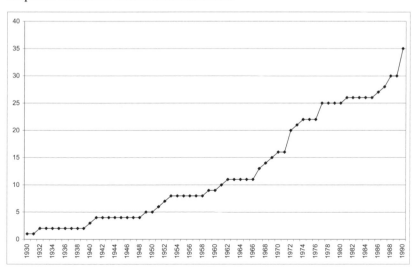

Sources: see tables 3.1 and 5.1.

Graph 6.2. Diversification and research-based diversification.

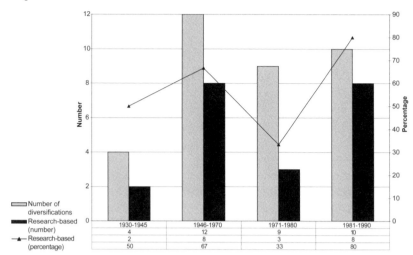

	1930-1945	1946-1970	1971-1980	1981-1990
Number of diversifications	4	12	9	10
Research-based (number)	2	8	3	8
Research-based (percentage)	50	67	33	80

Sources: see tables 3.1 and 5.1

Note: Both the + and ++ diversifications have been counted as research-based for this graph.

but soon after improved the ammonium sulphate process. Technology acquisitions complemented internal capabilities, as in the case of nitro phosphates and the once-through urea process. The Central Laboratory was established before the Second World War, but embarked on a process of growth in the 1950s. Research became increasingly important, both initiating and enabling diversifications, and the successes of research contributed to its growing importance.

In the 1970s, the importance of research for diversification declined. The research-based diversifications in that decade were in fine chemicals, a field DSM did not yet emphasise in its strategy at that time. DSM targeted further diversification in plastics and resins to expand and reach large-scale production, but purchased technology or took over companies to do so. Taking over other companies was a new means for DSM to diversify and expand, but the role of in-house research was as small as in technology acquisitions. After diversification, R&D optimised processes and improved product quality.

The 1980s were a renaissance for research.[7] The economic situation improved and research had more room to take initiatives and enable diversification. The jump in the number of research-based diversifications at the end of the 1980s reflects the output not only of the corporate development programmes but also of other research projects that had been started around the middle of the 1980s. In that decade, moreover, com-

THE COMPANY THAT CHANGED ITSELF

Table 6.2. Business strategy and R&D at DSM, 1925-1990.

Period	Business Strategy	Operational Translation	Role of R&D

1925-1960	Maximising value of available raw materials.	- Feedstock-driven diversification.	- Acquisition of technology main method of diversification before 1940.
			- Build-up of R&D:
			  - Meeting threats.
			  - Enabling diversification, particularly after 1945.
			- Strong integration of business strategy and research.

1960s	Expansion.	- Major capacity extensions for existing products. - Broadening/switching feedstock basis. - Diversification. - Internationalisation.	- Initiating: generation of options for management. - Enabling diversification: R&D necessary to enter markets. - Strong integration of business strategy and research.
1970s	The Large Leap Forward.	- Expansion, internationalisation. - Technology acquisitions.	Dependent: - Meeting threats: process improvements. - Absorptive capacity: helping technology acquisitions. - Research followed business strategy.
1980s	Towards products with high value-added.	- Focus on bulk chemicals with strong commercial/technological position. - Diversification: fine chemicals, performance materials.	- Initiating diversification. - Enabling diversification. - Strong integration of business strategy and research.

Compare: E. Homburg (2000). Epiloog: DSM Research op weg naar de 21e eeuw. H. Lintsen, Ed. *Research tussen vetkool en zoetstof.* Eindhoven/Zutphen: Stichting Historie der Techniek/Walburg Pers, 118-135.

plementary technology also became an argument for taking over other companies.

In all of the periods, DSM typically entered businesses late with a defensive innovation strategy, aimed at keeping up with the competition and if possible overtaking them (Table 6.1). In the case of fertilisers, particularly in the case of urea, and also in caprolactam, this proved to be a successful strategy. DSM tried to obtain a strong technological position, and from that position tried to market its products.

The only exceptions to this rule are lysine and Dyneema. Although they both built on elements of the technology base built around caprolactam, these projects entailed new markets and new technologies for DSM and such projects very often fail.[8] From this perspective the success of Dyneema, even though it took a long time, is perhaps more surprising than the failure of the lysine project.

As in the case of Dyneema, it took time before DSM could enter the fine chemicals field and could build a substantial business. The fragmented, low-volume businesses of the fine chemicals sector differed significantly from the bulk chemicals sector and the possibilities to acquire know-how were limited. The entry into fine chemicals built strongly on initiatives originating from research and in-house work. It could build on existing technological capabilities as DSM's strongholds in process research and catalysis were just as important for its fine chemical products as they were for bulk chemicals. The in-house work was small-scale in the 1970s, however, and the expansion of DSM's fine chemicals interests got a significant boost in the second half of the 1980s from the acquisition of Andeno and the establishment of aspartame production, which were typically defensive actions.

Although lysine was a new market and a new technology for DSM, its failure shows the limits of feedstock-driven and technology-driven research and diversification from a business point of view. The technological and feedstock links with caprolactam and the possibility to manufacture synthetic lysine fuelled an optimistic view of market development before any market development work had led to results. This optimism reigned not only in research but also in the production and marketing organisations, and in top management. Although research and marketing tried very hard and built a large network of relationships, the efforts to find a market lacked focus. Market development work covered a wide range of possibly interesting applications and market segments. This made it very hard to create a strong interface between research and marketing, which in turn contributed to the failure of the lysine project.

In the cases of urea and caprolactam, the target markets were clear, as were the demands set by customers. These markets, moreover, grew tremendously. The 1950s and 1960s were a unique time of high growth in the chemical industry and in this context a technology-based and feedstock-based strategy worked very well. There was not much need to worry over the question of whether products could be sold. Together with the failure of the lysine project, stagnating growth of markets led to the departure from existing practice formulated in the Large Leap strategy, with diversification issues being focused increasingly on the attractiveness of products rather than the availability of feedstocks and the potential to develop technology.

Causes of Waves

A wave-like pattern in the importance of research for diversification is not unique to DSM. The study of Du Pont by David Hounshell and John Smith shows a similar pattern for instance, although the boundaries of the periods differ slightly. Ernst Homburg's study of research in the Netherlands also shows a wave-like pattern.[9]

In the case of DSM, the wave-like pattern was caused by several factors. In the first place, market conditions and the company's results are important. In hard times, research is under pressure. DSM economised on research in the 1970s just as it economised on other functions. When the company's results improved in the 1980s, research gained more room again. In this way, the importance of research fluctuated with business results.

In the second place, Homburg has shown the importance of bandwagon behaviour in the directions companies chose for research management: firms follow their competitors. This perspective suggests that companies hold each other in a blind embrace, with no leaders and followers, but resulting in companies moving in the same direction.[10] Intriguing from this perspective is the direction companies choose in their diversification paths. Fertilisers in the 1930s, plastics and fibres in the 1950s and biotechnology and materials in the 1980s were all fashionable fields, attracting many firms. The example of DSM, with cases like urea and caprolactam, shows that such strategies can even be successful if markets grow fast enough and costs are cut as well. This perspective also highlights the difficulties encountered with lysine and Dyneema, cases in which there were few firms to follow.

A third factor in the wave-like pattern of the importance of research is management. The faith and confidence management had in research influenced the extent to which research could take initiatives. In the 1950s, the importance of research was beyond challenge, but this changed around 1970. The failure of the lysine project dented the self-confidence built over the previous years and led to a more critical attitude towards research, both inside and outside the Central Laboratory. Faith and confidence in the results of projects, and especially the sustained faith and confidence of the project leader, have been shown to be important factors contributing to the success of innovation. The example of DSM points to the importance of faith and confidence at business and top management levels.[11]

Graph 6.2 (page 252) shows the potency of having faith and confidence in research. The 1950s and 1960s were a time when many diversifications built on research. This shows that research needs room to take initiatives to reach such productivity. When this room was walled off and became smaller in the 1970s, productivity promptly declined but it grew again in the 1980s when room for research increased. An initiating role, or what Graham and Pruitt have called the formulation of a technical vision, is essential for research to play an important role in the long-term development of a company.[12]

In summary, research, diversification and management's views of research were strongly interrelated and varied in a wave-like pattern over time. The initiating role of research, the room business management gave to research, was a function of several parameters: economic circumstances, bandwagon behaviour, and the faith and confidence management had in research. Research contributed strongly to diversification in the 1950s and 1960s, and again in the 1980s; whereas in the 1970s, diversification took place mainly through technology acquisitions.

Unpredictability, Short-term and Long-term Research, and Business Management

In DSM's diversification process, the secondary effects of research projects have been important, but from a managerial perspective these effects make the results of research projects hard to predict. Of course, at the start of lysine research no-one expected that it would lead to alpha-picoline. Through research on the acrylonitrile-based lysine process, however, research on pyridine started and when that failed, it led to the establishment of alpha-picoline production. Making the example more narrow, even the failure of the pyridine project, which had a shorter time range than the lysine project, led to a successful, but unexpected, diversification. This example shows that secondary effects, along with problem shifts and unexpected turns and results, make the issue of the effectiveness of research a persistent one, basically because it is very hard to determine what the results of any one particular project are or will be.[13] Andries Sarlemijn and Marc de Vries argue that rationality in R&D is only piecemeal. Each step in the process that eventually leads to a new product might be managed rationally, but the overall results and directions of research develop over time and step by step.[14]

Nevertheless, management needs to find a response to this unpredictability. In the 1950s and 1960s, this response was simple and straightforward. Not only research management, but also top management and business management, accepted the unpredictability of research. In an atmosphere where faith and confidence in research was high, it was accepted that some projects would inevitably fail. This may have been only partly rational, because many projects failed, but from the perspective of the 1950s and 1960s such failures were more than offset by the successes. 'Research is a gamble', as Dick van Krevelen phrased it.[15]

From the late 1960s and early 1970s onwards, however, DSM increasingly attempted to manage this uncertainty. An important reason for this was the shift in focus towards markets, but the most crucial factor was the increased involvement of business management, the divisions. In the 1950s, the Central Laboratory was able to take the initiative towards the development of the HPO process without being influenced by production, but after 1970 such initiatives had to be coordinated with the divisions. The case of the HPO process also shows the merits of coordination. Business management became involved at a time when the process was ready to be commercialised, but at this point its judgement only threatened to make years of research useless.

The management literature has highlighted mismatches between the research and production functions of companies to argue that the research management practices of the 1950s and 1960s failed to integrate research, production and marketing.[16] The case of the HPO process, however, shows that the Central Laboratory did not take initiatives out of its own curiosity or out of scientific interest but on the basis of an analysis and a view of the long-term interests of the company. Researchers considered the production of ammonium sulphate alongside caprolactam as a threat, long before it became difficult to market ammonium sulphate and long before business management reached the same conclusion. On the basis of its analysis, the Central Laboratory conducted research to reduce or remove ammonium sulphate production. The relevance of this research became clear in the 1970s.

As business management showed no interest in the HPO process around 1960, the rational thing to do would have been to stop research. Similarly, researching Dyneema seemed to make little sense. The Central Laboratory had some experience and knowledge in the field of synthetic fibres through application research on caprolactam, but lacked the capabilities to introduce a new fibre. In the 1970s, moreover, neither the Plastics division, which was in principle related to Dyneema through polyethylene, nor the Chemical Products division, which was related through caprolactam, backed research into the new fibre.

The examples of Dyneema and the HPO process show the potency of having faith and simply continuing research. These examples also show that to some extent tensions between research and business are unavoidable. Crudely put, research will by nature focus more on the long term and business management more on the short and medium term, reflecting the different incentives and environments they face.

The issue of the relationship between research and business was not unique to DSM, although other companies perhaps had to confront it earlier. It is striking, however, that the issue of aligning the research and production functions gained considerable weight after DSM organised its divisions. In the 1950s, a triangle between top management (Jan van Aken), business management (Jef van Waes) and research management (Gé Berkhoff) was organised and this management triangle was an important bridge between research and production functions. In the 1960s, a more elaborate management structure developed, but top management involvement remained strong and put business and research management on an equal footing. The structure for research management became strained in the early 1970s when the divisions were established and the company made a quantum leap in chemical business growth. The balance of power tilted towards business management who, under the circumstances they were facing, were more interested in short-term incremental improvements than in long-term projects that might, but at the same time might not, lead to a new line of business or an improvement of an existing process or product. Some divisions shifted more to the short term than others but the heyday of long-term research had definitely passed. The failure of the lysine project had also dealt a blow to confidence in research.

Graham and Pruitt also note in their history of Alcoa research that the establishment of divisions pushed research to the short term.[17] At DSM, the stronger say of business management combined with stagnating market growth and declining confidence in research. In this way an organisational change reinforced already difficult circumstances for research. The matrix organisation of the Central Laboratory and the appointment of directors of research (*werkgebiedmanagers*), as well as stronger top management involvement toward the end of the 1970s, readjusted the balance of power more in favour of research. For the divisions, the matrix opened the black box of the laboratory at least to some extent, and the directors of research functioned as a bridge between research and production. The corporate development programmes of the mid-1980s similarly performed such a bridging function.

In her book about RCA, Graham implicitly pleads for a better understanding of research by business managers, but the example of DSM shows that the way in which the relationship between research and business is organised is important as well.[18] The management triangle of the 1950s and the research directors of the 1970s and 1980s provided a bridge between business and research, and an essential tool to align their diverging interests. Such alignment is open-ended but nevertheless necessary. It is not so much from the tensions between research and business that research derives its value, but from the process of alignment.

Hounshell has argued that all companies struggle to find a balance between research focused on the short term and research focused on the long term.[19] DSM is no exception, but the 1980s were a more balanced period than the 1950s and 1960s on the one hand and the 1970s on the other. In the 1950s and 1960s, research had much freedom to take initiatives and start projects, but at the same time, production and marketing functions were not involved in such initiatives. In the 1970s, by contrast, marketing and production issues pushed research toward short-term projects. In the 1980s, particularly through the corporate development programmes, DSM found a balance between short-term business interests and long-term research interests.

Meeting Threats: Research and Existing Businesses

Technological Maturity

Up to this point the related issues of diversification and the management of research have been emphasised, but enabling diversification was not the only role of research. A large part of the work consisted of improving and maintaining market positions. In the 1950s, researchers had to lower the amount of biuret in urea because of competitive threats. In the 1980s, researchers worked to reduce the amount of ammonium sulphate produced as a by-product of caprolactam through small changes to the process to improve the economics of caprolactam production. Although it was often not spectacular, the importance of such work can hardly be overestimated. The chemical industry is a competitive industry, and the markets for bulk chemicals are cyclical, requiring an ongoing effort to cut costs and improve product quality. Moreover, such work is hard to outsource.

Research in relation to existing businesses could have a narrow scope, and focus on small incremental improvements to a plant's processes, but could also have a broader scope, and include research on alternative processes. The Central Laboratory was the driving force work with a broad scope; in narrowly-scoped work, the staff engineers and operators of production plants played an important role alongside research. Chemiebouw played a role in both broadly-scoped and narrowly-scoped work for existing businesses, but the importance of this role declined somewhat after 1970 as Chemiebouw, like many other departments, was reduced in size through the company-wide economising programmes. DSM had hired engineering contractors mainly to acquire technology but after 1970, following a trend across the chemical industry, external firms were hired to do engineering work even in projects that relied on in-house technology.[20] In the narrow-scope area, the Central Laboratory conducted projects that were too large or too complex for staff engineers and Chemiebouw to handle, such as the reduction of ammonium sulphate by-product in caprolactam in the 1980s.

Broadly-scoped research projects in relation to existing businesses were set up in the 1950s and 1960s in particular. The results were mixed. In urea, the continuous effort to improve production technology paid off, but in caprolactam, the studies into the caprolactone process and a number of other alternative processes produced hardly any results. This type of research was constrained in the 1970s, but when it increased again in the 1980s, the results were again limited. New urea and caprolactam processes were investigated but could not be implemented. Work on urea was cut on the grounds of the supposed technological maturity of the stripping process. The fertiliser activities were in decline and consequently the research budget fell. In this increasingly tight budget, diversification got priority instead of research for existing businesses. This choice reflects DSM's refocus on innovation and diversification, but is striking in the light of the difficult position of the fertiliser division. One would sooner have expected a strategy of cost cutting and further rationalisation through incremental improvements. Research was successful and new products were introduced in 1990, but these activities were later sold off.

The case of urea shows that the opportunities to improve a technology decline in the long term: from the major leaps of the 1950s and 1960s, the opportunities to improve urea processes declined to relatively small steps in the 1980s. This is a life cycle or maturation process. With the urea stripping process, efficiency of urea production reached a high level, which in turn narrowed the window of opportunity for process improvements and new processes. Even the urea stripping process, however, had no 'shutdown economics' over other full recycle processes. Plotkin suggests that in the 1950s and 1960s, new processes reduced costs, or had other advantages that made it economical to shut down existing capacities or could force competitors out of business.[21] If there ever had been such processes, the urea stripping process was not one of them.[22] DSM introduced this process as markets grew. The fast growth of markets made it necessary to periodically expand capacities substantially, providing a chance to introduce new or improved processes. The growth of markets slowed down after 1970, and DSM's urea business got into trouble. The need for capacity additions declined, leading to a much more unfavourable environment for process innovation.

As the work of Utterback suggests, technological life cycles are coupled to the development of markets. Peter Hutcheson, Alan Pearson and Derrick Ball have applied Utterback's model to a study of innovation in ethylene production processes, arguing that the segmental stage occurred in the period between 1945 and 1970 and the systematic phase after 1970. Despite the obvious problem that it is difficult to speak of product innovations in a bulk chemical like ethylene, Hutcheson et al. show a pattern similar to urea, pointing to the catalytic effect of high market growth on process innovation in the chemical industry between 1945 and 1970.[23]

Utterback and Hutcheson et al. leave management out of the picture, however. By the 1980s, the stripping process was technologically 'mature' in the sense that major improvements and major cost reductions like those of the 1950s and 1960s were no longer possible. Research in the 1980s aimed at such a major leap but failed. Later, Stamicarbon showed that the stripping process could be further improved, but these improvements were based on engineering and less on research, and were relatively small. Research and business management chose innovation instead of rationalisation and failed to align research to the development of the market. This put further downward pressure on the position of urea production.[24]

The case of caprolactam is also interesting in this perspective. The HPO process rationalised the existing caprolactam process but did not provide such an advantage that replacement of existing capacities that had not yet reached the end of their life was viable. As market growth stagnated after 1970, incremental improvements could raise production enough to meet market growth and made existing processes a moving target for new processes. The success of incremental improvements narrowed the window of opportunity for broadly-scoped research for existing business after 1970.

The case of caprolactam also shows the increase in minimum viable scale of plants in the chemical industry. In 1952, DSM entered caprolactam with a plant of 3,600 tons per year but only about twenty years later it built the first HPO unit at a capacity of 70,000 tons per year. The risks involved in scaling up a process increased accordingly but, more importantly from a business management point of view, capital requirements also increased and made it expensive to introduce a new process. In the 1950s and 1960s, the minimum size at which a plant would be economical had also increased as a result of innovation and market growth.

Technological 'maturity', then, is primarily a function of the development of the market, the success of incremental improvements, and management's response to both. Technological maturity is not a static state reached at some point in time, but management has some room to respond and its response affects the maturation process. In the 1980s, management's focus on (high) growth in new products catalysed the maturation process in urea. The alternative would have been to align research and production in existing products very closely and put emphasis on engineering.

Acquisitions: Absorptive Capacity
In the case of urea and caprolactam, research had established the business and continued afterwards to maintain or improve DSM's commercial and technological positions. But research in relation to existing businesses was also important in businesses that had not been built on in-house research. The first of DSM's innovations was the improvement of the acquired ammonium sulphate process, which was important to meet pressure from

competitors. Research was central in a defensive innovation strategy to maintain market position, but particularly to improve that position. Research was crucial for catching up and overtaking competitors.

Research on acquired technologies also helped anchor these technologies in DSM's technology base. Berkhoff's work on ammonium sulphate enlarged and extended DSM's base in fertilisers, like Chemiebouw's work on the first once-through process laid a foundation to develop recycle processes. ASED's once-through process fitted with DSM's existing technological capabilities. The process was established, but had to be developed to industrial scale, which required some process research but mainly development and engineering work. In this way it provided a stepping-stone to the expansion of the technology base in fertilisers.

This mechanism also worked in some of the cases where companies were taken over. The acquisition of Andeno fitted well with both DSM's business and its research in fine chemicals. It could therefore stimulate DSM's own research and business in this sector. Chem-Y, on the other hand, presented both new markets and new technologies for DSM and little research was done for Chem-Y in Geleen. The company was divested in the end.

Although acquisitions were typically a much faster route to diversification, the example of Chem-Y shows that acquisitions could also fail, just like research projects. Anchoring technology and company acquisitions in market and technology bases is vital for the success of these acquisitions. Research provided an important part of the absorptive capacity necessary to track, acquire and integrate external technology and companies. Research in itself provided no guarantee for success however. In the case of ABS, for instance, research worked on product and process improvements, but ABS could nevertheless not maintain its position in DSM's portfolio.[25]

Other Roles of Research

In the introduction, several roles of industrial research were distinguished. The case of DSM shows that meeting threats and enabling diversification were the most important roles of R&D. The Central Laboratory functioned as a training house for future managers as well. Business and top managers usually started their careers at DSM in the research organisation. Some remained a researcher only for a short time, while others remained for a longer period and then moved to a business management function. The highest research managers, like Berkhoff and Van Krevelen, did not move into top management, however.[26]

Another role of industrial research is that it enabled companies to control the rate and direction of technological change, primarily by means of patents.[27] In the case of Dyneema, patenting provided a strong defence against competitors. Conversely, patents of other companies often provided the starting point for in-house R&D. The HPO project started from patents of Spencer Chemical, like the caprolactone project started from patents of Union Carbide. The Central Laboratory could depart from patented technology and build an independent position, as in the case of the HPO process. R&D sometimes failed to build an independent position or to invent around patented technology, as in the case of caprolactone. The in-house work could also provide bargaining power to obtain a license, or to obtain favourable licensing terms. In EPDM, DSM's own work, its patent position and its licenses were tools to bend Montecatini's position.

Viewed from the perspective of Montecatini, the case of EPDM shows that patents were typically insufficient to prevent competition and to control technology in the chemical industry. Even in polypropylene, the patents of the Italian firm did not prove strong enough. DSM had a similar experience in the case of its urea stripping process. Snam Progetti patented ammonia stripping, and in this way worked around DSM's carbon dioxide stripping patents. Patents on processes are typically weaker than product patents. In this way, firms in the bulk chemicals sector of the chemical industry, which relied strongly on process technology for their competitiveness, were handicapped in using patents to control technological change. Typically, many companies worked in a particular field, always threatening each other, and always requiring a large effort even to keep up. Finally, markets were so often so large that it was impossible for one firm, or a combination of firms, to build a monopoly.

The control of technological change is related to an industry's structure. The absence of such control and the impossibility of any one company gaining a monopoly position are defining characteristics of the bulk chemical industry, particularly in the period after the Second World War.

On the other hand, patents, combined with the know-how of how to engineer an industrial plant, could build an attractive licensing business. In the case of DSM, the urea stripping process is an excellent example of the mechanisms of licensing. This process was a breakthrough, but Stamicarbon started to license it immediately. The urea market was very large and several other companies and engineering contractors were offering technology. A potential producer would always find a source of technology. From the perspective of DSM, *not* licensing would not have meant less competition.[28] Stamicarbon sold large numbers of licenses on DSM's urea process and also on other DSM technologies (see graph A3 in the appendix). Licensing developed into a profitable business.

Stamicarbon also played an important role in DSM's R&D. It was initially the only party to show an interest in the HPO process. In the 1980s, it also stimulated, and partly paid for, fertiliser research, particularly the work on urea. Conversely, R&D on integrated urea and ammonia production stopped when Stamicarbon reached the same, negative, conclusion as DSM's fertiliser production unit. For the Central Laboratory, Stamicarbon provided an extra outlet for its research and sometimes also an extra source of funds.

Stamicarbon projects also provided an opportunity to learn. The first HPO plants were built for other companies, for instance, and the first two licensed stripping plants had larger unit capacities than DSM's own plant. Stamicarbon was also more international than DSM in the 1960s and 1970s. They worked for many foreign companies and had contacts with many engineering contractors that specialised in the engineering and construction of plants for the chemical industry. These contacts could be valuable: a tender for a caprolactam project in Mexico in 1980 triggered an evaluation of DSM's own technology. Stamicarbon's international outlook provided a setting for training managers as well. Leo Kretzers and Ruud Selman, for instance, had worked for Stamicarbon before becoming responsible for the management of production units (plastics in Kretzer's case, and fine chemicals in Selman's case).

Research and the Development of DSM

In an article from 1996, Simon de Bree, then chairman of DSM's Managing Board, paraphrased a researcher of the company who had said that PV = RT (the law of Boyle and Gay-Lussac) really means that the product of price and volume (in other words, turnover) equals the product of research and technology.[29] This 'law' is one way of saying that research played a central and crucial role in the development of DSM, both in enabling and initiating diversification, and in maintaining and improving established market positions.

In the first place, research enabled many diversifications for the company and contributed substantially to DSM's three transformations. Acquisitions, either of technology or of companies, competed with research in its role of enabling diversification. Like research projects, however, acquisitions can also fail. In fine chemicals, for instance, the lysine project of the Central Laboratory failed, but so did the acquisition of Chem-Y. Successful acquisitions depended on starting research on what the company had bought and on buying what fitted the company.

The importance of research in enabling diversification shifted with management attitudes towards research in a wave-like pattern over time. After a build-up phase in the 1930s and 1940s, management gave research much room in the 1950s and 1960s to take initiatives and to work on subjects research thought relevant. The Central Laboratory played a crucial role in many diversifications after the Second World War. The room management gave research decreased in the 1970s, but again increased in the 1980s, although not to the levels of the 1950s and 1960s. After 1970, the importance of research for diversification similarly declined and increased again. This wave-like pattern also shows that the management of research is an open-ended process: bridging research and business interests, as well as long-term and short-term interests, remain crucial challenges.

A second role of research in the development of DSM was the maintenance of existing businesses. Research worked with the engineering department and plant staff to cut costs and improve product quality. This type of research was, and remains, of paramount importance for competing in the chemical industry and is an inevitable in-house function of firms.

After 1970, however, the slowdown in growth of many markets combined with the increased minimum viable size of plants to make the introduction of improved processes risky and difficult. In the 1980s, moreover, DSM also emphasised innovation and diversification in relation to established lines of business, and this further narrowed the opportunities for broadly-scoped research in relation to existing businesses. Management also plays an important role in research on existing products and processes.

This review of the role of research in diversification and in the maintenance of existing businesses at DSM shows a pattern that differs from that of the R&D pioneers and the large companies that have been studied so often in the history of industrial research. DSM established a research organisation in response to diffuse threats, and its research organisation grew out of works laboratories and existing (but small scale) research work. After the Second World War, research did not diverge from other company functions. Business strategy and research were closely related and integrated. DSM's research organisation played an important role in diversification but also in the maintenance of existing businesses.

On the other hand, DSM's wave-like pattern followed a general pattern. The example of DSM shows that 1970 was a turning point. Compared to the 1950s and 1960s, research got less room to initiate and enable diversification, while broadly scoped research for existing businesses became more difficult. The period between 1945 and 1970 was exceptional, however.[30] Markets grew at unprecedented rates while technology developed fast; the opportunities for innovation seemed endless. The 1970s and early 1980s were a more difficult period, but research at DSM recovered to some extent after 1985. The next chapter, a short epilogue, investigates whether this trend continued in the 1990s.

Notes

1 L. Küchler (1963). Wandel in der chemischen Technik. *Wandel in der chemischen Technik: Karl Winnacker zum 60. Geburtstag gewidmet 21. September 1963.* Frankfurt: Farbwerke Hoechst AG, 1-24. There 1. C. H. Kline (1984). Breaking Through to New Technologies. *Chemtech* 14(3), 148-151, in particular 151.

2 See A. van Rooij (2004). *Building Plants: Markets for Technology and Internal Capabilities in DSM's Fertiliser Business, 1925-1970.* Amsterdam: Aksant. Dissertation Eindhoven University of Technology. 195-229.

3 For fertiliser related build-up of technological capabilities compare: Van Rooij 2004, op. cit. 234-237.

4 Also Van Rooij 2004, op. cit. 201-203.

5 E. Homburg (2003). *Speuren op de tast: Een historische kijk op industriële en universitaire research.* Maastricht: Universiteit Maastricht. Inaugural lecture, 31 October 2003. 27.

6 For plastics and rubbers at DSM see: T. van Helvoort (2000). Staatsmijnen gaat polymeriseren, 1945-1970. H. Lintsen, Ed. *Research tussen vetkool en zoetstof: zestig jaar DSM Research 1940-2000.* Eindhoven/Zutphen: Stichting Historie der Techniek/Walburg Pers, 44-59.

7 Cf. F. Veraart. *De renaissance van research (1980-1990).* Veldman & Van Royen report J.

8 E. Roberts & C. Berry (1985). Entering New Businesses: Selecting Strategies for Success. *Sloan Management Review* 26(3), 3-17. J. Faber (2000). Wetenschappelijke kennisverwerving en diversificatie: Noury & Van der Lande. *Scientiarum Historia* 26(1-2), 217-230.

9 D. A. Hounshell & J. K. Smith (1988). *Science and Corporate Strategy: Du Pont R&D, 1902-1980.* Cambridge: Cambridge University Press. Homburg 2003, op. cit.

10 Homburg 2003, op. cit. 44-45.

11 B. G. Achilladelis, P. Jervis & A. B. Robertson (1971). *Project SAPPHO: A study of Success and Failure in Innovation.*

12 M. B. W. Graham & B. H. Pruitt (1990). *R&D for Industry: A Century of Technical Innovation at Alcoa.* New York: Cambridge University Press. 10, 501-504.

13 D. A. Hounshell (1998). Measuring the Return on Investment in R&D: Voices from the past, Visions of the Future. *Assessing the Value of Research in the Chemical Sciences: Report of a Workshop.* Washington: National Academy Press. Chemical Sciences Roundtable, National Research Council, 6-7. G. P. Pisano (2000). In Search of Dynamic Capabilities: The Origins of R&D Competence in Biopharmaceuticals. G. Dosi, R. R. Nelson & S. G. Winter, Eds. *The Nature and Dynamics of Organizational Capabilities.* New York: Oxford University Press, 129-154.

14 A. Sarlemijn & M. J. de Vries (1992). The Piecemeal Rationality of Application Oriented Research: An Analysis of the R&D History leading to the Invention of the Philips Plumbicon in the Philips Research Laboratories. P. A. Kroes & M. Bakker, Eds. *Technological Development and Science in the Industrial Age.* Dordrecht: Kluwer Academic Publishers, 99-131.

15 D. W. van Krevelen (1950). Chemische industrie en research Staatsmijnen. *De Zakenwereld,* 108-111, in particular 109.

16 P. A. Roussel, K. N. Saad & T. J. Erickson (1991). *Third Generation R&D – Managing the Link to Corporate Strategy.* Boston: Harvard Business School Press. R. Varma (1995). Restructuring Corporate R&D: From Autonomous to Linkage Model. *Technology Analysis and Strategic Management* 7(2), 231-247.

17 Graham & Pruitt 1990, op. cit. 500. Also: N. S. Argyres & B. S. Silverman (2004). R&D, Organization Structure, and the Development of Corporate Technological Knowledge. *Strategic Management Journal* 25, 929-958.

18 M. B. W. Graham (1988). *The Business of Research: RCA and the VideoDisc.* London: Cambridge University Press. Graham & Pruitt 1990, op. cit.

19 Hounshell 1998, op. cit.

20 A. van Rooij & E. Homburg (2002). *Building the Plant: A History of Engineering Contracting in the Netherlands.* Eindhoven/Zutphen: Stichting Historie der Techniek/Walburg Pers. 96-97.

21 J. S. Plotkin (2003). Petrochemical Technology Development. P. H. Spitz, Ed. *The Chemical Industry at the Millennium: Maturity, Restructuring, and Globalization.* Philadelphia: Chemical Heritage Press, 51-84.

22 Cf. R. B. Stobaugh (1988). *Innovation and Competition: The Global Management of Petrochemical Products.* Boston: Harvard Business School Press. 20-22.

23 J. M. Utterback (1994). *Mastering the Dynamics of Innovation: How Companies Can Seize Opportunities in the Face of Technological Change.* Boston: Harvard Business School Press. Particularly 83-101. P. Hutcheson, A. W. Pearson & D. F. Ball (1995). Innovation in Process Plant: A Case Study of Ethylene. *Journal of Product Innovation Management* 12, 415-430.

24 Cf. E. Homburg, with contributions by A. van Rooij (2004). *Groeien door kunstmest. DSM Agro 1929-2004.* Hilversum: Verloren. 301-303.

25 E. Homburg (2000). Epiloog. DSM Research op weg naar de 21e eeuw. H. Lintsen, Ed. *Research tussen vetkool en zoetstof: zestig jaar DSM Research 1940-2000.* Eindhoven/Zutphen: Stichting Historie der Techniek/Walburg Pers, 118-135, in particular 124. Draft of this chapter, July 2000, 11-12. Van Rooij 2004, op. cit. 37, 243-246.

26 This changed in 1998 with J. Zuidam's appointment to the Managing Board. Zuidam had been manager of DSM Research before this appointment.

27 L. S. Reich (1977). Research and the Struggle to Control Radio: A Study of Big Business and the Uses of Industrial Research. *Business History Review* 51(2), 230-235.

28 Van Rooij 2004 op. cit., 246-247.

29 S. de Bree (1996). Technologie is de motor van DSM. *Chemisch Magazine*, 222-225, in particular 222.

30 Cf. Hobsbawn's view of the 20th century as progressing from a period of crisis via a brief 'Golden Age' (1947-73) to another period of crisis. E. Hobsbawn (1996). *The Age of Extremes: A History of the World, 1914-1991.* New York: Vintage Books. First edition 1994.

7
Epilogue: the 1990s

In July 1988, Hans van Liemt, the then chairman of DSM's Managing Board, said at a press conference: 'Our large competitors are so aggressive that we have to concentrate on seven or eight areas, and not on twenty.'[1] This statement signalled a change of course: DSM embarked on a process of focus, both in its business and in its research.

The Chemical Industry and DSM in Transition

The chemical industry changed profoundly in the 1990s. Companies in Western Europe, Japan and the United States continued to suffer from cost disadvantages in raw materials and labour, and continued to face increasingly stringent environmental regulations. In addition, stock markets added pressure to improve (short-term) profitability and to decrease cyclical ups and downs in financial results. Internationalisation tied national economies together and shifted production around the world. For European chemical companies, the United States and Asia became focal areas in their efforts to increase sales outside their home region.[2]

In response to these structural changes, chemical companies sought new, profitable businesses for growth, a continuation of the innovative strategies of the 1980s. They also retreated from areas outside their core and from areas they considered unattractive. Companies sought leadership positions based on what they considered to be their core competencies. A wave of mergers, divestments and acquisitions changed the landscape of the chemical industry. Some well-known and old companies like Hoechst and ICI ceased to exist in their previous forms while other companies changed their portfolio substantially.[3]

At DSM, top management reached the conclusion that the company could build a strong competitive position only if it focused on a limited number of core activities. Leadership (both commercial and technological) and growth potential were important parameters in choosing the company's strategic direction. Moreover, DSM aimed at internationalisation to spread turnover across Europe, Asia and the United States. Turnover in countries outside Europe should double.[4]

The strategy of focus and internationalisation changed the company's course. In the late 1980s, activities in fertilisers had already been scaled down through the divestment of several production sites.[5] DSM also gradually retreated from its energy-related activities and sold its interests in plastics processing.[6]

Expansion in fine chemicals continued, however. In 1992, DSM formed a Fine Chemicals division, and a year later this division drafted a strategy that aimed at substantially boosting turnover. Top management approved this strategy. Research intensified and the acquisition of companies speeded up as well (Table 7.1), leading to a sharp increase in fine chemicals turnover after 1993. The acquisition of Gist-brocades in 1998 enabled DSM to take the next step in its reorientation from bulk to fine chemicals. This Dutch company produced penicillin and ingredients for the food industry, including flavour enhancers and preservatives. The takeover brought fermentation and enzyme technologies as well. Gist-brocades had much experience with the use of enzymes in food and feed products and complemented DSM's work in this field. In other words, DSM's capabilities in fine chemicals ensured the fit with Gist-brocades.[7]

DSM paid 2.9 billion Dutch guilders (about 1.3 billion euro) for Gist-brocades. The company became the world's largest supplier of intermediates for pharmaceutical and food products. DSM merged its existing activities in fine chemicals with Gist-brocades into a Life Science Products cluster, reflecting the broadening scope and the strategic importance attached to these activities. With Gist-brocades, the turnover of Life Science Products more than doubled and accounted for about 26% of DSM's total turnover. Operating profits in this cluster made a similar jump (see also graphs 7.1 and 7.2.). DSM's takeover of Gist-brocades was a major one.[8]

Besides fine chemicals, DSM also included performance materials in its core businesses. Amidst other performance products, Dyneema grew into an important business. Stanyl also flourished, after a number of difficult years. DSM also bought several companies to boost its performance materials business.[9]

In the early 1990s, top management included bulk polymers such as polyethylene in DSM's core, but in 2000 it reached the conclusion that restructuring in the chemical industry in the 1990s had left DSM vulnerable. Competitors in bulk polymers often had their own feedstock base and they were more focused and very large. In fact they had only grown larger and more focused in the 1990s. Moreover, DSM had been fully state-owned until 1989, when the Dutch state sold two-thirds of its interest in the company, and was fully privatised in 1996 when the state sold the remaining third. Top management concluded that the cyclical nature of bulk chemicals made the company's stock unattractive. DSM embarked on a new course, focusing on fine chemicals, specialties and performance materials. In 2002, the company sold its interests in polyethylene, polypropylene

Table 7.1. DSM's acquisitions in fine chemicals, 1977-2002.

Company	Acquired	Remarks
Chem-Y	1977	Sold to Kao Co. in October 1992
Aspartame	1985	Technology joint venture with Tosoh
Andeno	1987	
Plaine Chemicals SA	1988	Closed in 1997
ACF Chemie	1991	
Fine chemicals of Bristol-Myers Squibb	1993	
Chemie Linz	1996	Majority share
	1998	Full ownership
Deretil (pharmaceutical intermediates)	1996	Majority share
Alpha Drug India Ltd.	1997	Majority share
Gist-brocades	1998	
Catalytica Pharmaceuticals	2000	
Roche Vitamins and Fine Chemicals	2003	

Sources: DSM annual reports 1988, 1997. Q. B. Broxterman, W. H. J. Boesten, H. E. Schoemaker & B. Schulze (1997). DSM gets the biocatalysis bug. *Speciality Chemicals* 17(6), 186-188, 190, 193, in particular 186. E. Homburg (2000). Epiloog. DSM Research op weg naar de 21e eeuw. H. Lintsen, Ed. *Research tussen vetkool en zoetstof: zestig jaar DSM Research 1940-2000.* Eindhoven/Zutphen: Stichting Historie der Techniek/Walburg Pers, 118-135, in particular 129. Draft of this chapter, July 2000, 18. H. Strijkers (2002). DSM, een koninklijke eeuwling: kroniek van de laatste 25 jaar. *Het Land van Herle* 52(3), in particular 64, 74, 79, 81, 92. Nieuwsfeiten. *Business Value* 2002, 16(5), 5, 7, 9-10, in particular 10.

and ethylene to the Saudi company SABIC and used the revenues to buy the vitamins and fine chemicals activities of the Swiss pharmaceutical firm Hoffmann-La Roche, a deal that was formally closed in 2003.[10]

DSM paid 1.8 billion euro for Roche's vitamins and fine chemicals division, making it the largest takeover by a Dutch company in 2002, and added 7,500 employees in more than fifty countries to its Life Science Products cluster.[11] Like the acquisition of Gist-brocades, the takeover added a big chunk to DSM's turnover and operating profit. Turnover in Life Science Products and Nutritional Products, the name DSM gave to the former Roche division, added up to 49% of total turnover in 2004. Operating profits from these two clusters amounted to 56% of total profits (Graphs 7.1 and 7.2).

With the acquisition of Roche's division, the takeover of Gist-brocades and the divestment of bulk polymers, DSM completed its third transformation. From coal-mining, the company had stepped into fertilisers and then diversified into chemicals, and around 1975 it had started a careful search for high value-added products. This search came to full maturation in the 1990s and transformed the company from a producer of mainly bulk chemicals to a producer of mainly fine chemicals and performance materials. Melamine and caprolactam remained in the portfolio as important industrial chemicals.

Research played a major role in this third transformation. The Central Laboratory had pushed DSM's entry into fine chemicals in 1969 and started a process of capability building that ensured the fit with Gist-brocades and the vitamins and fine chemicals division of Hoffman-La Roche. The Central Laboratory similarly pushed the development of strong polyethylene fibres, resulting in the commercialisation of Dyneema. Capabilities in materials provided the foundation for expansion in the 1990s.

Graph 7.1. DSM turnover profile, 1997-2004.

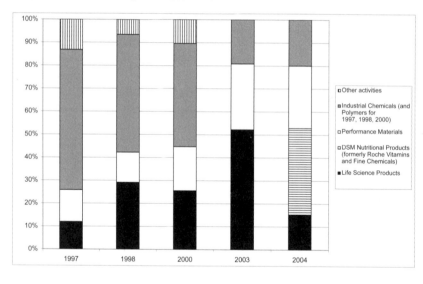

Sources: DSM annual reports 1998, 2000, 2003 and 2004. Notes:
- The graph shows the years before and after the acquisition of Gist-brocades and Roche's vitamins and fine chemicals division. The year 2000 was added for reference. The annual reports do not offer enough details to regroup figures for earlier years in the clusters DSM adopted in 1998.
- Fourth quarter turnover from Roche's division is omitted from the figures for 2003.

THE COMPANY THAT CHANGED ITSELF

Graph 7.2. Operating profit profile DSM, 1997-2004.

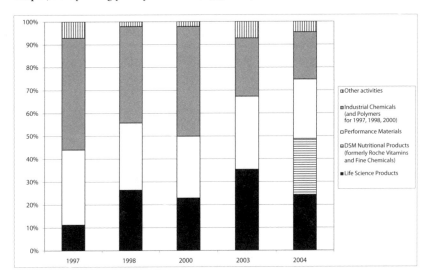

Sources: DSM annual reports 1998, 2000, 2003 and 2004.

Notes: see graph 7.2 and:

– DSM's 'other activities' incurred losses in 2003 and 2004.

– Fourth quarter profits from Roche's division are omitted from the figures from 2003.

– Profit figures for 2000, 2003 and 2004 follow the EBIT standard, which compares best with figures from 1997 and 1998.

Business and Research in the 1990s

DSM's shifting business strategy also had consequences for DSM Research. In the early 1990s research expenditure had grown somewhat, reaching 4.7% of chemical turnover in 1993, but it declined after that year. Research expenditure remained relatively stable between 3.5 and 4%, well above the level of the 1970s and early 1980s (see graph A2 in the appendix). Within the research budget, the share of corporate funds fell and DSM's business units paid for a larger part of the budget. Moreover, increasing amounts were spent on fine chemicals and specialties.[12]

The issue of the alignment of research and business reappeared on the agenda. In 1993, DSM Research replaced its functionally-organised departments by seven sectors. Six of these sectors had a direct link with DSM's business units. For instance, research on fine chemicals was now concentrated in one specialised sector instead of being spread across several departments. The seventh sector of DSM Research consisted of several generic research activities that were too small to split up among the six business-oriented sectors. This seventh sector included analysis, for instance.

Jan Zuidam, who had become head of DSM Research in 1991, wanted to secure the links between research and business and improve the market-orientation of research. At the same time, he wanted to prevent short-term marketing issues from becoming dominant. According to Zuidam, research should be a 'partner in business' and should fit in with business strategy. Supporting DSM in its efforts to excel in its core activities became a key goal of research.[13]

In the 1990s, the trend towards decentralised research continued and gained momentum. DSM's divisions increased their own research through acquisitions of companies with substantial research facilities. This led to the growth of research on locations outside Geleen, where DSM's central research facilities were located. After the acquisition of Gist-brocades, the number of DSM researchers employed in Geleen was less than 50% of the overall R&D workforce (Graph 7.3). Decentralisation also meant in-ternationalisation because DSM bought several foreign companies with research facilities. As a result of this decentralisation and internationalisa-tion, research became more fragmented than before 1990. After the acqui-sition of Gist-brocades, DSM Research started to develop new procedures to coordinate centralised and decentralised research, and to keep the lines between research and business short.[14]

Decentralisation and market orientation were developments that had started after 1970. In the 1990s, structural changes in the chemical industry and acquisitions added further weight to them. The takeover of Gist-bro-cades in particular was important in this respect. Business interests were emphasised more than in the 1980s, but not as much as in the 1970s. DSM sought a balance between short-term and long-term interests and research. Other companies chose a similar course and emphasised the link with business and markets in the conduct of research. Some companies chose a stronger decentralisation of research, however.[15]

At other Dutch-based companies, too, the relative importance of R&D outside the Netherlands increased. This trend caused concern, as indus-trial research seemed to be relocating abroad. However, the increase in R&D conducted outside the Netherlands was due mainly to takeovers of foreign companies with research facilities. The research efforts of the acquired firms typically came on top of the effort in the Netherlands. Nev-ertheless, growth in R&D typically occurred abroad.[16] For DSM, the more fragmented and decentralised R&D practice across locations in various countries meant a break with the period before 1990. DSM's research fa-cilities in Geleen had long been the centre of the company's research. In the 1990s, research at Geleen continued to be important, but no longer was the centre of gravity of DSM's research.

Graph 7.3. Number of researchers at DSM's central research facility in Geleen (Netherlands) and at other research facilities.

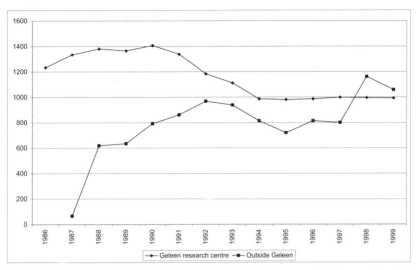

Cf. E. van Royen (2000). Steenkolenveredeling en industriële research bij Staatsmijnen. H. Lintsen, Ed. *Research tussen vetkool en zoetstof: zestig jaar DSM Research 1940-2000.* Eindhoven/Zutphen: Stichting Historie der Techniek/Walburg Pers, 12-29, in particular 27. Source for total number of researchers: DSM annual reports 1987-1999.

'Growing Ideas': Internal and External Research

DSM stabilised the budget for fundamental research in 1994. Increasingly, however, DSM Research sought contacts with researchers at universities, research institutes and other companies. In the 1980s, DSM Research had started to seek such cooperation to compensate for DSM's increasing diversification and the increasing diversity of the knowledge fields that were of interest to the company. Contacts were established mainly with Dutch universities. In the 1990s, by contrast, DSM increasingly sought international contacts. Moreover, the company's increasing focus in business and research led to a similar focus in external research. DSM Research sought to generate new opportunities for DSM at lower costs. Funding of university research and joint research with other companies and research institutes were to generate tangible results for DSM's business units. This also meant that business units paid part of the costs of external research.[17]

In the Netherlands, the relationships between universities and companies also changed through the establishment of so-called Leading Technological Institutes (LTIs, *Technologische Top Instituten*) in which several companies, the Dutch government and universities participate. DSM is involved in the Dutch Polymer Institute (DPI) and the Wageningen Cen-

View of chemical plants at Geleen (The Netherlands), near DSM's headquarters. On this site DSM built its first chemical plants. Today, DSM is active in 49 countries and shares the Geleen site with other companies.

tre for Food Sciences (WCFS). Cooperation between industry and universities is closer than in the IOP structure of the 1980s. DSM, and the other companies involved, participated in drafting research programmes for the DPI and the WCFS. Research is fundamentally oriented, but broadens DSM's own work.[18]

DSM not only made more use of university research, but also continued to cooperate with other companies in the field of research. The company started to emphasise corporate venturing as well. Corporate venturing built a business development function to find potentially profitable ideas and start-up companies that might develop into a DSM business unit. In order to qualify as venturing targets for DSM, these start-ups had to have strategic value, fit with DSM's technologies or markets, and promise financial performance; on the other hand they were offered access to DSM's capital and to its resources in the field of management, marketing and research. Besides business development, corporate venturing built mechanisms to spin out ideas that did not fit the company.[19] The Venturing unit's task was to generate growth for DSM by 'growing ideas into flourishing businesses'.[20]

The combination of corporate venturing, cooperation with other companies and use of university research gave rise to a more 'open' research and innovation process at DSM in the 1990s.[21] This trend can be seen at other companies as well, in varying degrees and forms. The decrease in in-house fundamental research has caused concern however, even though it might be compensated by increasing collaboration with universities. With the increased emphasis on business interests and market orientation, the declining level of fundamental research might lead to a similarly strong short-term orientation of research, and might also damage DSM's ability to integrate external knowledge and to translate it into an advantage in its business. This integration and translation capability, which has been called 'absorptive capacity' in economics, lay at the heart of some of DSM's innovation successes of the past. In the case of Dyneema, spinning and marketing know-how relating to synthetic fibres had to be integrated. In the case of urea and caprolactam, DSM used external knowledge as a springboard for the development of in-house technologies.[22]

In the 1990s, the wave-like pattern in the importance of research continued as business interests were again emphasised within DSM Research and within top management. Takeovers, and external research more broadly, played an important role. The continuation of this wave-like pattern further emphasises the uniqueness of the period between 1945 and 1970, and the open-ended nature of research management. A continuing effort is required to balance research and business. Key parameters are mutual commitment and room for research to develop its own vision of the company. Or, as DSM Research's management put it in an introductory brochure for new researchers in the early 1990s: "The tension between applied science on the one hand and the dynamics of the business on the other is what makes working at DSM Research so fascinating."[23]

Notes

1   Quoted in E. Homburg (2000). Epiloog. DSM Research op weg naar de 21e eeuw. H. Lintsen, Ed. *Research tussen vetkool en zoetstof: zestig jaar DSM Research 1940-2000.* Eindhoven/Zutphen: Stichting Historie der Techniek/Walburg Pers, 118-135, in particular 127. Ernst Homburg provided his notes for this chapter and thereby provided extra input into this chapter. Permission to use these notes is gratefully acknowledged.

2   H. Albach, D. B. Audretsch, M. Fleischer, R. Greb, E. Höfs, L.-H. Röller & I. Schulz (1996). *Innovation in the European Chemical Industry:* Discussion Paper FS IV 96 - 26, Wissenschaftszentrum Berlin. http://skylla.wz-berlin.de/pdf/1996/iv96-26.pdf. Accessed 25 November 2004. 52-54. F. Aftalion (2001). *A History of the International Chemical Industry: From the "Early Days" to 2000.* Philadelphia: Chemical Heritage Foundation. Second Edition. 374-405, particularly 378. K. E. Sluyterman (2003). *Kerende kansen: Het Nederlandse bedrijfsleven in de twintigste eeuw.* Amsterdam: Boom. 284-306.

3   Albach et al. 1996, op. cit. 35-54. V. Walsh & G. Lodorfos (2002). Technological and Organisational Innovations in Chemicals and Related Products. *Technology Analysis and Strategic Management* 14(3), 273-298.

4   DSM 2000: minder speerpunten en verder internationaliseren. *DSM Nieuws* (20 December 1990), 4-5. Homburg 2000, op. cit. 127-129.

5   See: E. Homburg, with contributions by A. van Rooij (2004). *Groeien door kunstmest. DSM Agro 1929-2004.* Hilversum: Verloren. 292-298.

6   Homburg 2000, op. cit. 127.

7   D. J. Venderbos, 1 July 2005. *128 Years of Gist-Brocades: Harvesting the Invisible.* Sheets from a presentation, May 1998. R. Mulders (2002). De metamorfose van DSM: Van steenkolenboer naar fijnchemist. *Management Team* (MT #21-13/12/02). http://www.mt.nl/magazine/104282/102866. Accessed 7 August 2003. H. Strijkers (2002). DSM, een koninklijke eeuwling: kroniek van de laatste 25 jaar. *Het Land van Herle* 52(3). 9.

8   DSM 1998 annual report.

9   DSM annual reports 1995, 1997. Homburg 2000, op. cit. 130.

10 Mulders 2002, op. cit. Strijkers 2002, op. cit. 92. W. Buitelaar & J. P. van den Toren, with contributions by P. van der Meché (2002). *DSM: Portret van een Maaslandse reus.* Amsterdam: Mets & Schilt. 28-29.

11 DSM annual reports 2003, 2004. Wereldspeler na overname Roche. *DSM Magazine* (December 2002), 10.

12 Personal papers of Dr S. E. Schaafsma: De R&D van DSM in de periode 1980-2000. DSM Research, ERP, S.E. Schaafsma, 1 May 2000.

13 G. Dekker (1993). DSM Research: brug tussen business en onderzoek. *De Ingenieur* (3), 26-29. Quote translated from 26.

14 Personal papers of Dr S. E. Schaafsma: De R&D van DSM in de periode 1980-2000. DSM Research, ERP, S.E. Schaafsma, 1 May 2000. DSM Research: Een Revolutie in Wording. *Match* (May 2000), 14-17. Buitelaar et al. 2002, op. cit. 48-49.

15 M. Cornet & M. Rensman (2001). *The Location of R&D in the Netherlands: Trends, Determinants and Policy.* The Hague: CPB Document 14, 29 November 2001. http://www.cpb. nl/nl/pub/document/14/doc14.pdf. Accessed 21 February 2005. 9-19. E. Homburg (2003). *Speuren op de tast: Een historische kijk op industriële en universitaire research.* Maastricht: Universiteit Maastricht. Inaugural lecture 31 October 2003. 48-49.

16 Cornet & Rensman 2001, op. cit. 20-24. See figure 2.3, 22 for the distribution of R&D spending of large Dutch companies across countries. The exception to the pattern is Royal Dutch/Shell, which divested several R&D intensive chemical divisions. Foreign R&D spending consequently declined.

17 Afdeling "Universitaire en Wetenschappelijke Contacten" (UWC) bij DSM Research: Venster op de buitenwereld. *DSM Magazine* (114, May 1993), 28-31. F. van Steijn (1994). De vierde generatie R&D. *Chemisch Weekblad* (5 March 1994), 4.

18 DSM annual reports 1996-1999. Homburg 2003, op. cit. 48-50.

19 D. Jacobs & J. Waalkens (2001). *Innovatie²: Vernieuwingen in de inovatiefunctie van ondernemingen.* Deventer: Kluwer. Achtergrondstudies van de AWT, 23. 65-66, 71-78. P. L. A. Hamm (2002). DSM Venturing & Business Development. *Chemical Analysts Conference. Vaalsbroek, September 19/20, 2002.* Heerlen: DSM Investor Relations, 5.1-5.31. *Boosting DSM's Growth.* Promotional material DSM Venturing & Business Development, 2005.

20 Paraphrased from "Grow your idea into a flourishing business." Promotional material DSM Venturing & Business Development, 2005.

21 Interview with Professor E. M. Meijer, 21 June 2004.

22 Jacobs & Waalkens 2001, op. cit. 12-13, 16. Homburg 2003, op. cit. 50-51,

23 *DSM Research: Where Knowledge Turns into Business.* DSM Corporate Public Relations. No year of publication. Probably from the early 1990s.

Appendix

Managers of Central Laboratory, CRO and DSM Research

1. Research as part of DSM's chemical sector (Chemische Bedrijven), 1940-1949.

– Heads of the Chemical Sector:

D. P. Ross van Lennep	1930-1947	Reported to top management.
J. S. A. J. M. van Aken	1947-1949	

– Research managers:

G. Berkhoff	1940-1949	Reported to head of chemical sector.

– Financial and personnel director, Central Laboratory:

H. A. J. Pieters	1940-1948	Reported to Berkhoff.

2. Research as a corporate activity, from 1949 onwards.

– R&D managers:

G. Berkhoff	1949-1961	Reported to top management.
F. L. J. Sixma	1961-1963	
L. J. Revallier	1963-1980	
D. H. E. Tom	1978-1985	Between 1978 and 1980, together with Revallier.
D. J. Venderbos	1985-1992	
J. Zuidam	1992-1998	
E. M. Meijer	1998-2005	

– Heads of Central Laboratory:

D. W. van Krevelen	1948-1959	Reported to R&D manager (Berkhoff). Responsible for research process.
J. Selman	1948-1955	Reported to R&D manager (Berkhoff). Responsible for finance and personnel.
		In 1955 Van Krevelen took over Selman's job.
F. L. J. Sixma	1959-1961	After Berkhoff left, Sixma took over his tasks, combining the positions of R&D manager and head of the Central Laboratory.

Sources:

F. J. G. Kwanten (1993). *Onderzoek bij Staatsmijnen in Limburg/ DSM Centraal Laboratorium/DSM Research 1940-1990.* DSM Research Report R 89 8061 (1 September 1993). 14, 18, 28, 29, 42. E. Homburg (2000). Epiloog: DSM Research op weg naar de 21e eeuw. H. Lintsen, Ed. *Research tussen vetkool en zoetstof: zestig jaar DSM Research 1940-2000.* Eindhoven/Zutphen: Stichting Historie der Techniek/Walburg Pers, 118-135, in particular 131. H. Strijkers (2002). DSM, een koninklijke eeuwling: kroniek van de laatste 25 jaar. *Het Land van Herle* 52(3). 131. E. Homburg, with contributions by A. van Rooij (2004). *Groeien door kunstmest. DSM Agro 1929-2004.* Hilversum: Verloren. 306.

Graph A1: Research personnel, 1950-1999

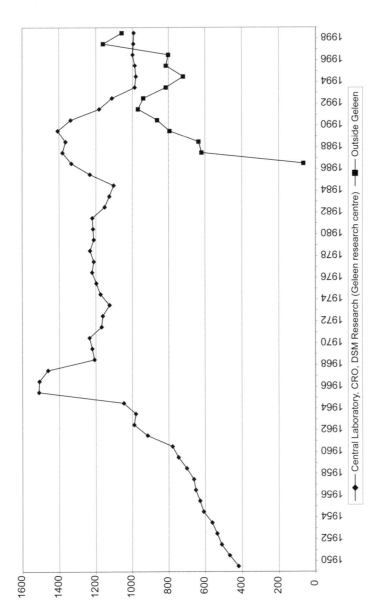

Cf. E. van Royen (2000). Steenkolenveredeling en industriële research bij Staatsmijnen. H. Lintsen, Ed. *Research tussen vetkool en zoetstof: zestig jaar DSM Research 1940-2000.* Eindhoven/Zutphen: Stichting Historie der Techniek/ Walburg Pers, 12-29, in particular 27. Source for total number of researchers: DSM annual reports 1987-1999.
Notes: The peak in 1966 is caused by the integration of the Central Experimental Station (coal-related research) with the Central Laboratory.

Graph A2: Research expenditure as a percentage of turnover, 1949-1999

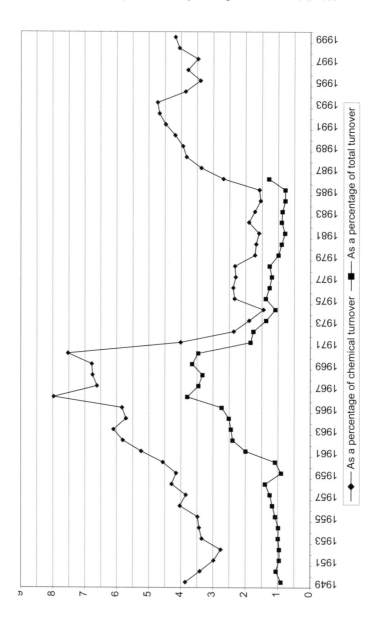

Sources: Turnover figures from RAL, 17.26/18B inv. no. 83: Bedrijfseconomisch Verslag 1950-1956, and DSM annual reports 1957-1999. Frank Veraart compiled research costs for the period 1949-1970. Research cost for 1970-1999 compiled by Siep Schaafsma.
Notes: see next page.

THE COMPANY THAT CHANGED ITSELF

Notes:

Chemical turnover is the sum of DSM's chemical activities. Turnover from energy (coal, coke, coke oven gas, natural gas, oil), electricity, construction, and the item 'other activities' from the annual reports are excluded.

The declining ratio of research expenditure to chemical turnover until 1953 was caused by rapidly-increasing turnover.

The peak in 1966 was caused by the integration of the Central Experimental Station (coal-related research) with the Central Laboratory.

In 1987, DSM deconsolidated its natural gas activities, and consequently chemical activities now represented a much higher percentage of DSM's turnover. The difference between research costs as a percentage of chemical turnover and as a percentage of total turnover became negligible after this year.

Graph A3: Licenses on DSM's chemical processes sold by Stamicarbon, 1935-1999 (Five-year moving average).

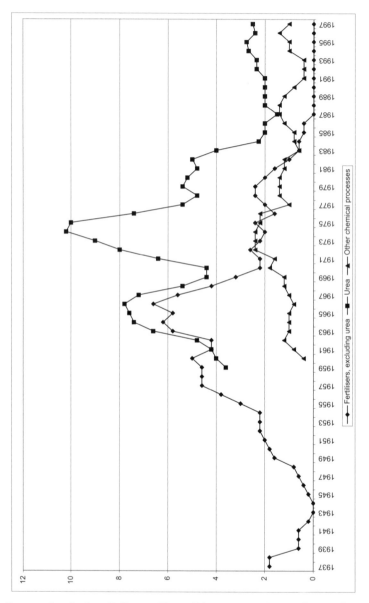

Sources: Stamicarbon Reference List, 1 February 1985. Stamicarbon Reference List at: www.stamicarbon.com. Accessed 5 July 2005.

Note: Stamicarbon included plants of DSM and its subsidiaries in its reference lists. These plants have been excluded from this graph, however.

Sources

Interviews

Dr H. G. Bakker	16 March 2005	
Dr J. A. Bigot	8 December 2003	
	7 February 2005	Discussion of draft chapter.
D G. Evens	26 July 2005	
J. T. J. van Goolen	5 December 2003	With D. J. van Waes.
	18 January 2005	Discussion of draft chapter.
Dr R. van Hardeveld	29 August 2005	
R. Kirschbaum	7 January 2005	Interview/discussion of draft chapter.
Professor E. M. Meijer	21 June 2004	
Dr L. J. Revallier	18 January 2005	
Dr B. C. Roest	29 July 2005	
Professor A. H. de Rooij	8 December 2003	With D.J. van Waes.
	7 February 2005	Discussion of draft chapter.
	23 May 2005	Discussion of draft manuscript.
Dr S. E. Schaafsma	27 June 2003	
	22 January 2004	Discussion of draft chapter.
	21 April 2004	Discussion of draft chapter.
R. E. Selman	27 June 2003	
	19 July 2005	Discussion of draft manuscript.
Professor J. J. Steggerda	8 August 2005	
D. J. Venderbos	1 July 2005	Discussion of draft manuscript.
W.J.W. Vermijs	29 August 2005	
Dr H. de Vries	29 July 2005	
D. J. van Waes	15 July 2003	With E. Homburg
J. Zuidam	27 July 2005	Discussion of draft manuscript.

E-mail correspondence:

Dr S. E. Schaafsma	28 February 2005
	9 March 2005
D. J. van Waes	28 January 2005

Interviews during previous projects (with E. Homburg):

J. Barendse	22 September 1999
J. Damme	23 November 2000
J. P. M. van Waes	4 April 2000
	17 May 2000

Note: Dutch academic titles for which there is no exact English equivalent have been omitted.

Archives

State archives, Maastricht:

Abbreviation:	RAL		
Archive code:	17.26/	18	Finance
		19	Commerce
		21	Organisation
		34	SBB
		35	Chemische Bedrijven (production unit)
		36	Central Laboratory
		38	Lysine
		40	Mijnraad
		46	Polychemie (production unit for plastics)

Corporate archives, DSM headquarters, Heerlen:

Abbreviation: CADH   Corporate archives on research.

Archives of top management:
- Minutes of top management meetings: 1949-1990.
- Appendixes to these minutes (references starting with D.V. and RvB).

Personal papers:

Dr H. G. Bakker

Dr J. A. Bigot

Dr L. J. Revallier

Dr S. E. Schaafsma

Serials and Journals

Annual reports:

DSM   1970-1990

Central Laboratory   1948-1949, 1951-1967, 1970-1971 (including research programmes)

Company newsletters:

DSM Magazine	1974-1990
DSM Nieuws[i]	1970-1974
Nieuws DSM Zuid-Limburg	1974-1975
Nieuws DSM Limburg	1975-1976
DSM Limburg Nieuws	1976-1980
Nieuws DSM Limburg	1980-1984
DSM Limburg Nieuws	1984-1990
DSM Nieuws	1990

Trade journals:

Chemical & Engineering News	1970-1990
Chemische Industrie	1970-1990

[i] successive titles listed.

Unpublished Reports Concerning the History of DSM and DSM Research

F. J. G. Kwanten (1993). *Onderzoek bij Staatsmijnen in Limburg/DSM Centraal Laboratorium/DSM Research 1940-1990*. DSM Research report R 89 8061 (1 September 1993).

H. J. Merx (1950). *Overzicht van de ontwikkeling van de productie en de afzet van meststoffen, teerproducten, benzolkoolwaterstoffen en enkele andere producten der Chemische Bedrijven van de Staatsmijnen in Limburg*. Heerlen: Staatsmijnen.

H. J. Merx (1955). *Chronologisch overzicht van de geschiedenis van de Cokesfabrieken en het Gasdistributiebedrijf 1912-1952*. Heerlen: Archief van de Staatsmijnen in Limburg.

H. J. Merx (1955). *Chronologisch overzicht van de geschiedenis van het Stikstofbindingsbedrijf 1925-1952*. Heerlen: Archief van de Staatsmijnen in Limburg.

G. F. te Roller (1990). *Een halve eeuw Centraal Laboratorium. Een serie gesprekken met oud-researchdirecteuren van DSM*. Heerlen: DSM Corporate Public Relations. Unpublished manuscript.

F. W. R. Röthig (1959). *Archiefdocumentatie betreffende de algemene gang van zaken bij de ontwikkeling van de projecten "Fenol - Caprolactam - Nylonzout" van de Staatsmijnen in*

Limburg van 1937 t/m 1959 (oktober). Heerlen: Staatsmijnen, Bureau Secretariaat en Correspondentie.

F. W. R. Röthig (1960). *Het ureumproject van de Staatsmijnen in Limburg (Archiefdocumentatie 1940-1960).* Heerlen: Staatsmijnen.

F. W. R. Röthig (1960). *De algemene gang van zaken bij de ontwikkeling van het polyolefinenproject van de Staatsmijnen in Limburg van 1935 t/m 1959. Deel I: ethyleen.* Heerlen: Staatsmijnen, Bureau Secretariaat en Correspondentie.

F. W. R. Röthig (1960). *De algemene gang van zaken bij de ontwikkeling van het polyolefinenproject van de Staatsmijnen in Limburg van 1935 t/m 1959. Deel II: polyethyleen - algemeen en hogedruk-polyethyleen.* Heerlen: Staatsmijnen, Bureau Secretariaat en Correspondentie.

F. W. R. Röthig (1960). *De algemene gang van zaken bij de ontwikkeling van het polyolefinenproject van de Staatsmijnen in Limburg van 1935 t/m 1959. Deel III: lagedruk-polyetheen.* Heerlen: Staatsmijnen, Bureau Secretariaat en Correspondentie.

F.W.R. Röthig (1965). *De contacten van de Staatsmijnen met derden op het gebied van melamine, melamine-harsen, en melamine-perspoeders.* Heerlen: Staatsmijnen, Centraal Archief.

F.W.R. Röthig (1966). *Chronologisch overzicht van het ontstaan en de organisatie van het Centraal Laboratorium van de Staatsmijnen, Geleen.* Heerlen: Staatsmijnen, Centraal Laboratorium.

F. W. R. Röthig (1968). *Toepassing lysine voor menselijke voeding en als therapeuticum. Contacten CL/DSM met derden.* Heerlen: Staatsmijnen, Centraal Laboratorium.

H. Strijkers. *DSM en melamine.* Unpublished and undated manuscript.

P. F. G. Vincken (2000). *Van Staatsmijnen in Limburg tot DSM Chemie.* Unpublished manuscript.

Draft chapters for: H. Lintsen, Ed. (2000). *Research tussen vetkool en zoetstof: zestig jaar DSM Research 1940-2000.* Eindhoven/Zutphen, Stichting Historie der Techniek/Walburg Pers.

- T. van Helvoort. *Omzien in verwondering: Chemische expansie van Staatsmijnen en de rol van research* (1945-1967). Veldman & Van Royen report B. Undated.
- T. van Helvoort. *De omarming van de polymeer-chemie: polyetheen* (1952-1967). Veldman & Van Royen report F. Undated.
- T. van Helvoort. *Synthetische rubbers: de verlokkingen van een enorme markt.* Veldman & Van Royen report G. Undated.
- E. Homburg. *Epiloog: DSM Research op weg naar de 21ste eeuw.* Draft, July 2000.
- J. Schueler. *Diversificatie en de plaats van research in de DSM-organisatie* (1967-1980). Veldman & Van Royen report I. Undated.
- E. van Royen. *De Nederlandse Staatsmijnen, chemie en research* (1901-1945). Veldman & Van Royen report A. Undated.
- F. Veraart. *Fenol* (1939-1964). Veldman & Van Royen report C. Undated.

THE COMPANY THAT CHANGED ITSELF

- F. Veraart. *Het ureumstrippingproces*. Veldman & Van Royen report D. Undated.
- F. Veraart. *Melamine uit ureum*. Veldman & Van Royen report E. Undated.
- F. Veraart. *Lysine* (1957-1969). Veldman & Van Royen report H. Undated.
- F. Veraart. *De renaissance van research* (1980-1990). Veldman & Van Royen report J. Undated.

References

References without an author are listed first, in chronological order.

Staatsmijnen 1902-1952. Gedenkboek bij gelegenheid van het vijftigjarig bestaan. Heerlen: Staatsmijnen. 1952.

Let's Pin a Dollar Sign on Industrial Research. *Chemical Engineering* (15 December 1958), 88.

Lysine Prospects Brighten. *Chemical & Engineering News* (20 April 1959), 25.

Afscheid van dr. ir. H. A. J. Pieters. *Nieuws van de Staatsmijnen* 1962, 11(2), 8.

Kirk-Othmer Encyclopedia of Chemical Technology. London: Wiley-Interscience. Second edition, 22 volumes, 1963-1977.

Owners Shout "Si" to Montecatini Edison. *Chemical & Engineering News* (4 April 1966), 66-70.

Dr. van Aken: kracht putten uit research en samenwerking. *Chemisch Weekblad* 1968, 44, 17-19.

Ureum capaciteit naar 450.000 ton per jaar. *Staatsmijnen Nieuws* 1968, 17(17), 1,2.

Naam is alléén DSM. *DSM Nieuws* 1969, 18(25), 1.

New Construction. *Chemical & Engineering News* (12 January 1970), 27.

New Construction. *Chemical & Engineering News* (16 February 1970), 24.

Stamicarbon develops new high density polyethylene process. *Chemical & Engineering News* (20 April 1970), 38.

Auch Holland hat jetzt einen Chemie-Großkonzern. Die Akzo und ihre Möglichkeiten. *Chemische Industrie* 1970, XXII(2), 8-85.

Keltan onderdelen in wasautomaten. *DSM Nieuws* 1971, 20(5), 4.

Bouwindustrie gaat Keltan voor dakbedekking en bassinbekleding gebruiken. *DSM Nieuws* 1971, 20(5), 4.

Structuur DSM wordt afgestemd op marktgerichte stijl van werken: Vraaggesprek met president-directeur dr. A. Rottier. *DSM Nieuws* 1971, 20(13), 1, 2.

Organisatie van DSM in 1973. *DSM Nieuws* 1971, 20(13), 2-4.

Eerste stap op 1 september 1971. *DSM Nieuws* 1971, 20(13), 4, 5.

Ir. R.E. Selman nieuwe 'general manager' van Nypro (U.K.) Ltd. *DSM Nieuws* 1971, 20(18), 4.

Dr. J.A. Bigot chef Speciale Producten. *DSM Nieuws* 1971, 20(18), 4.

Veiligheidsbumper van kunstrubber Keltan. *DSM Nieuws* 1971, 20(21), 1.

Compactproces van Groep Polymeren staat op het punt product af te leveren. *DSM Nieuws* 1972, 21(6), 1, 6.

Vlotte start van proefbedrijf voor zuivering afvalwater van onze chemische bedrijven. *DSM Nieuws* 1972, 21(17), 5.

Nieuwe fabriek voor lagedichtheid polyetheen. *DSM Nieuws* 1972, 22(20), 1.

Researchgroep ontwikkelt nieuwe centrale zuiveringsinstallatie. *DSM Nieuws Extra, Externe editie* (28 April 1972), 1, 4.

Afdeling Milieutechniek van Stamicarbon doet goede zaken. *DSM Nieuws* 1973, 23(20), 1, 2.

Grondstoffenbesparing en productievergroting door nieuwe katalysator in ACN. *DSM Nieuws* 1973, 23(24), 1.

DSM kan krakergas 'propeen' volledig gaan benutten voor hoogwaardig eindproduct. *DSM Nieuws* 1973, 23(24), 1, 2.

Dr. C. Bokhoven van CL 25 jaar in dienst. *Nieuws DSM Zuid-Limburg* 1974, 24(18), 2.

DSM-concern past per 1 april '75 zijn structuur aan. *Nieuws DSM Zuid-Limburg* 1974, 24(24), 4-5, 7.

Research in de aanval tegen bruine pluim. *DSM Informatie* 4 (29 March 1974), 4.

Accenten bij industriële research zullen geleidelijk aan anders worden gelegd. *DSM Magazine* (8, July 1975), 4-7.

DSM-concern kan in rond eenzesde deel van wereldcaprolactambehoefte voorzien. *DSM Magazine* (9, September 1975), 5-8.

Ein Aufschwung bei Chemiefasern ist keinesweg sicher. *Chemische Industrie* 1976, XXVIII(2), 80.

Reorganisatie in fasen van de Concerndienst Research en Octrooien: Geleidelijke invoering van matrix-organisatie. *Nieuws DSM Limburg* 1976, 26(4), 6.

HPO-fabriek van Groep Organische Producten in bedrijf genomen. *DSM Limburg Nieuws* 1976, 26(17), 1, 2.

Afvalwaterstripper NAK 3 gaat stankhinder rigoureus te lijf: Ook loogneutralisator voor zelfde doel in opstart. *DSM Limburg Nieuws* 1977, 27(14), 5.

SP neemt eerste eenheid van nieuwe fabriek voor hoogwaardige fijnchemicaliën in bedrijf. *DSM Limburg Nieuws* 1977, 27(14), 6.

Eerste straat IAZI opgestart. *DSM Limburg Nieuws* 1977, 27(17), 1.

Technisch partner van polymerenafnemers. *DSM Magazine* (17, January 1977), 22-24.

Directeur Grotens van Divisie Kunststoffen: DSM heeft voor de productie van grondstoffen voor volgproducten zowel NAK 3 als NAK 4 nodig. *DSM Limburg Nieuws* 1978, 28(3), 6-7.

Chem-Y brengt nieuwe technologie in huis. *DSM Magazine* (24, April 1978), 19-21.

Akzo auf dem Wege der Besserung. *Chemische Industrie* 1979, XXXI(6), 401-403.

Milieuresearch: veelzijdige afdeling met één gericht doel. *DSM Limburg Nieuws* 1979, 29(9), 6-7.

KAS-Granulatiefabriek SBB maakt eerste produkt. *DSM Limburg Nieuws* 1979, 29(10), 1.

Werkverdeling Raad van Bestuur per 1 januari 1979. *DSM Magazine* (29, February 1979), 3.

Groepsdirecteur van Polymeren: stalen zenuwen? *DSM Limburg Nieuws* 1980, 30(2), 3.

De opstart van systeem 16: nog in de jaren zeventig. *Nieuws DSM Limburg* 1980, 30(3), 1, 2.

Nieuw miniplant-complex op CRO. *Nieuws DSM Limburg* 1980, 30(14), 1.

Productie-activiteiten geconcentreerd en verdubbeld in nieuw complex te Emmerich. *DSM Magazine* (38, September 1980), 8-11.

Biotechnology - Seeking the Right Corporate Combinations. *Chemical Week* (30 September 1981), 36-40.

Belangrijke uitbreiding KELTAN-productie in Beek. *Nieuws DSM Limburg* 1981, 31(17), 1, 4.

De heer J.A. Thoma wordt directeur van de Groep Organische Producten. *Nieuws DSM Limburg* 1981, 31(20), 1.

Major Growth Ahead for Carbon Fibers. *Chemical & Engineering News* (17 May 1982), 18.

Voortgaan op biotechnologische weg. *DSM Magazine* (50, October 1982), 9-11.

Nieuwe omlegging caprolactamfabriek: Dertig jaar oud fabriekgedeelte geheel gerenoveerd. *Nieuws DSM Limburg* 1982, 32(24), 5.

Milieuresearch: waakzaam en beschikbaar. *DSM Magazine* (55, July 1983), 22-24.

Energierekening kan f 70 miljoen omlaag: Omvangrijke campagne volgende week van start. *Nieuws DSM Limburg* 1983, 33(5), 1.

Wat is energiebewaking? *Nieuws DSM Limburg* 1983, 33(5), 3.

Ronfalin EST. DSM ontwikkelde nieuwe kunststof. *Nieuws DSM Limburg* 1983, 33(6), 4.

DSM ontwikkelde kunststof voor fabricage van brandstoftanks. *Nieuws DSM Limburg* 1983, 33(11), 1.

DSM presenteerde nieuwe typen kunststoffen. *Nieuws DSM Limburg* 1983, 33(20), 1, 5.

'Winstherstel, saneren, excelleren.' Caprolactam op breukvlak in de tijd. *Nieuws DSM Limburg* 1983, 33(22), 4.

Renovatie caprolactamfabrieken. *DSM Limburg Nieuws* 1984, 34(23), 1, 2.

Stanyl: nieuwe nylon, product van innovatie. *DSM Magazine* (61, July 1984), 9-11.

UKF: its origins and development. *Nitrogen* 1984, (147), 14-16.

DSM wil Aspergillus 'temmen'. *DSM Magazine* (65, March 1985), 26-27.

Drs. D.H.E. Tom, scheidend directeur Concerndienst Research en Octrooien: Uniek laboratorium in Nederland. *DSM Magazine* (67, July 1985), 7-9.

Ullmann's Encyclopedia of Industrial Chemistry. Weinheim: VCH. Fifth edition, 36 volumes, 1985-1996.

Speciale Producten bruist. *DSM Limburg Nieuws* 1986, 36(5), 4.

Ruim f 200 miljoen bespaard in 3 jaar. *DSM Limburg Nieuws* 1986, 36(6), 1.

Nieuw 'Gel-lab' geopend. *Nieuws DSM Limburg* 1986, 36(13), 1.

Nieuw lab geopend bij DSM Research: Proeftuin voor composieten. *DSM Limburg Nieuws* 1986, 36(20), 1.

Niet alleen 'schouder aan schouder'. In ARTS werkt men bovendien 'arm-in-arm'. *DSM Limburg Nieuws* 1986, 36(22), 4.

HSC, Holland Sweetener Company: de 'weight-watchers' van DSM. *DSM Magazine* (72, May 1986), 3-5.

Sulfaatfabriek begeeft zich op nieuwe markten. De tweede jeugd van een 'oud product'. *DSM Limburg Nieuws* 1987, 37(1), 3.

STAPRON in opmars. *DSM Limburg Nieuws* 1987, 37(6), 1, 4.

Eerste grote multi-purposefabriek: Bij business-eenheid Speciale Producten. *DSM Limburg Nieuws* 1987, 37(10), 1, 3.

Andeno: de aandrijving van de pharma. *DSM Magazine* (79, August 1987), 18-20.

Licht en sterk: Dyneema. *DSM Magazine* (80, October 1987), 22-24.

DSM start productie van specialty aminozuren. *DSM Limburg Nieuws* 1988, 38(21), 1.

Speciale gerechten uit de 'keuken van de fijnchemie': Miniplant 2 onmisbaar voor ontwikkeling specialties SP. *DSM Limburg Nieuws* 1989, 39(13), 5.

Een supersterk verhaal... *DSM Magazine* (89, March 1989), 8-11.

DSM Research: Where Knowledge Turns into Business. DSM Corporate Public Relations. No year of publication. Probably from the early 1990s.

Gouden research, DSM Research 50 jaar: 1940-1990. DSM Corporate Public Relations. 1990.

Ir. R.E. Selman: Ruimte voor research. *DSM Magazine* (May 1990), 4-7.

Dyneema zit gebeiteld. *DSM Nieuws* 1990, 40(23), 4-5.

Maatregelen tegen dumping aspartaam. *DSM Nieuws* 1990, 40(24), 3.

De 'alfabet-fabriek' en het ABC van de kunststoffen. *DSM Nieuws* 1990, 40(24), 4-5.

DSM 2000: minder speerpunten en verder internationaliseren. *DSM Nieuws* (20 December 1990), 4-5.

Kirk-Othmer Encyclopedia of Chemical Technology. London: Wiley-Interscience. Fourth edition, 16 volumes, 1991-1996.

Afdeling "Universitaire en Wetenschappelijke Contacten" (UWC) bij DSM Research: Venster op de buitenwereld. *DSM Magazine* (114, May 1993), 28-31.

Stamicarbon: The Know-How People: Urea. Geleen: Stamicarbon. Undated, probably from 1999.

DSM Research: Een Revolutie in Wording. *Match* (May 2000), 14-17.

Nieuwsfeiten. *Business Value* 2002, 16(5), 5, 7, 9-10.

Wereldspeler na overname Roche. *DSM Magazine* (December 2002), 10.

Industrieel erfgoed – Dankzij particulier initiatief werd in het Zeeuwse Dreischor een originele 'Pasveersloot' in oude staat hersteld. *TNO Magazine* 2003, (3), 28.

Novo Nordisk History, undated.
http://www.novonordisk.com/images/about_us/history/history_uk.pdf. Accessed 9 February 2004.

B. G. Achilladelis, P. Jervis & A. B. Robertson (1971). *Project SAPPHO: A Study of Success and SFailure in Innovation.*

B. Achilladelis, A. Schwarzkopf & M. Cines (1990). The Dynamics of Technological Innovation: The Case of the Chemical Industry. *Research Policy* 19, 1-34.

F. Aftalion (2001). *A History of the International Chemical Industry: From the "Early Days" to 2000.* Philadelphia: Chemical Heritage Foundation. Second Edition.

J. S. A. J. M. van Aken (1960). Management's View on Research in Chemical Industry. *TVF* 31, 57-64

H. Albach, D. B. Audretsch, M. Fleischer, R. Greb, E. Höfs, L.-H. Röller & I. Schulz (1996). *Innovation in the European Chemical Industry.* Discussion Paper FS IV 96 - 26, Wissenschaftszentrum Berlin. http://skylla.wz-berlin.de/pdf/1996/iv96-26.pdf. Accessed 25 November 2004.

J. R. Anchor (1985). Managerial Perceptions of Research and Development in the UK chemicals industry, 1955-1981. *Chemistry and Industry* (1 July 1985), 426-430, (15 July 1985), 459-464, (5 August 1985), 498-504.

N. S. Argyres & B. S. Silverman (2004). R&D, Organization Structure, and the Development of Corporate Technological Knowledge. *Strategic Management Journal* 25, 929-958.

H. van Baal (1996). Nieuwe technologie maakt ureumproductie goedkoper. *Chemisch Magazine* (October 1996), 416.

D. G. H. Ballard (1986). The Discovery of Polyethylene and its Effect on the Evolution of Polymer Science. R. B. Seymour & T. Cheng, Eds. *History of Polyolefins: The World's Most Widely Used Polymers.* Dordrecht: D. Reidel Publishing Company, 9-53.

P. Baggen, J. Faber & E. Homburg (2003). Opkomst van een kennismaatschappij. J. W. Schot et al., Ed. *Techniek in Nederland in de Twintigste Eeuw.* Eindhoven/Zutphen: Stichting Historie der Techniek/Walburg Pers. Vol. 7, 141-173.

T. C. N. Belgraver (1970). *70 jaar Nederlandse Rubberindustrie: Uitgave ter gelegenheid van het 50-jarig jubileum van de Nederlandse Vereniging van Rubberfabrikanten 29 oktober 1970.*

H. Benninga (1990). *A History of Lactic Acid Making: A Chapter in the History of Biotechnology.* Dordrecht: Kluwer.

G. Berkhoff (1947). Research in bedrijven. *De Ingenieur* 59(43), A371-A373.

G. Berkhoff & J. H. Ottenheym (1961). Verbetering van de voedingswaarde van eiwitten door toevoeging van lysine en methionine. *Voeding* 22(7), 292-306.

J. A. Bigot (1980). Heden en toekomst van de Nederlandse fijnchemie. *Chemisch Magazine* (November 1980), m 729-m 732.

A. Boccone (2003). Specialty Chemicals. P. H. Spitz, Ed. *The Chemical Industry at the Millennium: Maturity, Restructuring, and Globalization.* Philadelphia: Chemical Heritage Press, 85-110.

I. de Boer, Ed. (1974). *Boer en markt: Ontwikkeling van de Nederlandse land- en tuinbouw en de Cebeco-Handelsraad organisatie in de periode 1949-1974. Een uitgave van Cebeco-Handelsraad ter gelegenheid van zijn 75-jarig bestaan.*

K. Boersma (2002). *Inventing Structures for Industrial Research: A History of the Philips Nat. Lab. 1914-1946.* Amsterdam: Aksant. Dissertation, Eindhoven University of Technology.

K. Boersma & M. de Vries (2003). De veranderende rol van het Natuurkundig Laboratorium van het Philipsconcern gedurende de periode 1914-1994. *NEHA Jaarboek* 66, 287-313.

D.-J. Böning (1969). *Bestimmungsfaktoren der Intensität industrieller Forschung und Entwicklung.* Clausthal-Zellerfeld: Bönecke.

J. L. Bower (1986). *When Markets Quake: The Management Challenge of Restructuring Industry.* Boston, MA: Harvard Business School Press.

S. de Bree (1996). Technologie is de motor van DSM. *Chemisch Magazine*, 222-225.

A. M. Brownstein (1976). *Trends in Petrochemical Technology: The Impact of the Energy Crisis.* Tulsa: Petroleum Publishing Co.

A. Budzinski (1981). Pyridin hat noch Wachstumschancen. *Chemische Industrie* XXXIII (September), 529-531.

W. Buitelaar & J. P. van den Toren, with contributions by P. van der Meché (2002). *DSM: Portret van een Maaslandse reus.* Amsterdam: Mets & Schilt.

W. Buschmann, Ed. (1993). *Koks, Gas, Kohlechemie: Geschichte und gegenständliche Überlieferung der Kohleveredlung.* Essen: Klartext Verlag.

K. Chapman (2000). Industry Evolution and International Dispersal: The Fertiliser Industry. *Geoforum* 31, 371-384.

W. M. Cohen & D. A. Levinthal (1990). Absorptive Capacity: A New Perspective on Learning and Innovation. *Administrative Science Quarterly* 35, 128-152.

E. Corcoran (1992). Redesigning Research: Trends in Industrial Research. *Scientific American* 266(6), 72-80.

M. Cornet & M. Rensman (2001). *The Location of R&D in the Netherlands: Trends, Determinants and Policy.* The Hague: CPB Document 14, 29 November 2001. http://www.cpb.nl/nl/pub/document/14/doc14.pdf. Accessed 21 February 2005.

J. J. Dahlmans (1975). Enzymen in de organische proces-industrie. *Chemisch Weekblad* (28 November 1975), 24-26.

J. J. Dahlmans, W. H. J. Boesten & G. Bakker (1980). Enzymatische scheiding van D- en L-aminozuren op technologische schaal. *Chemisch Magazine* (May 1980), m 322-m 323.

J. Damme, J. T. van Goolen & A. H. de Rooij (1972). Cyclohexanone Oxime Made Without Byproduct $(NH4)_2SO4$. *Chemical Engineering* (10 July 1972), 54-55.

M. Davids (1999). *De weg naar zelfstandigheid: de voorgeschiedenis van de verzelfstandiging van de PTT in 1989.* Hilversum: Verloren. Dissertation Erasmus University Rotterdam.

G. Dekker (1993). DSM Research: brug tussen business en onderzoek. *De Ingenieur* (3), 26-29.

M. A. Dennis (1987). Accounting for Research: New Histories of Corporate Laboratories and the Social History of American Science. *Social Studies of Science* 17, 479-518.

L. L. van Dierendonck (1970). *Vergrotingsregels voor gasbelwassers.* Enschede: Dissertation Twente Technical College.

A. Dijkgraaf (2003). Volgende caprolactamfabriek wordt goedkoper. *Chemisch2 Weekblad* (6 December 2003), 14-15.

W. B. Duncan (1982). Lessons from the Past, Challenge and Opportunity. D. H. Sharp & T. F. West, Eds. *The Chemical Industry.* Chichester: Ellis Horwood, 15-30.

M. Eckstut & P. H. Spitz (2003). Strategy Development in the Chemical Industry. P. H. Spitz, Ed. *The Chemical Industry at the Millennium: Maturity, Restructuring, and Globalization.* Philadelphia: Chemical Heritage Press, 111-144.

P. Ellwood (1968). Melamine Process Uses Low-Pressure Reactor to Achieve Low Costs. *Chemical Engineering* (20 May 1968), 124-126.

P. Erker (1990). Die Verwissenschaftlichung der Industrie: Zur Geschichte der Industrieforschungen in den europäischen und amerikanischen Elektrokonzernen. *Zeitschrift für Unternehmensgeschichte* 35(2), 73-94.

W. Eschenmoser (1997). 100 years of progress with Lonza. *Chimia* 51(6), 259-267.

J. Faber (2000). Wetenschappelijke kennisverwerving en diversificatie: Noury & Van der Lande. *Scientiarum Historia* 26(1-2), 217-230

J. Faber (2003). Het Nederlandse Innovatie Systeem, 1870-1970. *NEHA Jaarboek* 66, 208-232.

M. Fransman (1992). *Biotechnology: Generation, Diffusion and Policy.* UNU/INTECH working paper #1.

C. Freeman (1974). *The Economics of Industrial Innovation.* Harmondsworth: Penguin Books. First edition.

H. I. Fusfeld (1994). *Industry's Future: Changing Patterns of Industrial Research.* Washington: American Chemical Society.

L. Galambos (1992). Theodore N. Vail and the Role of Innovation in the Modern Bell System. *Business History Review* 66(1), 95-126.

B. Gales (2000). Houwen en stof bijten? Maakbaarheid in een mijnstreek. *Studies over de sociaal-economische geschiedenis van Limburg* XLV, 27-64.

F. Gambrelle (ca. 1995). *Innovating for Life: Rhône-Poulenc 1895-1995.* Paris: Éditions Public Historie Albin Michel.

J. T. J. van Goolen (1976). Development and Scaling-Up of a Three-Phase Reactor. *Chemical Reaction Engineering: Proceedings of the 4th international symposium, 6-8 April 1976, Heidelberg.* Frankfurt am Main: Dechema, 309-407.

M. B. W. Graham (1985). Industrial Research in the Age of Big Science. *Research on Technological Innovation, Management and Policy* 2, 47-79.

M. B. W. Graham (1985). Corporate Research and Development: The Latest Transformation. *Technology in Society* 7, 179-195.

M. B. W. Graham (1988). *The Business of Research: RCA and the VideoDisc.* London: Cambridge University Press.

M. B. W. Graham & B. H. Pruitt (1990). *R&D for Industry: A Century of Technical Innovation at Alcoa.* New York: Cambridge University Press.

P. M. E. M. van der Grinten (1984). Vergrijzing en verjonging in de chemische industrie. *Chemisch Magazine* (November 1984), 677-680.

E. Gwinner (1978). *Wirtschaftliche Aspekte der Biochemie, Bioenergie und Biotechnologie.* Düsseldorf: Handelsblatt Verlag für Wirtschaftsinformation.

J. Hagedoorn (2002). Inter-firm R&D Partnerships: An Overview of Major Trends and Patterns Since 1960. *Research Policy* 31(4), 477-492.

H. Hagen & H. Domininghaus (1961). *Polyäthylen und andere Polyolefine.* Hamburg: Brunke Garrels. Second edition.

P. L. A. Hamm (2002). DSM Venturing & Business Development. *Chemical Analysts Conference. Vaalsbroek, September 19/20, 2002.* Heerlen: DSM Investor Relations, 5.1-5.31.

C. van Heerden (1966). Research in de chemische industrie. *Chemisch Weekblad* 66, 290-296.

H. Heerings & W. Smit (1986). *Internationale herstrukturering in de kunstmestsector: Nederlands overheidsbeleid en de gevolgen voor ontwikkelingslanden.* Amsterdam: Stichting Onderzoek Multinationale Ondernemingen (SOMO).

T. van Helvoort & F. Veraart (2000). Grondstoffen voor kunststoffen, 1945-1970. H. Lintsen, Ed. *Research tussen vetkool en zoetstof: zestig jaar DSM Research 1940-2000.* Eindhoven/Zutphen: Stichting Historie der Techniek/Walburg Pers, 30-43.

T. van Helvoort (2000). Staatsmijnen gaat polymeriseren, 1945-1970. H. Lintsen, Ed. *Research tussen vetkool en zoetstof: zestig jaar DSM Research 1940-2000.* Eindhoven/Zutphen: Stichting Historie der Techniek/Walburg Pers, 44-59.

J. F. den Hertog & E. Huizenga (2000). *The Knowledge Enterprise: Implementation of Intelligent Business Strategies.* London: Imperial College Press.

E. Hobsbawn (1996). *The Age of Extremes: A History of the World, 1914-1991.* New York: Vintage Books. First edition 1994.

F. Hoelscher (1972). *Kautschuke, Kunststoffe, Fasern: Sechs Jahrzehnte Technische Herstullung synthetische Polymere.* Ludwigshafen: BASF.

J. P. Hogan & R. L. Banks (1986). History of Crystalline Polypropylene. R. B. Seymour & T. Cheng, Eds. *History of Polyolefins: The World's Most Widely Used Polymers.* Dordrecht: D. Reidel Publishing Company, 103-115.

E. Homburg (1992). The Emergence of Research Laboratories in the Dyestuffs Industry. *British Journal for the History of Science* 25, 91-111.

E. Homburg (2000). Epiloog: DSM Research op weg naar de 21e eeuw. H. Lintsen, Ed. *Research tussen vetkool en zoetstof: zestig jaar DSM Research 1940-2000.* Eindhoven/Zutphen: Stichting Historie der Techniek/Walburg Pers, 118-135.

E. Homburg, A. van Selm & P. Vincken (2000). Industrialisatie en industriecomplexen: De chemische industrie tussen overheid, technologie en markt. J. W. Schot & et al., Eds.

Techniek in Nederland in de twintigste eeuw. Eindhoven/Zutphen: Stichting Historie der Techniek/Walburg Pers. Vol. 2, 377-401.

E. Homburg (2003). *Speuren op de tast: Een historische kijk op industriële en universitaire research.* Maastricht: Universiteit Maastricht. Inaugural lecture 31 October 2003.

E. Homburg & A. van Rooij (2004). Die Vor- und Nachteile enger Nachbarschaft: Der Transfer deutscher chemischer Technologie in de Niederlande bis 1952. R. Petri, Ed. *Technologietransfer aus der deutschen Chemieindustrie (1925-1960).* Berlin: Duncker & Humblot, 201-251.

E. Homburg, with contributions by A. van Rooij (2004). *Groeien door kunstmest: DSM Agro 1929-2004.* Hilversum: Verloren.

D. A. Hounshell & J. K. Smith (1988). *Science and Corporate Strategy: Du Pont R&D, 1902-1980.* Cambridge: Cambridge University Press.

D. A. Hounshell (1992). Du Pont and the Management of Large-Scale Research and Development. P. Galison & B. Hevly, Eds. *Big Science: The Growth of Large-Scale Research.* Stanford: Stanford University Press, 236-261.

D. A. Hounshell (1996). The Evolution of Industrial Research in the United States. R. S. Rosenbloom & W. J. Spencer, Eds. *Engines of Innovation: U.S. Industrial Research at the End of an Era.* Boston: Harvard Business School Press, 13-85.

D. A. Hounshell (1998). Measuring the Return on Investment in R&D: Voices from the past, Visions of the Future. *Assessing the Value of Research in the Chemical Sciences: Report of a Workshop.* Washington: National Academy Press. Chemical Sciences Roundtable, National Research Council, 6-17.

J. Howells, A. James & K. Malik (2003). The Sourcing of Technological Knowledge: Distributed Innovation Processes and Dynamic Change. *R&D Management* 33(4), 395-409.

P. Hutcheson, A. W. Pearson & D. F. Ball (1995). Innovation in Process Plant: A Case Study of Ethylene. *Journal of Product Innovation Management* 12, 415-430.

J. J. Hutter (1984). Nederlandse Laboratoria 1860-1940, een kwantitatief overzicht. *Tijdschrift voor de geschiedenis der geneeskunde, natuurkunde, wiskunde en techniek* 9(4), 150-174.

M. J. N. Jacobs (1999). *Creep of Gel-Spun Polyethylene Fibres: Improvements by Impregnation and Crosslinking.* Eindhoven: Dissertation Eindhoven University of Technology.

D. Jacobs & J. Waalkens (2001). *Innovatie²: Vernieuwingen in de inovatiefunctie van ondernemingen.* Deventer: Kluwer. Achtergrondstudies van de AWT, 23.

P. J. C. Kaasenbrood & J. D. Logemann (1969). DSM's Urea Stripping Process. *Hydrocarbon Processing* 48(4), 117-121.

W. W. Kaeding (1964). How Dow Makes Phenol From Toluene. *Hydrocarbon Processing* 43(11), 173-176.

J. Kamphuis, J. A. M. van Balken, H. E. Schoemaker, E. M. Meijer & W. H. J. Boesten (1988). Biotechnologische productie van optisch actieve aminozuren. *I2-Procestechnologie* 4(9), 31-41.

J. Kamphuis, W. H. J. Boesten, B. Kaptein, H. F. M. Hermes, T. Sonke, Q. B. Broxterman, W. J. J. van den Tweel & H. E. Schoemaker (1995). The Production and Uses of Optically Pure Natural and Unnatural Amino Acids. A. N. Collins, G. N. Sheldrake & J. Crosby, Eds. *Chirality in Industry: The Commercial Manufacture and Applications of Optically Active Compounds.* Chichester: John Wiley & Sons, 187-208.

R. P. van de Kasteele (1979). *R&O: research en ontwikkeling en de Nederlandse onderneming.* Deventer: Kluwer.

C. H. Kline (1976). Maximising Profits in Chemicals. *Chemtech* 6(February), 110-117.

C. H. Kline (1983). Surviving the Petrochemical Collapse. *Hydrocarbon Processing* 62(2), 84-A-H.

C. H. Kline (1984). Breaking Through to New Technologies. *Chemtech* 14(3), 148-151

H. J. Kolowski (1983). Abbau der Synthesefaser-Kapazität in Westeuropa. *Kunststoffe* 73, 724-726.

L. M. Kretzers (1980). Markt en technologie als drijfveer voor de Nederlandse chemische industrie. *Chemisch Magazine* (November 1980), m 701-m 705.

D. W. van Krevelen (1950). Chemische industrie en research. *De Zakenwereld*, 108-111.

D. W. van Krevelen (1958). Het Centraal Laboratorium, chemisch research centrum van de Staatsmijnen in Limburg. *De Ingenieur* 70(39), Ch 79-87.

D. W. van Krevelen (1980). Bij het scheiden der wegen: Voordracht bij het afscheid van het Centraal Laboratorium der Staatsmijnen, te Geleen op 25 augustus 1959. *In retrospect: Een keuze uit de voordrachten.* Amsterdam: Meulenhoff, 43-47.

D. W. van Krevelen (1993). Vijftig jaar activiteit in de chemische technologie. *Werken aan scheikunde: 24 memoires van hen die de Nederlandse chemie deze eeuw groot hebben gemaakt.* Delft: Delftse Universitaire Pers, 243-263.

L. Küchler (1963). Wandel in der chemischen Technik. *Wandel in der chemischen Technik: Karl Winnacker zum 60. Geburtstag gewidmet 21. September 1963.* Frankfurt: Farbwerke Hoechst AG, 1-24.

V. Laguna & G. Schmid (1975). Snamprogetti's Newest Urea Process. *Hydrocarbon Processing* 54(7), 102-104.

N. R. Lamoreaux & K. L. Sokoloff (1999). Inventors, Firms and the Market for Technology in the Late Nineteenth and Early Twentieth Century. N. R. Lamoreaux, D. M. G. Raff & P. Temin, Eds. *Learning by Doing in Markets, Firms and Countries*. Chicago: Chicago University Press, 19-57.

R. Landau (1998). The Process of Innovation in the Chemical Industry. A. Arora, R. Landau & N. Rosenberg, Eds. *Chemicals and Long-Term Economic Growth: Insights from the Chemical Industry*. New York: John Wiley & Sons, 139-180.

P. L. Layman (1982). Surfactants - A Mature Market with Potential. *Chemical & Engineering News* (11 January 1982), 13-16.

P. L. Layman (1982). Aramides, Unlike Other Fibers, Continue Strong. *Chemical & Engineering News* (8 February 1982), 23-24.

P. L. Layman (1985). European Custom Chemical Makers Shift Focus to Specialisation. *Chemical & Engineering News* (27 May 1985), 30-31.

J. A. de Leeuw den Bouter, L. L. van Dierendonck & W. O. Bryan (1978). Computer-Aided Development of the Cyclohexane Oxidation Process. V. W. Weekman & D. Luss, Eds. *Chemical Reaction Engineering: 5th International Symposium, Houston, Texas, March 13-15, 1978*. Washington, D.C.: American Chemical Society, 348-358.

H. Lintsen, Ed. (2000). *Research tussen vetkool en zoetstof: zestig jaar DSM Research 1940-2000*. Eindhoven/Zutphen: Stichting Historie der Techniek/Walburg Pers. Besides the following chapters with Lintsen as leading author, see: Van Helvoort 2000, Van Helvoort & Veraart 2000, Homburg 2000, and Van Royen 2000.

H. Lintsen (2000). Proloog: Research en DSM in ontwikkeling. H. Lintsen, Ed. *Research tussen vetkool en zoetstof: zestig jaar DSM Research 1940-2000*. Eindhoven/Zutphen: Stichting Historie der Techniek/Walburg Pers, 6-11.

H. Lintsen, T. van Helvoort & P. Vincken (2000). Intermezzo: Research en de opbouw van een chemisch concern. H. Lintsen, Ed. *Research tussen vetkool en zoetstof: zestig jaar DSM Research 1940-2000*. Eindhoven/Zutphen: Stichting Historie der Techniek/Walburg Pers, 60-69.

H. Lintsen, F. Veraart & P. Vincken (2000). De onvervulde belofte: Lysine. H. Lintsen, Ed. *Research tussen vetkool en zoetstof: zestig jaar DSM Research 1940-2000*. Eindhoven/Zutphen: Stichting Historie der Techniek/Walburg Pers, 70-81.

H. Lintsen, J. Schueler & F. Veraart (2000). Naar een heroriëntatie van de research, 1970-1985. H. Lintsen, Ed. *Research tussen vetkool en zoetstof: zestig jaar DSM Research 1940-2000*. Eindhoven/Zutphen: Stichting Historie der Techniek/Walburg Pers, 82-103.

H. Lintsen & F. Veraart (2000). De nieuwe bloei van research, 1985-1990. H. Lintsen, Ed. *Research tussen vetkool en zoetstof: zestig jaar DSM Research 1940-2000*. Eindhoven/Zutphen: Stichting Historie der Techniek/Walburg Pers, 104-115.

A. van Loen (1966). *De betekenis van lysinesuppletie als directe benadering van het proteinmal-nutrition-probleem in de wereld.* Heerlen: Staatsmijnen/ DSM.

U. Marsch (2000). *Zwischen Wissenschaft und Wirtschaft: Industrieforschung in Deutschland und Großbritannien 1880-1936.* Paderborn: Ferdinand Schöningh.

H. Martin (2002). *Polymere und Patente: Karl Ziegler, das Team, 1953-1998: Zur wirtschaftlichen Verwertung akademischer Forschung.* Weinheim: Wiley-VCH.

J. J. McKetta (1976-1999). *Encyclopedia of Chemical Processing Design.* Basel: Dekker. 68 volumes.

F. McMillan (1979). *The Chain Straighteners: Fruitful Innovation: The Discovery of Linear and Stereoregular Synthetic Polymers.* London: The MacMillan Press.

R. R. van der Meer (1980). *Biotechnologie en innovatie: Advies uitgebracht aan de Minister voor Wetenschapsbeleid door het CIVI (Centraal Instituut voor Industrieontwikkeling) te 's-Gravenhage.* 's-Gravenhage: Publicatie van de Voorlichtingsdienst Wetenschapsbeleid.

P. G. Meerman (1978). Tien jaar research aan integrale afvalwaterzuivering. Van 1:100.000.000 naar 1:1. *DSM Magazine* (26, August 1978), 4-8.

E. M. Meijer (1985). Diversificatie naar speciale chemische producten. *Biotechnologie in Nederland* 2, 98-100.

E. M. Meijer, W. H. J. Boesten, H. E. Schoemaker & J. A. M. Van Balken (1985). Use of Biocatalysts in the Industrial Production of Specialty Chemicals. J. Tramper, H. C. van der Plas, J. A. M. van Balken & P. Linko, Eds. *Biocatalysts in Organic Synthesis: Proceedings of an International Symposium Held at Noordwijkerhout, 14-17 April 1985.* Amsterdam: Elsevier, 135-156.

E. M. Meijer (1987). *Biokatalyse en fijnchemie: grenzen en perspectieven.* Eindhoven: Eindhoven University of Technology. Inaugural lecture, 15 May 1987.

E. M. Meijer (1987). Aspartaam en aminozuren. *Biotechnologie in Nederland* 4(1), 15-16.

J. L. Meikle (1991). Plastics. S. G. Lewin, Ed. *Formica & Design: From the Table Top to High Art.* New York: Rizzoli International Publications, 39-57.

J. L. Meikle (1995). *American Plastic: A Cultural History.* New Brunswick, New Jersey: Rutgers University Press.

F. A. M. Messing (1988). *Geschiedenis van de mijnsluiting in Limburg: Noodzaak en lotgevallen van een regionale herstructurering 1955-1975.* Leiden: Martinus Nijhof.

G. Meyer-Thurow (1982). The Industrialization of Invention: A Case Study from the German Chemical Industry. *Isis* 73, 363-383.

C. G. M. van de Moesdijk (1979). *The Catalytic Reduction of Nitrate and Nitric Oxide to Hydroxylamine: Kinetics and Mechanism.* Eindhoven: Dissertation Eindhoven Technical College.

C. G. M. van de Moesdijk (1986). Development of a Continuous Process for Substituted Pyridines and other Heterocycles. *Chemistry & Industry* (4), 129-134.

D. C. Mowery & N. Rosenberg (1998). *Paths of Innovation: Technological Change in 20th-Century America.* Cambridge: Cambridge University Press.

K. Mulder (1992). *Choosing the Corporate Future: Technology Networks and Choice Concerning the Creation of High Performance Fiber Technology.* Dissertation Rijksuniversiteit Groningen.

R. Mulders (2002). De metamorfose van DSM. Van steenkolenboer naar fijnchemist. *Management Team* (MT #21-13/12/02). http://www.mt.nl/magazine/104282/102866. Accessed 7 August 2003.

K. F. J. Niebling, R. E. Pourier, R. A. Fisher & N. B. F. Telders, Eds. (1990). *Innovatiegericht Onderzoekprogramma Biotechnologie (IOP-b) 1985-1990.* Eindverslag. Leidschendam: Programmabureau Biotechnologie. Two volumes.

A. G. Nill (2000). *The History of Aspartame: Food and Drug Law/Third Year Paper, Professor Peter Hutt. Harvard Law School.* http://leda.law.harvard.edu/leda/data/244/. Accessed 14 August 2003.

D. F. Noble (1977). *America by Design.* New York: Knopf.

R. Olin (1973). R&D Management Practices: Chemical Industry in Europe. *R&D Management* 3, 125-135.

D. A. O'Sullivan (1977). West European Man-Made Fibre Outlook is Grim. *Chemical & Engineering News* (21 February 1977), 16-20.

K. Oyama (1995). The Industrial Production of Aspartame. A. N. Collins, G. N. Sheldrake & J. Crosby, Eds. *Chirality in Industry: The Commercial Manufacture and Applications of Optically Active Compounds.* Chichester: John Wiley & Sons, 237-247.

E. T. Penrose (1959). *The Theory of the Growth of the Firm.* Oxford: Basil Blackwell.

E. Penrose (1971). The Growth of the Firm. A Case Study: The Hercules Powder Company. *Growth of Firms, Middle East Oil and Other Essays.* London: Frank Cass & Co. Ltd., 43-63. Originally published in: *Business History Review* 1960, 34, 1-23.

H. A. J. Pieters & M. J. Mannens (1929). Winning van pyridine en van phenol uit ruwe benzol. *Chemisch Weekblad* 26(20), 286-290.

H. A. J. Pieters (1929). Het Centraal Laboratorium der Staatsmijnen. *Chemisch Weekblad* 26(23), 318-321.

G. P. Pisano (2000). In Search of Dynamic Capabilities: The Origins of R&D Competence in Biopharmaceuticals. G. Dosi, R. R. Nelson & S. G. Winter, Eds. *The Nature and Dynamics of Organizational Capabilities*. New York: Oxford University Press, 129-154.

J. S. Plotkin (2003). Petrochemical Technology Development. P. H. Spitz, Ed. *The Chemical Industry at the Millennium: Maturity, Restructuring, and Globalization*. Philadelphia: Chemical Heritage Press, 51-84.

P. Puype, G. Beauchez & M. Jongsma (1979). *Van kiem tot korrel: Nederlandse Stikstof Maatschappij N.V. 1929-1979*. Kloosterzande: Duerinck-Krachten.

J. B. Quinn (1959). *Yardsticks for Industrial Research: The Evaluation of Research and Development Output*. New York: The Ronald Press Company.

B. Cornils & M. Rasch (1997). *Geschichte der Forschung der Ruhrchemie AG und des Werkes Ruhrchemie (1927-1997)*. Frankfurt/M.: Hoechst AG; unpublished manuscript.

W. J. Reader (1970-1975). *Imperial Chemical Industries: A History*. London: Oxford University Press. Two volumes.

L. S. Reich (1977). Research and The Struggle to Control Radio: A Study of Big Business and the Uses of Industrial Research. *Business History Review* 51(2), 230-235.

L. S. Reich (1985). *The Making of American Industrial Research: Science and Business at GE and Bell, 1876-1926*. Cambridge: Cambridge University Press.

C. Reinhardt (1997). *Forschung in der chemischen Industrie: die Entwicklung synthetische Farbstoffe bei BASF und Hoechst, 1863 bis 1914*. Freiburg: Dissertation Technische Universität Freiburg.

C. Reinhardt (1998). An Instrument of Corporate Strategy: The Central Research Laboratory at BASF, 1868-1914. E. Homburg, A. S. Travis & H. G. Schröter, Eds. *The Chemical Industry in Europe, 1850-1914: Industrial Growth, Pollution and Professionalization*. Dordrecht: Kluwer Academic Publishers, 239-259.

E. Roberts & C. Berry (1985). Entering New Businesses: Selecting Strategies for Success. *Sloan Management Review* 26(3), 3-17.

A. H. de Rooij, C. Dijkhuis & J. T. J. van Goolen (1977). A Scale-up Experience: The DSM Phosphate Caprolactam Process. *Chemtech* 7(5), 309-315.

A. van Rooij (1998). *"De rest kunt u vergeten. Op de band komt het aan!" Een onderzoek naar het beeld van de fietsband tussen 1900 en 1960 als bijdrage tot de materiaalgeschiedenis van rubber*. Maastricht: Faculteit der Cultuurwetenschappen. Master thesis.

A. van Rooij & E. Homburg (2002). *Building the Plant: A History of Engineering Contracting in the Netherlands*. Eindhoven/Zutphen: Stichting Historie der Techniek/Walburg Pers.

A. van Rooij (2003). Aangekochte technologie en industriële research bij het Stikstofbindingsbedrijf van de Staatsmijnen in de jaren 1930. *NEHA Jaarboek* 66, 263-286.

A. van Rooij (2004). *Building Plants: Markets for Technology and Internal Capabilities in DSM's Fertiliser Business, 1925-1970.* Amsterdam: Aksant. Dissertation Eindhoven University of Technology.

L. D. Rosenberg & C. H. Kline (1981). Should Management Seek More Profits Downstream? *Hydrocarbon Processing* 60(12), 158-167.

P. A. Roussel, K. N. Saad & T. J. Erickson (1991). *Third Generation R&D – Managing the Link to Corporate Strategy.* Boston: Harvard Business School Press.

E. van Royen (2000). Steenkolenveredeling en industriële research bij Staatsmijnen. H. Lintsen, Ed. *Research tussen vetkool en zoetstof: zestig jaar DSM Research 1940-2000.* Eindhoven/Zutphen: Stichting Historie der Techniek/Walburg Pers, 12-29.

A. Sarlemijn & M. J. de Vries (1992). The Piecemeal Rationality of Application Oriented Research: An Analysis of the R&D History Leading to the Invention of the Philips Plumbicon in the Philips Research Laboratories. P. A. Kroes & M. Bakker, Eds. *Technological Development and Science in the Industrial Age.* Dordrecht: Kluwer Academic Publishers, 99-131.

A. C. M. Schakenraad & J. Hagedoorn (1988). Industriële R&D-samenwerking op biotechnologisch gebied. *Biotechnologie in Nederland* 5(6), 313-316.

A. Schmidt (1966). Herstellung von Melamin aus Harnstoff bei Atmosphärendruck. *Chemie-Ingenieur-Technik* 38(11), 1140-1143.

A. E. Schouten & A. K. van der Vegt (1966). *Plastics: Hoofdlijnen van de huidige kennis en toepassing van synthetische macromoleculaire materialen.* Utrecht & Antwerpen: Prisma-Boeken.

H. G. Schröter (1991). Privatwirtschaftliche Marktregulierung und Staatliche Interessenpolitik. Das internationale Stickstoffkartell 1929-1939. H. G. Schröter & C. A. Wurm, Eds. *Politik, Wirtschaft und internationale Beziehungen: Studien zu ihrem Verhältnis in der Zeit zwischen den Weltkriegen.* Mainz: Philipp von Zabern, 117-137.

J. Schuijer (2001). Van Nylonkous tot GSM. H. van Bekkum, J. Reedijk & S. Rozendaal, Eds. *Chemie achter de dijken: Uitvindingen en uitvinders in de eeuw na van 't Hoff.* Amsterdam: Koninklijke Nederlandse Akademie van Wetenschappen (KNAW), 92-93.

J. Selman (1952). Over de ontwikkeling van het researchwerk. M. Kemp, Ed. *Mijn en Spoor in goud.* Maastricht: Publiciteitsbureau Veldeke, 73-89.

R. B. Seymour (1986). Introduction to the History of Polyolefins. R. B. Seymour & T. Cheng, Eds. *History of Polyolefins: The World's Most Widely Used Polymers.* Dordrecht: D. Reidel Publishing Company, 1-7.

R. A. Sheldon (1987). Biokatalyse en fijnchemie in Nederland. *Biotechnologie in Nederland* 4(1), 18-19.

H. Siedel (1982). Feinchemikalien: bei Schering wächst eine neue Unternehmensbereich heran. *Chemische Industrie* XXXIV (July), 488.

K. J. Skinner (1975). Enzymes Technology. *Chemical & Engineering News* (18 August 1975), 23-41.

K. E. Sluyterman (1995). *Driekwart eeuw CSM: cash flow, strategie en mensen.* Diemen: CSM.

K. E. Sluyterman (2003). *Kerende kansen. Het Nederlandse bedrijfsleven in de twintigste eeuw.* Amsterdam: Boom.

J. K. Smith (1990). The Scientific Tradition in American Industrial Research. *Technology & Culture* 31, 121-131.

H.A.M. Snelders. Verweij, Evert Johannes Willem (1905-1981). *Biografisch Woordenboek van Nederland.* http://www.inghist.nl/Onderzoek/Projecten/BWN/ lemmata/bwn3/verweij Last update: 5 September 2003. Accessed 10 March 2005.

P. H. Spitz (1988). *Petrochemicals: The Rise of an Industry.* New York: Wiley.

P. H. Spitz (2003). Restructuring: The First Wave. P. H. Spitz, Ed. *The Chemical Industry at the Millennium: Maturity, Restructuring, and Globalization.* Philadelphia: Chemical Heritage Press, 9-50.

F. van Steijn (1994). De vierde generatie R&D. *Chemisch Weekblad* (5 March 1994), 4.

R. Stobaugh & P. Townsend (1975). Price Forecasting and Strategic Planning: The Case of Petrochemicals. *Journal of Marketing Research* 12, 19-29.

R. B. Stobaugh (1988). *Innovation and Competition: The Global Management of Petrochemical Products.* Boston: Harvard Business School Press.

H. Strijkers (1992). *DSM Chemicals: een terugblik, 1975-1991.* DSM.

H. Strijkers (1994). *Van hobby naar hoeksteen: 25 jaar Speciale Produkten bij DSM.* Geleen: DSM Fine Chemicals, Special Products.

H. Strijkers (2002). DSM, een koninklijke eeuwling: kroniek van de laatste 25 jaar. *Het Land van Herle* 52(3).

P. Tans (1977). Van Staatsmijnen tot DSM. Hoofdlijnen van de ontwikkeling. *Land van Herle* 27(3), 87-103.

E. G. M. Tornqvist (1986). Polyolefin Elastomers – Fifty Years of Progress. R. B. Seymour & T. Cheng, Eds. *History of Polyolefins: The World's Most Widely Used Polymers.* Dordrecht: D. Reidel Publishing Company, 143-161.

J. M. Utterback & W. J. A. Abernathy (1990). A Dynamic Model of Process and Product Innovation. C. Freeman, Ed. *The Economics of Innovation.* Cheltenham: Edward Elgar, 424-441. Originally published in *Omega* 1975, 3(6).

J. M. Utterback (1994). *Mastering the Dynamics of Innovation: How Companies Can Seize Opportunities in the Face of Technological Change.* Boston: Harvard Business School Press.

R. Varma (1995). Restructuring Corporate R&D: From Autonomous to Linkage Model. *Technology Analysis and Strategic Management* 7(2), 231-247.

R. Varma (2000). Changing Research Cultures in U.S. Industry. *Science, Technology, & Human Values* 25(4), 395-416.

J. Verhoog & H. Warmerdam (1994). *Melkzuur?... natuurlijk! 25 jaar PURAC Biochem BV 1969-1994.* Noordwijk: Van Speijk.

J. G. de Voogd (1937). Verslag van de 65ste algemene vergadering van gasfabrikanten in Nederland. *Chemisch Weekblad* 34(37), 589-592. There: H. A. J. Pieters. Het procédé der Staatsmijnen voor de zoogenaamde natte gaszuivering, 591-592.

V. Walsh & G. Lodorfos (2002). Technological and Organisational Innovations in Chemicals and Related Products. *Technology Analysis and Strategic Management* 14(3), 273-298.

W. Wimmer (1994). „*Wir haben fast immer was Neues": Gesundheitswesen und Innovationen der Pharma-Industrie in Deutschland, 1880-1935.* Berlin: Duncker & Humblot. Dissertation Freie Universität Berlin.

M. Wolf (1993). *Im Zeichen von Sonne und Mond: von der Frankfurter Muenzscheiderei zum Weltunternehmen Degussa AG.* Frankfurt am Main: Degussa.

J. L. van Zanden (1997). *Een klein land in de 20e eeuw: economische geschiedenis van Nederland 1914-1995.* Utrecht: Het Spectrum.

List of Figures, Graphs and Tables

Index

Economic Affairs, Ministry of 121, 200, 221
Edison 173
Eindhoven Technical College see Eind-
    hoven University of Technology
Eindhoven University of Technology 71,
    206, 207
electronics 13, 15, 59, 198
Emmerich 160, 161
EMS Dottikon 214
Enjay Chemical see Exxon
ENKA 42, 83
EPDM 29, 30, 62-64, 99, 106-109, 114, 124,
    178-181, 63
EPM rubber 106-108
epsilon-aminocapronitrile 96, 97
Erickson, Tamara 16, 67
ethylene 49, 54, 62, 99-102, 106, 107, 109,
    140, 164, 179, 181, 233, 260
explosives 13, 24, 46
Exxon 107

FAO 117, 122, 123
Far East 92, 208, 223
Fauser, Giacomo 78
fertiliser passim
Fibre Intermediates department 12, 27, 63,
    67, 82, 85, 92-95, 98, 109, 126, 127, 139, 141,
    205, 235, 245, 246
fine chemicals 9, 12, 27, 29-31, 125, 138, 147,
    149-155, 159, 161-164, 184, 185, 198, 200,
    212, 214, 219, 221, 223, 235-237, 245, 246,
    248-254, 262, 264, 270-273
First World War 13, 16, 17, 36
Flixborough 174, 223
formaldehyde 60, 109, 110, 112, 113, 196
Foster Wheeler 53
Foundation for the History of Technology 9
France 214
Freeman, Chris 18, 19

Galambos, Louis 18, 19, 22
gamma-cyanobutyraldehyde 153, 156-158
gas, natural 65, 67, 113, 139, 140, 166, 230,
    283
G.D. Searle & Co. 214
Geleen 26, 46, 91, 152, 159, 175, 177, 178,
    202, 218, 224-227, 231, 262, 274-276
gel spinning 205-207, 211
Germany 13, 19, 26, 44, 48, 73, 82, 84, 102,

104, 105, 115, 153, 160, 207, 226
Gist-brocades 118, 154, 220, 221, 270-272,
    274
glutamic acid 154, 155
Goodrich, B.F. 107
Goris, Johan 42, 43, 48, 49, 53, 70, 83, 87, 93
Graham, Margaret 15, 18, 19, 21-23, 67, 127,
    137, 149, 256, 258
Griesheim-Elektron 21
Groningen University 204

Hagendoorn, John 221
Hall Keynes, Matthew 216
HDPE 60, 64, 99, 101, 103, 105-107, 109,
    182, 183, 235
Heerden, Cor van 73, 128, 137
Helvoort, Ton van 9
Hercules Powder Company 24, 198
heterocyclics 155
Hibernia 102, 104
Hinselmann 36
Hirschfeld, Willem 118
HMD (hexamethylene diamine) 82, 83,
    96-98
Hoechst 26, 105, 269
Hoffmann-La Roche 237l
Holland Sweetener Company 215, 216
Holzverzeckerungs AG. Zorn 88, 89
Homburg, Ernst 9, 10, 15, 17, 19, 21, 22, 255
Hoogstraten, Wim 9
Hounshell, David 14, 17, 19, 22, 23, 125, 149,
    255, 258
HPDE 106, 114, 183
HPO (Hydroxylamine Phophate Oxime)
    166, 167, 169-278, 184, 185, 224, 227, 228,
    257, 261, 263, 264
Hurry-up Programme 208
HVA (Verenigde HVA-Maatschappijen)
    159, 160
hydrogen 38, 43, 49, 67, 227, 249
hydroxylamine 84, 85, 88, 167-170, 175

ICI 45, 62, 64, 76, 92, 99-101, 156, 158, 168,
    205, 269
IG Farben 39, 44, 45, 50, 51, 62, 73, 82-84,
    88, 167
IJmuiden 45
ILOB (Instituut voor Landboukundig
    Onderzoek van Biochemische Producten)
    118, 120

—